THEFT OF THE CITY

THEFT OF THE CITY

Readings on Corruption in Urban America

Edited with Introductions

BY

John A. Gardiner and **David J. Olson**

INDIANA UNIVERSITY PRESS   BLOOMINGTON • LONDON

Library of Congress Cataloging in Publication Data
Gardiner, John A 1937–   comp..
        Theft of the city. *Readings on Corruption*
        Bibliography: p.430   *in Urban America,*
    1. Corruption (in politics)—United States—   *Bloomington,*
Addresses, essays, lectures.   2. Municipal government   *Indiana*
    —United States—Addresses, essays, lectures.   *University*
    I. Olson, David J., joint comp.   II. Title.   *Press, 1974.*
        JS401.G37   329′.00973   73–16519
            ISBN 0–253–35860–4
            ISBN 0–253–35861–2 (pa.)

CONTENTS

v

Part II: The Targets of Corruption

Part III: Causes and Consequences of Corruption

Contents   vii

PREFACE

This book of readings on corruption in American cities has been assembled for several reasons. For the first time it provides under one cover the most important writings about municipal corruption. Although works on this subject are numerous, they have appeared in widely scattered locations, often as unpublished reports and documents and even more frequently in obscure publications. In addition to making these readings more accessible, we have tried to organize them in a manner that will draw attention to the complexities surrounding the issue of corruption and the continuities between contemporary and past corrupt practices. Definitional and conceptual problems are explored, the historical background and the targets of corruption are reviewed, and the volume concludes with an assessment of various causes and consequences of corruption. Perhaps most important, the book demonstrates that corruption is a major and enduring problem that has plagued the conduct of American politics in the past and in all likelihood will continue to do so in the post-Watergate era. Corruption is not confined to municipal jurisdictions, but municipal corruption is illustrative of the kinds of corruption that occur throughout the American political system.

Social scientists have paid scant attention to the subject of corruption in government. The most detailed and perceptive accounts of corruption in the twentieth century have come primarily from exposés by journalists, the findings of government commissions, and testimony during trials of government officials and only secondarily from research conducted by social scientists. Social scientists have a narrow vision of political reality. Their inattention to corruption has left them unprepared for several undeniable governmental crises, such as the race crisis of the 1960s and the environmental-energy crisis of the 1970s. Whether due to social scientists' implicit confidence in the rectitude of public officials and the propriety of their acts or to the difficulties inherent in studying the subject, there is a gap in understanding the impact of corruption on American politics that is in need of correction. As a first step toward that end, we have gathered a combination of original source materials (often as told by the participants themselves), the few research studies that have been conducted, and theoretical works that seek to integrate these materials into a broader framework.

Students of American politics should be interested in corruption for several reasons. First, it is a fact of American political life and has been a central aspect of American politics at least since the turn of the last century; as Lincoln Steffens declared in *The Shame of the Cities*, "The spirit of graft and of lawlessness is the American spirit." Indeed, subsequent comparisons of American politics with that of Western European nations often note the frequency of American scandals exposing official abuse of power; the bribery, extortion, and kickbacks involved in awarding government jobs and contracts; and the use of politics to secure personal advantage. Second, to the extent that these observations are accurate, it is necessary to study corruption simply to gain a more complete understanding of how American political life operates. When corruption is involved in the decision-making process it affects who gets what, when, and how; it influences the shape of public policy and the kind and amount of services delivered in government programs; and it is part of the determination of how the day-to-day governance of the society is conducted. Finally, and perhaps most important in the end, the degree of support or cynicism citizens hold toward the legitimacy of their government is directly influenced by the degree of corruption among those charged with the affairs of state.

Corruption has been observed in almost all societies throughout recorded history. In America, the patronage and bank scandals in the 1830s under the Jackson administration, the Whisky Ring and Star Route frauds in the Grant administration, the Teapot Dome and Elk Hills oil scandals in the Harding administration, and the events associated with the Watergate scandal in the Nixon administration are but four instances when national politics seemed to be dominated by illegal and unethical practices, and similar abuses of public trust have occurred in most of the fifty states. We have ignored these instances of corruption in order to examine intensively several facets of municipal corruption, all of which have their equivalents at the state and national levels. By this means we hope that the reader will gain a more detailed understanding of how corruption works.

Municipal corruption can be traced back at least as far as the 1820s, when greedy local officials seeking instant prosperity for their crossroads hamlets were more than willing to sell out to promoters of rail and water transportation schemes. Steffens revealed similar rapacity in dealings between local governments and the mushrooming public utilities at the beginning of the twentieth century. Today, perhaps because most capital improvements have been completed or involve federal funding and thus federal auditing, local corruption seems to center on the enforcement of criminal laws and regulations and the awarding of government contracts, although suburbs and the rapidly growing metropolitan areas of the Midwest and Southwest still see the development of payoffs common in older cities fifty years ago. Concentrating on city-level corruption thus allows us to address a major area where corruption has been common and permits us to examine in detail the relationships between corruption and the political systems in which it arises.

The extent and persistence of corruption as a component of political life in urban America raise a number of basic questions. The reader will want to keep them in mind as an aid to understanding, explaining, and evaluating the nature of municipal corruption and in considering various reform recommendations. What constitutes a corrupt act? Is corruption a necessary or even valuable component of the political process, or should it be written off as the deviant acts of a few individuals who fail to accept and abide by the values of the society? Has the extent and severity of municipal corruption increased or decreased in the current period? How does corruption affect local political life? What are the costs and benefits for the individuals involved in corruption (corrupters and corruptees)? Are there broader consequences for some or all of the uninvolved residents of the city? If it is concluded that corruption should be reduced, what are the available and most effective avenues of attack? Are the most critical elements facilitating schemes of corruption the individual participants (mayors, policemen, purchasing agents, and so forth) or the surrounding environments (laws, public attitudes, political structures, community norms, and so forth) within which corrupt individuals operate? Satisfactory answers to these questions are not easy to come by because of the complexities surrounding the issue of corruption itself.

Part I of this book introduces the nettlesome problem of defining corruption. There is seldom a black-and-white distinction between cor-

rupt and legitimate bases for making political and governmental decisions, whether they involve the selection of officeholders, the awarding
of contracts or other privileges, or the application and enforcement of
laws and regulations. The affairs of government seldom permit the
mechanical application of clear rules covering all situations, so the
exercise of discretion and selection from among competing values must,
of necessity, be a commonplace occurrence. It is often difficult, both
factually and conceptually, to identify the acts that are based upon
corrupt motives or to sort out the corrupt from the legitimate motives
inherent in a particular act. The selections in chapter 1 offer several
bases for making these distinctions. In chapter 2 we begin to describe
the nature of corruption as it has affected the growth and development
of American cities in the twentieth century. The readings in this chapter describe the classic cases of cities that have been overwhelmed by
patterns of corruption, sometimes sustained for more than a generation.

The targets of corruption are dealt with in Part II. Chapter 3 exam-
ines in detail law enforcement and its nullification, and chapter 4 reviews the kinds of corruption periodically involved in the awarding of
government contracts and other privileges. From these materials the
reader can attempt to sort out what the *goal* of the corruption was,
who the *participants* involved in corrupt schemes were, and the *environmental factors* that influenced how the corruption was carried out.

The selections in Part III deal with the process of evaluation and
recommendation. Two contrasting explanations of corruption are given
in the works in chapter 5, with one set of articles stressing individual
culpability and the other emphasizing the environmental settings
within which corruption is found. Those subscribing to the first explanation propose to curb corruption by limiting the opportunities for
individual deviance, while adherents of the latter explanation argue
that long-range possibilities for reform lie only in changes that minimize
conflicts between public values and the functions governments are
asked to perform. The concluding section, chapter 6, focuses on the
mysterious problem of identifying the costs and benefits of corruption,
both to the persons involved and to the political systems in which they
live.

The studies reprinted in this book come from a variety of sources:
scholarly books and articles, reports of government commissions, government documents, magazine and newspaper articles, and several
previously unpublished works. Many of the works listed in the bibliography at the end of the book were considered for inclusion but were
not reprinted in this volume because of space limitations. The reader

interested in pursuing additional aspects of urban corruption is urged
to consult these articles as well as the general discussions of corruption
listed there.

By their very nature, the materials contained in this volume touch
upon values and expectations regarding the goals of government and
the conduct of its officials. To the best of our ability, we have attempted to select and present these materials in as objective a manner
as possible, leaving to the reader the tasks of making judgments and
arriving at conclusions about the issues that are raised. It is impossible,
however, to remain neutral on a subject like corruption, and we preface
the readings by acknowledging the values that have informed our work
on this volume: as might be surmised from the title we have chosen,*
we feel that official corruption constitutes a dangerous substitution of
private for public values; it has contributed to the erosion of public
confidence in the institutions of government; and it has weakened the
potential of city governments for addressing the problems of urban
America. We hope that the presentation of this book will contribute to
a greater understanding of the problem of corruption and assist in efforts to combat it.

J.A.G.
D.J.O.

* With acknowledgment to our friend Donald R. Cressey, whose book
*Theft of the Nation: The Structure and Operations of Organized Crime in
America* (New York: Harper and Row, 1969) did much to bring to the
attention of the American public the problems of organized crime and
corruption.

ACKNOWLEDGMENTS

The impetus for publication of this volume grew out of our interest in corruption and research in several municipalities over the past eight years. Our views on corruption have developed through discussions with countless individuals—news reporters, city employees, public officials, lawyers, and concerned citizens.

The content of this volume reflects the comments and suggestions we received from many colleagues and associates. We have profited particularly from the advice of Donald R. Cressey of the University of California at Santa Barbara; Martin B. Danziger, former associate deputy attorney-general, U.S. Department of Justice; Arnold Heidenheimer, Washington University; Patrick V. Murphy, former police commissioner of New York City; Paul E. Peterson, University of Chicago; Leroy N. Rieselbach and York Willbern, Indiana University; and Henry S. Ruth, Jr., former deputy director of the President's Commission on Law Enforcement and the Administration of Justice. Robert Goehlert and Richard C. Rich undertook useful research in unfamiliar areas; and Marion Lovelace and Marianne Platt prepared the manuscript copy through several versions.

The points of view and opinions expressed in this volume are those of the editors and authors of the individual selections, and do not necessarily reflect the official positions or policies of Indiana University or the National Institute of Law Enforcement and Criminal Justice, Law Enforcement Assistance Administration.

PART ONE

INTRODUCTION

(1)

The Problem of Corruption

CORRUPTION IN POLITICAL AFFAIRS is not new to the current era nor can any particular political system validly claim to be free from it, yet basic questions about the nature of corruption remain unanswered and attempts to provide answers have been plagued by seemingly unresolvable difficulties. This chapter introduces several of these difficulties and directs attention to the critical importance of how questions about corruption are posed. As is the case with most social and political issues, the way in which questions about corruption are initially framed in large part determines the kinds of conclusions eventually arrived at. The readings in this chapter represent a variety of formulations about fundamental aspects of corruption, and each comes to somewhat different conclusions about the subject. In weighing the strength of an author's argument, it is therefore necessary to give close scrutiny to the explicit and implicit assumptions that are made about the nature of corruption.

Political corruption poses a host of problems for the society in which it occurs, for those who desire to construct institutional arrangements to diminish its frequency and severity, and for those who simply seek to understand it. We begin the task of understanding the nature of corruption by focusing on what is meant by the term *corruption*. Although that would seem to be an easy matter, there is no agreement on its meaning, perhaps because it is so commonly and loosely used in the daily political lexicon.

From the different definitions in the existing literature one can pretty much pick and choose a definition according to one's own preferences. There are no universally acceptable criteria or standards that can be employed to judge political acts as corrupt or legitimate. We do not pre-

3

tend to be able to resolve this problem here. In fact, it may be unresolvable in any ultimate sense. As long as different individuals maintain conflicting evaluative criteria and standards over what constitutes a corrupt act, the meaning of corruption will itself remain a matter of public dispute. We can, however, review various definitions that have been offered and show the implications involved in each.

One set of authors has offered very broad definitions of corruption. In 1934 V. O. Key provided a general definition of graft engaged in by public officials: "It may be defined as the abuse of control over the power and resources of the government for the purpose of personal or party profit."[1] Key was quick to point out that the kind of profit received by public officials need not be limited to cash payments.[2] Costikyan's more recent definition is similarly all-encompassing: "In short, corruption is the exercise of government power to achieve nongovernmental objectives."[3] The absence of specification of what constitutes "the abuse of control" in Key's definition and "nongovernmental objectives" in Costikyan's allows different individuals to place different constructions on corrupt acts. This open-ended implication is inherent in broad definitions of corruption, as Wilson recognizes when offering a similar formulation: "In general, corruption occurs whenever a person, in exchange for some private advantage, acts other than as his duty requires," and then adding: "The only problem with this definition is that by its test almost all politicians are corrupt in some measure."[4]

Narrow definitions of corruption, usually tied to laws enacted by the legislature, executive orders, and administrative rules, involve a set of opposite implications. What is corrupt becomes what is in violation of formal and legal rules. Consider, for example, Scott's statement: "we

1. V. O. Key, Jr., "The Techniques of Political Graft in the United States" (Chicago: Unpublished Ph.D. dissertation, University of Chicago Libraries, 1936), p.5.
2. In addition to cash payments corrupt officials may receive the following considerations: gifts, jobs or promises of future jobs, friendship, political support, campaign endorsements and contributions, honorific appointments, and ill-defined debts and obligations available for redemption later, to mention only a few. It may be useful to introduce here the distinction between corruption for personal gain and corruption for power augmentation. Most of the considerations we have listed contribute to the personal gain of the officeholders. Yet many instances of corruption result in little personal gain for the officials involved, but in considerable consolidation of power. Watergate and most of its related events illustrate corruption of the latter type.
3. See "The Locus of Corruption," in chapter 4.
4. See "Corruption Is Not Always Scandalous," in this chapter.

may define corruption as: behavior which deviates from the formal duties of a public role (elective or appointive) because of private-regarding (personal, close family, private clique) wealth or status gains: or violates rules against the exercise of certain types of private-regarding influence."[5] Political acts which transgress formal duties and rules are clearly corrupt under this definition, but it fails to address the possibility that corrupt acts may become institutionalized through the decrees, laws, and rules adopted by public officials themselves. Thus the legal-centered definition adequately covers acts which are illegal and calculated to benefit public officeholders. Its virtue is its precision. Its major limitation is its uncritical acceptance of state-enacted laws and rules as *the* single standard for judging whether public officials' acts are corrupt or not. Perhaps needless to say, allowing those whose behavior is to be judged corrupt or legitimate to establish the standards of judgment opens the very real possibility of public officials' rigging the system of evaluation in a manner that allows otherwise corrupt acts to pass as legitimate simply because they do not violate state law. The legal-centered definition is also inadequate because different governmental jurisdictions may adopt different definitions of corruption. Thus what is legal and thus corruption-free in one jurisdiction may be illegal and thus corrupt in another. By overlooking and confusing variations between jurisdictions and changes that may occur within jurisdictions over time, the legal definition of corruption proves to be less than universally acceptable.

Both narrow and broad definitions of corruption contain distinct advantages and disadvantages. The former offer specific criteria for determining the existence of corruption, but exclude significant areas of political behavior; the latter provide comprehensive coverage of potentially relevant behavior, but lack precision in identifying standards of evaluation. This definitional paradox is inherent to the subject of political corruption because the subject itself involves fundamental questions of opinions, judgments, and values about which there is rarely agreement. Yet the issue of how corruption is defined is highly important because it partially determines how much and what kind of corruption is found.

In view of these definitional problems, the reader will benefit by paying close attention to the orientations the authors of the following

5. James C. Scott, *Comparative Political Corruption* (Englewood Cliffs, N.J.: Prentice-Hall, Inc., 1972), p.4. Scott recognizes and discusses some of these same problems with this definition, ibid., pp. 3–6.

selections adopt toward corruption. Each author approaches the study of corruption with a different set of values informing his work, and the kinds of conclusions he arrives at may depend partly on his initial perspectives. Readers will also benefit by resisting the tendency to view corruption exclusively in black-and-white terms. Studies of corruption often yield "gray areas," where matters of fact and value are necessarily intermingled. The gray areas appear with considerable frequency because the affairs of government seldom permit the mechanical application of clear rules governing all situations, as our review of definitions of corruption also has shown.

In the first selection in this chapter we are introduced to George Washington Plunkitt's classic distinction between "honest graft" and "dishonest graft." His earthy observations were recorded by the journalist Riordon at the turn of the century, at a time when Plunkitt occupied a key leadership position in Tammany Hall, then the dominant Democratic party organization in New York City. Plunkitt offers the ultimate practical justification for the way he capitalized on his positions as an elected official and party leader with the words "I seen my opportunities and I took 'em." In the second selection, Leys uses cases drawn from American and African political experiences to show that determinations of what constitutes a corrupt act are often too simplistic, and that students of corruption need to search for more complex standards and criteria by which corruption may be judged. Heidenheimer's discussion draws attention to various definitions of corruption and the different normative implications involved in the use of each. His concern for precision in the use of the term corruption should be kept in mind when reading this volume and applied to each article in order to understand its author's set of assumptions. In the next selection, Key provides a straightforward definition of political graft and a useful taxonomy of the techniques commonly employed in schemes of corruption. Wilson's discussion of the problem of corruption concludes this chapter by emphasizing the importance of the circumstances surrounding corrupt acts and the different consequences flowing from various forms of corruption. As an introduction to the substantive chapters which follow, these selections should alert the readers to the problematical nature of corruption and disabuse them of preconceived notions that corruption is a simple, clear-cut matter.

HONEST GRAFT
William L. Riordan

Everybody is talkin' these days about Tammany men growin' rich
on graft, but nobody thinks of drawin' the distinction between honest
graft and dishonest graft. There's all the difference in the world between
the two. Yes, many of our men have grown rich in politics. I have myself.
I've made a big fortune out of the game, and I'm gettin' richer every day,
but I've not gone in for dishonest graft—blackmailin' gamblers, saloonkeepers, disorderly people, etc.—and neither has any of the men who
have made big fortunes in politics.

There's an honest graft, and I'm an example of how it works. I might
sum up the whole thing by sayin': "I seen my opportunities and I took
'em."

Just let me explain by examples. My party's in power in the city, and
it's goin' to undertake a lot of public improvements. Well, I'm tipped
off, say, that they're going to lay out a new park at a certain place.

I see my opportunity and I take it. I go to that place and I buy up
all the land I can in the neighborhood. Then the board of this or that
makes its plan public, and there is a rush to get my land, which nobody
cared particular for before.

Ain't it perfectly honest to charge a good price and make a profit on
my investment and foresight? Of course, it is. Well, that's honest graft.

Or supposin' it's a new bridge they're goin' to build. I get tipped off
and I buy as much property as I can that has to be taken for approaches.
I sell at my own price later on and drop some more money in the bank.

Wouldn't you? It's just like lookin' ahead in Wall Street or in the
coffee or cotton market. It's honest graft, and I'm lookin' for it every
day in the year. I will tell you frankly that I've got a good lot of it, too.

I'll tell you of one case. They were goin' to fix up a big park, no matter where. I got on to it, and went lookin' about for land in that neighborhood.

I could get nothin' at a bargain but a big piece of swamp, but I took it fast enough and held on to it. What turned out was just what I counted on. They couldn't make the park complete without Plunkitt's swamp, and they had to pay a good price for it. Anything dishonest in that?

Up in the watershed I made some money, too. I bought up several bits of land there some years ago and made a pretty good guess that they would be bought up for water purposes later by the city.

Somehow, I always guessed about right, and shouldn't I enjoy the profit of my foresight? It was rather amusin' when the condemnation commissioners came along and found piece after piece of the land in the name of George Plunkitt of the Fifteenth Assembly District, New York City. They wondered how I knew just what to buy. The answer is—I seen my opportunity and I took it. I haven't confined myself to land; anything that pays is in my line.

For instance, the city is repavin' a street and has several hundred thousand old granite blocks to sell. I am on hand to buy, and I know just what they are worth.

How? Never mind that. I had a sort of monopoly of this business for a while, but once a newspaper tried to do me. It got some outside men to come over from Brooklyn and New Jersey to bid against me.

Was I done? Not much. I went to each of the men and said: "How many of these 250,000 stones do you want?" One said 20,000, and another wanted 15,000, and another wanted 10,000. I said: "All right, let me bid for the lot, and I'll give each of you all you want for nothin'."

They agreed, of course. Then the auctioneer yelled: "How much am I bid for these 250,000 fine pavin' stones?"

"Two dollars and fifty cents," says I.

"Two dollars and fifty cents!" screamed the auctioneer. "Oh, that's a joke! Give me a real bid."

He found the bid was real enough. My rivals stood silent. I got the lot for $2.50 and gave them their share. That's how the attempt to do Plunkitt ended, and that's how all such attempts end.

I've told you how I got rich by honest graft. Now, let me tell you that most politicians who are accused of robbin' the city get rich the same way.

They didn't steal a dollar from the city treasury. They just seen their opportunities and took them. That is why, when a reform administration comes in and spends a half million dollars in tryin' to find the public robberies they talked about in the campaign, they don't find them.

The books are always all right. The money in the city treasury is all right. Everything is all right. All they can show is that the Tammany heads of departments looked after their friends, within the law, and gave them what opportunities they could to make honest graft. Now, let me tell you that's never goin' to hurt Tammany with the people. Every good man looks after his friends, and any man who doesn't isn't likely to be popular. If I have a good thing to hand out in private life, I give it to a friend. Why shouldn't I do the same in public life?

Another kind of honest graft. Tammany has raised a good many salaries. There was an awful howl by the reformers, but don't you know that Tammany gains ten votes for every one it lost by salary raisin'?

The Wall Street banker thinks it shameful to raise a department clerk's salary from $1500 to $1800 a year, but every man who draws a salary himself says: "That's all right. I wish it was me." And he feels very much like votin' the Tammany ticket on election day, just out of sympathy.

Tammany was beat in 1901 because the people were deceived into believin' that it worked dishonest graft. They didn't draw a distinction between dishonest and honest graft, but they saw that some Tammany men grew rich, and supposed they had been robbin' the city treasury or levyin' blackmail on disorderly houses, or workin' in with the gamblers and lawbreakers.

As a matter of policy, if nothing else, why should the Tammany leaders go into such dirty business, when there is so much honest graft lyin' around when they are in power? Did you ever consider that?

Now, in conclusion, I want to say that I don't own a dishonest dollar. If my worst enemy was given the job of writin' my epitaph when I'm gone, he couldn't do more than write:

"George W. Plunkitt. He Seen His Opportunities, and He Took 'Em."

WHAT IS THE PROBLEM
ABOUT CORRUPTION?

Colin Leys

Under what circumstances are actions called corrupt? It seems best to start from some examples.

(1) In the spring of 1964 the (Republican) Secretary of State of Illinois died. Under the State constitution the (Democratic) Governor temporarily filled his place by appointing a young (Democratic) official to the office. Within a few weeks a substantial number of State civil servants appointed by the late Secretary of State were dismissed, and their jobs were filled by Democratic Party supporters.

(2) In Chicago about the same time a controversy was taking place concerning school desegregation. Active desegregationists alleged that they were prevented from attending in force a meeting of the City Council as part of their campaign, because all the public seating was filled by council employees who had for this purpose been given a holiday by the city administration.

(3) In Kampala, Uganda, in August 1963 the City Council decided to award a petrol station site to a majority-party member of the Council, who offered the lowest price, £4,000; the highest offer was for £11,000. It was alleged in the National Assembly that the successful purchaser resold the plot to an oil company at a profit of £8,000.

(4) In Port Harcourt, Nigeria, in 1955, there were people in the Town Hall drawing labourers' salaries not provided for in the estimates; they were employed on the personal recommendation of individual councillors.

(5) In New York City, in 1951, it was estimated that over $1 million per annum was paid to policemen (for overlooking illegalities) by a bookmaking syndicate.

From Colin Leys, "What Is the Problem about Corruption?" *Journal of Modern African Studies* 3: 2 (August 1965), pp. 217–224. All footnotes deleted.

(6) In Lagos, Nigeria, in 1952, the practice of giving an unofficial cash gift or a fee for services rendered was fairly authoritatively stated to be found

> in hospitals where the nurses require a fee from every in-patient before the prescribed medicine is given, and even the ward servants must have their 'dash' before bringing the bed-pan; it is known to be rife in the Police Motor Traffic Unit, which has unrivalled opportunities on account of the common practice of overloading vehicles; pay clerks make a deduction from the wages of daily paid staff; produce examiners exact a fee from the produce buyer for every bag that is graded and sealed; domestic servants pay a proportion of their wages to the senior of them, besides often having paid a lump sum to buy the job.

One thing which all these events have in common is that someone regards each of them as a bad thing. Equally, however, it is clear that at least someone else—i.e. those involved in the acts in question—regards each of them as a good thing. Writers of the moralist school accept this, but they are convinced that such behaviour is always against the 'public interest'. But what is the 'public interest'? Some substantial arguments have been put forward to suggest that the public interest may sometimes *require* some of these practices. The most famous of these is probably the American defence of patronage, as in case (1) above, and 'honest graft'. This argument turns essentially on the view that democratic politics in 'mass' societies can only be ensured by the integration of a multitude of interests and groups into political parties, capable of furnishing leadership and coherent policies; this involves organisation and inducements, both of which cost money; therefore politics must be made to pay. From this point of view the political role of money is to serve as a cement—'a *hyphen* which joins, a *buckle* which fastens' the otherwise separate and conflicting elements of a society into a body politic; 'the greater the corruption, the greater the harmony between corruptor and corruptee', as one candid critic recognised. And Professor Hoselitz has argued that the early years of the life of a nation are dominated by these 'persistent integrative needs of the society', and that

> Much of the alleged corruption that Western technical advisers on administrative services of Asian and African stages encounter, and against which they inveigh in their technical reports with so little genuine success, is nothing but the prevalence of these non-rational norms on the basis of which these administrations operate.

This can be taken a stage further. The moralist school of thought may recognise that some of the activities recorded above indirectly

serve these broadly beneficial purposes. But they generally assume that
the economic price paid is a heavy one. For instance:

> The sums involved in some of the proved cases of corruption in Africa
> would have brought considerable benefits to people for whom 'under-
> privileged' is too mild a word, if they had been properly spent.

But spending public money properly does not guarantee that it will
benefit the poor. The Uganda Minister of Information was much criti-
cised for giving a lucrative and unusual monopoly of television set sales
to an American contractor, in return for building a transmission station
at cut rates: even had corruption been involved the policy did produce
a television station much more quickly and cheaply than the policy
adopted in neighbouring Kenya. To take another example, one may ask
whether the Russian consumer would be better off without the operations of the illegal contact men who derive illegal incomes in return for
their aid in overcoming bottlenecks in the supply of materials for production. Even in the case of petty bribery or extortion it is relevant to
ask, What is the alternative? Could an equally efficient and socially
useful administration be carried on if effective means of eliminating
perquisites were found and all concerned were required to live on their
salaries? Would the pressure for higher salaries be no greater? Could
it be resisted? If it could not, would increased taxation fall on those
most able to pay and would this, or reduced services, be in the public
interest? To ask these questions is to realise that the answers call for
research and analysis which is seldom undertaken, and that they are
likely to vary according to circumstances. One also becomes aware
that near the heart of the moralists' concern is the idea that the public
interest is opposed to anything that heightens *inequality*. But we also
have to ask how far equality and development are themselves compatible ideals. The régime most committed to both of them—the
U.S.S.R.—found it necessary to postpone its concern with equality in
order to achieve development. This is not to say that all kinds of inequality promoted by all kinds of corruption are beneficial from the
point of view of development; it is merely to challenge the assumption
that they are invariably bad.

But we still have not answered the question, Under what circumstances are actions called corrupt? What is at issue in all the cases
cited above is the existence of a standard of behaviour according to
which the action in question breaks some rule, written or unwritten,
about the proper purposes to which a public office or a public institution may be put. The moralist has his own idea of what the rule should

be. The actors in the situations concerned have theirs. It may be the same as the moralists' (they may regard themselves as corrupt); or quite different (they may regard themselves as behaving honourably according to their standards, and regard their critics' standards as irrelevant); or they may be 'men of two worlds', partly adhering to two standards which are incompatible, and ending up exasperated and indifferent (they may recognise no particular moral implications of the acts in question at all—this is fairly obviously quite common). And in addition to the actors there are the other members—more or less directly affected—of their own society; all these positions are possible for them too.

The Analysis of Corruption

The following questions suggest themselves as a reasonable basis for the analysis of any case in which corruption is alleged:

(1) What is being called corrupt and does it really happen? In the case of the African Continental Bank it became clear that no one was able to formulate a clear enough allegation against Dr. N. Azikiwe showing precisely what was the rule which he had broken. A precise statement is required of the rule and the sense in which it is said to have been perverted. It may turn out, as in the case of the African Continental Bank, that there is really no clear idea of what the rule is; or that there is a clear rule but that it has not clearly been broken (this was Lord Denning's verdict on the Profumo case).

(2) Who regards the purpose which is being perverted as the proper or 'official' purpose? It may be so regarded by most people in the society, including those who pervert it; or it may be so regarded by only a few people (e.g. state political patronage is regarded as corrupt by only a relatively small group of American reformers).

(3) Who regards the allegedly corrupt action as perverting the official purpose? This is not necessarily the same question as question (2) above. For example, in a subsequent debate in the Uganda National Assembly on the petrol station site mentioned above, the Minister of Regional Administrations accepted the principle that the Council ought not to accept offers lower than the official valuer's valuation of the property, but held that they were by no means obliged to accept the highest offer and that the Council were justified in preferring to give a 'stake' in the city to a poor man rather than to a rich one. The opposition took the view that it was the man's politics rather than his poverty which actuated the majority on the Council, and that the loss

to the public revenue was too high a price to pay for assisting one individual member of the public. They also took the view that the official object should be to accept the highest bid, unless circumstances of public importance not present in this case dictated otherwise. Thus the nature of the rule was also a matter of controversy, but both sides to the dispute to some extent made the distinction between the rule on the one hand, and the question of what amounted to breaking it on the other.

(4) What are the short-term and long-term consequences of the behaviour in question, both of each particular case and of such behaviour generally? The answer might usefully, if roughly, be broken into two parts: (a) objective consequences, and (b) subjective consequences. Under (a) will come such questions as, What resources are directed from what applications to what other applications? What are the real as opposed to the theoretical opportunity costs of the alleged corruption? What are the effects for income distribution? And what consequential effects are there on the pattern of loyalties, the scope of party activities, the incentives to economic activity? etc. etc. Under (b) will come such questions as e.g., What effect does behaving in this way have on the work of civil servants who regard themselves as behaving corruptly? and, What effect does observing such behaviour have on the attitudes and/or behaviour of others? etc. etc.

It is natural but wrong to assume that the results of corruption are always both bad and important. For instance it is usually assumed that a corrupt civil service is an impediment to the establishment of foreign private enterprise, which has enough difficulties to contend with without in addition having to pay bribes. This may be clearly the case, but sometimes also the reverse appears to be true. Where bureaucracy is both elaborate and inefficient, the provision of strong personal incentives to bureaucrats to cut red tape may be the only way of speeding the establishment of the new firm. In such a case it is certainly reasonable to wish that the bureaucracy were simpler and more efficient, but not to argue that bribery *per se* is an obstacle to private economic initiative. On the other hand the results may be unimportant from any practical standpoint, even if they are not particularly nice.

From such questions one may go on to pose another which is clearly the central one for the scientific study of the problem: In any society, under what conditions is behaviour most likely to occur which a significant section of the population will regard as corrupt? Some obviously relevant points are:

(1) The 'standing' of the 'official purpose' of each public office or

institution in the society. This involves the diffusion of understanding of the idea generally, and within particular relevant groups (e.g. civil servants or police); how strongly supported this conception is, generally, and within particular groups; and what effect distance and scale have on both these dimensions. For example, ordinary people in England did not immediately condemn the Ferranti company for wanting to keep over £4 million windfall profits on a defence contract, because it was an incomprehensibly vast sum gained in highly unfamiliar circumstances; but the same people would instantly condemn a local contractor who made a windfall profit of £40,000 on laying a drainpipe for the Rural District Council. And the 'standing' of the 'official purpose' of anything is also affected by the 'standing' of other rival conceptions of its purpose, e.g. the competing moral claims of relatives on a civil servant who is making junior appointments.

(2) *The extent to which action which perverts or contravenes such official purposes is seen as doing so*—another complex problem of research into attitudes.

(3) *The incentives and disincentives to corrupt the official purposes of an office or institution*. For instance, the size of the profits to be made by bribery, or the losses liable to be incurred by refraining from it, compared with the penalties attached to being caught and exposed.

(4) *The ease with which corruption (once defined) can be carried on*. This involves such things as the case of a particular type of corruption, and the extent to which ordinary people are exposed to opportunities for it (which is among other things affected very much by the range of the activities of the state).

All these aspects clearly interact with each other.

DEFINITIONS, CONCEPTS
AND CRITERIA
Arnold J. Heidenheimer

Any attempt to analyze the concept of corruption must contend
with the fact that in English and other languages the word *corruption*
has a history of vastly different meanings and connotations. In some
eras, for instance the 1900s in the United States, corruption was one
of the most frequently employed terms in the political vocabulary.
According to a critic contemporary with this period, Robert C. Brooks,
party orators, journalists, reformers, political philosophers, and historians "stigmatize[d] in this way transactions and conditions of very
different kinds . . . [with] little disposition to inquire into the essential
nature of corruption and to discriminate in the use of the word." The
only connotaton that the many usages of the word *corruption* had in
common in this period was that it was somehow the antithesis of
reform, rationality, and the demands of the public weal.

Thus, even the more thoughtful and objective writers of this earlier
era would have been nonplussed had they read Samuel Huntington's
judgment in a 1968 publication that "corruption may thus be functional to the maintenance of a political system in the same way that
reform is." As is implied in Huntington's usage and elsewhere in the
contemporary social science literature, the term *corruption* has developed a more specific meaning with regard to kinds of behavior and
a much less polarized meaning with regard to ethical connotations. At
times, indeed, it is employed in a context that is almost totally value-
free, as in this passage by the economist, Nathaniel Leff:

> Corruption is an extra-legal institution used by individuals or groups to
> gain influence over the actions of the bureaucracy. As such the existence

Reprinted with the permission of the publisher from Introduction to
Arnold J. Heidenheimer, ed., *Political Corruption: Readings In Compara-
tive Analysis,* pp.3–9, copyright © 1970 by Holt, Rinehart and Winston,
Inc. References to other readings and some footnotes deleted.

of corruption *per se* indicates only that these groups participate in the decision-making process to a greater extent than would otherwise be the case.

Varieties of Meanings

A careful examination of what past and present writers seem to have intended when they employed the term *corruption* in political contexts reveals an even broader catalog of usages and potential ambiguities. Some reasons for this become more apparent by referring to the *Oxford English Dictionary*, where we find that only one of nine commonly accepted definitions for the term is applicable to political contexts: "Perversion or destruction of integrity in the discharge of public duties by bribery or favour; the use or existence of corrupt practices, especially in a state, public corporation, etc."

The *OED* categorizes the nine meanings of corruption as follows:

1. *Physical*—for example, "The destruction or spoiling of anything, especially by disintegration or by decomposition with its attendant unwholesomeness and loathsomeness; putrefaction."

2. *Moral*—the "political" definition already given comes under this category. Another definition in this category is: "A making or becoming morally corrupt; the fact or condition of being corrupt; moral deterioration or decay; depravity."

3. *The perversion of anything from an original state of purity*—for example, "The perversion of an institution, custom, and so forth from its primitive purity; an instance of this perversion."

The present usage of the term *corruption* in political contexts has obviously been colored by the meanings in the "moral" category, and in earlier times usage was frequently colored by the meanings in the two other categories, especially by those in the third category. Thus the author of a nineteenth-century encyclopedia article entitled "Corruption in Politics" developed his discussion essentially in terms of meanings derived by way of Montesquieu from Aristotle, who, for instance, conceived of *tyranny* as a "corrupted" variant of monarchy.

Contemporary Social Science Definitions

The variety of definitions employed by contemporary social scientists interested in corruption fortunately does not cover as wide a span as those given in the *OED*. Among them we can identify usages that seek to define corruption in terms of one of three kinds of basic models or concepts. The largest group of social science writers follow the

OED definition and relate their definitions of *corruption* essentially to concepts concerning the duties of the public office. A smaller group develop definitions that are primarily related to demand, supply, and exchange concepts derived from economic theory; while a third group discuss corruption more with regard to the concept of the public interest.

Public-Office-Centered Definitions

Definitions of corruption that relate most essentially to the concept of the public office and to deviations from norms binding upon its incumbents are well illustrated in the work of three authors—David H. Bayley, M. McMullan, and J. S. Nye—who have concerned themselves with the problems of development in various continents. According to Bayley's definition of the word . . . ,

> Corruption, while being tied particularly to the act of bribery, is a general term covering misuse of authority as a result of considerations of personal gain, which need not be monetary.

M. McMullan says that

> A public official is corrupt if he accepts money or money's worth for doing something that he is under duty to do anyway, that he is under duty not to do, or to exercise a legitimate discretion for improper reasons.

J. S. Nye defines corruption as

> . . . behavior which deviates from the normal duties of a public role because of private-regarding (family, close private clique), pecuniary or status gains; or violates rules against the exercise of certain types of private-regarding influence. This includes such behavior as bribery (use of reward to pervert the judgement of a person in a position of trust); nepotism (bestowal of patronage by reason of ascriptive relationship rather than merit); and misappropriation (illegal appropriation of public resources for private-regarding uses).

Market-Centered Definitions

Definitions in terms of the theory of the market have been developed particularly by those authors dealing with earlier Western and contemporary non-Western societies, in which the norms governing public officeholders are not clearly articulated or are nonexistent. Leff's definition, cited earlier, would fall into this category, as would the definitions of Jacob van Klaveren and Robert Tilman. Van Klaveren . . . states that

> A corrupt civil servant regards his public office as a business, the income of which he will . . . seek to maximize. The office then becomes a "maximizing unit." The size of his income depends . . . upon the market situation and his talents for finding the point of maximal gain on the public's demand curve.

Robert Tilman . . . holds that

> Corruption involves a shift from a mandatory pricing model to a free-market model. The centralized allocative mechanism, which is the ideal of modern bureaucracy, may break down in the face of serious disequilibrium between supply and demand. Clients may decide that it is worthwhile to risk the known sanctions and pay the higher costs in order to be assured of receiving the desired benefits. When this happens bureaucracy ceases to be patterned after the mandatory market and takes on characteristics of the free market.

Public-Interest-Centered Definitions

Some writers feel that the first set of definitions is too narrowly conceived and the second set too broadly conceived. They tend to maintain that the embattled concept of "public interest" is not only still useful but necessary to illustrate the essence of concepts like corruption. Carl Friedrich, for instance, contends that

> The pattern of corruption can be said to exist whenever a power-holder who is charged with doing certain things, i.e., who is a responsible functionary or officeholder, is by monetary or other rewards not legally provided for induced to take actions which favour whoever provides the rewards and thereby does damage to the public and its interests.[1]

Arnold A. Rogow and H. D. Lasswell . . . maintain that

> A corrupt act violates responsibility toward at least one system of public or civic order and is in fact incompatible with (destructive of) any such system. A system of public or civic order exalts common interest over special interest; violations of the common interest for special advantage are corrupt.

Whose Norms Set the Criteria?

The definitions employed in the first and third of the categories just discussed directly raise the question encountered in all normative

1. Carl J. Friedrich, "Political Pathology," *Political Quarterly*, 37 (1966), p.74.

analysis: Which norms are the ones that will be utilized to distinguish corrupt from noncorrupt acts? If the definitions are public-office-
centered, then which statement of the rules and norms governing
public officeholders is to be employed? If the definitions are public-
interest-centered, then whose evaluation of the public's interest is to
be operationalized? Definitions couched in terms of market theory appear to bypass this problem, but in fact they do not. They too imply
that somewhere there is an authority that distinguishes between the
rules applicable to public officials and those applicable to businessmen
operating in the free market, or that there are certain characteristics
that distinguish a "black market" from the free market.

Political scientists of an earlier generation tried to deal with the
problem of norm setting with reference to the legal rules provided by
statute books and court decisions. Thus behavior was judged by James
Bryce to be either permissible or corrupt in accordance with the criteria established by legislators and judges:

> Corruption may be taken to include those modes of employing money to
> attain private ends by political means which are criminal or at least
> illegal, because they induce persons charged with a public duty to trans-
> gress that duty and misuse the functions assigned to them.[2]

But most contemporary social scientists would echo the skepticism that
Robert Brooks articulated in 1910 . . . as to whether legal definitions
alone would suffice:

> Definitions of corrupt practices . . . found in every highly developed
> legal code . . . are scarcely broad enough to cover the whole concept as
> seen from the viewpoint of political science or ethics. The sanctions of
> positive law are applied only to those more flagrant practices which
> past experience has shown to be so pernicious that sentiment has crystal-
> lized into statutory prohibitions and adverse judicial decisions. Even
> within this comparatively limited circle clearness and precision are but
> imperfectly attained.

The author of the article on "Corruption, Political," in the *Encyclopedia of the Social Sciences* agreed that "the question of formal legality . . . is not the essence of the concept." The normative judgments
that should be used as criteria, he thought, were the judgments of the
elite: "Where the best opinion and morality of the time, examining the

---

2. James Bryce, *Modern Democracies*, II, New York: St. Martin's,
1921, p.524.

intent and setting of an act, judge it to represent a sacrifice of public for private benefit, then it must be held to be corrupt."[3]

The definition suggested by Senturia raises numerous problems, namely those related to the difficulties of identification, operationalization, and uniqueness. Although social scientists often select particular elite groups with reference to status and other criteria, few claim to have developed specific techniques for identifying in any society a sample that would represent "the best opinion of the time." Even if this were accomplished, Senturia's particularistic emphasis would require that this fairly large body of elites serve as a jury for each particular case. Their findings, in effect, would relate only to their society of that particular era.

A consensus of the "best opinion" in a time and place, such as Britain in 1960, could presumably establish criteria beyond which private-regarding behavior would be considered corrupt in the contemporary setting. However, it would then be impossible to compare either the extent or the varieties of political corruption between the situations prevailing of Britain in 1960 and in 1860 because of the uniqueness of the suggested definition. This difficulty would apply equally to attempts to compare, say, bureaucratic corruption in nineteenth-century Russia and twentieth-century Chicago. Another difficulty in relying too much on any one elite opinion is that the incumbent elite may change drastically as the result of revolution or decolonization. Thus, in the course of decolonization, the criteria by which the colonial rulers had punished corruption among native officials and subjects were radically diluted within a short time when the opinion of the postcolonial native politicians de-emphasized many of the taboos that had been attached to private-regarding behavior. Still later, in many African and Asian countries, behavior that was widely accepted by the ruling politicians one month was heavily stigmatized the next month after spartan-minded officers successfully carried through a coup d'état.

Western versus Non-Western Standards

If one does not accept the criteria established by law or the norms of a small elite group as delimiting political corruption, how far can one go in delineating the relevant norms with reference to the standards of a more diverse set of reference groups and codes? At present this

3. Joseph J. Senturia, "Corruption, Political," *Encyclopedia of the Social Sciences,* IV. New York: Crowell-Collier-Macmillan, 1930–1935, p. 449.

problem presents itself most directly for those social scientists who
have sought to analyze corruption in developing countries where mores
rooted in two very distinct milieus govern the standards of political and
bureaucratic behavior. David H. Bayley . . . has outlined the resultant
problem posed for the objective investigator:

> It not infrequently happens . . . in developing non-Western societies
> that existing moral codes do not agree with Western norms as to what
> kinds of behavior by public servants should be condemned. The Western
> observer is faced with an uncomfortable choice. He can adhere to the
> Western definition, in which case he lays himself open to the charge of
> being censorious and he finds that he is condemning not abhorrent behav-
> ior, but normal acceptable operating procedure. On the other hand, he
> may face up to the fact that corruption, if it requires moral censure, is
> culturally conditioned. He then argues that an act is corrupt if the sur-
> rounding society condemns it. This usage, however, muddies communi-
> cation, for it may be necessary then to assert in the same breath that an
> official accepts gratuities but is not corrupt.

Given this alternative, authors like Bayley prefer to build upon the
"Western denotative meaning of corruption," even in analyzing non-
Western systems. This "imposition" on the rest of the world of Western
standards in evaluating behavior may well be, at this stage of research
and theory building, a prerequisite to meaningful comparative analysis
of political corruption phenomena. In general terms (more with regard
to bureaucratic than to electoral corruption) there probably does exist
today a broad consensus among Western elites and non-elites as to
which kinds of behavior are clearly conceived of as corrupt. This consensus has gradually developed over the past century as will be traced
in the subsequent section. But the norms embodied in a definition such
as that of Nye, quoted earlier, are surely built upon more than the
personal preferences of a small clique of academic political moralizers.
It is highly probable that any elite or even mass survey of attitudes in
Western countries would result in overwhelming support for the proposition that the kinds of deviations from public rules and the kinds of
self-regarding behavior that are included in Nye's definition should be
labeled corrupt, and guilty practitioners stigmatized accordingly.
Writers such as Bayley admit that this consensus is limited rather than
universal, but they argue that the norms expressed by it are the only
ones that can possibly be applied cross-culturally and that we should
go ahead and do so. In further defense of his strategy, Bayley argues
that:

> the intelligentsia, and especially top-level civil servants, in most under-
> developed nations are familiar with the Western label "corruption," and

they apply it to their own countries. . . . It is not unfair, therefore, to make comparative statements between West and non-West based upon Webster's definition. Such judgements will be readily understood by the nation-building elites in most developing countries.

TECHNIQUES OF POLITICAL GRAFT

V. O. Key, Jr.

Certain conclusions and hypotheses may be drawn from the data which have been presented. A classification of the techniques of graft may be formulated, the functions of graft may be sketched, certain tentative remarks relative to the "causes" of graft may be offered, and some of the trends in graft and counter trends may be suggested.

The Techniques of Graft

The general scheme followed in presenting the descriptive material has precluded the formulation of a classification of the techniques of graft, but it should be obvious by the time this point is reached that there are certain common types which recur in all the activities of government. It is believed that practically all instances of graft may be grouped into several fundamental types of techniques of graft. The point may be raised that the patterns of behavior which are set forth as the basic techniques of graft involve such minute situations as to be meaningless. But in the precise analysis of social phenomena, it is necessary to break the indeterminate total situation into its component parts. It will be recalled that in the beginning graft was defined as an abuse of power for personal or party profit. It was noted that graft usually involved a relationship between the official exercising the power which is abused and some other individual or individuals and

From V. O. Key, Jr., "The Techniques of Political Graft in the United States," Chicago, Ill.: University of Chicago Libraries, 1936, pp.386–395. All footnotes deleted.

that the techniques of graft are the methods employed in these relationships plus the methods used in cases of graft involving only a single individual.

Bribery to influence official action is the most obvious technique of
graft. The name which a particular payment in money or other value
for this purpose takes is immaterial. Some campaign contributions cannot be differentiated from bribes. Business and professional relationships may conceal bribery. When a corporation secures its bonds or
insurance, for example, from a political leader, it cannot be assumed
that this is done because the "boss" sells the best insurance. Any favor
secured as a result of such relationships is secured by bribery. Bribery
is fundamentally the same whether employed in relation to legislators,
administrators, judges, other public officials, "bosses" exercising their
power or private individuals acting in agency positions. It is the same
on all levels of government and in all functions. The act of bribery, as
has been observed from some of the instances recounted, is a matter
requiring considerable skill. In the process there is often considerable
preliminary negotiation in order to achieve an intimate relationship
with the person to be bribed. He is given "good" and plausible reasons
for doing what he is being bought to do. Sometimes advantage is taken
of his financial needs, and he may be in a way "coerced" to accept. In
other cases, of course, bribery is a more or less cold-blooded commercial transaction.

The converse of bribery is extortion, i.e., the abuse or threat of
abuse of a power in such a way as to secure response in payment of
money or other valuable thing. This technique is the same whether it
is exercised by a legislative coterie through a "sand-bagging" bill or by
a building inspector through a trivial "shake-down." In extortion the
initiative is clearly with the public official or the person exercising his
power. Legislators may hold a "regulator" or a "revenue-raiser" over
the heads of persons directly interested in the proposed legislation and
subtly intimate that it might be put quietly away by payments to the
right persons. A licensing official may threaten revocation of a saloon
license if a campaign contribution is not made. A disbursing officer may
threaten to delay a payment justly due if some gratuity is not forthcom-
ing. The assessment of public employees usually takes the form of extortion although it is actually carried on with widely varying degrees
of subtlety. In all these and other similar situations the behavior pattern
involved is the same, although, of course, in making threats and demands for money various shades of bluntness in communication prevail.

In individual instances it may be difficult to distinguish between extortion, solicitation of a bribe and bribery. Business men usually claim that all their bribes are "protection" money which they are compelled to pay. Others take the view that there is really no extortion, but that it is all bribery. It seems quite evident that there are both types of relationships.

"State-bribery" is a term which may be applied to those instances where control of various public properties and of the expenditure of public funds is abused—or perhaps more accurately misused—for the purpose of creating power or control relationships. Analyzed to the ultimate any instance in which one individual controls another is a power situation or relationship. Thus, state-bribery includes the control of the political organization, its candidates and to some extent its policies, by the control of patronage. A rebellious district leader or ward committeeman may discover that his printing contracts or his fire hose business has been cut off by the men "higher-up" in the organization and that it is too late to mend his ways. Control by state-bribery may extend to electors as in the employment of election officials and the hiring of polling places with the tacit understanding, if not express, that the ballots will be cast "right." This type of control may extend to the political attitudes of community leaders, such as bankers, through the distribution of deposits of public funds. The construction of public works, the distribution of subsidies may be in the nature of state-bribery, to control the electoral behavior of particular groups, territorial or functional. An executive may "buy" a legislator with an appointment. These examples are not intended to exclude others but are merely illustrative. The common element running through all of them is the element of control secured by an abuse—a perversion of the purpose—of the power granted to the official concerned. The object of the control need not be to influence a person with reference to his political behavior, but it generally is. The widespread acquiescence in the practice of various forms of state-bribery does not change their real nature. The relationship is without doubt one of bribery with public funds.

Another fundamental form of graft is political discrimination in the formulation and administration of law or rules of behavior, that is to say, the power to make or administer law. The consideration is a political attitude rather than a payment of money or other value. Law making and law enforcing may be lumped together in this category for when law making is unequivocally employed for this purpose, as in administration, the individual case is dealt with rather than broad interests. The effect of abuse in this category may be to create lines of control within the political organization as when a ward committeeman or a district leader is permitted to operate a gambling house. The boss of the organization is certain of the support of this leader for he can order the police to close the place, if he wishes. In smaller matters the effect of this discriminatory administration of law may be to create "friends" among the electorate, as when tickets for violating traffic ordinances are "fixed." Political discrimination of this sort may come either as the result of the initiative of the official concerned or on petition of the person favored. The relationship may resemble either bribery or intimidation.

Discrimination in the administration of service functions for political purposes is a fifth fundamental technique of graft. The standards set up for the administration of services in individual cases are departed from and the criteria become political. Republicans are discriminated against in favor of Democrats in granting unemployment relief, for example. The Republican party functionary is given preference in the selection of stalls in the public markets. Abuses in the service functions may be differentiated from state-bribery in that abuses in the latter category are usually incident to some appointive or contractual relationship whereas abuses in the service activities are incident to a service relationship between citizen and government. Abuses in service relationships differ from abuses in the administration of law for in the latter a norm of conduct is applied through penal sanctions.

A final type of technique of graft may be denominated "auto-corruption." In bribery, extortion, state-bribery and the other types which have been described, relationships between two or more individuals are involved. In auto-corruption the public official or person exercising the power of such official, boss or whatever he may be, in a sense plays the role of both parties in the other situations involving two or more persons. He secures for himself the administrative privilege which would be secured by an outsider by bribery. He awards contracts to himself, perhaps using dummy corporations, which would go to reward a contractor in the organization. He appropriates public property which might be used to reward some other member of the political organization. At times in all types of auto-corruption the gains may trickle into the political organization through campaign contributions and by various other means, but there is a fundamental distinction between this and the other forms of graft. However, in some instances auto-corruption may be a single link in a chain of individual cases which create a "ring" formation of power. The spoils are divided by individuals in their respective official positions, but the series of events bind together all the participants in the political machine. In auto-corruption cases often occur in which the personal gain far outweighs the group or party advantage. Matters of this kind, of course, have no place in the well regulated machine.

In addition to these fundamental techniques of graft there are employed in conjunction with the primary methods various subsidiary or ancillary techniques, which have been described in considerable detail in connection with the various activities of government. The methods of maintaining secrecy, which is essential in most types of graft, are fairly obvious. In the first instance as little evidence as possible is created. When bribes are passed only the giver and the receiver are present, or perhaps the money passes through several hands from briber to bribee. Some of the individuals through whose hands it passes may be more or less ignorant of what the purpose is. The terms of an agreement to give some particular privilege may be vague, indefinite or merely implied. Non-verbal symbols may be employed. As little documentary evidence as possible is created. When payments have to be made from corporate or firm funds, false entries are made. A bribe may be charged as repairs to steamers or roadbed maintenance. Double records—one false, one true—may be kept. Dummy corporations have a multiplicity of uses. Business and professional relationships may conceal bribery. In the maintenance of secrecy much depends on the "right" relations with opposition politicians and with newspapers which might ferret out and disclose unsavory matters.

The various methods of camouflage and counter-propaganda constitute another subsidiary technique. In nearly every instance of alleged graft the accused has an explanation differing from the interpretation offered by the prosecutor. The meanest sort of "steal" is sometimes transformed by the graft artist into a great deed for the promotion of the public welfare or at least a bit of harmless pillaging of the rich for the benefit of the poor. If this cannot be done, sufficient dust may be raised to create confusion and doubt. Foreign wars to allay domestic uprisings is a political theme on which there are many variations. Grafters as well as other political technicians have been thoroughly aware of this principle of politics. We have the spectacle of "Big Bill" Thompson sallying forth to kick King George "on the snoot" after his cohorts had virtually carried away the city hall stone by stone. Grafting political organizations have managed their activities as if public opinion mattered, whether it did or not.

The evasion of legal requirements, such as those in civil service laws and in regulations governing the award of public contracts, is a subsidiary method which varies with the legal regime concerned. Certain types of evasion, however, recur. Legislation cannot anticipate every possible contingency and exceptions to the general rule are usually provided. These exceptions may be utilized to such an extent as to nullify the general rule. Temporary appointees are named under the provisions of the civil service laws providing for emergency appointments. In awarding contracts orders are divided and made under the legal provisions allowing purchases without calling for bids when the amount is less than $1000 or $500. Discretion may be abused. Thus, who is the lowest responsible bidder? General terms may be used to indicate specific things as in the manipulation of contract and purchase specifications. Probably more important than these verbalistic techniques designed to give a color of legality is the outright disregard of legislation governing the administration.

The master strategy of the political machine consists in the political consolidation of the beneficiaries of the graft system together with others who may be brought into the combination by some other appeal. Thus, graft as it has been defined may be either sporadic or systematic. The individual instances are the same in either case, or on any level of government, or in any country, but in any instance it is contended that it is virtually impossible to rule by graft alone. Other techniques must be employed to win the support of persons who do not obviously benefit as a result of graft. At any rate the technique of combination of various interests into a governing bloc is not peculiar to organizations specializing in corrupt political techniques. It consists in welding together all the interests benefiting by the privileges given as a result of bribery, the receivers of state-bribes, and beneficiaries of political discrimination into the most powerful combination in the political life of a jurisdiction. It may include the suppression of opposition by methods often akin to intimidation as by a threat to skyrocket an individual's tax bill. Regardless of the techniques employed this procedure has to be consummated in order to attain and retain power. The aspect of a corrupt power combination which may be peculiar is that the combinations and alliances are effectuated by the application of sanctions and controls with compelling force directly to the individual. When some other types of techniques are employed successful combinations may be effectuated to a greater extent by group appeals. But the sole function of these power techniques is not to place a given set of individuals in power.

CORRUPTION IS NOT
ALWAYS SCANDALOUS

James Q. Wilson

The problem with corruption is that it tends to become the Problem of Corruption. Moral issues usually obscure practical issues, even when the moral question is a relatively small one and the practical matter is very great. This is especially true in an era when the amount of corruption in governing is declining but our moral sensibilities about that which remains are getting keener.

In 1964, Paul Screvane, an earnest, personally honest, somewhat colorless public official with a long record of competent public service, was named as the receiver of a $50,000 bribe in a purchase of parking meters for the city. Though the story was later admitted to be a complete fabrication, Screvane was the object for some months of a "scandal."

In 1967, John V. Lindsay, an earnest, personally honest, rather colorful public official, learned that one of his department heads, James L. Marcus, had been accused along with five other men—one of whom the F.B.I. described as a Mafia leader—in a bribery conspiracy involving a reservoir-cleaning contract. The Lindsay administration was, in the standard newspaper phrase, "rocked by scandal."

In each of these cases, whatever was good or bad about the official —however competent or incompetent he had been in the conduct of public affairs, however profound or superficial in the analysis of the city's problems—all that was in large measure obscured by the fact, real or imagined, that public power had been used for private purposes.

If the ability to achieve important results for a city can be easily offset by a modest moral blemish (or if the utter inability to achieve anything can be hidden behind the unstained vestments of personal purity), the temper of the American electorate would appear to be less pragmatic and more puritanical than some have imagined. And worse, the standard of value implied by such sentiments can be exploited by anyone sufficiently ruthless to countenance lying and sufficiently daring to risk a possible perjury charge.

All the opposition party need do is hire someone who, falsely but persuasively and using lots of details about bills of small denomination, secret meeting places and juggled records, will accuse a prominent public official of corruption. The newspapers will print it immediately of course—it is dramatic and, for the newspaper, not libelous. The public will be aroused, the politician will issue a futile denial, the existence of the denial will give the accuser an opportunity to repeat and embroider his charges, and the leaders of the opposition party, while not committing themselves to the truth of the charges, can view with alarm and point with dismay. By the time the hoax is exposed—if it is exposed—the public official is ruined and the accuser, if he is clever enough to avoid actually making the charges under oath before a grand jury, may get off scot-free.

The bolder, more imaginative variant on this strategem is to plant the accuser inside the opponent's administration, much as the C.I.A. might plant an *agent provocateur* in Castro's Cabinet. At the appropriate time, the official is "exposed" in a way that suggests that the man who appointed him is at least stupid and perhaps larcenous. For the charge to command attention, the official need not even steal anything, though if he could be persuaded to take a few bucks it might add a note of verisimilitude.

The public's response to scandal, real or fancied, and the possibility of taking advantage of that response by inventing scandals, suggest that we ought to sort out our reactions so that we can distinguish between harmful and not-so-harmful varieties of corruption, allowing our moral outrage to be proportional to the problem, not simply triggered full force by a "breath of scandal." I suggest this not to weaken our moral capacities but to encourage discrimination between corruption that has practical consequences and corruption that does not and between those forms of corruption that impede the attainment of social objectives and those that may facilitate it.

In general, corruption occurs whenever a person, in exchange for some private advantage, acts other than as his duty requires. The only problem with this definition is that by its test almost all politicians are corrupt in some measure. Offering a judgeship to a Senator to get his vote on a legislative measure, putting a plumber on the party's ticket in order to get the backing of leaders of organized labor in the election, trading a favorable vote by Councilman A on one appropriation item in exchange for a favorable vote by Councilman B on another item— all are, strictly speaking, actions based on motives other than duty. Even college professors are not immune. Female students often get higher grades than males (around Harvard it is called the "Radcliffe B") partly because professors wish to avoid having to confront a weepy coed. And I suspect Negroes may get higher grades than whites, other things being equal, out of some measure of professional guilt or moral cowardice. (Under the impact of the Black Power movement, the "Negro B" may even become the "Negro A-minus.")

But ordinarily we do not think of these acts as cases of corruption— they are not experienced as moral problems or so considered, nor does the law penalize their commission. What is regarded and treated as corruption is vulgar bribery—acting other than as one's duty requires *in exchange for cash* (or something readily convertible into cash, such as a fur coat or a color TV). Money, for reasons I do not fully understand, converts a compromise or an exchange of favors into a corrupt act.

But cash transactions do not all have the same moral or practical meaning; indeed, some are not thought of by the participants as bribery at all. In this borderline area we find campaign contributions, "office expense funds" and expensive gifts tendered without reference to, or even in expectation of, any *quid pro quo*. Many otherwise intelligent and prudent politicians—Sherman Adams and Richard Nixon come to mind—have learned to their sorrow that money payments are always suspect whatever the motives of the parties, although the most deliberate and cynical exchange of favors not involving money (logrolling, patronage judgeships, ticket balancing and the like) is likely to go unnoticed or if noticed, to be regarded approvingly as evidence of "shrewdness" or "real professionalism."

Even with respect to vulgar bribery, there are different social consequences, depending on the circumstances. An emphasis on the moral and legal issues raised by bribery tends to obscure these consequences, not all of which are equally undesirable. On this point, it is difficult to avoid being misunderstood. The argument I am making is not that a bribe that produces a beneficial effect becomes morally right—becomes, in effect, a noble way in which to spend one's money. Corruption by definition is wrong. But so are many other public actions (incompetence, for one, and unfairness for another). In evaluating these other ills, we normally take into account the circumstances and consequences. (Was the incompetent hired to prevent a harmful split in the governing party? Did the nominally unfair act nonetheless produce some kind of rough justice?) The same sort of calculation, I argue, ought to be made in evaluating the various forms of corruption.

The most frequently mentioned distinction, the author of which was the semilegendary George Washington Plunkitt of Tammany Hall, is between honest and dishonest graft. Roughly speaking, honest graft entails a money benefit for the recipient but no money cost to the public. Every city must buy insurance or deposit funds in banks. The premiums charged or the interest paid are usually everywhere the same; indeed, they are often set by law. Thus, it may make no difference to the city which company gets the business but it may make a great deal of difference to the company—so much so that the company is willing to pay to get it, either with money or by putting a key politician on its board or hiring him as its "lawyer."

Sometimes these arrangements exist solely for the private advantage of a particular politician; other times they are ways by which a political party attracts support and necessary campaign funds from the business community. This is honest graft. "Dishonest graft" costs the public money—the city buys something it does not need, or pays more for it than it should. In my opinion, there has been a rather sharp decline in the amount of dishonest graft over the last 30 or 40 years, but probably much less decline in the amount of honest graft.

A second distinction is between graft involved in capital formation and graft involved in operating economies. Large sums may be paid (and certainly have been paid) for the privilege of building a subway, installing a municipal lighting system or acquiring the land for an airport. Sometimes these vast civic projects would not have been undertaken at all if somebody had not spread a lot of cash around to buy off the many different persons and groups who had they acted solely on the basis of duty, might well have been unable to agree on either the need for the project or its form. Samuel Insull used graft to create various municipal utilities around the turn of the century; indeed, hardly a single subway, city hall or port in a large (and especially old) American city was the result of a virgin birth. Graft involved in this kind of capital formation was often expensive, thus increasing— sometimes substantially—the cost of the enterprise. But it is an open question, to be answered only by examining the particular cases, whether this excess cost did or did not purchase something of value (an early decision to undertake a risky project, a willingness to innovate, etc.).

Graft involved in the operation of many of these enterprises, however, must be judged by quite different standards. Subways, airports and electric-power generators are complex mechanisms that require, for their efficient operation, closely coordinated activities and the employment of skilled professionals. Paying people to act in ways other than those required by the needs of the organization or appointing unqualified party hacks to important posts can play havoc with such facilities. Perhaps one of the reasons for the increased stress on morality in government is that today, unlike the situation 50 years ago, the maintenance of operating efficiency—not the formation of new enterprises or the granting of franchises—has become (rightly or wrongly) the primary concern of government.

A third distinction is between integrative and disintegrative corruption. Corruption, when used to obtain compliance among formally independent sources of authority or to increase the compliance of nominal subordinates, is integrative; it serves to concert the actions of many in accordance with the intentions of one or a few. In American cities, it has been the characteristic of those political machines which arose primarily because the fragmented and legally weak institutions of government could scarcely operate at all unless somebody ("the boss") put together—on the basis of patronage and similar forms of bribery—an informal government to do what the mayor and city council, on their own, could not do.

Whether a machine, once constructed, will serve desirable or undesirable ends is another matter. But we note that Mayors Richard J. Daley and David Lawrence ran Chicago and Pittsburgh, respectively, in ways that attracted much favorable national publicity; by contrast, on the eve of Mayor Lindsay's inauguration, New York City was described by sociologist Nathan Glazer as "ungovernable," and Mayor Yorty of Los Angeles has had to resort to television publicity to achieve what the absence of both formal authority and a strong party prevents him from achieving otherwise.

Disintegrative corruption occurs when a public official, acting alone, or at least without the sanction of the mayor or party leader, sells his discretionary authority to a private party. The official benefits, but not in ways that serve the ends of his organization or further the policies of his superiors. Distintegrative corruption is often widespread when, as in the Soviet Union or certain underdeveloped nations, bureaucratic authority becomes so rigid and all-encompassing that various "black markets" emerge to handle necessary transactions illicitly. Soviet corruption, called *"blat,"* is a constant concern to the regime and results from the fact that, formally, the Government is *too* centralized, *too* integrated, *too* tightly controlled to permit sufficient freedom of action at the lower levels.

But disintegrative corruption can occur in weak political systems as well. Building inspectors who sell their approval to landlords, police officers who sell their authority to criminal syndicates, and licensing officials who sell their seals and forms to contractors or liquor stores are operating in many cases to line their own pockets without reference to the goals of their organizations. I suspect that disintegrative corruption, at least in the United States, is an especially prevalent transitional form following on the collapse of an old-style party machine and preceding the emergence of any "good government" alternative to it. Since the formal institutions of government are rarely strengthened sufficiently to achieve legally that which the political machine can achieve illegally, well-organized, integrative corruption becomes freelance, individualistic, disintegrative corruption. Habits of thievery are harder to change than institutions of thievery.

A final distinction is between corruption that has high symbolic costs to society and that which has low symbolic costs. The $10 bill taken by the police officer to overlook the numbers runner may be more costly to society (in symbolic terms) than the $10 bill taken by the same police officer in exchange for checking a merchant's door every night to make sure it is locked. In one case, a privileged class of lawbreakers is being created; in the other, a reward is paid for doing what it is the duty of the officer to do anyway (but which, for lack of time, he probably would not do, or do as faithfully). Intermediate between the two cases would be the $10 bill taken to allow a doctor to park in a no-parking zone in front of his office. Law-violation is being countenanced, but we think of that law, unlike the one against gambling, as a trivial one, designed (arbitrarily) to regulate matters of mere convenience.

We know the least about such symbolic values, for the cost is intangible and subjective and not (primarily) something that can be measured as an unnecessary addition to the tax bill. Accounts of Negro slum life often suggest that law enforcement is experienced as arbitrary, and thus held in contempt, because slum residents believe that the police are tough in regulating the residents' street conduct but look the other way when the gamblers and dope pushers set up shop. (Whethers this implies that the police should stop "bothering" non-gamblers or stop giving immunity to the gamblers is not clear.)

In all of these distinctions, however, one factor is easily overlooked.

Evaluating the costs and benefits of various forms of corruption is one thing when the only participants are the citizens, the officials and the individual interests which benefit from the corruption.

However, the evaluation of costs and benefits may lead to quite different conclusions if the benefiting interests are not individual but highly organized instead, and if these organized interests are not engaged in otherwise innocent enterprises but are engaged instead in a criminal conspiracy. Ten thousand dollars from a highway contractor means one thing, $10,000 involving a member of the Mafia means something else indeed. The reason is that bribery involving organized crime is the most disintegrative form imaginable—it is not simply that a few officials cease to do their duty, but that a rival, covert government is thereby helped to come into being.

We know very little about the conditions which give rise to the worst forms of corruption—graft that affects operating economies has high symbolic costs and leads to the disintegration of legitimate authority and the emergence of an illegitimate and criminal covert government. One possibility is that when political power is centralized in the hands of a strong executive—whether he be a party boss, a powerful mayor or a dominating city manager—the man at the top will find it to his advantage either to eliminate corruption entirely or confine it to the least objectionable forms. The very meaning of centralization, of course, is that the top man can get his way on matters of importance to him; that being so, he will presumably not want his subordinates to subvert his power either by selling out to persons offering bribes or by creating embarrassing scandals for which the boss will have to take responsibility. A centralized city government, then, may be the kind best able to resist subversion by a criminal syndicate.

Such accounts as we have seem to suggest that cities with decentralized politics—a party composed of warring factions, for example, or a weak governmental structure—are especially vulnerable to the most costly forms of corruption. Chicago in the late 19th and early 20th centuries was both the scene of contending party cliques and the prey of racketeers, vice lords and exploitive businessmen. Kansas City has off and on been the object of various exposés of vice and gambling conditions and the Democratic party there has, concomitantly, been in a state of chronic disrepair. In the nineteen-forties, Oakland, Calif., had weak nonpartisan political leadership and cautious city managers; large-scale gambling enterprises began to flourish. A very strong city manager who came to power in the nineteen-fifties was able to put a stop to it.

But centralized governments have another characteristic. What a centralized government does is very much up to the man in charge, and the tastes and interests of such men may vary considerably. Edward Crump ran Memphis with an iron hand, but he would not tolerate organized rackets and closed down the city's red-light district. Bootlegging existed, but there were apparently no shakedowns; money for politics was raised primarily from assessments levied on city employes.

Frank Hague, at the height of his power as a city boss, once described Jersey City as "the most moralest city in America"—by which he meant not only that vice and indecency were vigorously suppressed (there were no brothels or even taxi-dance halls) but that other threats to public morals, such as Socialists and labor organizers, were also kept out of town. On the other hand, Hague saw nothing wrong with gambling, and so Jersey City became one of the largest centers for bookies and horse parlors in the country. Westbrook Pegler once referred to Hague's Jersey City as the "Hourse Bourse" of the nation.

Some city bosses have had more latitudinarian views. Until it was torn down by Governor Rockefeller to make way for a new complex of state government buildings, the "Gut" in Albany was famous throughout the Northeast as a major center of brothels, dives and bookies. But even though Dan O'Connell, who has led the Albany Democratic party without interruption and almost without challenge since 1923, may have been tolerant of prostitutes and gamblers, he has not been tolerant of rivals. Accordingly, the vice industry was never allowed to fall into the hands of any organization other than the party. As even O'Connell's strongest critics concede, no criminal syndicate or even any outsiders ever operated in Albany. Now that the Gut is almost gone and only two dozen or so bookies remain, no underworld exists to attempt the disintegrative corruption of particular public officials. The party has its own sources of money.

Other centralized political regimes may have had different experiences. Some bosses or mayors may have had centralized power and then sold it en bloc to the highest bidder. Others may have condoned individualized bribery or used their offices to practice dishonest graft. Tom Pendergast, one-time boss of Kansas City, was sent to jail because, unlike Ed Crump, he had a personal weakness—a love of the ponies which led him to steal in order to support his betting habits. Of 20 city bosses described in a study published in 1930, only eight remained free from prison, trial or indictment. The bosses who, like Crump or Richard Daley of Chicago, have survived unscathed have not been greedy

in ways that which excite either the envy of subordinates or the suspicion of investigators. Such men, like good businessmen, are rare.

Indeed, sometimes the businessmen who offered the bribes have
been more statesmanlike than the politicians who received them.
Charles T. Yerkes, the Chicago traction magnate of the 1890's, was
constantly being victimized by aldermen and ward leaders who would
practice extortion on him by threatening not to renew his franchises or
to charter rival companies with even better franchises. Tiring of paying
the bribes necessary to avert this and disturbed by the financial costs
of this uncertainty, Yerkes decided to end the racket of which he was
the victim by sponsoring a bill in the state legislature that would not
only make his franchise secure but place the traction system under the
control of a state regulatory commission: better predictable bureaucrats than greedy politicians, Yerkes reasoned.

But to get the bill through the legislature, Yerkes of course had to
bribe its members. They balked when they realized that he was
bribing them to pass a bill that would make it impossible for them to
be bribed by him in the future. When his meaneuvers became public,
the bill failed. (The traction system was finally put on a sound basis
30 years later by Samuel Insull, but only after he had devised the most
intricate and costly stratagems to get the warring politicians together.)

The rate of corruption is no doubt less today than it was in the era
of Yerkes and Insull and very likely the form of that which remains has
changed—testimonial dinners, lawyers' fees, consultant contracts and
campaign funds have replaced the vulgar bribe. And these newer ways
of exchanging favors have altered the terms of trade—they are less
specific as to commitment, more diffuse as to effect, less binding as to
obligation than the straight-forward cash payoff for a particular vote
or action. But they are probably no less productive of disintegrative
tendencies in politics than the faction-ridden machines of old, partly
because they are (except perhaps in a few state legislatures) under no
central control and partly because they depend on no specific agreements or obligations.

But if the rate of corruption is declining and its form changing, the
problem of corruption for a mayor may be worse, if anything. Lacking
a strong party, he must rely on media appeal, personality and sales-
manship to get elected—he must rely, in short, precisely on those
qualities most vulnerable to scandal and rumors of scandal. A more
middle-classified society expects higher levels of probity than ever
before and is often unwilling to take into account the distinctions and
offsetting values which professors like to write about.

The recruitment of personnel into municipal service, once performed by the party, now must be performed by the mayor personally, often by taking into positions of the highest responsibility plausible but unknown persons who are "available." Formerly the party may have raised up its share of hacks and even thieves, but through long exposure to them in a variety of jobs the party leaders at least knew who the hacks and thieves were and could assign them accordingly. A new-style big-city mayor is not likely to know very much about anybody in his administration other than his immediate advisers. Perhaps it is partly to guard against unpleasant surprise that the mayors look for people whose paper credentials seem to place them above suspicion (and, in addition, provide some "style" to the administration). Accordingly, we find mayors recruiting (where they can) professors, big-business executives and young men fresh out of prestigious universities and law schools. Never mind that most such persons have had absolutely no political experience (or even among some of the younger ones, any experience doing anything at all). Never mind that their minds may be filled with untested ideas, academically popular nostrums or irrelevant analogies between business problems and government problems. They are available, their grammar is correct and they seem to be honest.

And finally, decentralization has become the new slogan of municipal reform, at least among many liberals. The governments of many large cities, already experiencing the greatest difficulty in deciding on —and especially in *acting* on—any policy for handling their problems, are now being told they must hand over control of the schools, police and other agencies to various neighborhood politicians. It was under precisely these circumstances that municipal corruption flourished in the past. Perhaps decentralization is desirable, even at the price of more corruption, but no one should suppose the price will not have to be paid.

It is no surprise that mayors find so many occasions to wonder why they got into this line of work.

(2)

The Legacy of Corruption

REVELATIONS OF SCANDAL and corruption in the Nixon administration evoked two contrasting sets of reactions. The first was characterized by shock, disbelief, and even incredulity that such wrongdoings could take place in American politics. The unmasking of numerous fraudulent election practices and former Vice President Agnew's use of county and state offices to extort cash for personal gain prompted the response that such activities were outrageous and flagrant abuses without precedent. Outrageous and flagrant they were, but to view them as unprecedented is to fail to appreciate the history of corruption in America. A second set of reactions assigned the misdeeds by important persons in positions of public trust to "politics as usual" and viewed these acts merely as extensions of, or refinements on, earlier illegal and unethical practices in American politics. To show that the second view is more accurate, this chapter looks at previous patterns of corruption in American cities.

Historical Cycles of Corruption

Are there periods in American history when municipalities have experienced more frequent and pervasive instances of corruption than at others? Answers to this question are hard to come by for several reasons. First, the frequency and severity of corruption in American cities has been little studied. Observers of cities have given research on corruption low priority, perhaps because of the problems inherent in studying it or merely because of a lack of interest. Second, information on the subject suffers from a host of inadequacies. What information is available comes from newspaper exposés, personal accounts and biographies, case studies of particular cities, and impressionistic sur-

39

veys of various time periods. As a consequence of these two limitations, we know relatively little about which eras experienced more corruption than others.

Third, the different kinds of corruption that flourished during different time periods make meaningful comparisons all the more difficult. During the Prohibition era (1919-1933), for example, there was unprecedented trafficking in illegal alcohol and nonenforcement of applicable laws. Another kind of corruption, collusive arrangements between businessmen and municipal legislators, proceeded at a rapid pace during the last quarter of the nineteenth century, when limits on business advancement were eased or ignored in return for payments to city officials. A final difficulty is an "iceberg problem"—what is revealed to public view about corruption may represent only a tiny portion of what actually occurs. Thus the actual frequency and severity of corruption may remain at a constant level while only public knowledge of such activities varies over time. Or, alternatively, perhaps our ability to know about corruption suffers so many limitations that it only appears as though corruption levels remain stable when in fact they vary considerably.

Despite these problems, several general observations concerning past instances of corruption may be made. Municipal corruption before the Civil War, while not unknown, appears to have been less common and less severe than during later periods partly because there were fewer urban dwellers, cities were smaller, and the rich Yankee elites who dominated municipal offices had less incentive to pillage the public treasury than later officials who were less wealthy. But an even more important reason is that before the Civil War cities engaged in few activities and thus provided only limited opportunities for corruption. Cities in the Northeast grew rapidly after the war, engaged in progressively more activities, and gained large numbers of propertyless immigrants. The opportunities for corruption increased accordingly, especially to the extent that cities provided more public services and economic notables were replaced in public office by political "bosses" from the lower classes. The bosses introduced machine-style politics to northern cities and institutionalized opportunities for corruption by dispensing material rewards and favors to their supporters and withholding them from their opponents. When the machine reached its zenith near the turn of the century, it found willing allies among robber-baron businessmen in concocting schemes of corruption beneficial to both parties. Business development proceeded with exorbitant profits, and political bosses amassed private fortunes while retaining elective office.

General affluence in the 1920s allowed similar business advancement in collusion with political bosses, and the simultaneous experiment with Prohibition created additional sources of corruption. If there was a period of decline in municipal corruption, it probably occurred in the period 1934 through 1945, for several reasons. The repeal of Prohibition in late 1933, economic scarcity during the depression, the nationalization and bureaucratization of welfare services in the Roosevelt administrations, and the mobilization of the economy for war cumulatively reduced the dominance of the machine and limited the opportunities for corruption. In succeeding years, new forms of corruption dealt with in later chapters of this book were added to previous ones, resulting in a general increase in corruption within American cities and suburbs.

This historical overview suggests that corruption accompanied the development of all cities at the same time. A more realistic assumption is that each city experienced its own cycle of corruption tied to its own pattern of historical development. The period in which cities were founded and developed varies considerably between regions of the country. For the most part cities in the Northeast were founded and developed long before their counterparts in other regions. Municipalities in the Midwest began to grow appreciably only after the Civil War, and it was not until this century that cities in the Southwest experienced similar growth patterns. While the periods of development vary, at similar stages in the development process opportunities for corruption were created that appear to be common to nearly all cities.

The developmental cycle of corruption may be illustrated by describing, albeit in an oversimplified manner, municipal growth stages and their accompanying opportunities for corruption. When cities are founded, the allocation of harbor and rail franchises creates avenues for corruption. So too does the provision of police and fire services, two of the initial activities cities engage in. Cities usually next develop the physical aspects of a community—paving streets, laying sewer and water lines, constructing public buildings, providing transportation networks, and generally engaging in public works. Each of these activities may require contracts that are vulnerable to the abuses identified in chapter 4. They also add to the value of real estate and allow those with inside information to speculate in "honest graft." The granting of leases and permits opens still more opportunities for cor-

ruption. Following physical development, cities tend to adopt two
types of regulations: those legislating public morals (alcohol, prostitution, gambling) and those concerning physical development (zoning,
permits, inspections). The nonenforcement of regulations of either type
usually involves large-scale corruption. Finally, cities adopt social welfare programs and other programs facilitated by intergovernmental
grants that may be undermined or abused by corrupt acts. Although
necessarily oversimplified, this brief description of the development
process suggests the numerous occasions when the acts of cities may
be subject to corruption.

Inducements to Corruption

The city development process reveals various occasions when corruption may take place, but it does not address the question of why
certain public officials have been prone to corruption while others
have not. Simplistic answers citing human fallibility and man's tendency toward evil fail to recognize the complex structural network of
political and economic relationships within which officials take part in
corrupt activities. Other explanations point to officials' thirst for fun
and profit, but to have fun and make a profit from public office presupposes the existence of structured opportunities to do so.

The number of opportunities for corruption within cities and the
inducements attaching to them are determined to some degree by state
governments. Cities are creatures of the states, owing their existence
to charters issued by the states and performing only those activities
specifically allowed in their articles of incorporation.[1] The form of
municipal organization, the powers granted, and the manner in which
those powers are exercised vary from state to state. The variation in
provisions for state auditing and reviewing of city budgets and accounts, civil service requirements, and competitive bidding procedures
may partially explain why such cities as Los Angeles, Milwaukee, and
Detroit have experienced relatively little corruption in recent years as
opposed to Chicago, Buffalo, and New York, where corruption has
surfaced periodically. Cities in California, Wisconsin, and Michigan
are restricted by "reform" statutes, while those in the state of Illinois
and New York exist under somewhat "unreformed" structures. State
regulations are not completely determinative of municipal corruption,

1. For additional discussion of this point see Edward C. Banfield and
James Q. Wilson, *City Politics* (Cambridge: Harvard University Press
and the M.I.T. Press, 1963), pp.63–73.

for cities in unreformed states have adopted measures to insure against corruption (as Peoria, Illinois did in the early 1950s) and cities in reformed states have experienced corruption (as San Francisco did in the 1950s).

Perhaps the most important inducement to municipal corruption over the past century was provided through machine-style politics. The machine party organizations were built on the votes of newly arrived immigrants given in return for favorable treatment and material rewards from the officials they helped elect. By distributing patronage, privileges, and other favors to their lower class supporters, machine "bosses" effectively organized an electoral base that allowed them to displace from office the previously dominant economic notables.[2] Instead of redistributing wealth or channeling government services to the lower class collectively, however, the bosses chose to reward their backers selectively, with only as many favors as were necessary for them to stay in office. For the most part they also used the prerogatives of office to amass large personal fortunes for themselves.

Besides bosses who pocketed governmental monies, the prime beneficiaries of machine politics were big businessmen. A symbiotic relationship developed between them and the bosses. The bosses received cash payments, gifts, and political support; in return the businessmen obtained privileges to operate unhindered by government regulations. The bosses' strong hierarchical control of party organizations and the centralization of political power and authority in the city facilitated schemes of corruption. With one boss or only a few party operatives to deal with, businessmen could easily negotiate permits, licenses, franchises, and other privileges for a price. Those in control, being few in number, could successfully conceal from public view the illicit bargains.

Since the turn of the century, reformers have appeared on the urban scene to challenge the bosses and the machine style of politics. Repulsed by the machine's dishonesty, inefficiency, vote-buying, and more generalized patterns of corruption, the reformers set an ambitious agenda for ridding cities of corrupting influences and structures offering opportunities for corruption.[3] Their impact may be seen in the

2. One of the best treatments of the urban machine is in J. David Greenstone and Paul E. Peterson, *Race and Authority in Urban Politics* (Beverly Hills, Cal.: Sage, 1973).

3. For a discussion of the goals of reformers see Eugene C. Lee, *The Politics of Nonpartisanship* (Berkeley: University of California Press, 1960).

extent to which nonpartisanship, at-large city council elections, and city manager forms of government have been adopted. The reformers paid particular attention to city bureaucracies, advocating the civil service system, adequate salaries, merit appointment and promotion, and permanent tenure as ways to insure against corruption. These measures, however, have produced extreme decentralization of authority and may allow corruption to take place unnoticed at lower bureaucratic levels, where fragmented structures serve to obscure illicit acts from public view. The exercise of administrative discretion within these newly autonomous departments also creates opportunities for corruption in the distribution of government grants and the implementation of government programs. Finally, the reformers tended to enact even more regulations and thereby created additional opportunities for corruption in the overlooking of such regulations.

The enhancement of politicians' careers provides another set of inducements to corruption. Corrupt practices can be utilized by officeholders to solidify their permanence in office or to build a base of support for pursuing higher office. Certainly the opposite strategy has been pursued periodically; public officials have fashioned careers around ousting corrupt officials. Mayor Fiorello H. LaGuardia of New York is an excellent case in point of a politician who built a popular reputation for "throwing the bums out." But for every LaGuardia there existed mayors of opposite orientations—such as "Big Bill" Thompson in Chicago, Frank Hague in Jersey City, and James Curley in Boston—who showed favoritism to friends and relatives in awarding city contracts, leases, permits, and franchises in order to build political support for themselves. That similar corrupt practices continue today may be seen from the conviction of three New Jersey mayors in the early 1970s for accepting kickbacks, extorting money from contractors, and neglecting to enforce gambling laws.[4]

The current struggle for power in many large cities between black and white community factions raises an issue that is as yet unresolved. Many cities in which blacks are attempting to replace whites in public office have a long history of corruption. The question arises whether blacks who do gain elective office will adopt and continue that legacy or break with it by establishing corruption-free administrations. Although little evidence is currently available, the limited information on a small number of cases (such as the Hatcher administration in

4. The cases are described in Thomas A. Hoge, "New Jersey—The Friendly State," in Nicholas Gage, ed., *Mafia, USA* (New York: Dell Publishing Co., 1972), p.280.

Gary and the Gibson administration in Newark) seems to indicate that significant departures from past patterns of corruption may take place with the succession to office of insurgent racial groups.

The readings in this chapter provide examples of past instances of corruption in American cities. The first three deal with Chicago: Wendt and Kogan focus on its machine at the turn of the century to show how ward-based politicians negotiated public favors encrusted with graft for big businesses. Landesco looks at the mutual dependence and assistance between politicians and gangsters and provides a useful compendium of tactics for corrupting elections. Royko's highly popular and contemporary account of shady politics in Chicago updates the first two selections and gives an excellent description of the current resources and operations of the machine. Next, the Kefauver Committee's investigation of connivance between criminal gangs and police officers in the early 1950s shows how official corruption facilitates organized crime. The following two selections discuss corruption in Newark, New Jersey: Cook takes the trial of Angelo DeCarlo as a point of departure for reviewing corruption and syndicate activities in that city from the Prohibition era to the present, while Porambo places greater emphasis on more recent schemes of corruption there, with particular reference to the role of law enforcement agencies. Gardiner's discussion of official corruption in Reading, Pennsylvania ("Wincanton") covers a fifty-year period and calls attention to election abuses and payoffs to buy protection from officials and the police. Finally, the limitations of attempts at reform are discussed by Martin, who analyzes the difficult transition Peoria, Illinois experienced when strict reformers tried to rid that city of its tradition of corruption.

BOSSES IN LUSTY CHICAGO
Lloyd Wendt and Herman Kogan

The lawmaking group into which Bathhouse John craved entry had about it, in 1892, an especially unsavory odor. The city's major legislative unit, the council, had deteriorated as Chicago had grown. Each ward elected its aldermen in alternate years for two-year terms and every twelvemonth, when half the aldermen were up for election, the city usually witnessed an influx into the council of inept burghers who more often than not joined the money-wise incumbents in sharing the copious graft. The ministers scorched the aldermen from their pulpits, the newspapers raved "Boodle! Boodle!" and on each election day called for aldermanic purges, but the councils grew steadily worse.

The opportunities for "tainted money" were limitless. In the First Ward alone in the three decades preceding 1890 the city fathers had disposed of twenty-five per cent of the streets to various railroads. Sixty companies, including department stores, junk shops, foundries, laundries and factories, had taken possession by city ordinance of 175 of the ward's thoroughfares. Eight new streetcar companies and elevated lines had come to the city to organize transportation. Three gas and electric companies had been formed and there were innumerable lesser groups shouting for rights in, under, and over the streets.

Few aldermen took the trouble to deny receiving money for backing ordinances which surrendered exclusive street rights to this railroad or that streetcar line. In the collective council mind these physical properties of the city were the aldermen's own and could be sold as they saw fit. When the public howled "Graft!" the city fathers responded loftily that their votes for various franchises encouraged a flow of capital into the city, greater transportation facilities, more jobs.

From *Lords of the Levee* by Lloyd Wendt and Herman Kogan, pp.34–40, copyright, 1943 by The Bobbs-Merrill Company, Inc. Reprinted by permission of the publisher.

The irksome aspect of boodling to the civic-minded was not only that the vicious system corrupted the whole of Chicago politics but that the city gained from the passage of boodle ordinances hardly a cent in compensation. Even the grafting aldermen, receiving as little as $100 or as much as $25,000,° actually were being paid only a small fraction of the real worth of the privileges they were selling. Big business was the beneficiary of this system, for it needed such favors to expand and grow rich. Once having created the system, business had no choice but to deal with the aldermen, and it was happy to do it under prevailing prices.

Boodle technique was simple. A favored method of securing passage of a graft measure was first to see to it that the ordinance was referred to a committee on which sat one or more influential boodlers who were susceptible to at least an occasional bribe. The promoter of the enterprise would send his representatives to these aldermen, who soon would suggest that the company hire one or more lawyers to "explain" the ordinance to the committee. The company then hired a member of the boodle gang's legal battery and paid an immense "fee" which would be apportioned among counsel and the boodlers. Should a rare honest alderman expose the scheme to the public, the company officials would profess to be as shocked as the voters. All they had done, these innocent-eyed gentelmen would protest, was to employ an attorney to straighten out difficulties the aldermen might have in expediting the ordinance. Usually there was a brief civic hullabaloo and the matter would be forgotten.

The small businessmen of Chicago might grumble at the virtual extortion practiced by the aldermen, but they paid. They paid for ordinances which would allow them to expand and they paid to smother shakedown ordinances which might harm them. The aldermen, rewarded at a rate of only three dollars a council meeting, owned mammoth houses, country places, racing stables, and when questioned publicly they insisted they were able to maintain these because of "good investments."

There were few in 1892 to dispute C. C. Thompson, of the city Chamber of Commerce, when he moaned: "If you want to get anything

---

° This latter amount was the price paid to each of four aldermen in 1890, according to exposés of the time, for their support of a measure giving valuable privileges to a railway corporation. Some others who joined them were said to have received $8,000 each. The all-time high, according to Chicago political legend, was the payment of $100,000 and two pieces of property to a high city official who insured passage of a boodle ordinance.

out of the council, the quickest way is to pay for it—not to the city, but to the aldermen."

There was one man in Chicago who wanted plenty and was willing to pay for it.

He was Charles Tyson Yerkes, emerging rapidly as the czar of midwest traction and the financial boss of municipal Chicago. Yerkes had come to Chicago in 1882 after a flashy rise—resulting in a prison term—in his home town of Philadelphia.

The son of a Philadelphia bank president, Yerkes had started his business career as a clerk and in 1859 had opened a brokerage office. Three years later he started his own banking house and soon became known as a financial genius. In 1868 he gained considerable fame throughout the nation through his operations in municipal bonds, and by 1871 he was recognized as a financial power in Philadelphia. In the panic that year which followed the great fire in Chicago, however, Yerkes was caught short when called upon to deliver money he had received from the sale of some Philadelphia bonds. Tried and convicted of embezzlement, he was sentenced to two years and nine months in prison but was pardoned after serving only seven months.

Yerkes went to Chicago. Supplied with funds by Philadelphia bankers, he invested in Chicago transportation, and soon won control of several traction lines. Early in his Chicago career, he incurred the enmity of Joe Dunlap, publisher of the Chicago *Dispatch*, a paper notorious for its scandalous exposés. Dunlap sent a reporter with a pressroom proof of an article exposing Yerkes as an ex-convict.

"The boss wants you to look this over and see if it's all true," the reporter stated.

Yerkes' sharply etched face went livid. "You're damn right it's true," he snorted. "And you tell that God-damned Dunlap that if he ever publishes a line or tells a soul I'll kill him the first time I see him."

The story was not used.

It was this ruthless, forceful Yerkes who, by devious means, by rich payments to the aldermen, grew to a position of power. When he arrived in Chicago the city's transportation had been in a woeful state. Although Chicago was expanding rapidly, it still depended for the most part on tiny stretches of car lines which served limited neighborhoods. It took almost as long to get from the city limits to the city hall as from Chicago to Milwaukee by steam train.

Borrowing more money from A. B. Widener, the Philadelphia traction king, Yerkes had organized his own traction line, the North

Chicago Street Railway, and using the stock of this company as collateral for further loans, had built an empire of subsidiary transportation companies from which, by complex juggling and watering of stocks and bonds, he derived great profits while stockholders invariably were left with ornate stock certificates and little else. A builder as well as a plunderer, he had, in the decade since his arrival, replaced horsecars with cable lines, had added 500 miles of track to the city and applied electricity to some 250 additional miles, and was building Chicago's famous Loop.

Arrogant, contemptuous of the public, Yerkes' theory, simply expressed, was "Buy old junk, fix it up a little, unload it on the other fellow." Once, when a group of passengers smashed up a streetcar in protest against the poor service, he stopped all cars on the line until the public begged that service be resumed. When a friend suggested that he ought to run more cars on his lines, Yerkes replied, "Why should I? It's the straphangers who pay the dividends."

To expand and maintain his financial realm Yerkes needed special favors from the councils. Whether his mercenaries were Republicans or Democrats mattered little to Yerkes. He cared nothing for a man's political beliefs; all he craved was results. His payments to Republican hirelings were made through William Lorimer, one of Coughlin's boyhood friends, and by now a Republican chieftain popularly called "The Blond Boss."

Yerkes' man in the Democratic ring was John (Johnny de Pow) Powers, the alderman from the Irish-Italian Nineteenth Ward, who doted on funerals and reveled in the title, "Prince of Boodlers."

Of Johnny de Pow, the *Times-Herald* once wrote:

> Powers has piloted, either openly or covertly, nearly every boodle ordinance in the city council since the embodiment of the pernicious influence that has dictated municipal legislation for many years. In the Nineteenth, Mr. Powers is not called the Prince of Boodlers. He's called the Chief Mourner. The shadow of sympathetic gloom is always about him. He never jokes; he has forgotten how to smile. He never fails to visit the bedside of the dead, nor to distribute Christmas turkeys to the poor.
>
> Those who know Powers best will tell you that no meaner miser ever rivalled Shylock. The only way he can get votes is by hypocritical posing as a benefactor by filling the role of friend in need when death comes. He has bowed with aldermanic grief at thousands of biers. He is bloodless, personally unattractive. His demeanor is one of timid alertness and anxiety to please, but he is actually autocratic, arrogant, and insolent.

Like Coughlin a former grocery clerk, Powers later opened his own grocery and then went into the saloon business, a sure step toward a political career. In 1888 he was elected alderman and became a follower of Billy Whalen, then boodle boss of the council. Two years later when Whalen was killed in an accident, Powers staged a coup which set him up as Billy's successor. Whalen a few weeks prior to his untimely death had collected some $30,000 to be split with his associates as booty for a freshly passed franchise. The money was in a safe in Whalen's saloon and none but Powers knew this. He immediately purchased the entire furnishings of the saloon at a high price, moved out the safe, and a few days after Whalen's burial each of the aldermen in on the deal was paid his share. This deed established Powers as a "square guy" among his roughneck fellow legislators.

It was Powers who kept the boodlers in line and prevented them from selling out to two or more opposing interests simultaneously. He devised varied boodling refinements, one of them a system of granting a franchise a street block at a time so that the syndicates desiring such measures should ever be at the aldermen's mercy. He also worked out the plan of selling rights to a street not once but many times. If a transportation company, for example, had a horsecar franchise and decided to improve by installing cables, a new franchise became necessary. Similarly, council action was essential to substitute pony engines* for cable, or electricity for pony engines. Further, a company might obtain surface rights to a street at an exorbitant price only to find that the air rights above had been sold to an elevated line and the earth beneath transferred to a gas, electric, or tunnel firm.

Powers saw to it that Yerkes and his other benefactors received many favors. A favorite adjunct to the regular services was the fixing of personal property assessments which a powerful councilman like Powers, by greasing a palm here and there, could easily manage. Thus in one year, although Yerkes maintained a stable of fine horses and owned jewels and a lavish home containing a Japanese Room, a Yellow Room, an Empire Room, a palm garden, an art collection later sold for $769,200, a private museum and a library, his property for taxation purposes was assessed at only $1,337.

Yerkes' manager, D. H. Louderback, once publicly boasted that his chief controlled the city elections. The reform groups shouted this was so. And Johnny Powers, explaining to his constituents his friendship

---

* Steam engines, carried aboard the cars experimentally for several years. They were later discarded.

with Yerkes, once said, "You can't get elected to the council unless Mr. Yerkes says so."

Powers' explanation possibly was more shocking than it was true. For some, like Coughlin, had other backers, and many honest men occasionally became aldermen constituting a minority which was kept in check by Powers. One of these was John H. O'Neill; another, Martin Madden, later a distinguished United States congressman. Sometimes even such aldermen as Madden strayed. "I round up the boys and Madden talks to them," Powers is said to have boasted. But if some of the honest aldermen did find themselves often aligned with the boodlers, it was from necessity rather than conviction or greed. The golden rule of the council was reciprocity. "Either you go along with us," Powers would warn an alderman balking at a particularly heinous ordinance, "or you won't get a can of garbage moved out of your ward till hell freezes over."

ELECTION FRAUD
John Landesco

During primaries and elections, the evidence of the alliance of gangster and politician has again and again become a public scandal. The mutuality of their services is not difficult to discover. The gangster depends upon political protection for his criminal and illicit activities. He, therefore, has a vital business interest in the success of certain candidates whom he believes will be favorably disposed to him. The politicians, even the most upright, have a lively sense of the active part played in politics and elections by underworld characters. The gangsters and their allies always vote and bring out the vote for their friends, but the church people and other "good" citizens stay away from the polls, except for presidential elections and those occasional local elections, like the April 10, 1928, primary, when the issue of good citizenship versus organized crime was dramatically staged.

From John Landesco, "The Gangster and the Politician," in *Organized Crime in Chicago,* pp.183–189. Copyright © 1968 by The University of Chicago Press. Reprinted by permission of the publisher.

Election frauds are one of the ways in which gangsters and gun-men have repaid politicians for favors received. Fraudulent voting has been a perennial problem of municipal study in Chicago, and repeated investigations have been made. Only a summary is given here of the history of election frauds in Chicago. It is sufficient, however, to show the conditions responsible for the rise and persistence of election frauds and the failure of attempts to eliminate them.

An examination of vote fraud investigations since 1900 discloses the following facts:

(1) The geographic area within which vote frauds occur is limited and can be traced on the map of the city.

(2) The authorities over the election machinery, the county judge, the election commission, and the state's attorney's office, repeatedly carry on the same conflicts around the same legal points, arising out of duplication of function and overlapping and division of authority.

(3) The partisanship of the County Board of Commissioners de-termines its action in appropriating funds for special investigations.

(4) The incumbent state's attorney always opposes and impedes the appointment of special prosecutor and special grand jury to investi-gate election frauds if possible: (a) by efforts to stop the County Board's appropriation; (b) by efforts to gain priority in the appoint-ment of a favorable special prosecutor and a favorable grand jury. Re-peatedly there have been two or more special grand juries investigating vote frauds at the same time.

(5) The incumbent state's attorney tries to capture the services of the attorney general, who is in a position to take charge of as many grand juries as are in the field at any given time.

(6) When the dominant party is in the process of splitting into factions and factional bipartisan alliances occur, there is great activity in vote fraud investigation, with all the jockeying and maneuvering to capture the control of election machinery and prosecution and to se-cure advantageous publicity. This activity has seemed more often, in the past, to have as its aim factional advantage in political battle rather than the impartial suppression of vote frauds.

(7) The actual frauds that can be legally proved are committed by underlings. They refuse to testify as to the identity of their superiors in the conspiracy and it is, therefore, always impossible to convict the "higher-ups." The underlings under the gag of silence are usually sen-tenced for contempt of court by the county judge. Where prosecution is undertaken in a criminal court, it fails in a large number of cases be-cause of lack of evidence. The political bosses furnish the money and

attorneys to fight the cases, but they are seldom or never implicated by the testimony.

(8) The earlier centers of vote frauds were the areas in which dives, saloons, "flops," and rooming houses abounded, and the homeless or transient man was available in large numbers as purchaseable votes. This area was increased by the new immigration into territories dominated by political manipulators of the previous generations. Later, foreign leaders were developed under the tutelage of the earlier crooked politicians. In all of the foreign districts there have always been great numbers of immigrants who would stand aloof from politics because of what they regard as "low-down" local leaders and their crooked methods. The registration and the voting in these wards has always been small compared to the total population, and largely limited to the controlled vote. When racial or national group consciousness can be awakened through conflict situations, the politician can turn out a large number of legitimate votes.

(9) The young of the immigrant groups, beginning with the child at play in the street, were assimilated uncritically into all of the traditions of the neighborhoods in which they lived. Street gangs were their heritage, conflict between races and nationalities often made them necessary—conflict and assimilation went on together. The politician paid close attention to them, nurturing them with favors and using them for his own purposes. Gang history always emphasizes this political nurture. Gangs often become political clubs.

(10) Through every investigation the most constant element is the connivance of the police, witnessing and tolerating the vote frauds and resisting investigation by refusing to give testimony. Through it all is the evidence that the police defer to the politician because of his power over their jobs.

(11) Slugging and intimidation of voters is a chronic complaint through this entire period. With the advent of bootlegging arose the new phenomenon of the armed wealthy gun chief becoming the political boss of an area.

(12) While every fraud ever committed has been practiced within the last eight years, it can also be said that within the last few years there has been the most effective, impartial fight upon vote frauds through prosecution. For this, civic agencies, supported by private funds, and an honest county judge, impartially driving toward the objective of clean elections should be accredited; the more emphatically because of the disadvantages of the chaotic governmental machinery which the prosecution has to employ and the odds against them in

fighting the most powerful political organization in the history of Chicago.

The Technique

The technique of vote frauds during the entire period can be analyzed and listed under three heads: (a) irregular practices of election officials; (b) irregular activities of party workers; and (c) proceedings subsequent to the announcement of the election returns.

A. Irregular Practices of Election Officials.

　1. Padding Registration Books.
　　(a) The insertion of fictitious names in the register to enable fraudulent voters to vote those names on election day.

　2. Abuse of the Suspect Notice Provision.
　　(a) Deliberate failure to send notices to irregularly registered persons, fictious names and other names suggested by independent canvassers.
　　(b) Mailing notices to legal voters hostile to the machine on the expectation that they will neglect to answer the notice and consequently be barred.

　3. Substitution of Election Officials.
　　(a) A scheme by which the duly appointed election official is either kidnapped from the polls or intimidated into remaining away, so that a "machine" worker conveniently at hand is given the appointee's place in the polling place. The selection of the new official is made by the judges at the polling place.

　4. Failure to initial ballots.
　　(a) The intentional omission of the election officials' initials from the ballots handed to voters known to be hostile to the "machine," thus invalidating the ballot.

　5. Short-penciling, double marking.
　　(a) A trick whereby the election officials counting the ballots furtively fill in crosses opposite names left blank by the voter, or by double marking invalidate the vote cast by the voter. Double marking is a trick by means of which a vote cast is invalidated by marking a cross opposite the name of the opposing candidate for the same office. Since this can

occur even with the *bona fide* voter, there is little chance of detection.

6. Transposition of Totals on the Tally Sheet.
    (a) The apparently innocent and entirely plausible error of transposing the totals of votes with the benefit of the error going to favored candidates.

7. Alteration of Totals on the Tally Sheet.
    (a) The doctoring of totals while watchers are supposedly present during the count at the polling place.

8. Wholesale Changes on the Tally Sheet.
    (a) In the more notorious wards totals are inserted without regard to the number or distribution of votes cast. This requires the connivance of the entire staff and party watchers.

9. Substitution of Tally Sheets.
    (a) The substitution of the original sheet marked under the observation of the watchers for a false one marked by "machine" workers in accordance with instructions from party bosses.

10. Substitution of ballots.
    (a) The opening of sealed envelopes containing the ballots after they have left the polling place and the substitution of false ballots marked in accordance with the instructions of party bosses.

B. The Irregular Activities of the Party Workers.

1. Registration.
    (a) Non-resident vagrants registering under fictitious names and addresses.
    (b) Making false statement as to length of residence at correct address.
    (c) *Bona fide* voters of one precinct registering in another as a favor to some political boss in exchange for favors.
    (d) The actual housing of colonized vagrants for at least thirty days in order to conform with the lodging house law. This enables the ward bosses legitimately to control a large number of actually fraudulent votes.

2. Pledge Cards.
    (a) The use of pledge cards, obtained before election day, to determine the desirability of unregistered voters to party

interests, and if found favorable, the precinct boss somehow manages to have the names inserted after the registration books have been closed.

3. Ballot Box Stuffing.
    (a) Inserting a bundle of ballots already marked into the ballot
        box before the opening of the polling place.
    (b) Raids on polling places by armed thugs and the stealing of
        ballot boxes before the count begins.
    (c) The intimidation of election officials during the counting of
        the ballots while fraudulent ballots are being added.
    (d) The wholesale stealing of a large block of ballots before
        the opening of the polling place. These ballots are marked
        and later mixed with the valid ballots at counting time.

4. Irregular Voting.
    (a) Chain system—stringing. The first of a string of voters is
        given a marked ballot to take into the polling place and
        place in the ballot box. He brings out with him the blank
        ballot given him by the clerk, which is again marked by a
        worker on the outside and given to the next "stringer"
        voter, *ad infinitum.*
    (b) Voting for former residents who have left the precinct
        since registration.
    (c) Voting for registered voters who fail to vote.
    (d) Voting for registered voters who did not appear at the
        polling place until shortly before closing time. These
        voters are then refused the right to vote on the ground
        that they have already voted.
    (e) Removing ballots from the polling place avowedly for the
        use of bed-ridden voters, but actually for purposes of
        fraudulent marking.
    (f) Armed sluggers intimidating legal voters into leaving the
        polls without voting.
    (g) Shooting up of polling places and driving voters from the
        polls.
    (h) The purchase of votes by faction leaders, both from those
        who control the repeaters and from those counting the
        ballots.

5. Kidnapping of Workers.
    (a) This is resorted to when the party worker becomes too
        loud in his protest against the "machine" in the manipula-

tion of ballots or he is known to be an important, uncompromising worker for the opposition; also so as to instill fear into the opposing party so that their workers will refuse to come out for their faction at future elections.

6. Open Conflict of Workers.
   (a) When both factions employ thugs to control the polling place, open warfare sometimes takes place when the thugs of one faction resist the fraudulent practices of the other faction.

7. Liberation of Arrested Workers.
   (a) When the police do make an arrest of a fraudulent voter, the latter is usually released, either by armed thugs at the point of a gun, or by deputized bailiffs of the municipal court placed at the polls to insure order, or by a judge who is actively engaged in politics who holds court at the polling place or on the sidewalk, and frees the fraudulent voter by judicial process.

8. Control of the Police.
   (a) Forcing the police to do the bidding of the ward boss under the threat of demotion or on the promise of favorable mention to supervisors. Usually the policeman is called away from the polls on a ruse while the fraud is being committed. This leaves the police blameless.

9. Murder.
   (a) The deliberate assassination of party workers and political candidates of opposing factions where it is evident that such candidates are certain of election.

10. Support of Business Enterprises.
    (a) The owners of business profiting by the patronage of the gangs of hoodlums are required to furnish automobiles for the transportation of these fraudulent voters. Once the "hoodlum" is seated in the automobile, he can show little resistance to gangster persuasion.

C. Proceedings Subsequent to the Announcement of Election Returns.
   1. Recounts.
      (a) As a means of settling factional disputes and to discredit the opposing faction.
      (b) As a means of keeping the ballots from those seeking to have a recount made by the election commissioners.

   (c) As a means of keeping the ballots from special grand
        juries investigating ballot frauds.
   (d) Refusal by the custodian of the ballots to surrender them
        to the opposing faction or to the grand jury until com-
        pelled to by court order.

 2. Opposition of the State's Attorney.
   (a) Opposition in the impaneling of a special grand jury.
   (b) Opposition in the appointment of a special state's attorney.

 3. Opposition by the County Board.
   (a) Refusal to appropriate funds for a special grand jury or
        special state's attorney.
   (b) Injunction in the name of a taxpayer to enjoin the use of
        funds by the special state's attorney, already appropriated.
   (c) Refusal of the County Board to appropriate additional
        funds for the continuance of the vote fraud prosecution.

 4. Quashing Indictments.
   (a) After the indictments have been secured and the funds are
        exhausted, it is found that the indictments are faulty be-
        cause of some technicality.

 5. Challenging the Jurisdiction of the County Court in Handling
    of Vote Fraud Prosecutions.
   (a) Appealing convictions obtained by the County Court.
   (b) Obtaining writs for the release of convicted vote manipu-
        lators but applying to the Circuit or Superior Court with a
        consequent clash of judges over jurisdiction. The disap-
        pearance of the convicted persons pending an appeal to
        Supreme Court.

The long continued and prevailing nature of vote frauds in the river
wards is indicated by the nicknames by which persons engaging in the
various specialized activites are designated:

 1. *Stringer.* One who votes by the chain system.
 2. *Stinger.* An armed hoodlum who sometimes by threats and some-
    times by "floater" methods casts as many as one hundred ballots
    in one day.
 3. *Floater.* An amateur but usually homeless purchased voter, who
    votes many times during the day, going from precinct to precinct.
 4. *Repeater.* One who votes several times in the same precinct under
    fictitious names or in place of voters who fail to appear.

The repeated difficulties rising out of the election machinery and the technique of frauds, as listed above, are susceptible to correction and specialists in elections should be set to work to improve the election machinery and eliminate election frauds.

Conclusions

It will not be so simple or so easy a matter to disrupt the friendly relations of politician and gangster. The documents on the Ragen Colts and the testimonial banquet to John (Dingbat) Oberta show this fact unmistakably. These documents were selected from many others to indicate forms of neighborhood sentiment and standards of morality in the areas of vote frauds, far different from those of the lake front residence districts.

In the Dion O'Banion and Al Capone gangs is found a different and more sinister form of relation between the gangster and the politician. Neighborliness and friendly relations recede to the background. Operations in crime and political protection from its consequences are no longer local but city-wide. Immunity is no longer obtained by friendship, but from graft. Organized crime and organized political corruption have formed a partnership to exploit for profit the enormous revenues to be derived from lawbreaking.

DALEY'S MACHINE IN CHICAGO
Mike Royko

KUNSTLER: Mayor Daley, do you hold a position in the Cook County Democratic Committee?
WITNESS: I surely do, and I am very proud of it. I am the leader of my party.
KUNSTLER: What was that?
WITNESS: I surely do, and I am very proud of it. I am the leader of the Democratic party in Cook County.

From the book *Boss: Richard J. Daley of Chicago* by Mike Royko pp.59–69. Copyright © 1971 by Mike Royko. Published by E. P. Dutton & Co., Inc. and used with their permission.

KUNSTLER: Your honor, I would like to strike from that answer anything about being very proud of it. I only asked whether he had a position in the Cook County Democratic party.

HOFFMAN: I will let the words "I surely do" stand. The words after those may go out and the jury may disregard the expression of the witness that he is very proud of his position.

The Hawk got his nickname because in his younger days he was the outside lookout man at a bookie joint. Then his eyes got weak, and he had to wear thick glasses, so he entered politics as a precinct worker.

He was a hustling precinct worker and brought out the vote, so he was rewarded with a patronage job. The Hawk, who had always loved uniforms but had never worn one, asked his ward committeeman if he could become a member of the county sheriff's police department. They gave him a uniform, badge, and gun, and declared him to be a policeman.

But the Hawk was afraid of firearms, so he asked if he could have a job that didn't require carrying a loaded gun. They put him inside the County Building, supervising the man who operated the freight elevator. He liked the job and did such a good job supervising the man who operated the freight elevator that the Hawk was promoted to sergeant.

When a Republican won the Sheriff's office, the Hawk was out of work for one day before he turned up in the office of the county treasurer, wearing the uniform of a treasurer's guard. His new job was to sit at a table near the main entrance, beneath the big sign that said "County Treasurer," and when people came in and asked if they were in the county treasurer's office, the Hawk said that indeed they were. It was a good job, and he did it well, but it wasn't what he wanted because he really wasn't a policeman. Finally his committeeman arranged for him to become a member of the secretary of state's special force of highway inspectors, and he got to wear a uniform that had three colors and gold braid.

The Hawk is a tiny piece of the Machine. He is not necessarily a typical patronage worker, but he is not unusual. With about twenty-five thousand people owing their government job to political activity or influence, nothing is typical or unusual.

The Hawk keeps his job by getting out the Democratic vote in his precinct, paying monthly dues to the ward's coffers, buying and pushing tickets to his ward boss's golf outing and $25-a-plate dinners. His reward is a job that isn't difficult, hours that aren't demanding, and as long as he brings out the vote and the party keeps winning elections, he well remain employed. If he doesn't stay in the job he has, they will find something else for him.

Some precinct captains have had more jobs than they can remember. Take Sam, who worked his first precinct forty-five years ago on the West Side.

"My first job was as a clerk over at the election board. In those days to succeed in politics you sometimes had to bash in a few heads. The Republicans in another ward heard about me and they brought me into one of their precincts where they were having trouble. I was brought in as a heavy, and I took care of the problem, so they got me a job in the state Department of Labor. The job was . . . uh . . . to tell the truth, I didn't do anything. I was a payroller. Then later I went to another ward as a Democratic precinct captain, where they were having a tough election. I did my job and I moved over to a job as a state policeman. Then later I was a city gas meter inspector, and a pipe fitter where they had to get me a union card, and an investigator for the attorney general, and when I retired I was an inspector in the Department of Weights and Measures."

The Hawk and Sam, as precinct captains, are basic parts of the machine. There are some thirty-five hundred precincts in Chicago, and every one of them has a Democratic captain and most captains have assistant captains. They all have, or can have, jobs in government. The better the captain, the better the job. Many make upwards of fifteen thousand dollars a year as supervisors, inspectors, or minor department heads.

They aren't the lowest ranking members of the Machine. Below them are the people who swing mops in the public buildings, dump bedpans in the County Hospital, dig ditches, and perform other menial work. They don't work precincts regularly, although they help out at election time, but they do have to vote themselves and make sure their families vote, buy the usual tickets to political dinners, and in many wards, contribute about two percent of their salaries to the ward organization.

Above the precinct captain is that lordly figure the ward committeeman, known in local parlance as "the clout," "the Chinaman," "the guy," and "our beloved leader."

Vito Marzullo is a ward committeeman and an alderman. He was born in Italy and has an elementary school education but for years when he arrived at political functions, a judge walked a few steps behind him, moving ahead when there was a door to be opened. Marzullo had put him on the bench. His ward, on the near Southwest Side, is a pleasant stew of working class Italians, Poles, Mexicans, and blacks. A short, erect, tough, and likable man, he has had a Republican opponent only once in four elections to the City Council. Marzullo has about four hundred patronage jobs given to him by the Democratic Central Committee to fill. He has more jobs than some ward bosses because he has a stronger ward, with an average turnout of something like 14,500 Democrats to 1,200 Republicans. But he has fewer jobs than some other wards that are even stronger. Marzullo can tick off the jobs he fills:

"I got an assistant state's attorney, and I got an assistant attorney general, I got an electrical inspector at twelve thousand dollars a year, and I got street inspectors and surveyors, and a county highway inspector. I got an administrative assistant to the zoning board and some people in the secretary of state's office. I got fifty-nine precinct captains and they all got assistants, and they all got good jobs. The lawyers I got in jobs don't have to work precincts, but they have to come to my ward office and give free legal advice to the people in the ward."

Service and favors, the staples of the precinct captain and his ward boss. The service may be nothing more than the ordinary municipal functions the citizen is paying taxes for. But there is always the feeling that they could slip if the precinct captain wants them to, that the garbage pickup might not be as good, that the dead tree might not be cut down.

Service and favors. In earlier days, the captain could do much more. The immigrant family looked to him as more than a link with a new and strange government: he was the government. He could tell them how to fill out their papers, how to pay their taxes, how to get a license. He was the welfare agency, with a basket of food and some coal when things got tough, an entree to the crowded charity hospital. He could take care of it when one of the kids got in trouble with the police. Social welfare agencies and better times took away many of his functions, but later there were still the traffic tickets to fix, the real estate tax assessments he might lower. When a downtown office didn't provide service, he was a direct link to government, somebody to cut through the bureaucracy.

In poor parts of the city, he has the added role of a threat. Don't vote, and you might lose your public housing apartment. Don't vote, and you might be cut off welfare. Don't vote, and you might have building inspectors poking around the house.

In the affluent areas, he is, sometimes, merely an errand boy, dropping off a tax bill on the way downtown, buying a vehicle sticker at City Hall, making sure that the streets are cleaned regularly, sounding out public opinion.

The payoff is on election day, when the votes are counted. If he produced, he is safe until the next election. If he didn't, that's it. "He has to go," Marzullo says. "If a company has a man who can't deliver, who can't sell the product, wouldn't he put somebody else in who can?"

Nobody except Chairman Daley knows precisely how many jobs the Machine controls. Some patronage jobs require special skills, so the jobholder doesn't have to do political work. Some are under civil service. And when the Republicans occasionally win a county office, the jobs change hands. There were more patronage jobs under the old Kelly-Nash Machine of the thirties and forties, but civil service reform efforts hurt the Machine. Some of the damage has been undone by Daley, however, who let civil service jobs slip back into patronage by giving tests infrequently or making them so difficult that few can pass, thus making it necessary to hire "temporary" employees, who stay "temporary" for the rest of their lives. Even civil service employees are subject to political pressures in the form of unwanted transfers, withheld promotions.

On certain special occasions, it is possible to see much of the Machine's patronage army assembled and marching. The annual St. Patrick's Day parade down State Street, with Daley leading the way, is a display of might that knots the stomachs of Republicans. An even more remarkable display of patronage power is seen at the State Fair, when on "Democrat Day" thousands of city workers are loaded into buses, trains, and cars which converge on the fairgrounds outside Springfield. The highlight of the fair is when Daley proudly hoofs down the middle of the grounds' dusty racetrack in ninety-degree heat with thousands of his sweating but devoted workers tramping behind him, wearing old-fashioned straw hats and derbies. The Illinois attorney general's staff of lawyers once thrilled the rustics with a crack manual of arms performance, using Daley placards instead of rifles.

Another reason the size of the patronage army is impossible to measure is that it extends beyond the twenty to twenty-five thousand government jobs. The Machine has jobs at racetracks, public utilities, private industry, and the Chicago Transit Authority, which is the bus and subway system, and will help arrange easy union cards.

Out of the ranks of the patronage workers rise the Marzullos, fifty

ward committeemen who, with thirty suburban township committeemen, sit as the Central Committee. For them the reward is more than
a comfortable payroll job. If they don't prosper, it is because they are
ignoring the advice of their Tammany cousin George Washington
Plunkitt, who said, "I seen my opportunities and I took 'em." Chicago's
ward bosses take 'em, too.

Most of them hold an elective office. Many of the Daley aldermen
are ward bosses. Several are county commissioners. Others hold office
as county clerk, assessor, or recorder of deeds and a few are congressmen and state legislators. Those who don't hold office are given top
jobs running city departments, whether they know anything about the
work or not. A ward boss who was given a $28,000-a-year job as head
of the city's huge sewer system was asked what his experience was.
"About twenty years ago I was a house drain inspector." "Did you
ever work in the sewers?" "No, but many a time I lifted a lid to see if
they were flowing." "Do you have an engineering background?" "Sort
of. I took some independent courses at a school I forget the name of,
and in 1932 I was a plumber's helper." His background was adequate:
his ward usually carries by fifteen thousand to three thousand votes.

The elective offices and jobs provide the status, identity, and
retinue of coat holders and door openers, but financially only the
household money. About a third of them are lawyers, and the clients
leap at them. Most of the judges came up through the Machine; many
are former ward bosses themselves. This doesn't mean cases are always
rigged, but one cannot underestimate the power of sentimentality. The
political lawyers are greatly in demand for zoning disputes, big real
estate ventures, and anything else that brings a company into contact
with city agencies. When a New York corporation decided to bid for a
lucrative Chicago cable TV franchise, they promptly tried to retain the
former head of the city's legal department to represent them.

Those who don't have the advantage of a law degree turn to the old
reliable, insurance. To be a success in the insurance field, a ward boss
needs only two things: an office with his name on it and somebody in
the office who knows how to write policies. All stores and businesses
need insurance. Why not force the premium on the friendly ward boss?
As Marzullo says, everybody needs favors.

One of the most successful political insurance firms is operated by
party ancient Joe Gill. Gill gets a big slice of the city's insurance on
public properties, like the Civic Center and O'Hare Airport. There are
no negotiations or competitive bidding. The policies are given to him
because he is Joe Gill. How many votes does Prudential Life deliver?

The city's premiums are about $500,000 a year, giving Gill's firm a yearly profit of as much as $100,000.

Another firm, founded by the late Al Horan, and later operated by his heirs and County Assessor P. J. Cullerton gets $100,000 a year in premiums from the city's park district. Since Cullerton is the man who sets the taxable value of all property in Cook County, it is likely that some big property owners would feel more secure being protected by his insurance.

When the city's sprawling lake front convention hall was built, the insurance business was tossed at the insurance firm founded by George Dunne, a ward boss and County Board president.

Another old-line firm is operated by John D'Arco, the crime syndicate's man in the Central Committee. He represents the First Ward, which includes the Loop, a goldmine of insurable property. D'Arco has never bothered to deny that he is a political appendage of the Mafia, probably because he knows that nobody would believe him. A denial would sound strained in light of his bad habit of being seen with Mafia bosses in public. Besides, the First Ward was controlled by the Mafia long before D'Arco became alderman and ward committeeman.

D'Arco's presence in the Central Committee has sometimes been an embarrassment to Chairman Daley. Despite D'Arco's understandable efforts to be discreet, he can't avoid personal publicity because the FBI is always following the people with whom he associates. When D'Arco announced that he was leaving the City Council because of poor health, while remaining ward committeeman, the FBI leaked the fact that Mafia chief Sam Giancana had ordered him out of the council in a pique over something or other. Giancana could do that, because it is his ward; D'Arco only watches it for him. One of Giancana's relatives has turned up as an aide to a First Ward congressman. Another Giancana relative was elected to the state Senate. At Daley's urging, the First Ward organization made an effort to improve its image by running a young banker for alderman. But the banker finally resigned from the council, saying that being the First Ward's alderman was ruining his reputation.

When he is asked about the First Ward, Daley retreats to the democratic position that the people elect D'Arco and their other representatives, and who is he to argue with the people? He has the authority, as party chairman, to strip the First Ward, or any ward, of its patronage, and there are times when he surely must want to do so. Raids on Syndicate gambling houses sometimes turn up city workers, usually sponsored by the First Ward organization. While he has the authority to take away the jobs, it would cause delight in the press and put him in the position of confirming the Mafia's participation in the Machine. He prefers to suffer quietly through the periodic flaps.

The question is often raised whether he actually has the power, in addition to the authority, to politically disable the Mafia. It has been in city government longer than he has, and has graduated its political lackeys to judgeships, the various legislative bodies, and positions throughout government. While it no longer is the controlling force it was in Thompson's administration, or as arrogantly obvious as it was under Kelley-Nash, it remains a part of the Machine, and so long as it doesn't challenge him but is satisfied with its limited share, Daley can live with it, just as he lives with the rascals in Springfield.

Ward bosses are men of ambition, so when they aren't busy with politics or their outside professions, they are on the alert for "deals." At any given moment, a group of them, and their followers, are either planning a deal, hatching a deal, or looking for a deal.

Assessor Cullerton and a circle of his friends have gone in for buying up stretches of exurban land for golf courses, resorts, and the like. Others hold interests in racetracks, which depend on political goodwill for additional racing dates.

The city's dramatic physical redevelopment has been a boon to the political world as well as the private investors. There are so many deals involving ranking members of the Machine that it has been suggested that the city slogan be changed from *Urbs In Horto*, which means "City in a Garden," to *Ubi Est Mea*, which means "Where's mine?"

From where Daley sits, alone atop the Machine, he sees all the parts, and his job is to keep them functioning properly. One part that has been brought into perfect synchronization is organized labor—perhaps the single biggest factor in the unique survival of the big city organization in Chicago. Labor provides Daley with his strongest personal support and contributes great sums to his campaigns. Daley's roots are deep in organized labor. His father was an organizer of his sheet-metal workers' local, and Bridgeport was always a union neighborhood. With politics and the priesthood, union activity was one of the more heavily traveled roads to success. Daley grew up with Steve Bailey, who became head of the Plumbers' Union, and as Daley developed politically, Bailey brought him into contact with other labor leaders.

Thousands of trade union men are employed by local government. Unlike the federal government and many other cities, Chicago always pays the top construction rate, rather than the lower maintenance scale, although most of the work is maintenance. Daley's massive public works projects, gilded with overtime pay in his rush to cut ribbons before elections, are another major source of union jobs.

His policy is that a labor leader be appointed to every policy-making city board or committee. In recent years, it has worked out this way: the head of the Janitors' Union was on the police board, the park board, the Public Buildings Commission, and several others. The head of the Plumber's Union was on the Board of Health and ran the St. Patrick's Day parade. The head of the Electricians' Union was vice-president of the Board of Education. The Clothing Workers' Union had a man on the library board. The Municipal Employees' Union boss was on the Chicago Housing Authority, which runs the city's public housing projects. The head of the Chicago Federation of Labor and somebody from the Teamsters' Union were helping run the poverty program. And the sons of union officials find the door to City Hall open if they decide on a career in politics.

The third major part of the Machine is money. Once again, only Daley knows how much it has and how it is spent. As party chairman, he controls its treasury. The spending is lavish. Even when running against a listless nobody, Daley may spend a million dollars. The amount used for "precinct money," which is handed out to the precinct captains and used in any way that helps bring out the Democratic vote, can exceed the entire Republican campaign outlay. This can mean paying out a couple of dollars or a couple of chickens to voters in poor neighborhoods, or bottles of cheap wine in the Skid Row areas. Republicans claim that the Democrats will spend as much as $300,000 in precinct money alone for a city election. To retain a crucial office, such as that of county assessor, hundreds of thousands have been spent on billboard advertising alone. Add to that the TV and radio saturation, and the spending for local campaigning exceeds by far the cost-per-vote level of national campaigning.

The money comes from countless resources. From the patronage army, it goes into the ward offices as dues, and part of it is turned over to party headquarters. Every ward leader throws his annual $25-a-head golf days, corned beef dinners, and picnics. The ticket books are thrust at the patronage workers and they either sell them or, as they say, "eat them," bearing the cost themselves.

There are "ward books," with page after page of advertising, sold by precinct workers to local businesses and other favor-seekers. Alderman Marzullo puts out a 350-page ad book every year, at one hundred dollars a page. There are no blank pages in his book. The ward organizations keep what they need to function, and the rest is funneled to party headquarters.

Contractors may be the biggest of all contributors. Daley's public works program has poured billions into their pockets, and they in turn have given millions back to the party in contributions. Much of it comes from contractors who are favored, despite the seemingly fair system of competitive bidding. In some fields, only a handful of contractors ever bid, and they manage to arrange things so that at the end of the year each has received about the same amount of work and the same profit. A contractor who is not part of this "brotherhood" refrains from bidding on governmental work. If he tries to push his way in by submitting a reasonable bid, which would assure him of being the successful low bidder, he may suddenly find that the unions are unable to supply him with the workers he needs.

Even Republican businessmen contribute money to the Machine, more than they give to Republican candidates. Republicans can't do anything for them, but Daley can.

The Machine's vast resources have made it nearly impossible for Republicans to offer more than a fluttering fight in city elections. Daley, to flaunt his strength and to keep his organization in trim, will crank out four hundred thousand primary votes for himself running unopposed. His opponent will be lucky to get seventy thousand Republicans interested enough to cast a primary vote.

OFFICIAL CORRUPTION
AND ORGANIZED CRIME
Kefauver Committee

In May 1950 the U. S. Senate created a special committee to investigate organized crime in interstate commerce. It became known as the Kefauver Committee after its chairman, Senator Estes Kefauver of Ten-

From the Third Interim Report of the Special Committee to Investigate Organized Crime in Interstate Commerce, 82d Cong., 1st session, Senate Report No. 307. Published by Arco Publishing Co. as Senator Kefauver's *Crime Committee Report*, pp.183–186.

nessee. It held hearings in fourteen cities and interviewed more than 600 witnesses. This portion of its report summarizes the Committee's findings on ties between public officials and criminal syndicates.

The most shocking revelations of the testimony before the committee is the extent of official corruption and connivance in facilitating and promoting organized crime. Nevertheless, it should not be assumed that our revelations cast doubt as to the integrity of the great preponderance of law enforcement and other public officials. On the contrary, our findings and conclusions relate only to a small but disturbing minority of such officials. The committee found evidence of corruption and connivance at all levels of government—Federal, State, and local. The evidence of the corruption of Federal Government officials is primarily in connection with the enforcement of the income-tax laws. Certain officials of the Bureau of Internal Revenue in California conceived the scheme of selling stock which they owned in a company that they controlled to persons who were likely to have trouble with their income taxes. The stock was worthless, but its purchase assured immunity from a too-careful scrutiny of income-tax returns. This is not an indictment of the Bureau as a whole; most of these employees have been discharged and some have been indicted by a Federal grand jury.

The evidence of corruption and connivance with organized crime in State and local government is present in four different forms:

(1) Direct bribe or protection payments are made to law-enforcement officials, so that they will not interfere with specific criminal activities.

(2) Political influence and pressure of important officials or political leaders is used to protect criminal activities or further the interests of criminal gangs.

(3) Law-enforcement officials are found in the possession of unusual and unexplained wealth.

(4) Law-enforcement officials participate directly in the business of organized crime.

Just before his death, James Ragen, head of Continental Press, told the State's attorney that over a 3-year period, the wire service had in the past paid out $600,000 in political contributions.

Evidence of Direct Payments to Officials

At the local level, the committee received evidence of corruption of law-enforcement officers and connivance with criminal gangs in every city in which it held hearings. The testimony at the Tampa hearings indicates that Sheriff Culbreath, of Hillsborough County, was the center of the criminal conspiracy to violate the gambling laws. Evidence was received of direct and regular payments of protection money by gamblers to Culbreath and to other law-enforcement officials in Tampa.

The sordid story of direct payments to law-enforcement officials in return for the protection of criminals is repeated in Philadelphia, where the "bag" man for a Captain Elwell would come into the station house with his pockets bulging with money. Three thousand dollars to four thousand dollars a month was alleged to have been paid in each of 38 police districts or approximately $152,000 a month, not counting payments to the higher ups. In New York City it has been estimated that the Gross bookmaking empire paid over $1,000,000 a year for police protection. In Dade County, Fla., a deputy sheriff is alleged to have turned over to the wife of the sheriff seven, eight, ten, and eleven thousand dollars at a time in cash and obtained signed receipts therefor. In Jackson County, Mo. (K. C.), some deputy sheriffs were on the payrolls of slot-machine distributors and taverns that violated the liquor laws. In Los Angeles, at least half a dozen police officers "borrowed" money from the Guarantee Finance Co., a big bookmaking operation. One suspended officer worked as a collector from bookmakers for the Guarantee Finance Co. during the period of his suspension. An entry of $108,000 on the books of the Guarantee Finance Co. for "juice" undoubtedly indicates payoffs to law enforcement officials. The strong box which Sheriff Grosch of Orleans Parish, La., bought with such elaborate precautions at a time when he was a city detective was intended to keep not his legitimate earnings but the fruits of his betrayal of the public trust—protection money from law violators. But his official behavior was similar to that of many other important law-enforcement officials in the New Orleans area. This is illustrated by the extraordinary story of Moity who discovered that he could not stay in the slot-machine business without paying "ice."

There is also the case of former Police Chief George Reyer, of New Orleans, who once was president of the International Association of Police Chiefs. Squeezed by a change in administrations, Reyer took his pension and switched to the wire service payroll at $100 a week without the loss of a payday.

Law enforcement has been an easy road to affluence for many law-enforcement officials. The case of Dan "Tubbo" Gilbert, "the richest police officer in the world," who was chief investigator in the State attorney's office in Chicago, is well known. Such officials as "King"

Clancy, sheriff of Jefferson Parish, La., and Walter Clark, sheriff of Broward County, Fla., have grown rich, powerful, and arrogant from their association with the underworld elements who ran the gambling and prostitution enterprises in their jurisdictions. There are many other illustrations in the testimony before the committee. Typical of this is the fortunate economic position of John English, the city commissioner in charge of the police department of East St. Louis, who was able to obtain a $100,000 summer home, various interests in real estate in East St. Louis, interests in a restaurant and a gas station, on a salary of $4,500 to $6,000. The fact that the city was wide open for years and only two or three gambling arrests were made in 1950 may have some relation to the commissioner's wealth.

Politics Used to Paralyze Police

The attempt to paralyze law enforcement by political means is encountered again and again in the testimony before the committee. The success of mobster Frank Costello in exercising control over the New York County Democratic organization is typical of what one can expect from the alliance between politics and crime. Mobster Joe Adonis' influence upon the Kings County (Brooklyn, N. Y.) Democratic organization may go far to explain why neither he nor a major subordinate like Anastasia was ever subjected to prosecution and punishment. The committee developed at great length the extraordinary attempt by Binaggio, a powerful political leader, to acquire control of the Police Board of Kansas City so that he could install his candidate Braun as chief of police. Binaggio finally offered a substantial bribe to one of the commissioners who had refused to go along with his program. Gene Burnett, police chief of Granite City, Ill., was apparently willing to close down the gambling places and the handbooks in his town, but the orders from the mayor were to let them operate as that is how the city council wanted it. There is more than a remote connection between the orders to Police Chief Short of Miami to "lay off" gambling, "although the city could be closed in a matter of hours," and the fact that one of Miami's councilmen had had many extremely profitable deals with Harold Salvey, a member of the S and G Syndicate. The story of Governor Fuller Warren of Florida is told elsewhere. After accepting a huge campaign contribution from William H. Johnston, who has close connections with present and past members of the Capone syndicate, Warren allowed the power of his office to be used by the Capone syndicate in its successful effort to muscle into Miami Beach gambling. Most recently

Warren has reinstated Sheriff James Sullivan of Miami without any satisfactory explanation of the serious evidence and charges brought against Sullivan before this committee.

There was considerable evidence before the committee concerning contributions to political campaigns by gamblers and gangsters. For example, Molasky contributed $2,500 to the gubernatorial campaign in Missouri in the hope that he would be given the right to name a member of the St. Louis Police Board. When he was unable to do so he claimed to have been double-crossed. Pat Noonan, an associate of the mobsters in the Binaggio gang, did considerable political work in the campaign to elect Governor Smith. Much of his expenses were paid by persons involved in violations of the gambling laws. The fact that Emilio Georgetti, "the Gambling King of San Mateo County," worked "like hell" for the election of Sheriff McGrath and "accumulated a little money for the campaign," did not hurt him in his gambling operations.

Evidence has also been presented to the committee that certain law-enforcement officials or their relatives not only received protection money from gangsters but that they actually ran gambling operations themselves. The bookmaking operation which was run right in Sheriff Culbreath's office by his brother and an employee of the sheriff may or may not have been as insignificant as the sheriff tried to show. But the same thing cannot be said for the partnership which Sheriff Clark of Broward County had in the Broward Novelty Co. This company operated bolita games (policy) and slot machines and provided the sheriff with his principal source of income. The participation of public officials in the New Orleans area in the operation of slot machines has almost come to have the status of an established institution.

It is obvious that law-enforcement officials who are themselves engaged in gambling operations will have no special desire to enforce gambling statutes.

WHO RULES NEW JERSEY?
Fred J. Cook

The headline-making trial begins. U.S. Attorney Frederick B. Lacey
—a commanding 6 feet 4 and 225 pounds, a man who walks at a trot—
rises and asks Judge Robert Shaw: "Your Honor, may I use the lectern?
I have so many notes." The judge nods and Lacey wheels the lectern to
a spot front and center, before the jury box.

The jurors are brought in. They settle themselves with the usual
self-conscious bustle and look up at Lacey and the judge, the sober
citizens composing themselves with an air of appropriate seriousness as
they prepare to listen to a fanstastic story of gangland intrigue and
brutality.

The Federal prosecutor goes into his opening address, and it quickly
becomes apparent that the business with the lectern was just a bit of
expert stage-managing. Frederick Lacey does not need such a prop for
his notes; his case is in his head. He speaks in a deep, resonant voice,
clearly and distinctly, leaning casually across the lectern toward the
jury. When he reaches an especially dramatic point, he rests his right
elbow on a corner of the lectern, his lower arm and pointed finger stabbing at the jury. He captures and holds all eyes.

The tale that he unfolds is one that, varying only in details, is to
be repeated again and again in the Federal Courthouse in Newark during the next two years. In a series of trials just beginning, jury after jury
will be asked to decide cases which, in their cumulative effect, are expected to provide the most graphic study in American criminal annals
of the complete subversion of a city—and, indeed, of much of a state—
by the money and muscle of the underworld.

The case Lacey outlines to the Newark jury on this particular day
deals with the international financial machinations of a shady Newark
insurance broker, Louis Saperstein, who departed this world in late

November, 1968, mysteriously loaded with "enough arsenic to kill a mule." It is a tale that involves literally hundreds of thousands of dollars in an international stock scheme. The money for this gambit in high finance—all cash—had been obtained, Lacey says, from Angelo De-Carlo, variously known as "Ray" and "the Gyp," who is identified as a capo in the Jersey Mafia family headed by the late Vito Genovese. DeCarlo's favorite racket over the years had been loansharking, and he and three associates are on trial for having tried to collect thousands of dollars a week in "vigorish" (the loan shark's term for usurious interest) from Saperstein, allegedly beating him in the process "until his face turned purple and his tongue bulged out."

As Lacey speaks, there reposes in the courtroom behind the prosecution table what can only be described as a time bomb. It is an aluminum file cart, much like the kind used in supermarkets, and it is piled high with some 1,200 pages of white printed transcripts, the product of four years of industrious Federal Bureau of Investigation wiretapping and bugging of the phone and premises of Angelo DeCarlo. The transcripts are records of conversation in which DeCarlo and his associates brag about having a stranglehold on the city of Newark and much of New Jersey. Before the day is out, Judge Shaw will make the transcript public.

Throughout the drama of Lacey's speech, Angelo DeCarlo sits impassively, to all appearances the most unflappable man in the courtroom. He resembles nothing so much as a simple Italian *paisano*—67 years old, silver-haired, short and stocky, with an impressive paunch. He is wearing a shapeless gray suit with a light brown sweater under the coat to guard against the winter's chill. He has a heavy face, a long, sharp nose and a shelving chin; and when he waddles out into the corridor among his waiting henchmen, his lips curve around a big cigar in an almost cherubic smile. But there is nothing cherubic about him now. He swivels around in his chair at the defense table, turning his back on Lacey with a kind of bored indifference, his tight lips twisted in a hard travesty of a smile while the cold remote eyes, devoid of any trace of humor, stare out at the courtroom spectators with never a blink.

Such is the scenario. It is one that will be repeated almost endlessly in the coming months as U.S. Attorney Lacey and his young assistants wade through a mushrooming pile of indictments that, on their face, outline the most complete network of crime and official corruption that has yet to be brought to trial in an American courtroom. There has been nothing remotely comparable to this since the Murder, Inc., trials of 1940; and by comparison even Murder, Inc., was pallid stuff.

The late William O'Dwyer, who rode to glory on that exposé, contented himself with sending to the electric chair the expendable strong arms of gangdom; he never touched their bosses, Joe Adonis and the late Albert Anastasia. Nor did he disturb the political superstructure without whose complaisance the organized underworld could not exist. In this perspective, the current Jersey investigation harbors a far more explosive potential.

The potential began building almost half a century ago—from that time to this, to put it bluntly, Newark has been dominated by the mob —and it is a remarkable and notable fact of life in Newark that no underworld mogul of the first rank has ever suffered much more than a gentle slap on the wrist from the forces of the law. When a big-time mobster gets in deep trouble, something almost invariably happens.

The story goes back to Prohibition days to the nineteen-twenties. Newark—New Jersey's largest city and only a short truck haul from the thirsting fleshpots of Manhattan, became virtually the bootleg capital of the Eastern seaboard. In the gangland wars of the era, a czar of czars emerged. He was Abner (Longie) Zwillman, a Newark Jew who came to rule one of the toughest mobs in gangland history. Zwillman's underworld rivals seemed to meet their Maker in the most gory fashion, but the mob ruler himself was always leagues removed from the awful deed.

His free use of muscle and a native organizational genius made Zwillman the most important bootlegger on the East Coast. In Port Newark, then far more isolated from the central city than it is today, his rum-running fleets operated on almost a regular ferry schedule; and all up and down the inlet-dented New Jersey shoreline, especially in Monmouth and Ocean Counties, Longie's men ran a gantlet of unseeing Coast Guardsmen until they could reach haven in the arms of local policemen and sheriffs. The magnitude of the Zwillman operation may be gleaned from official estimates that his mob reaped a $50-million bonanza from bootlegging between 1926 and 1931, and that at the peak of its operation it was importing about 40 per cent of the bootleg liquor flowing across the nation's borders.

Such rapidly accumulated millions catapulted Zwillman into a position of enormous (and not too secret) political power. He became known as the Democratic boss of Newark's old Third Ward and his money helped to finance many a state gubernatorial campaign. The scuttlebutt of the times was that Longie Zwillman requested just one little favor from gubernatorial candidates who benefited from his largesse—the right to name, or at least to approve, the new Attorney General. There was never any proof of such a deal, but events frequently lent credence to the rumors. Mobsters were rarely inconvenienced in New Jersey, and the state became increasingly a haven for gangsters.

The path of an underworld chieftain is never smooth, however, and so it was with Longie. As he rose in power, so did a rival, Ruggiero (Richie the Boot) Boiardo. Just as Zwillman became the political power of the Third Ward, Boiardo achieved dominance in the First. And there was no love lost between them.

They were oddly contrasting types. Boiardo was the flashy Prohibition mobster, complete with a $5,000 diamond-studded belt buckle. Zwillman was the suave businessman of crime, a strangely dual personality. He had married into society; he knew how to conduct himself like a gentleman, and his heart bled all over his public sleeve for the poor. In the blackest pit of the Depression, he reached into his bootleg millions and paid the cost of running a soup kitchen for the impoverished in Newark's Military Park. He later established a similar soup kitchen at a Catholic church. There was, however, nothing benevolent about him when the issue was a test of underworld power, and this fact Richie the Boot Boiardo was to learn at great expense.

The bloodletting was preceded, as is so often the case in the treacherous quicksands of the underworld, by a great show of fraternity. Longie and Richie the Boot announced in 1930 that they had composed their differences, and just to show how much they loved each other, they threw a bash that was to become the talk of Newark. The party roared into its second sunset and terminated then only because the Newark News had begun to show some interest in the merriment. It spoke much about the political climate in Newark that gangsters and politicians mingled indiscriminately; among the politicians present were a former U.S. Commissioner, a candidate for the State Assembly and—most unfortunately—Paul Moore, a Democrat who was running for Congress. Moore committed the indiscretion of having his picture taken with the Boot and his belt buckle. Moore's rival, the late Representative Fred Hartley, had thousands of copies of the picture distributed in the Eighth Congressional District, and Moore later lamented that the photograph had played a large role in his defeat.

If Richie the Boot thought that the two-day wassail had made Longie Zwillman his bosom pal, he was soon to be disabused of the notion. Shortly after the party the Boot stepped out into the daylight at 242 Broad Street and encountered a hail of bullets sprayed from a sniper's nest across the street. Sixteen slugs perforated Boiardo's anatomy, and his life was probably saved by his $5,000 diamond belt buckle. "The shot that almost certainly would have killed him, ripping through his intestines, hit that belt buckle and ricocheted away," says a man who remembers the incident.

When Richie recovered, he was sent to prison for 2½ years because he had been carrying a gun himself when he was put upon on Broad Street. But prison was not the tough ordeal for the Boot that it is for most. He was packed off to Trenton State Prison in March, 1931. However—though regulations provided that prisoners must serve at least one-third of their sentences before they could be considered for less rigorous confinement—Richie the Boot was whisked away to the minimum security Bordentown Prison Farm after only four months. And rumors soon began circulating that witnesses had seen the Boot, as big as life, circulating in his old Newark haunts, especially at night and on weekends. The police investigated—but, of course, found no proof.

Freed after 16 months at Bordentown, the Boot returned to his old racket leadership in the First Ward, and he and Longie evidently agreed to divide Newark between them; the law remained a bystander.

Just how ineffectual the law was during this period was illustrated in 1939, when Richie got into difficulties with the State Alcoholic Beverage Control office. The A.B.C. seemed to have the irrational notion that the Boot, as a convicted gangster, had no business operating a tavern called the Vittoria Castle. In the subsequent hearings, some high police officials testified to Boiardo's estimable character. Acting Capt. Joseph Cocozza of the Essex County Prosecutor's staff testified that he and his wife often dined with the Boot and the latter's wife, and he added: "We have never connected him with any gang in our work." The deputy police chief in Newark and the sergeant in charge of the morals squad added their voices to the chorus, testifying that Richie was simply "trying to earn an honest living."

Reality, of course, bore no resemblance to these official pronouncements. Last summer the Government released transcripts produced in four years of surveillance of Simone Rizzo (Sam the Plumber) De-Cavalcante, who, says the F.B.I., is a Mafioso of the first water. In the DeCavalcante tapes, the real story of Richie the Boot, still active at 80, began to emerge. The revelation came when some of the boys got together in Sam's office to talk over the finer points of murder. Participants in the conversation, according to the F.B.I., were Sam the Plumber, Ray the Gyp DeCarlo and Anthony (Tony Boy) Boiardo, Richie's son and heir. It went like this:

TONY BOY: How about the time we hit the little Jew.

RAY: As little as they are they struggle.

Tony Boy: The Boot hit him with a hammer. The guy goes down and comes up. So I got a crowbar this big, Ray. Eight shots in the head. What do you think he finally did to me? He spit at me and said, "You ———"

The tapes released at DeCarlo's trial Jan. 6 add another startling dimension to the picture. Richie the Boot's private citadel is a great stone mansion (built in part with slabs his wrecking company crews had torn from the old Newark Post Office when it was demolished) that sits upon a wooded plot of several acres in Livingston, N.J. The mansion is approached by a drive at least two city blocks long, and at one turn the startled visitor comes upon a monument to megalomania. There, life-size and in full color on a life-size white horse, sits a stone Richie in all his splendor, while around and below him, mounted on stone pedestals, are nine busts—also in full, glorious color—of members of his family. The Boiardo castle, isolated behind a thick screen of trees at the end of the drive, is an eerie place; and, according to the F.B.I.'s transcripts, some shudderingly sinister things have happened there.

On Jan. 7, 1963, according to the F.B.I. tapes, DeCarlo and Anthony (Little Pussy) Russo—a mobster who once bragged that he had Long Branch in his hip pocket—discussed some of the macabre events that had taken place on the Boiardo estate. Russo warned DeCarlo never to go near the place alone if Boiardo tried to lure him there. According to Russo and DeCarlo, there was an incinerator for human bodies at the rear of the estate, up behind the Boiardo greenhouse. ". . . Ray, I seen too many," said Little Pussy. "You know how many guys we hit that way up there?"

DeCarlo: What about the big furnace he's got back there?
Russo: That's what I'm trying to tell you! Before you go up there . . .
DeCarlo: The big iron grate.
Russo: He used to put them on there and burn them.

Little Pussy and Ray the Gyp agreed that Richie the Boot was "a nut" because he disposed of not only the bodies that resulted from his own business endeavors, but also those that any other mob chief chose to pass on. According to Russo, the late Thomas (Three-Finger Brown) Luchese, for years the ruler of one of New York's five Mafia families, used to turn over the bodies of his victims to Boiardo for burning. ". . . He'd give them to me and we'd take them up," Russo told DeCarlo.

The picture that emerges from the transcripts contradicts the bland contentions of Newark policemen that Richie the Boot was an estimable character trying to earn an honest living. Of course, back in 1939 the police did not have F.B.I. tapes to apprise them of the facts of life, but still there were events that seemed to speak for themselves. In the election of November, 1932, for example, the 11th District of Longie Zwillman's Third Ward gave all the Republican candidates except Herbert Hoover just eight votes; Hoover got nine. And the Democrats, almost to a man, registered 587.

The suspiciously stuffed ballot boxes were impounded but somehow managed to flit past bemused guards and out of the City Hall basement as if they had been carried on a witch's broomstick. Few people in Newark had any doubt that the witch who had performed this magical deed was Longie Zwillman, and there was a terrific hullabaloo that included a number of indictments. Then, of course, nothing happened. Nobody was convicted.

This "no conviction" refrain became familiar in Newark as scandal after scandal whimpered to a silent and forgotten end. More than 20 indictments have been returned against public officials over the years; officials have been criticized and censured; business firms and contractors doing business with the city have been indicted. But seldom has anyone had the misfortune to be convicted.

Perhaps it is just a coincidence, but during these decades when the law and the courts seemed unable to fight their way out of a paper bag, the buddy-buddy relationship of the underworld with Newark's politicians remained one of the world's worst-kept secrets. The love affair probably never received greater public exposure than at the wedding of Tony Boy Boiardo in 1950. More than 2,000 guests turned out, and among them were Mayor Ralph Viliani, now president of the City Council; Hugh J. Addonizio, then a Congressman, now the indicted Mayor of Newark, and Rep. Peter W. Rodino, still a Democratic Congressman from the 10th District.

Such is the background of Newark. After decades of scandals, after the sputtering of innumerable exposés that have fizzled like pieces of punk in a cloudburst, Newark has once more been propelled into the spotlight as a graphic study in mob rule and political corruption.

The reasons go back to the Newark riot of 1967. On July 12 of that year the predominantly Negro Central Ward exploded in one of the worst race riots in the nation's history. The outburst lasted for days, left 26 persons dead and inflicted property damage estimated at $10.4 million. Even today, large sections of the Central Ward stand in blackened, boarded-up ruins, resembling nothing so much as the gaping chasms left in a city destroyed by war.

In an effort to determine the causes of the Newark outbreak, Gov. Richard J. Hughes appointed a commission headed by Robert D.

Lilley, executive vice president of American Telephone and Telegraph. The Lilley commission's report in February, 1968, was a shocker. It found that an important underlying cause of the 1967 riot was "a pervasive feeling of corruption" in Newark, and declared: "A former state official, a former city official and an incumbent city official all used the same phrase: 'There is a price on everything at City Hall.'"

Though the commission did not go into specifics, its blast at Newark touched off widespread reaction. Essex County Prosecutor Joseph P. Lordi began an 18-month grand jury investigation, and state legislative hearings were held. Prof. Henry S. Ruth, who had been deputy staff director of the President's Commission on Law Enforcement and the Administration of Justice, touched sensitive political nerves when he declared that, in his opinion, "Official corruption in New Jersey is so bad that organized crime can get almost anything it desires." Another expert witness assured flabbergasted officials that Professor Ruth was absolutely right. And, capping all, William J. Brennan 3d (the son of the Supreme Court Justice) remarked in a speech in December, 1968, that a number of legislators were entirely "too comfortable" with organized crime.

Brennan's remark almost prostrated the New Jersey Legislature, but events were to vindicate the young prosecutor. The Nixon Administration came to office on the cry of law and order and a pledge to fight crime. A new U.S. Attorney for New Jersey was to be appointed, and Senator Clifford Case, for years the best Republican vote-getter in the state, recommended Frederick Lacey.

At 48, Lacey was a partner in the law firm of Shanley and Fisher. His roots go deep in Newark. His grandfather was at one time a Republican Freeholder in Essex County; his father was Newark police chief for eight years; his mother still lives in the Vailsburg section of Newark, where he was born and went to school. A Phi Beta Kappa graduate of Rutgers University and a graduate of the Cornell Law School (where he was editor of the Law Review), a lieutenant commander in the Navy, a former city councilman in Glen Ridge, Lacey had moved at a furious pace to the top of his profession and was considered an expert on cases involving aerial and medical law. He specialized in trial work, was generally considered brilliant at it and represented some of the largest corporations in the nation in especially difficult cases.

When the bid came from Washington, he went down to the capital to discuss the proposition with Attorney General John N. Mitchell. "I was making big money, really big money at the time," he says, and he didn't see how he could take the $29,000-a-year U.S. Attorney's post. He was about to reject the offer when he received a call from William Sutherland, a 73-year-old lawyer.

"When you're my age," Lacey says Sutherland told him, "and you look back on your life, your pride will not be the size of the estate you are going to leave, but what you have accomplished. I know that you have an extremely lucrative law practice, but when you get to this point the money you didn't make won't seem to matter so much. What you might have accomplished in a few years as U.S. Attorney could well be the one thing in your life you would be proud of."

This conversation with Sutherland, Lacey says, "pried my thinking and had a lot to do with changing my mind."

There was another consideration. Lacey, as a young lawyer, had had one direct and shocking confrontation with big-league New Jersey crime. Throughout the nineteen-forties and into the fifties—until the Kefauver investigation threw a wrench into the machinery—the Mafia families of New York and New Jersey had run a veritable capital of crime in Duke's Restaurant, opposite the Palisade Amusement Park. Here a working crime council held daily conclave. It consisted of Joe Adonis, Frank Costello's partner, as chairman of the board; Albert Anastasia, the enforcer; the Moretti brothers, Willie and Solly, and Anthony (Tony Bender) Strollo, the right arm of Vito Genevese. On Tuesdays, the council met with some of the top czars of the national syndicate. Longie Zwillman might come up from Newark; Frank Costello from New York; Meyer Lansky from Florida. When Zwillman wasn't present, his proxy was voted by Gerardo (Jerry) Catena. After Zwillman committed suicide in 1959, Catena rose in power and is now reputed to be the ruler of the Jersey wing of the Genevese family. New York detectives, Internal Revenue agents and Federal Bureau of Narcotics agents were aware of the pivotal importance of Duke's Restaurant, but when they tried to go over to New Jersey for a little sleuthing, they were often chased out of town by local policemen.

When the lid finally blew off, under the threat of a Federal investigation, it caused a scandal that rocked the New Jersey State House. The charge was that the Adonis-Moretti combine had paid Harold John Adonis, a clerk in Gov. Alfred E. Driscoll's office and no relation to gangdom's Joe, $228,000 over a period of 19 months for protection at the state level. Frederick Lacey, a young assistant U.S. Attorney, inherited the chore of prosecuting both Harold Adonis and Albert Anastasia, and he got convictions against both.

"In that case," Lacey says now, "I found conditions shocking—and

I hadn't considered myself all that naive. But I had never encountered the broad evidence of corruption of public bodies, business and labor unions. It became my fixed and firm convicton that organized crime was taking us over. And everything that I have seen so far in this office reinforces that conviction."

When he decided to accept the U.S. Attorney's post, Lacey says, he had a firm understanding with Attorney General Mitchell. First, he explains, there is one theory that a U.S. Attorney should simply prosecute the cases handed to him by Federal investgative agencies; Lacey thinks a U.S. Attorney should be aggressive and actively develop cases if the situation seems to warrant it. The Attorney General agreed. "Next," Lacey continues, "I was assured I would have a free hand in selecting my staff and in the direction we would go. Wherever our leads take us, that's where we will go."

Lacey believes that the public, so long apathetic about syndicated crime, must be shocked and aroused, must be made to understand that when it places a $2 bet with a bookie or plays the numbers it is feeding the treasury of the underworld—and paying for the corruption of its own officials. In a speech to a bar association gathering at Seton Hall University in South Orange on Nov. 29, some three weeks before his investigation exploded in a rash of indictments, Lacey told his audience: "I want to challenge you—indeed, to goad you—to accept obligations, to assume responsibilities . . . unless you, as leaders, arouse an apathetic public to stem the tide of crime in this nation, our society as we know it is doomed."

He added: "Organized crime is, in the vernacular, taking us over. First, it corrupts law enforcement and office holders. Second, it corrupts unions and makes a mockery of the collective-bargaining concept. Third, it corrupts the businessman. Organized crime . . . cannot operate without law enforcement personnel. I flatly state that it will not even go into a municipality unless and until it has bought its protection against raids and arrests."

This was the reasoning that led Lacey to commit his most controversial act so far, his advocacy of the release of the DeCarlo tapes. Though he stood mute in open court as the DeCarlo defense fought public disclosure, he is known to have strongly favored full publicity. Governor Hughes, who left office Jan. 20, and many legal experts and concerned citizens have been aroused by this action, appalled at the damage that may be done to innocent persons through the publication of the chitchat of gangsters. Lacey, however, feels that the public good outweighs any possibility of individual harm. He takes the attitude that the only way the public can be made acutely aware of the reality of the criminal menace is by publication of the recorded words of the mobsters themselves.

The man who takes these attitudes remains something of a conundrum to many. "I don't think they know what they're letting themselves in for, he's a dynamo," said one of his law partners when Lacey was appointed. The prosecutor is the kind of man who does his push-ups every morning to keep in shape. He has worked for years on a 60-hour-a-week schedule. He likes to drop remote classical allusions into routine press conferences, perhaps quoting Alexander Pope or some other favorite authority. One day baffled newsmen had difficulty getting the point, and one of them said: "Oh, don't mind him. He's a Phi Beta Kappa and he has to show off his learning." This leads some people to think Lacey a bit pompous, but he tells the anecdote himself, chuckling about it in high good humor.

As for the future, he says flatly: "I do not entertain any political ambitions. When I took this job, I gave a commitment to Senator Case and Attorney General Mitchell that I would stay as long as I could afford to do so financially, or until I felt I had the office organized and matters well in hand. Then all I want to do is to return to my private trial practice in New York and New Jersey."

Law enforcement, Lacey feels, is primarily the responsibility of the localities and the states; it is not a job for Federal authority alone. Federal prosecutors, he believes, can set standards, can goad and stimulate, but in the final analysis the bulk of the burden must be borne by local and state agencies. And so he has proposed a series of remedial laws for New Jersey.

One proposal that goes to the roots of the gangland structure would impose a stiff jail sentence upon anyone convicted in connection with organized gambling—the bookie or the numbers runner, for instance. In the past, all too many judges have considered such offenders to be small fry of little consequence and have imposed only minor fines; but Lacey argues that their activities are basic to the system that pours an estimated $50-billion into the coffers of the crime syndicate each year.

Lacey's other proposals include the adoption of a state antitrust law modeled after the Federal Sherman Antitrust Act; it would give the state the power to act in cases in which gangland money has infiltrated legitimate business and then, by extortion and threat, driven out all competition. Another cardinal Lacey proposal calls for the creation of an organized crime unit in the State Attorney General's office. The unit would be under the direction of a Deputy Attorney General and would have the authority to investigate anywhere in the state—a provision that should make it more difficult for the underworld to establish its customary fixes on the local and county levels.

All of this, however, will represent no final solution, Lacey feels, unless the public can be aroused from apathy. In a recent interview, he explained his philosophy.

"In our schools and colleges," he said, "we teach political science in terms of defining the powers of various offices and office holders, the requirements to vote and so forth—and all of this is largely irrelevant. Relevant instruction in political science today is going to have to be aimed at getting at the roots, at showing and explaining the decaying moral fiber of those who are elected to office, those who are in law enforcement.

"If the younger generation and the university groups finally come to the terminal point in their thinking—that any government that is so corrupted isn't worthy of survival—then we who have done nothing to stop this, we who have consented to the existence of such a system by our inaction, will have only ourselves to blame. This is the evil of organized crime. It corrupts and it destroys. It destroys the officeholder, and therefore destroys the confidence of the public in its government and representatives.

"This is what I think is happening in our society today."

So the vital question raised by the current Newark probe is this: Will the public be stirred from its decades-long apathy by the flood of indictments and the inside-the-mob revelations?

The answer is mixed. There is indignation in Newark, and there is also indifference. A two-month public-opinion poll in which a group known as Focus on Newark questioned 4,000 persons indicated that if Mayor Addonizio had been running for re-election in November or December he would have been favored, 2 to 1, over his nearest rival. Newsmen interviewing Newark residents came up with some who expressed shock and indignation, but others were like the man who shrugged his shoulders and said: "This has been going on for a long time. Frankly, I don't care. I don't really care."

If the impact of the more damaging DeCarlo tapes or the upcoming trial of Mayor Addonizio (who's been indicted in an alleged kickback scheme involving mob-dominated businesses) should change this attitude, the Newark municipal election this year will probably resolve itself along racial lines. In that event, City Councilman Anthony Imperiale, the karate instructor and white militant in the heavily Italian North Ward, is seen as the probable white candidate against Kenneth A. Gibson, the Negro former city engineer. Though this shabby industrial city of some 407,000 is estimated to be more than 60 percent Negro and Spanish-speaking, there are many who feel that Imperiale just might win in such a contest—a result that would certainly intensify the racial polarization of Newark.

Even Lacey concedes that the reaction to his probe falls short of the universal cry of outrage he might have wished. On the one hand, he has been highly praised by responsible citizens, and an encouraging number of tips have come from the public. "We have received many letters and telephone calls offering information," he says. "Most of these are anonymous, but in cases where people are willing to identify themselves we keep their identity absolutely confidential, of course. Some of the tips obviously come from crackpots, but there have been, nevertheless, what I would regard as a startling number of good leads."

This is encouraging. Far less so is the old bromide that Lacey hears time and again: "You are always going to have crime and corruption." The implicit corollary to that is, of course, "So why are you getting so excited about it?"

The prosecutor shakes his head in vexation and retorts:

"To that, I say, 'Yes, but you are always going to have people who are willing to fight it. It is true that there always have been and always will be people who have frailties and who yield to temptation, but that is only part of the story. If our system is to survive, there must also be people who are willing to fight, willing to oppose, this kind of corruption.'"

AN AUTOPSY OF NEWARK
Ron Porambo

Nowhere are the ashes of the Newark riot thicker than at the city's administrative roots, those scattered by the mayor's office and the police department. Both have been, to put it mildly, infiltrated by the influence of organized crime. What began in the 1930's—Mafia kingpins leaving New York City to set up headquarters in Jersey City and Newark—soon developed into the phenomenon of institutionalized crime. That the Mafia, in a real sense, actually ran Newark cannot be denied. At the highest echelons, they still control gambling in the city. They control the flow of narcotics. And they control the numbers game. This is no different than in most big cities, but what made Newark unique is that the Mafia also controlled the mayor's office, main facets of the administrative government, and also enjoyed a candid relationship—a euphemism—with the Newark Police Department.

Untroubled by the Democratic regime in Trenton—with Governor Hughes and Attorney General Sills both under mob control, according to the words of Mafiosi recorded by the FBI—the Mafia through local political affiliations and boundless generosity made inroads into the Newark city administration. Old friendships with Mayor Addonizio and Police Director Spina that went back many years did not hurt their cause.

Newark's particular brand of corrupt politics goes back to 1949 when the city operated under a city commission form of government, and lovable Ralph Villani was elected mayor. Villani was the first of Italian heritage to be so honored. He was also the first mayor of Italian heritage to be accused by a grand jury of taking part in a shakedown racket four years later when he was turned out. Unfortunately, the amiable gentleman could not be prosecuted because of a statute of limitations. That the electorate didn't learn by this lesson was obvious from the election of a fourteen-year congressman, Hugh Addonizio, as mayor in 1962. Addonizio, a paunchy but otherwise honest-looking individual, was the second Italian to be elected mayor of Newark and the second Italian to be ass-deep in corruption.

"The only reason I came back to Newark is because I wanted to help a city in trouble and because I wanted to be closer to my family," Hughie later explained.

However, to an accomplice in extortion Addonizio had a different explanation: "There's no money in being a congressman but you can make a million bucks as mayor of Newark."

The way had been well paved for Addonizio's homecoming by Mafia bribery, threats, and job promises, which were used to get him elected and to have Dominick Spina, his diligent campaign worker, appointed as police director. Thus did Newark become an open city for criminal activity.

The biggest threat posed to Addonizio's election, as it happened, was from Michael Bontempo, then City Council president and another outstanding example of Italian civic virtue. The incumbent, Mayor Leo P. Carlin, a wily politician, promised Bontempo Police Director Joseph Weldon's job if he would enter the mayoralty race, thereby splitting the Italian vote. Bontempo reported to Mafia kingpin Angelo "Ray" DeCarlo of his intention to run. He also said he would drop out if the fix could be made with Governor Hughes to have him appointed director of motor vehicles, a reward for his presence of mind. Instead, Bontempo had to settle for $5,000 and promise of a job licking stickers at a Newark motor vehicle inspection station, should he ever be in need.

As campaign workers the Mafia's head men were diligent, at least as far as fund raising was concerned. Anthony "Tony Bananas" Caponigro contributed $5,000 toward Addonizio's election, Anthony "Tony Boy" Boiardo a whopping $10,000, Ham Dolasio $5,000, DeCarlo another $5,000, and three others $5,000 apiece.

Even before Addonizio had been elected Spina went to him—according to FBI recorded tapes—and tried to get Hughie to allow organized gambling in the city, should he become mayor. Addonizio denied the request. If Addonizio's avarice wasn't fully developed then, he quickly made up for lost time. As mayor, Addonizio soon learned what fun municipal government in a decaying city could be when he began selling everything at City Hall except the building. As one Mafia chieftain put it: "The guy's [Addonizio] taking $400, $500 for little jobs."

Addonizio and Tony Boiardo had grown up together in the same neighborhood and, long-time friends, their seemingly divergent occupations soon became mutually beneficial.

No sooner had Addonizio settled into the mayor's chair than Boiardo and his lieutenants set up a phony supply company and began shaking down contractors doing business with the city for 10 percent of their contracts. The middle man running the "company," whose address was actually a vacant lot, sent phony bills to the victimized contractors and, after payment checks were deposited in a bank, the money was withdrawn and returned to Boiardo. A good slice of the action then went to Addonizio and eventually a host of city officials, including eight of nine members of the City Council. By the time they were through, Boiardo, Addonizio and company had milked more than $1.4 million in kickbacks. What else they managed to collect must be left to the imagination.

In addition, soon after the election, Spina began pestering Ray De-Carlo to have Addonizio appoint him as police director, a situation that came to pass and made the picture complete. Thus did Newark become a sanctuary for organized gambling, which enterprise financed the heavy narcotic traffic and other Mafia hobbies.

Spina, a career police officer who would work his way up to deputy chief, had married into the well-to-do family of contractor Joseph Nesto. Authorities believed that Spina's sister-in-law, who gave the same home address as the police director, was involved in the operation of a gambling enterprise out of the Office Lounge Tavern in the East Ward. They also believed that her helpers were Angelo Ferrante and one of his sons, Daniel Ferrante. Another son, Police Captain Rocco Ferrante, the apple of Spina's eye, was marked by the police director to succeed him. Accordingly, Rocco was named by Spina to head —of all things—the intelligence division of the Newark police, whose function it was to keep track of gambling and vice violations.

Rocco, a likable, brawny individual not renowned for his thinking capacity, was also Addonizio's bodyguard, an arrangement that helped the right hand know what the left was doing. The Nesto family was thus in the best political position it had enjoyed since 1945, when Ralph Villani, then a city commissioner, had helped it to a $100,000 construction contract. A grand jury later chastised Villani in this affair for failing to "protect the interests" of the city.

Serving during the post-riot period, a further tribute to the intelligence of Newark's electorate, was a group of councilmen whose intelligence and integrity were open to question. Still hanging around was Villani, and their choice of the oldtimer to serve as council president both in 1962 and 1966 is indicative of their level of so-called thought.

From the city's highest executive office, to the City Council, to most administrative offices, the corruption spread, reaching even the office of corporation counsel, whose job was to make the dirty work look legal. When the Hughes report stated that *everything* was for sale at City Hall it was not merely using a figure of speech. The Mafia controlled the unions working on city projects, city officials awarded contracts to friends like Boiardo, who also shared in shakedowns of other contractors. Sometimes the victimized contractors got even by charging for work never performed. The drugged electorate paid the bills, possibly the most permissive captive citizenry in the history of this country.

The situation became so routine that the Mafia no longer had to remain under cover. Tony Boy Boiardo was listed as a "salesman" for

Valentine Electric Company, a modest little enterprise that opened its doors fully funded in 1958. Aided by the greatest salesman since Jesus Christ, the company prospered. In ten years it became the largest electrical contractor in the area. Valentine was awarded half the contracts of the Newark Housing Authority and was soon doing better than $5 million annually. The city's other electrical outfits regarded many city jobs as "locked up" with few if any even bothering to submit bids. What was locked up was Newark—lock, stock and barrel—in the hands of the Mafia, and Valentine's star salesman was regarded by insiders as "the real boss of Newark."

Throughout this period, Addonizio was enjoying himself on many luxurious vacations in Puerto Rico and Florida for which he never paid a cent. Newark's mayor gambled frequently, often losing heavily, also without paying. In effect, Hughie could vacation and gamble when he pleased with his "many, many good friends" picking up the tabs.

Once Spina was named police director the morale of the department started to decline, largely because of his personal handling of crucial assignments to the detective division, one method utilized by corrupt law enforcement officers to negate the effectiveness of their own agencies. Although assignment as a detective amounts to a promotion—a $300-annual-salary increase and added prestige—no examination was required when the assignment system was instituted in 1955. Spina's predecessor, Joseph Weldon, established evaluation criteria when he took over in 1958. Evaluation under Weldon, who had a reputation for honesty, consisted of a written examination, a rating system, and recommendations of deputy chiefs.

Spina replaced this system with his personal choices. Men made the team for being good police officers, or avid spies in department politics and in the black community. Fondness for spaghetti was not a handicap. With incentive redefined, the department morale nosedived. Its members grouped as supporters or opponents of Spina. The anti-Spina faction included a group that backed Deputy Chief John Redden, the only police officer with the leadership, character, and understanding of the city's problems to reverse the losses of the Spina regime.

"A large segment of the Negro people," the Hughes Report stated, "are convinced that the single continuously lawless element operating in the community is the police force itself, and its callous disregard for human rights."

White people may never know the bitterness and frustration that set in when a law enforcement agency outdoes criminals in lawlessness. In crying foul at the words of the Hughes Report, Spina, Imperiale and the PBA only tainted their own credibility. If anything, the report was only frosting on the cake.

The ghetto's streets are crime-infested, a way of life individual police officers routinely take advantage of. Frequent gambling parties, after-hours liquor spots, dope pushers, and hustlers are easy marks for shakedowns. Some police rationalize that if criminal activities can't be curtailed—as they can't be under the circumstances—then they can at least be used for personal gain. The cancer of lawlessness eating through the ghetto touches and finally infects all who come in contact with it. The necessary surgery of effective prosecution would cut away a large chunk of the police department itself. "The real money starts up around the top," one former officer told me. "The money patrolmen pick up is little stuff."

Once the lower police echelons realize that organized crime is licensed, they cut themselves in. Taking a cut from such rackets as numbers, the police form a virtual partnership. They are controlled from the upper echelons by assignments and the money is passed upward.

Many black policemen in Newark are hated in the ghetto not for serving the power structure but because they victimize their own people and often operate brutally in the process. Although there are only approximately 230 blacks on the force (which has an authorized quota of 1,512 and is currently at least 200 short), many of them are accomplished thieves. Black officers, particularly detectives, know the numbers carriers, junkies, and pushers on sight, and use their knowledge to shake them down. For a pusher, a payoff of a few hundred dollars is well spent if it prevents being fingerprinted and photographed.

White police start with an information disadvantage in the ghetto, but they quickly learn the knack of shakedowns and payoffs, known in the trade as "juice." Once in the ghetto, where the opportunities are so plentiful, white officers are seldom anxious to leave, particularly ranking officers who can take their cut while sitting behind a desk.

"There are some policemen that are interested in this sort of thing," Assemblyman Richardson testified before the Hughes Commission, referring to graft, payoffs, extortion. "Despite all the dangers of being involved in this all-black community, you couldn't run some of the white officers away from there. In my estimation, that is the reason why Captain Williams has not been assigned to one of those Negro precincts, because of obvious pressures from other people that have certain influences in the city."

Whether corruption spread from the city administration to the police department or vice versa is an interesting but moot question. Corruption in each has grown apace, increasing at about the same rate that whites retreated from the decaying city. Thus non-writes were not only cheated of political control while gaining numerical superiority. They were also forced to watch as leeches sucked the city's blood.

Since the city administration and the police were virtual partners in illicit activity, neither was about to blow the whistle on the other. Each looked the other way, and was aided in this endeavor by the legal guardians of the city—the prosecutor's office and the magistrates sitting in municipal court.

* * *

Spina's involvement in organized gambling and the corrupt dealings of Addonizio and others within the administration have been well documented by FBI recording devices. Their connections with Mafia kingpins Simone "Sam the Plumber" DeCavalcante, Ray DeCarlo, Gerardo "Jerry" Catena, Ruggiero "Richie the Boot" Boiardo, and his son, Tony Boy, are now a matter of record.

"You know Hughie Addonizio got hold of me," Tony Boy Boiardo told DeCavalcante and DeCarlo in early 1963. "He said, 'Look, tell DeCarlo that the FBI knows about Irving Berlin.' I'll tell you how much the FBI knows about Irving Berlin. This kid Vic [Pisauro] turned himself in. The prosecutor [Brendan Byrne] told the FBI that he's one of my boys and that I made him give himself up to the director [Spina]."

Boiardo was referring to the killing of bartender James Del Grosso at the West Side Tavern on South Orange Avenue earlier in 1963, an event that brought to light two Mafia factions within the city, as well as the pride that Boiardo took in controlling his men. One faction belonged to the Boiardos and the other included Angelo Bruno and one of his lieutenants, Carmine Battaglia, who had set up gambling in the tavern.

Pisauro, one of Boiardo's men, visited the tavern with Miss Patricia Fiore, who had known Del Grosso. Early in the morning, Del Grosso made advances to her and she rebuffed him. In the ensuing fight, he was killed by a blow over the head and his body was punctured by numerous stab wounds. Because it was in his territory, according to the tape, Battaglia "went around screaming about it." Though there were no known witnesses to the fight, police had teletypes out for Miss Fiore and Pisauro. Shortly thereafter, Boiardo told Pisauro and the girl to go to Spina and give themselves up, which they did.

"The FBI went to see Byrne and asked about this Pisauro—about how come he gave himself up," Boiardo said. "Byrne told them, 'We had Carmine Battaglia in here and told him if we don't get this man here—' Byrne said, 'We had him affiliated with Carmine but we found out we were wrong. This is Tony Boy's man.'"

On October 30 a jury acquitted both Pisauro and Miss Fiore of the Del Grosso murder, justifying Boiardo's faith in law and order.

Another portion of the FBI tape related the conversation of Boiardo, DeCavalcante, and DeCarlo on a 14th Street gambling operation of Ham Dolasco:

> BOIARDO: You know Dick Spina asked me, "Why don't you and Ray [DeCarlo] get together and open up?" I said, "What is there to open up?"
>
> DeCAVALCANTE: You know, Tony, thirty or thirty-five years ago if an— was even seen talking to a cop they looked to hit him the next day. They figured he must be doing business with the cop.
>
> DeCARLO: Today if you don't meet them and pay them you can't operate.
>
> BOIARDO: The only guy I handle is Dick Spina. Gino [Farina] and them guys handle the rest of the law. About seven or eight years ago I used to handle them all.
>
> DeCAVALCANTE: Did you see the way Ham operates on Fourteenth Street?
>
> DeCARLO: For five thousand dollars Ham and Tony [Anthony "Bananas" Caponigro, another Essex County chieftain] thought they bought a license.
>
> DeCAVALCANTE: This was before the five thousand dollars.
>
> DeCARLO: They walk into precincts and everything. You can't have a man and be seen with him. He's no good to you then.
>
> DeCAVALCANTE: And how long do you think it will take the federal men to find out?

As long as it took to play the tapes—and they've been playing them for seven years now.

Organized gambling is Newark's biggest business. Estimates based on evidence seized by agencies other than the Newark police, in two raids alone, show the extensive activity in the city. One raid conducted in the second precinct in early 1966 showed that a lottery operation limited to one quarter of Newark brought in a weekly take of $130,000 collected by some 400 writers. The yearly take from this single operation amounted to $6.7 million. Experts have projected that the yearly take for the entire city approaches $27 million, a figure that does not include the lucrative take of bookmaking and gambling parties. Widely known organized gambling figures come and go in Newark with impunity while trafficking in the illicit business.

So broad is the license to operate that lottery pick-up men make little effort to conceal their activity. One man was arrested making pick-ups totaling $7,000 in lottery play on a busy corner in the Fourth Precinct.

Evidence of a law enforcement breakdown in the city is ample and clear. The total of lottery and bookmaking raids in 1965 was 142. In 1966 the number dropped to eighty-five and in 1967 to forty-eight. During this period gambling activity was rapidly increasing. If the Newark police were reluctant to make raids, the prosecutor's detectives were willing, with embarrassing results to the police. One raid by the prosecutor's men in 1965 resulted in the transfer of the entire fifth precinct's plainclothes squad to other duties, and on December 4, after a further series of prosecutor raids, Mayor Addonizio angrily abolished plainclothes gambling squads in all precincts. The prosecutor's men were doing a job and Hughie figured they didn't need any help.

The prosecutor's detectives said that when they told the Newark police of proposed raids, they arrived to find they were playing cops and robbers with themselves. The gambling operations had suddenly vanished. It is no surprise that the prosecutor's office then kept any information it uncovered on gambling activity to itself. Likewise, after the FBI tapes, neither were the federal people anxious to communicate with either the Newark police or the city administration on such criminal matters.

Four Essex County grand jury presentments between 1961 and 1965 had asserted police corruption and police reacted by continuing business as usual.

The April 1965 presentment charged political interference with the police department and lack of enforcement of Newark gambling laws, and drew attention to open activity of Harry "Tip" Rosen, a public relations man for People's Express. This local trucking company is jointly owned by Jerry Catena, Mafia chief of Newark, and Ralph Damco, who in November of 1967 threw a banquet for newly appointed Police Captain Rocco Ferrante, Spina's right-hand man. Rosen also happened to be public relations man for the Newark Police Department, a combination of roles that seems practical but one which the grand jury found unsettling. Instead of being rewarded for efficiency, Rosen was fired. The presentment observed the following:

> We have a lack of confidence in the Newark Police Department's enthusiasm for a crackdown on the underworld. Nowhere has our attention been focused on any policy statement by the police department vigorously attacking organized crime. . . .
> There are things which to us, as laymen, are disturbing. They include: A) Political considerations seem to override all else in the assignment of officers to plainclothes and gambling details. We refer to the testimony Director Dominick A. Spina stated, that he makes the decisions regarding the transfers of personnel and he uses his own standards, particularly in regard to appointments to rank of plainclothesman and detective.
> All of this has been weighed in the light of Mayor Hugh A. Addonizio's testimony, which indicated that he has made recommendations for appointments and transfers of various individuals to positions in the police department, and in many instances these were grounded in political motivations. . . .
> B) Commanders have little say regarding the composition of their own divisions or squads in a sensitive field of gambling enforcement.

As a result of their probe, the grand jury recommended:

> That transfers and assignments, as distinguished from raises in grades provided by Civil Service, should be made on the basis of merit and the good of the service. They should not be made through personal, political, or private motivations.

Despite this recommendation, Spina's private promotion system remained unchanged. Deputy Chief Eugene O'Neill said that within a month of taking command of the bureau of investigation in March 1968 he analyzed his men's productivity in raids and arrests. He then recommended that fifteen to twenty detectives and five lieutenants—almost half the men assigned to him—be transferred out of the division. Spina *never took action* on the recommendation. It might have been too costly. One Mafia figure said on FBI tapes he was paying $12,000 monthly for police protection.

A second presentment in December of 1965 again noted flagrant gambling violations and Spina reacted quickly to the new attack, tossing out a few slices of bologna for the public appetite. He labeled the presentment "vicious" and challenged Prosecutor Byrne to show him any organized gambling in Newark, a thoughtless move even in the name of expediency. Within forty-eight hours Byrne raided two apartments and charged fifteen people with operating a lottery.

✿ ✿ ✿

The polarization that pervaded post-riot Newark included the police department, though here it was limited to a low murmur. On one side was the fifty-seven-year-old Spina and on the other, Deputy Chief Redden, who since 1962 had been watching with growing disgust as Addonizio and Spina helped turn Newark into a corrupt whorehouse. For the forty-eight-year-old Redden, the riot had been the last straw and his Irish anger flared. He called city officials bastards to their faces. He told them he'd testify before a grand jury and before the Hughes Commission.

While public attention was drawn to the evil black man, LeRoi Jones, and the ranting of Imperiale in the North Ward, the real struggle in post-riot Newark was a silent one. Few understood that, as far as Spina and organized crime were concerned, John Redden was the most dangerous man in Newark.

Police Chief Oliver Kelly went on terminal leave before his retirement on December 29, 1968, leaving the position open to one of three deputy chiefs, Anthony Barres, Eugene O'Neill, and Redden. Ordinarily the New Jersey Civil Service Commission would have scheduled a promotion exam, but the commission was not notified of the vacancy until after Kelly had left. Spina had five other deputy chiefs appointed after Kelly's departure, hoping that they would be at their new posts a year before an exam for the chief's position was held, thus fulfilling eligibility requirements.

In December of 1967 Spina said he had asked the commission to hold exams as early as possible in 1968. The director of classification for the Newark office, however, said he had received no such communication. Spina then said he had not asked for the exam because he wanted to choose from a "wider field" than the men then eligible. More accurately, he wanted to avoid appointing Redden, who had finished *first* on the list in the last two exams.

Newark's flagrant gambling activity, particularly because of Redden's testimony, was aired in the Hughes Report: "Based on my own experience, based on the statement—the public statement—of a man such as former Assistant Attorney General [John] Bergin, I would say that it was very prevalent," Redden testified. "It is a very large business." Redden further pointed out the assigning of personnel for "political reasons."

Badly stung by the Hughes Report, Mayor Addonizio ordered a special gambling squad into existence shortly afterward to save face and imprudently placed Redden in command. Between March and mid-April, the nine-man unit made twenty-two arrests and confiscated

$15,370 in lottery play, two shotguns, six pistols, and $10,000 in stolen merchandise. They also confiscated $16,389 in cash. In six weeks the squad had collected more cash than the entire police department had in the previous three years. In one of their most successful forays on March 15, Redden's squad raided Frisco's Luncheonette. They arrested five men and confiscated a paper bag that contained $6,934 in cash, $498 worth of lottery play, some medicine, an apple, and—now what do we have here?—twelve tickets to Mayor Addonizio's birthday party.

Redden said his squad had also uncovered evidence of widespread loan-sharking in the city and that several big raids were being planned. They were never carried out. The end of the special gambling squad was first announced informally during a preliminary court hearing when a widely known professional gambler told squad members that there would be "changes" within a week. There were changes within a week. While the squad was out on a raid, a teletype order from Spina disbanded the group—much to the surprise of Addonizio, who had never been informed.

Spina said the men on the squad were needed elsewhere because of "a manpower shortage" but squad members told a different story:

"The number of arrests could have been tripled, but we had trouble getting search warrants."

"We were stepping on too many toes."

"We were getting close to the big people."

Addonizio was vacationing at Miami Beach when he heard of the disbanding of a squad he had ordered. "Spina discussed it with me before I left," the mayor stated. "He said they hadn't produced anything." Commenting on Redden's loan shark discoveries, he said, "Redden should take it up with Director Spina. I'm sure Director Spina is just as interested in arresting gamblers as he is."

Addonizio may have been joking but Essex County Prosecutor Joseph P. Lordi, who had succeeded Byrne, wasn't. The day following Spina's abolition of the gambling squad, Lordi said he would call for a special grand jury to investigate what was going on in Newark. The real question was, what wasn't going on.

THE STERN SYNDICATE
IN WINCANTON

John A. Gardiner

For at least fifty years, Wincanton has had something of a reputation as a "sin city." One worker on the staff of the National Crime Commission recalled that when he was growing up in a nearby city, Wincanton was where men went to raise hell on Saturday night—if their wives would let them out of the house. Physically, it hardly looks the part; lacking either verdant resorts or quaint "Oldtown" or Greenwich Village charm, Wincanton looks mostly like an old, rather decayed factory town. A journalist who visited the city in 1967 summed it up as

> an almost museum piece nineteenth century industrial, immigrant-inhabited, red brick mill town. Except for a few 1930 tall business buildings, it retains exactly the look of unreconstructed 1890–1900—huddles of workers' houses nestling under overhead wires up to railroad tracks and long black factories with tall black chimneys. An Englishman from the midlands would feel perfectly at home, the abrupt descent from rich green rolling highlands and countryside to packed-in proletarian obsolescence. . . .[1]

While the physical appearance of Wincanton hasn't changed much in the twentieth century (although several upper-middle-class suburbs have grown up since World War II), a number of changes have taken place in the economic, social, and political characteristics of the city. A spurt of industrialization in the late nineteenth century transformed a rural marketplace and trading center into a bustling center for manu-

From chapter 2 (pp.6–13) and chapter 3 (pp.17–31) of *The Politics of Corruption: Organized Crime in an American City* by John A. Gardiner, © 1970 by Russell Sage Foundation, New York. References to other chapters and some footnotes deleted.

1. Nathaniel Burt, "Report from Wincanton," *Philadelphia Magazine*, November, 1967.

facturing, with a population exceeding 110,000 in the 1920s. Textile mills and leather-working industries dominated the local economy for many years. While the city has not known a serious depression during the last forty years (only 2.5 percent of the labor force was unemployed in 1965), it hasn't known any growth either; the central city population has been declining slowly since 1930, with a net loss of 11,000 residents between 1950 and 1960. Several textile mills and most of the leather industries have gone out of business or moved to the South, balanced somewhat by the postwar construction or expansion of machine works and electronics assembly plants.

Wincanton's postwar economy has been both diversified and dominated by national rather than locally owned corporations. The major industries today include steel processing, heavy machinery, textiles, and food products; seven corporations have more than 1,000 employees. Most of the major industries are now parts of nationwide corporations, and are operated by salaried managers rather than owner-entrepreneurs. Descendants of the original artisan-industrialists can still be found in the area, but they are primarily active in banking, investment corporations, and the law, having since the 1930s sold their stock in the family corporations.

Data from the 1960 Census show that Wincanton's population was somewhat older and had a higher proportion of lower-middle-class residents than other middle-sized cities. The Negro and Puerto Rican populations were small, and there was relatively little substandard or overcrowded housing. While there was little extreme poverty in Wincanton, there was also little great wealth within the city's boundaries. Only 11 percent had incomes over $10,000, and only 27 percent had completed high school. The vast majority of Wincanton residents belonged to the lower-middle and middle classes, with incomes between $3,000 and $10,000. There has been little in-migration to the city in recent years; 88 percent of the 1960 residents were born in this state, and more than 60 percent were living in the same homes that they had occupied in 1955. This stability has encouraged the continuation of the separate identities of the various nationality groups: the Germans, Poles, Italians, and Negroes still have their own neighborhoods, stores, restaurants, social clubs, and political leaders.

Politics in Wincanton

During the years when American cities were controlled by highly centralized political machines, it was possible for men seeking illegal privileges to control the entire city government by simply bribing the boss, who then arranged for the "cooperation" of low-level policemen, councilmen, judges, and so forth; uncooperative subordinates quickly found themselves deprived of their offices or patronage. In more recent years, some city charters have given mayors a few of the powers of the old-time bosses, but nonpartisanship, the formal fragmentation of metropolitan government, civil service, the growth of unions within the municipal bureaucracy, and the separate election of many city officials have meant that few mayors today are able to guarantee the acquiescence of all parts of the city government in any policy, whether legal or illegal.

Where, as is often the case in American cities today, the local political system is not centralized enough to give total control to one or a few men, the next best hope for a crime syndicate seeking protection for its illegal activities is a political system which is so decentralized that *no* political force is powerful enough to challenge any individual officials who have been corrupted. For reasons that will be discussed later, such fragmented systems seem both to attract more temptable leaders and to contain fewer forces, such as party organizations, interest groups and elite associations, which might persuade tempted officials to conform to legal norms.

Wincanton is an almost perfect example of such a weak, fragmented system in terms of both its formal governmental structure and its informal political processes. Many governmental functions are handled by independent boards and commissions, each able to veto proposals of the mayor and city council. The city government is a modified version of the commission plan, with a council composed of the mayor and four councilmen. In odd-numbered years, two councilmen are elected (on a partisan ballot) to four-year terms. The mayor is directly elected by the voters for a four-year term. Every two years, following local elections, the five members of the council meet to decide who will control which departments (with the statutory requirement that the mayor *must* control the police department). Thus the city's affairs can be shared equally by the five men, or a three-man majority can control most important departments. (In one not atypical occurrence, a councilman disliked by his colleagues found himself controlling only garbage collection and the Main Street comfort station!) After the biennial allocation of city departments, each department head (mayor or councilman) has fairly strong control over the actions of his departments; while the entire council must formally ratify most personnel and budgetary matters, a "gentlemen's agreement" usually leads to council approval of the requests of department heads. Thus official decision-making in Wincanton is for all practical purposes divided into a series of "decision centers" dominated by the individual city departments and the councilmen who control them; the mayor and other council members seldom intervene in departmental decisions, so there is little co-ordination of city activities, and councilmen can follow whatever policies are satisfactory to their bureaucracies and relevant interest groups.

Supplementing the commission structure in producing a corruptible local government in Wincanton is the limited nature of state supervision of local affairs. The state civil service laws do little to constrain official actions, since they apply only to the police, engineering, and electrical departments and building and health inspectors; within the police department, the mayor has complete authority to promote and demote officers, including the chief, although men can only be *removed* from the force "for cause." Every election leads to a wholesale reorganization of the police department; patrolmen have been named chief and former chiefs have been reduced to walking a beat. As will be seen later, the state police seldom enter a city unless asked to do so, thus allowing local officials to set whatever law-enforcement policies they wish. The state's municipal bidding law also contains many loopholes inviting fraud. Cities are not required, for example, to seek competitive bids for "emergency work," "patented and manufactured materials," insurance policies, personal or professional services, or contracts involving less than $1,500. Even when bids are sought, the city is free to reject the lowest bidder where others are felt to offer superior judgment, skill, or promptness, and courts will only set aside such contracts if a complainant can *prove* that the city acted corruptly or in bad faith.

Just as these formal qualities of Wincanton government have led to a decentralization of official authority, a number of informal characteristics of Wincanton politics have also minimized the likelihood that any nongovernmental group can or will control city officials or their policies. Since the 1940s, when the Socialist Party faded from view, the Democratic Party has easily won most local elections, and there are now about two registered Democrats for each Republican in the city. Neither party organization has, however, been able to control primary elections or voting in city council meetings. Council voting has crossed party lines as often as it has followed them. Although both party organizations have had ample patronage to dispense from state, county, and local positions, their endorsements have never guaranteed victory in the primaries. No Wincanton mayor has ever succeeded himself in of-

fice; four of the last five mayors have been defeated in bids for re-
election, often unable to survive even their own party's primary.
Primary election contests have seldom offered a confrontation of issue-
or program-based factions; candidates tend rather to appeal to the
voters on the basis of their personalities, ethnic background, or ability
to deliver such favors as street improvements, playgrounds, or city jobs.
Local custom requires every politician to visit the ethnic associations,
ward clubs, and voluntary firemen's associations during campaign time
—buying a round of drinks for all present and leaving money with the
club stewards to hire poll watchers to advertise the candidates and to
guard the voting booths.

No private interest groups (other than the crime syndicates) have
dominated Wincanton politics in recent years. Labor unions support
Democratic candidates in the general elections, but are often split in
the primaries, with the industrial unions backing liberal or reform
candidates and the trade unions endorsing "regulars." The unions' influence in Wincanton politics has been weakened by the fact that
leaders of the local labor council have been more interested in state
and national issues (minimum wage and right-to-work laws, working
conditions, etc.) than in control of the city government. The newspapers, business organizations, and "good government" groups almost
always support Republican candidates, but they have only been able
to overcome the normal Democratic majority when monumental
scandals have shaken the confidence of registered Democrats. . . .

A number of Wincantonites interviewed in 1966 felt that even if
the party organizations and unions didn't control local politicians,
there was a small cabal of bankers and industrialists who "really"
dominated local politics. Members of this supposed elite are amused
by these persistent legends, feeling that few local politicians care much
about their opinions. One felt that his *father* could have called a meeting "to settle everything"—as current folklore says he and his friends
are now capable of doing—but that no one has this sort of power
today. Why is this elite no longer able to control Wincanton politics?
For one thing, the structure of the Wincanton economy has changed:
local families no longer own the major industries, and thus lack the
political resource of control over jobs. Furthermore, most members of
the financial-business-managerial community live in the suburbs and
are ineligible to vote for or hold city office, although they contribute
regularly to Republican candidates. Finally, control over local officials,
if obtainable, would offer few rewards to these men; they live in beautiful suburbs which provide excellent schools, parks, playgrounds,

musuems, etc., so central city policies have little impact on their personal lives.

One major exception to both the political inactivity of these men and the irrelevance of city policies to them concerns the issue of economic development. As the focus of the elite has moved from the ownership of industry to the management of money, the bankers and investors have been particularly interested in the attractiveness of the Wincanton area to possible industrial developers. Since World War II, although they have been detached from policy-making in other matters, the leaders of the Wincanton business community have been quite concerned about policies related to urban redevelopment, industrial land banks, and other schemes for bringing new industry into the city. Frequently, plans for such economic growth have been developed outside the city government through urban renewal authorities, advisory panels on economic problems, and economic development corporations. This separation from the city council and electoral politics has somewhat increased the potential for elite influence, and each of these agencies has usually been dominated by members or representatives of the business and financial communities.

If the elites of Wincanton have become dissociated from all political activities except those involving economic growth (whether this dissociation has been voluntary or involuntary is here beside the point), why should they be mentioned in this discussion of law enforcement, corruption, and organized crime? Most of the time, the inactivity of the Wincanton elites has had only a negative impact, leaving politics and power to lower-middle-class politicians and voters; upper-middle-class attitudes toward crime and law enforcement are thus less often presented either in campaign oratory or in official deliberations. The elites have, however, maintained an interest in the *image* of the city, and have reacted indignantly when scandals have exposed the extent of corruption and organized crime in Wincanton. One manufacturer told of attending a convention in California at which he was called upon to defend not the quality of his products but the honor of Wincanton. ("You're from Wincanton?" a conventioneer is supposed to have asked. "Boy, have I heard about the hoodlums and crooked politicians you've got there!") This national image of corruption, some bankers and industrialists said, has kept potential investors from choosing Wincanton as a site for the location of new industry. Whether we attribute the elite's concern for the city's image to economic self-interest ("We must keep the city growing to find investment opportunities for our capital") or to *noblesse oblige* boosterism ("Our families made this city great and we don't want cheap politicians and crooks giving it a bad name"), Wincanton elites have been interested in corruption and law-enforcement policies, at least when they become notorious enough to give the city a bad name.

The Wincanton political system is thus fragmented, both formally and informally. Five virtually autonomous councilmen share in the management of city affairs. The mayor, while guaranteed control over the police department, has little power over the bureaucracies headed by other councilmen. The party organizations, while well provided with money and patronage, have been unable to control primary contests, council voting, or the activities of city officials. Unions, the newspapers, and business groups have been similarly unable to dominate local politics, so each candidate has been forced (and free) to develop his own constituency of neighbors, fellow ethnics, social clubs, and city workers, most of whom are only interested in his ability to deliver petty favors. The men attracted to city office have been predominantly locally oriented men with lower-middle-class backgrounds, although there has been some variation between parties. Republican candidates have usually been small businessmen of English or German ancestry; Democratic candidates have more frequently represented the Irish, Italian, and Polish neighborhoods. Recent "regular" officeholders have included two tavern owners, two accountants, a liquor salesman, and several union leaders; candidates running on *reform* Democratic slates, however, have usually been school teachers. Neither party, it will be noticed, has drawn candidates from big business or industry.

Since the early 1930s, the story of gambling and corruption in Wincanton has centered around the activities of Irving Stern. Born in Russia in 1898, Stern emigrated to the United States and settled in Wincanton in 1904. After he had worked for a few years at his family's fruitstand, Prohibition arrived and Stern became a bootlegger for Heinz Glickman, then controlling beer distribution throughout a three-state region. Once after hijacking a shipment of illicit alchol, Stern was ambushed and shot at by his infuriated rivals; Stern quickly identified his assailants for the police. At the ensuing trial, however, Stern was "unable" to recognize the defendants, and the outraged judge slapped a two-year perjury sentence on him. In 1933, shortly after Stern's release from prison, gang warfare led to the murder of Glickman; Stern seized control of part of his business and continued to sell untaxed liquor after the repeal of Prohibition in 1933. Stern was convicted on liquor violation charges several times in the late 1930s, and spent over one year in federal prison.

Coming out of prison around 1940, Stern announced to the world that he had reformed and was taking over the family's produce business. While Stern did in fact quit the bootlegging trade (legal competition and the zeal of federal enforcement agents was making bootlegging rather unprofitable), he turned his attention to the field of gambling, for Wincanton had developed a "wide-open" reputation, and state and local police were ignoring gamblers and prostitutes. Stern started with a numbers bank and soon added horse betting, a dice game, and slot machines to his activities. Former bootlegging friends from New York provided technical advice, and the family produce store served as a legitimate "cover." During World War II, officers from a nearby army base closed down Wincanton's brothels, but Stern was unaffected, since he had already concluded that possible profits from prostitution would not compensate for the threats which the houses posed to his gambling activities; public reprisals against prostitution might carry over to gambling, and besides, gamblers had more public legitimacy or "status" than pimps. In the course of federal investigations in 1951, it was estimated that Wincanton gambling had become an industry with gross receipts of $5 million each year; from bookmaking alone, Stern had net profits of $40,000 per week, and Klaus Braun, a rival who controlled five hundred slot machines, was collecting $75,000 to $100,000 per year.

Irv Stern's activities in Wincanton collapsed abruptly in 1951 when these federal investigations brought about the election of a reform administration. . . . Republican Mayor Hal Craig decided to seek what he termed "pearl gray purity"—tolerating isolated prostitutes, numbers writers, and bookies, but driving out all forms of *organized* crime, all activities lucrative enough to encourage bribery of Craig's police officers. Within six weeks after he took office, Craig and his district attorney had raided enough of Stern's gambling parlors and seized enough of Klaus Braun's slot machines to convince both men that their activities were over—for four years at least. The Internal Revenue Service was able to convict Braun and Stern's nephew on charges of tax evasion and send both to jail. From 1952 to 1955 it was *possible* to place a bet or find a prostitute in Wincanton, but you had to know someone to do it and no one was getting very rich in the process.

Toward the end of Craig's administration, it was apparent to everyone that reform sentiment was dead and that the Democrats would soon be back in office. In the summer of 1955, Stern met with representatives of several East Coast "families" of the Cosa Nostra or "Mafia," and arranged for the rebuilding of his gambling empire. His experience during the 1940s and his brush with the Internal Revenue Service, however, suggested that a number of organizational changes were in order. Stern decided to consolidate *all* Wincanton vice and gambling under his leadership, but he also decided to turn the actual operation of most activities over to others. From 1956 until the next wave of reform swept Wincanton in 1964, Irv Stern generally succeeded in attaining these goals.

The Structure of the Stern Syndicate

The financial keystone of Stern's gambling empire was numbers betting. Records seized by the Internal Revenue Service in 1959 and 1960 indicated that Stern's gross receipts from the numbers business amounted to more than $100,000 per month, or about $1.3 million annually. Since the numbers are predominantly a poor man's form of gambling (bets range from a quarter to a dollar or more), and since payoffs are made daily, a large number of writers and very tight organization are required. Effective control demands that a maximum possible number of men be on the streets contacting bettors, that the writers report their bets honestly, and finally that no one man, if arrested, is able to identify others in the organization. During the "pearl gray purity" of Hal Craig, numbers betting was completely disorganized—isolated writers wrote bets for their friends but frequently had to renege if a popular number won; no individual was strong enough to insure against such eventualities. When reform ended in 1955, however, Stern's lieutenants notified each numbers writer in Wincanton that he was now working for Stern—or else. Those who objected were "persuaded" by Stern's men or else arrested by the police, as were any writers suspected of underreporting their receipts. Few held out for very long.

After Stern completed the reorganization of the numbers business, its structure was roughly this: Eleven sub-banks (each employing from five to thirty writers) reported daily to Stern's central accounting office (which was moved periodically to evade federal enforcement agents). Thirty-five percent of the gross receipts were kept by the writers. After deducting winnings and expenses (primarily protection payoffs to the police and other officials), Stern divided the net profits equally with the operators of the sub-banks, covering winnings whenever a popular number "broke" one of the smaller operators.

During the years after 1955, Irv Stern handled prostitution and several forms of gambling on a "franchise" basis. He took no part in the conduct of these businesses and received no share of the profits, but exacted a fee for protection from the police. Several horse-betting rooms, for example, operated regularly; the largest of these paid Stern $600 per week. While slot machines had permanently disappeared from the Wincanton scene after the 1951 federal investigations, a number of men began to distribute pinball machines which gave cash prizes to players. As was the case with numbers writers, these pinball distributors had been unorganized during the Craig administration. When Democratic Mayor Gene Donnelly succeeded Craig, he immediately announced that all pinball machines were illegal and would be confiscated by the police. A Stern agent then contacted the pinball distributors and notified them that if they employed Dave Feinman (Irv Stern's nephew) as a "public relations consultant," there would be no interference from the police. Several rebellious distributors formed an Alsace County Amusement Operators Association, only to see Feinman appear with two thugs from New York; after the Association president was roughed up, all resistance collapsed, and Feinman collected more than $2,000 each week to promote the "public relations" of distributors. (Stern, however, was never able to buy protection against *federal* action; after the Internal Revenue Service began seizing the pinball machines in 1956, the owners were forced to purchase the $250 federal gambling stamps for each machine as well as paying Feinman. Over two hundred Wincanton machines bore these stamps in 1961, and thus were immune from federal action.)

While maintaining direct control of Wincanton numbers betting, and an indirect interest in horse betting and pinball machines, Stern shared with two out-of-state syndicates in the operation and profits of two enterprises, a large dice game and the largest distillery found by the Treasury Department in the East since Prohibition. The dice game employed over fifty men—drivers to "lug" players into Wincanton from as far as a hundred miles away, doormen to check players' identities, loan sharks who "faded" the losers, croupiers, food servers, guards, etc. The 1960 payroll for these men was over $350,000. Irv Stern divided the game's profits with his out-of-state partners and received an extra $1,000 per week to secure protection from the police. While no estimate of the total gross receipts from this game is available, some indication can be found in the fact that $50,000 was found on the tables and in the safe when F.B.I. agents raided the game in 1962. Over one hundred players were arrested during the raid; one businessman had lost over $75,000 at the tables.

Similar profit-sharing arrangements governed the operation of a distillery erected in an old warehouse on the banks of the Wincanton River. Stern arranged for a city permit to link the still with the city's water and sewer systems, and provided protection from local police after it went into operation. With $200,000 in equipment, the still was capable of producing four million dollars' worth of alcohol annually, and served a five-state area until Treasury Department agents raided it after it had been in operation for less than one year.

The dice game and the distillery raise questions concerning the status of Irv Stern's Wincanton organization vis-à-vis the out-of-state syndicates. Newspapers and Republican politicians in Wincanton frequestly claimed that Stern was simply the local agent of the Cosa Nostra. Apart from the fact that Stern, being Jewish, was ineligible for membership in the Sicilian-dominated Cosa Nostra, the evidence suggests that Stern was far more than an agent for outsiders, even though he was regularly sending money to them. It would be more accurate to regard these payments as profit-sharing with coinvestors and as charges for services rendered.[2] The East-Coasters provided technical services in the operation of the dice game and still, and "enforcement" services for the Wincanton gambling operation. When deviants had to be persuaded to accept Stern domination, Stern called upon outsiders for "muscle"—strong-arm men who could not be traced by local police if the victim chose to protest. In 1941, for example, Stern asked for help in destroying a competing dice game; six gunmen came in and held it up, robbing and terrifying the' players. While a few murders took place in the struggle for supremacy in the 1930s and 1940s, only a few people were roughed up in the 1950s and no one was killed.

After Mayor Craig's reform era ended in 1956, Irv Stern was able

2. Just as we must wonder why Irv Stern did not close down Klaus Braun's slot-machine activities, the question arises why the East Coast families of the Costa Nostra did not attempt to take over Irv Stern's organization. Donald R. Cressey, in a private communication to the author, suggests three possibilities. First, Stern may have been allowed to remain independent as a reward for his services to the outsiders during Prohibition. Second, he may have been regarded as the only man who could arrange for official toleration of their Wincanton dice game and still. Third, they may have concluded that he was more valuable active than inactive (or alive than dead); his operations were, after all, yielding a tidy profit to the outsiders in layoff and "enforcement" fees. A fourth possibility, equally untestable, would be that the East Coast syndicates lacked the muscle or resources to destroy Stern even if they wanted to.

to establish a centralized system in which he alone determined which rackets would operate[3] and who would be allowed to operate them. How did he keep order within this system? Basically, three control techniques were operative—as a business matter, Stern controlled access to several very lucrative operations, and could quickly deprive an uncooperative gambler or numbers writer of his source of income. Second, since he controlled the police department, he could arrest any gamblers or bookies who were not paying tribute. (Some of the gambling and prostitution arrests which took place during the Stern era served another purpose—to placate newspaper demands for a crackdown. As one police chief from this era phrased it, "Hollywood should have given us an Oscar for some of our performances when we had to pull a phony raid to keep the papers happy.") Finally, if the mechanisms of fear of financial loss and fear of arrest failed to command obedience, Stern was always able to keep alive a fear of physical violence. As has been seen, numbers writers, pinball distributors, and competing gamblers were brought into line after outside enforcers put in an appearance, and Stern's regular collection agent, a local tough who had been convicted of murder of the 1940s, was a constant reminder of the virtues of cooperation. Several witnesses who had told grand juries or federal agents of extortion attempts by Stern received visits from Stern enforcers and tended to "forget" when called to testify against the boss.

The Process of Corruption

To continue to operate his various gambling enterprises, Irv Stern needed to be sure that law-enforcement agencies were immobilized. To this end, Stern worked to put cooperative men in office, to buy off those who occupied strategic enforcement positions, and to implicate most city officials in various forms of corruption so completely that they would be unable to turn upon him. Just as businessmen facing restrictions on their rates or operating practices will seek to control the choice of men who will serve on regulatory boards or commissions, so

3. Curiously, Stern never allowed narcotics to be sold (at least on a regular basis) while he controlled Wincanton. Explanations for this phenomenon are varied. Some Wincantonites feel that Stern had a healthy respect for federal narcotics agents. Close friends of Stern felt that the decision more likely came from a personal distaste for drugs and their users. There was also little evidence that Stern engaged in loan sharking, another lucrative activity favored by many crime syndicates, apart from one shark who catered to participants in the dice game.

Irv Stern was interested in the men who would set law-enforcement policy in Wincanton. To gain access to those *elected* officials involved with enforcement agencies, Stern early became active (if secretly) in Wincanton politics. . . . Most Wincanton election contests are decided in the Democratic primaries, and . . . endorsements from organizations are usually less important than support from ethnic and neighborhood blocs. Candidates devote much of their campaign time to visiting clubs and ward bars, buying drinks for all present (an expensive proposition if the visit has been well advertised), and leaving funds with the bartender or club steward to secure a good turnout of voters and poll-watchers on election day.

Success in this kind of electioneering requires either an exceptionally well known name or endorsements from most of the organizations with Democratic members—or a lot of money. No reliable figures are available (state campaign expense reporting laws are weak), but expenses for Wincanton primary candidates probably average around $5,000; the general election costs another $10,000 per man. In the chaos of the primaries, with three to five men seeking the mayoral nomination, and five or ten vying for the two seats on the council, few candidates can line up big legitimate money for media advertising or visits to the clubs. Knowing this well, Irv Stern often helped out men he felt would be tolerant if elected. In some years, he helped several candidates, not caring who won but wanting to guarantee access to all. In other years, when one candidate was particularly promising (or another particularly threatening), Stern concentrated his financial support on one man. A strange turnabout occurred in 1959, when Stern is alleged to have supported incumbent Mayor Donnelly in the primaries and asked challenging Councilman Walasek to withdraw; Walasek refused and went on to win the primary nomination. Never one to bear grudges, Stern is reported to have aided Walesek in defeating the Republican nominee in the general election.

Contributions during primary and general election campaigns gave Irv Stern access to many city officials; initial contact with others came later. Following Walasek's victory in 1959, for example, the question arose as to who would be named to top positions in the police department. Dave Phillips later told federal investigators that Stern's agents asked if he would be interested in the job; when he said that he was, Phillips was told that he would have to pay Stern $5,000 and that another $5,000 would be needed to give X a high position in the police department. Both men, of course, more than recouped their "investment" through payoffs from Stern and others protected by the police.

After insuring, during campaigns or otherwise, that accommodating men were in control of City Hall and the police department, Stern was careful to reward them regularly. Two basic strategies were used—to pay top personnel as much as necessary to keep them happy (and quiet), and to pay *something* to as many as possible, thus implicating them in the system and keeping them from talking. The range of pay-offs thus went from a weekly salary for the mayor to liquor and a Christmas turkey for many patrolmen. Records seized in a raid on the central numbers bank indicated payments totaling $2,400 each week to the mayor, police chief, and other city and county officials.

While the list of persons to be paid remained fairly constant, the amounts paid varied according to the gambling activities in operation at the time. While the dice game was running, the mayor was reportedly receiving $1,500 per week, the chief $100, and a few policemen lesser amounts. Payoffs were cut by 50 percent when the still and dice game were driven out of business.

While the number of officials receiving regular "salary" payoffs was quite restricted (only fifteen names were on the "payroll" found at the numbers bank), many other officials were paid off in different ways. Federal investigators found that Stern had given "mortgage loans" to a police lieutenant and a police chief's son. A judge recalled that shortly after being elected, he received a call from Dave Feinman, Stern's nephew. "Congratulations, judge. When do you think you and your wife would like a vacation in Florida?" "Florida? Why on earth would I want to go there?" "But all the other judges and the guys in City Hall—Irv takes them all to Florida whenever they want to get away." "Thanks anyway, but I'm not interested." "Well, how about a mink coat instead. What size coat does your wife wear? . . ." An assistant district attorney told of seeing Feinman walking up to his front door with a large basket from Stern's supermarket just before Christmas. "My minister suggested a needy family that could use the food," he recalled, "but I returned the liquor. How could I ask a minister if he knew someone that could use three bottles of Scotch?" (Some men were also silenced free of charge to Stern—low-ranking policemen, for example, kept quiet after they learned that men who reported gambling or prostitution were ignored or transferred to the midnight shift; they didn't have to be paid.)[4]

---

4. Studies of corruption in other cities suggest that when high-ranking police officials are on the syndicate's payroll, low-level policemen are likely to feel free to enter into free-lance shakedowns, demanding or accepting bribes from motorists, merchants, and others, secure in the knowledge that their superiors are in no position to complain.

Campaign contributions, regular payments to higher officials, holiday and birthday gifts—these were the bases of the system by which Irv Stern bought protection from the law. The campaign contributions usually ensured that tolerant officials were elected; regular payoffs usually kept their loyalty. In a number of ways, Stern was also able to enrich corrupt officials at no financial cost to himself. Just as the officials, being in control of the instruments of law enforcement, were able to facilitate Stern's gambling enterprises, so Stern, in control of a network of men operating outside the law, was able to facilitate the officials' "free-lance" corrupt enterprises. As will be seen shortly, some local officials were not satisfied with their legal salaries from the city and their illegal salaries from Stern, and decided to demand payments from prostitutes, kickbacks from salesmen, etc. Stern, while seldom receiving any money from these transactions, became a broker, bringing politicians into contact with salesmen, merchants, and lawyers willing to offer bribes to get city business, setting up "middlemen" who could handle the money without jeopardizing the officials' reputations, and providing enforcers who could bring delinquents into line.

From the corrupt activities of Wincanton officials, Irv Stern received little, at least in comparison with the profits of his gambling operations. Why then did he get involved in them? From Stern's point of view, the major virtue of the system of official extortion that flourished in Wincanton was that it kept down the officials' demands for payoffs directly from Stern. If a councilman was able to pick up $1,000 on a purchase of city equipment, he might demand a lower payment for the protection of gambling. Furthermore, since Stern knew the facts in each instance of extortion, the officials would be further implicated in the system, and thus less able to back out on the arrangements regarding gambling. Finally, as Stern discovered to his chagrin, it became necessary to supervise extortion to save officials from their own stupidity. Mayor Gene Donnelly was reported to have been cooperative, and remained satisfied with his regular "salary." Bob Walasek, who succeeded Donnelly, was more greedy, and seized many opportunities to profit from a city contract. Soon Stern found himself supervising many of Walasek's deals to keep the mayor from blowing the whole arrangement wide open. When Walasek tried to double the "take" on a purchasing of parking meters, Stern had to step in and set the contract price, provide an untraceable middleman, and see the deal through to completion. "I told Irv," Police Chief Phillips later testified, "that Walasek wanted $12 on each meter instead of the $6 we got on the last meter deal. He became furious. He said Walasek is going to fool around and wind up in jail. You come and see me. I'll tell Walasek what he's going to buy!"

The Extent of Corruption

Optimal protection for an extensive gambling operation requires control over many parts of local government. How successful was Stern? How many officials were under his control? How strong was that control? With the exception of the local Congressman and the city treasurer, it seems that a few officials at each level (city, county, and state) were involved either with Stern or with some form of free-lance corruption. Within the city administration, the evidence is fairly clear that several mayors and councilmen received regular payments from Stern and divided kickbacks on city purchases and sales. Key subcouncil personnel frequently shared in payoffs affecting their particular departments—the police chief shared in the gambling and prostitution payoffs and received $300 of the $10,500 kickback on parking-meter purchases. The councilman controlling one department may have received a higher percentage of kickbacks related to its operations than the other councilmen.

The fact that Stern had contacts in so many city departments does not, however, mean that all city employees were corrupt or that Stern had absolute control over those he supported. Both official investigations and private research lead to the conclusion that there is no reason whatsoever to question the honesty of the vast majority of the employees of the City of Wincanton. Certainly no more than ten of the 155 members of the Wincanton police force were on Irv Stern's payroll (although many of them accepted petty Christmas presents—turkeys or liquor). In each department, there were a few employees who objected actively to the misdeeds of their superiors, and the only charge which can justly be leveled against the mass of employees is that they were unwilling to jeopardize their positions by publicly exposing what was going on. When federal investigators showed that an honest (and possibly successful) attempt was being made to expose Stern-Walasek corruption, a number of city employees cooperated with the grand jury in aggregating evidence which could be used to convict the corrupt officials. Before these federal investigations began, however, it could reasonably appear to an individual employee that the entire machinery of law enforcement in the city was controlled by Stern, Walasek, *et al.*, and that an individual protest would be silenced quickly. This dilemma was documented in the momentary crusade conducted by Assistant District Attorney Phil Roper. When the district attorney left for a short vacation, Roper decided to act against local gamblers and prostitutes. With the help of the state police (who were astonished that *any* Wincanton official would be interested in a crackdown), Roper raided several large brothels. Apprehending on the street the city's largest distributor of punchboards and lotteries, Roper effected a citizen's arrest and drove him to police headquarters for proper detention and questioning. "I'm sorry, Mr. Roper," said the desk sergeant. "We're under orders not to arrest persons brought in by you." Roper was forced to call upon the state police for aid in confining the gambler. When the district attorney returned from his vacation, he quickly fired Roper for "introducing politics into the district attorney's office."

Just as the number of city employees corrupted by Stern was limited, so it must also be noted that several men who generally cooperated with Stern rebelled when his demands or external pressure became too great. One judge hated prostitutes and ordered city officials to close down several brothels protected by Stern; later, he asked for a state investigation of Stern's gambling activities after federal agents raided several bookies. Police Chief Phillips also changed his mind during his four years in office. After two years of ignoring gamblers and prostitutes, Phillips became frightened by increased federal interest in Wincanton and closed down Stern's horse-betting rooms. Finally, after a federal grand jury brought a perjury indictment against him, Phillips agreed to work for the federal government, secretly recording conversations with Stern and Walasek and testifying against them in subsequent trials.

Free-Lance Corruption

During most of the period after Prohibition, Wincanton officials tolerated Irv Stern's gambling activities. Much of the corruption in Wincanton, however, had little to do with Stern or gambling. Law books speak of at least three varieties of official corruption: nonfeasance ("failing to perform a required duty at all"), malfeasance ("the commission of some act which is positively unlawful"), and misfeasance ("the improper performance of some act which a man may properly do"). During the years in which Irv Stern was running his gambling operations, Wincanton officials were guilty of all of these. Some residents say that corrupt mayors came to regard their office as a brokerage, levying a tariff on every item that came across their desk; sometimes a request for simple municipal services turned into a game of cat and mouse, with the mayor sitting on the request, waiting to see how much would be offered, and the petitioner waiting to see if he could obtain his rights without having to pay for them. This kind of corruption was not as lucrative an enterprise as protecting gambling, but it offered a tempting supplement to low official salaries.

The most frequent form of corruption by Wincanton officials was the nonenforcement of the state's gambling laws against Irv Stern's men. Not all nonenforcement, of course, should be interpreted as corruption; police in many cities ignore violations of minor laws regarding traffic offenses, loitering, fornication, sales on Sunday, etc. In some cases, police inaction has been based on limited enforcement resources; in others, the police simply feel that no one in the community *wants* these laws enforced. Most instances of nonfeasance in Wincanton, however, were clearly based on bribery or extortion. A burlesque theater manager, under attack from high school teachers for his lurid advertising, was ordered to pay $25 per week to keep his "all-the-way" strip show open. All prostitutes were tolerated who kept up their protection payments. One madame who controlled more than twenty girls made protection payments of $500 per week. Another prostitute complained to a magistrate that she not only had to pay a city official $100 per week but also that "he had a couch in his office where we had to pay again."

If nonfeasance is the failure to do something you are required to do, malfeasance is the commission of an act you are forbidden to do. City and police officials regularly fixed traffic and parking tickets, at times for money, at times as political favors. One young Puerto Rican interviewed in 1966 told of being harassed by a patrolman for parking his car on the street at night; a quiet payment of $40 to a magistrate ended the harassment. Although state law offers no clear standards by which the mayor should make promotions within his police department, it was obviously improper for Mayor Walasek to name Dave Phillips as police chief on the basis of his payment of $5,000 to Stern. Decisions based on "political contributions," however, pose a serious legal and analytical problem in classifying the malfeasance of Wincanton officials, and indeed of politicians in many cities. Political campaigns cost money, citizens have a right to support the candidates of their choice, and officials have a right to appoint their backers to noncivil-service positions. At some point, however, threats or oppression convert legitimate requests for political contributions into extortion. Shortly after taking office in 1956, Mayor Gene Donnelly notified city hall employees that they would be expected "voluntarily" to contribute 2 percent of their salary to the Democratic Party. (It might be noted that Donnelly never forwarded any of these "political contributions" to the party treasurer.) A number of salesmen doing business with the city were notified that companies which had supported the party would receive favored treatment; Donnelly notified one salesman that in light of a proposed $81,000 contract for the purchase of fire engines, a "political contribution" of $2,000 might not be inappropriate. While neither the city hall employees nor the salesman had "rights" to their positions or their contracts, the "voluntary" quality of their contributions seems questionable.

One final example of malfeasance came in 1956 with Mayor Donnelly's abortive "War on the Press." Following a series of gambling raids by the Internal Revenue Service, the newspapers began asking why the local police had not participated in the raids. The mayor lost his temper and threw a reporter in jail, policemen were instructed to harass newspaper delivery trucks, and seventy-three tickets were written over a forty-eight-hour period for supposed parking and traffic violations. Donnelly soon backed down after national news services picked up the story and made him look ridiculous. Charges against the reporter were dropped, and the newspapers continued to expose gambling and corruption.

Misfeasance in office, says the common law, is the improper performance of some act which a man may properly do. City officials must buy and sell equipment, contract for services, and allocate licenses, privileges, etc. These actions can be said to be improperly performed either if the results are improper (e.g., if a building inspector were to approve a home with defective wiring, or a zoning board authorized a variance which had no justification in terms of land usage) or if a proper result is achieved by improper procedures (e.g., if the city purchased an acceptable automobile in consideration of a bribe paid to the purchasing agent). In the latter case, an improper result can usually be assumed as well—while the automobile will be satisfactory, the bribe-giver will probably have inflated the sale price to cover the costs of the bribe.

Given the previously noted permissive quality of the state's municipal bidding laws, it was relatively easy for council members to justify or disguise contracts in fact based upon bribes. The exemption for patented products facilitated bribe-taking in the purchase of two emergency trucks for the police department (with a $500 "campaign contribution" on a $7,500 deal), three fire engines ($2,000 was allegedly paid on an $81,000 contract), and 1,500 parking meters (involving payments of $10,500 plus an $880 clock for Mayor Walasek's home). Similar fees were allegedly exacted in connection with the purchase of a city fire-alarm system and police uniforms and firearms.

When contracts involved services to the city, the provisions in the state law regarding "the lowest *responsible* bidder" and excluding "professional services" from competitive bidding provided convenient loop-holes. One internationally known engineering firm refused to agree to a kickback in order to secure a contract to design a $4.5-million sewage disposal plant for the city; a local firm was then appointed which paid $10,700 of its $225,000 fee to an associate of Irv Stern and Mayor Don-nelly as a "finder's fee." Since the state law also excludes public works maintenance contracts from the competitive bidding requirements, most city paving and street-repair contracts during the Donnelly-Walasek era were given to a contributor to the Democratic party. Fi-nally, the franchise for towing illegally parked cars and cars involved in accidents was awarded to two garages which were then required to kick back one dollar for each car towed.

The handling of graft on the towing contracts illustrates the way in which minor violence and the "lowest responsible bidder" clause could be used to keep bribe-payers in line. After federal investigators began to look into Wincanton corruption, the owner of one of the garages with a towing franchise testified before the grand jury. Mayor Walasek immediately withdrew his franchise, citing "health violations" at the garage. The garageman was also "encouraged" not to testify by a series of "accidents"—wheels fell off towtrucks on the highway, steering ca-bles were cut, and so forth. Newspaper satirization of the "health viola-tions" charge forced the restoration of the towing franchise, and the "accidents" ceased. One final area of city powers abused by Walasek *et al.* covered discretionary acts such as granting permits and allowing zoning variances. On taking office, one man took control of the bureaus of building and plumbing inspection. With this power to approve or deny building permits, he "sat on" applications, waiting until the peti-tioner "contributed" $50 or $75 or threatened to sue to obtain his per-mit. Some building designs were not approved until a favored architect was retained as a "consultant." (It is not known whether this involved kickbacks or simply patronage for a friend.)

All of the activities detailed thus far involved fairly clear violations of the law. A brief discussion of "honest graft" will complete the picture of the abuse of office by Wincanton officials. This term was best defined by one of its earlier practitioners, New York State Senator George Washington Plunkitt, who loyally served Tammany Hall at the turn of the century.

> There's all the difference in the world between [honest and dishonest graft]. Yes, many of our men have grown rich in politics. I have my-self. I've made a big fortune out of the game, and I'm gettin' richer every day, but I've not gone in for dishonest graft—blackmailin' gam-

blers, saloonkeepers, disorderly people, etc.—and neither has any of the men who have made big fortunes in politics.

There's an honest graft, and I'm an example of how it works. I might sum up the whole thing by sayin': "I seen my opportunities and I took 'em."

Let me explain by examples. My party's in power in the city, and it's goin' to undertake a lot of public improvements. Well, I'm tipped off, say, that they're going to lay out a new park at a certain place.

I see my opportunity and I take it. I go to that place and I buy up all the land I can in the neighborhood. Then the board of this or that makes its plan public, and there is a rush to get my land, which nobody cared particular for before.

Ain't it perfectly honest to charge a good price and make a profit on my investment and foresight? Of course, it is. Well, that's honest graft.[5]

While there was little in the way of land purchasing—either honest or dishonest—going on in Wincanton during this period, several officials who carried on their own businesses while in office were able to pick up some "honest graft." Police Chief Phillips' construction firm received a contract to remodel the largest brothel in town. A councilman's company received a contract to construct all gasoline stations built in the city by a major petroleum company; some cities have concluded that the contract was the *quid pro quo* for the councilman's vote to award this company the city's gasoline contract.

Conclusions

. . . A police policy of not enforcing gambling laws may sometimes arise from a feeling that the maintenance of public order (preventing murder, muggings, etc.) is a task which consumes all available police resources; no one "has time," in other words, to worry about enforcing gambling, prostitution, or traffic laws. In Wincanton, the nonenforcement of gambling laws was instead based upon systematic corruption of public officials. The Stern syndicate both financed the election campaigns of tolerant candidates and made regular payoffs to city officials and senior police officers. Officials added to their syndicate payoffs by demanding bribes from individuals and companies doing business with the city or seeking legitimate city services. The result was not only the violation of many city and state laws but also the immobilization of the local law-enforcement apparatus. Reform . . . only came about when *outside* law-enforcement agencies destroyed the Stern syndicate and publicized its dealings with city officials.

5. William L. Riordan, *Plunkitt of Tammany Hall* (New York: E. P. Dutton, 1963), p.3.

THE TOWN THAT REFORMED
John Bartlow Martin

Over the years, Peoria, Illinois, has been known as a steamboat town, a whiskey town, a railroad town, a river town, a convention town, a wide-open town. At one time it seemed less a city than a vaudeville joke. Renowned for its gambling, prostitution and political corruption, it was accounted almost a classic case of American municipal decay.

Two years ago the citizens voted to get rid of the old aldermanic form of government and to install the city-manager plan. The new administration assiduously scrubbed the city clean, amid loud praise. And then, in an election a few months ago, the people issued a somewhat murky mandate that seemed to indicate they thought maybe reform wasn't so good after all. Why and how did all this come about?

On a hot day in June, down by the edge of the Illinois River, where diesels honk in the railroad yards and men make earth movers in clangorous factories, heat and smoke and the stench from the stockyards press down on the gray cottages and broken streets in the section of town known as The Valley. High on The Bluff and farther out in The Knolls, the air is cleaner and traffic moves quietly past the mansions along Moss Avenue. Peoria is built on steep-rising hills above the Illinois River, and it is sharply divided into The Valley and The Bluff— the workers in The Valley, the owners on The Bluff.

Tall office buildings rise near the courthouse, set on a bench of land above the river, and out in the wide one-way street a neat policeman prowls up and down, chalking the tires of parked automobiles. ("We're pushing our chalking program vigorously," says the young man in the city administration who is giving me a conducted tour.)

The City Hall was built in 1897–99, and the copper on its dome is peeling away, and water has come though the roof, cracking the ceiling of the grimy council chamber. The new administration has cleaned the tobacco juice of years from the marble walls of the first-floor hallways, has auctioned off the old spittoons, has put fluorescent lights and brand-new steel desks and business machines into the ancient offices.

Across the street from City Hall is a parking lot where once stood the headquarters of the gambling syndicate—a gambling casino, an accounting office and a tavern. Citizens who received traffic tickets used to go into the tavern and drop the tickets into a little box, and on Fridays someone would go over to City Hall and fix all the tickets. And from this headquarters, too, the gamblers brought their monthly tribute, paid directly into the city treasury—as much as $69,000 in one year.

"The town is down"—everyone says so. No more organized gambling, no more organized prostitution. The bars, once crowded, are almost deserted. The three large gambling casinos near City Hall which for years offered craps, poker, roulette and horse betting are closed. Slot machines have disappeared. The houses on The Line, the red-light district famed throughout the Midwest, are dark. A bartender says, "This used to be the best town in the country. Then we got a reform administration. Now it ain't worth a damn."

Students of local lore trace Peoria's predilection for frontier-style living to the roistering steamboat days. The town's recent history has been enlivened by gunplay and the periodic bombing of the homes of law-enforcement officials. Peorians talk about corruption the way people elsewhere talk about baseball.

Off and on, Ed Woodruff was Peoria's mayor for twenty-four years. An old-timer politician recalls fondly, "Old Ed Woodruff. There was a man that was a liberal. What made the town a wide-open liberal town was that Ed Woodruff started in 1903 and lasted till 1945. If some reformer got in for a while and the town was slowed up a little, he'd get back in and open her up. He poured out the jobs and seen that everybody made a little money and catered to The Valley and never paid any attention to the Association of Commerce. He never took a quarter himself. 'Course, he didn't mind his friends makin' some of it. And he made the gamblers bring it in at campaign time. But, hell, they overdid it. They put slot machines in drugstores and school zones and groceries and beauty parlors.

"Old Ed had an old houseboat called the Bumboat hauled up on the bank of the river, and he and his cronies used to run the city from it. That was where they chopped the heads off"—that is, dispensed patronage. "They'd go down there and they'd eat and drink and—you know, decide the city policies. He was a tough Republican, but he'd play with them Democrats. He didn't bar any holts."

There were no application forms for city jobs till the present administration came in. Excluding firemen and police, the city employed about 200 people, and they were swept out when the mayor's office changed hands. Even policemen were fired and replaced with friends of politicians. Who ran the police force? "Well," says a veteran policeman, "there were twenty-two aldermen. And each alderman had five friends. How many's that? About a hundred and ten?"

The present chief says, "I run the police department."

In 1951 the state legislature authorized Peoria to adopt the city-manager plan if it wished. Civic groups formed the Peorians for Council-Manager. They say that membership was open to the public, but PCM critics say PCM was a closed corporation. Mostly, PCM was led by men who live on The Bluff and represent the business interests of Peoria.

One of its young leaders, Joe Kelly, a customer's man in a stock-brokerage firm, a big, crew-cut man of thirty-two, has said, "They were all just good citizens sold on the idea of the need for the cleanup of the city—bad streets, bad street lighting, plus the general decrepitness of the city. The president of PCM and the campaign manager were both leading Jaycees. One was voted The Outstanding Young Man of 1951. We put out literature. We set up a speakers' bureau and talked to five hundred organizations. The opposition was terrific." It came from organized labor and old-fashioned politicians. But the plan was adopted, 15,000 to 7000.

The next step was to elect a mayor and eight councilmen in nonpartisan balloting. PCM decided to endorse candidates.

Kelly has said, "Not everybody thought we should. But there has to be some group to get good people to run for government. If not, the government will fall back to the grafters and crooks. To get a top industrialist or any honest man to run for public office is very, very hard. They won't subject themselves to politics."

For mayor PCM slated Robert Morgan, an upright man of forty-three, long active in civic affairs, a brother of the president of PCM and himself a leading lawyer who represents corporations in their dealings with labor unions. For councilmen PCM slated the president of the LeTourneau earth-moving-equipment-manufacturing company, the comptroller of a washing-machine company, the employee-relations manager of Caterpillar Tractor, a merchant, a mover, a newspaper distributor, the president of the Women's Civic Federation, and a banker.

Independent candidates filed against them. The campaign was noisy. PCM was accused of being a machine, trying to run the city. But

PCM elected the mayor and five councilmen, giving it a 6–3 majority in council.

Council, taking office in May of 1953, hired as the new city manager George Bean. Bean, a professional city manager of seventeen years' experience, was then managing Grand Rapids, Michigan, and could not come to Peoria till July. Mayor Morgan and council, however, lost no time in commencing reform.

Mayor Morgan recalls, "The job of sewer superintendent had for years been a sinecure for the retired head of the bricklayers union. We called him in and asked what his duties were. He said, 'I help Mr. Kosanovich.' Kosanovich was his assistant. We asked when he helped him. 'When he needs help.' So we just cut off his job and elevated Kosanovich. That made the bricklayers mad, of course." They also appointed a new police chief, fire chief, comptroller and street superintendent. And Mayor Morgan ordered the police to begin raiding gambling games and brothels.

Actually, big-time organized gambling had already stopped, ruined by political turnover, the enactment of a Federal law taxing gamblers, and the murder of the head of the gambling syndicate. Under Mayor Morgan the police closed the surviving poker games and lotteries. Prostitution, however, was still running wide open. "We had to root 'em out," police chief Frank Evans recalls. They made more than fifty raids on brothels.

The court fined the keeper and the inmates $200 apiece. This was costly; a raid might cost a madam $1800. (Fines have totaled about $25,000.) Moreover, after the police raided a house three times the city asked the state's attorney to obtain an injunction padlocking the house permanently as a public nuisance. Once somebody planted a dynamite bomb at the mayor's house and blew a hole in the foundation. But the police raids continued. Soon The Line was down. The police think a call-girl operation has begun. Now and then, they find a girl in a car or a tavern.

Such furtive operations do far less damage than a wide-open Line: they do not corrupt officials or spread disease. The month the raids started, 130 new venereal-disease cases were reported in Peoria, and the average for the preceding two years had been eighty-eight new cases a month. In 1955 it has been twenty-six.

When Manager Bean arrived he found the city's affairs in a deplorable state. This did not surprise him.

Bean, a tall, red-haired man of fifty-five, said recently, "The city-manager plan is a tool that desperate people reach for when everything else has broken down. Peoria's services were ineffective. There was a big backlog of needed physical improvements after forty years of neglect, and the city was broke—we had three hundred thousand dollars in unpaid bills. The budget had been unbalanced since 1948."

One of Bean's aides recalls, "Nearly all the department heads were about sixty-five years old. Everything was obsolete. They were using old incandescent lamps in the drafting department; I worked there awhile and kept getting headaches from the poor lighting. Some department heads never got to travel around to see what other cities were doing."

William Sommers, the new personnel officer, says, "In the old days the aldermen would hire men for the street department, then lay them off, mostly old men, couldn't work anywhere else, old winos, helpless drifters. So the street department was really a kind of relief agency. I felt sorry for the old guys. But you can't run a street department that way. We've been building up personnel files. We introduced physical examination, probationary six months' period, progress reports, training program and a merit system."

Manager Bean began his work in Peoria by recruiting a professional staff. All five of his recruits were young and all but one came from outside Peoria. Jake Dumelle was twenty-eight when he became Bean's administrative assistant, a mechanical engineer with a degree in public administration who had been assistant to another city manager. Dumelle brought in a classmate, Roy Anderson, a thirty-year-old certified public accountant, to replace the city comptroller. William Sommers, with a graduate degree from Harvard in public administration and experience with the Colorado Municipal League, became personnel officer at the age of twenty-seven. Dean DuBoff, an architect just out of the Navy, was the only local man; he became director of inspections. The youngest of all was Dan Hanson, who, at twenty-four, was hired away from the Chicago Motor Club to become Peoria's first traffic engineer.

The young administrators are bouncy and bright and eager. One of them said recently, "It's surprising how much we get done at staff meetings, considering the number of prima donnas there are among us." On an average they possess two college degrees each. Their average age is now twenty-nine, all but Dumelle are married. They sometimes refer to themselves as "the crew-cuts."

Watching them at work, you get the impression they care more deeply about the city than many people who have lived here all their lives. Their youth and eagerness have led them to make some "boners," as they term them. Manager Bean has said, "Young people tend to go too fast." Once the traffic engineer, Dan Hanson, began enforcing the parking-meter ordinance on Monday until nine o'clock at night, something that hadn't been done for years. Police handed out 300 tickets in one night. Amid loud public outcry, council changed the ordinance.

Dumelle recalls, "Once council bought some parking meters to be paid for at two thousand dollars a month out of revenue. The comptroller thought this was silly and asked the manufacturer for a five per cent discount for cash, got it, issued tax-anticipation warrants, and paid them off. Council didn't find out about it till the end of the year. The comptroller hadn't consulted them and they were indignant. He couldn't understand that as a private CPA he had had only one boss, but now, as a public official, he had more than a hundred thousand. A lot of public relations is needed in this work. You get in a town like this, you can't change it all overnight."

When Hanson, the traffic engineer, came to Peoria he spent about six months compiling facts about traffic—accident statistics, law violations, traffic flow—then waded in. He installed new street-name signs throughout the city. He adopted a city-wide through-street plan. He changed bus routes. He painted forty-five miles of center stripes and lanes. Perhaps his biggest job was removing a lot of stop signs.

Hanson said recently, "Under the old form of government, aldermen were deluged with requests for stop signs. Stop signs were erected at every place where a near miss occurred, or where there was a school, or where the alderman's wife was involved in an accident. The city has sixteen hundred street intersections and it had over thirteen hundred stop signs. We went to the council with a plan to remove three hundred and ten signs. They adopted it. Since then we've had only three petitions asking that signs be reinstalled."

A blond young man, crew-cut, pink-cheeked, short and compact, Hanson spends as much time as he can driving around and looking for traffic trouble spots. One day recently he left the downtown district and headed up The Bluff on Knoxville Avenue, traffic swirling smoothly along on new pavement, and he said, "Along here is the first place in the city that we installed rush-hour parking control. They'd tried it several years ag and it lasted thirty days—too many complaints from the neighbors. When we got ready to do it, the captain of traffic and I went to every house along here, door to door, and explained why it was necessary. We've had very few complaints."

Driving on, Hanson pointed to a set of traffic lights and said, "Here's a new intersection we synchronized. We put in green arrows to let them turn on the red and head for downtown; then we laned it off-center to give 'em room to turn, and we took off parking on one side. That's the kind of stuff we're always looking for."

In an outlying neighborhood, seeing a motorcycle policeman lying in wait for stop-sign violators, he said, "He's not there just because he happens to live nearby or anything. He's there because they've analyzed the accident reports of several months and found that they were caused by stop-sign violation at about this time of day. It's really scientific now."

Enforcement and engineering were getting results. Last year only three people were killed in traffic accidents—fewer than ever before. Injuries and accidents declined. In 1953 the National Safety Council ranked Peoria's traffic-safety program forty-third out of fifty cities. Last year it ranked third. "So," Hanson said, "we feel something's beginning to happen. Of course, it's slow. You can't move any faster than the town will let you."

At the end of its first year in office the new administration issued a report to the people, pointing proudly to its achievements. Peoria had been termed an "All-American City" by the National Municipal League. The administration had improved the city's housekeeping, bought new equipment, bought a new police headquarters, improved law enforcement, cut accidents, taken politics out of city service, and balanced the budget. It had balanced its current budget by funding $300,000 of unpaid bills, by re-enacting a city vehicle license which the outgoing aldermen had repealed, and by imposing a new cigarette tax.

But it still had not solved its basic financial problem. The city badly needed $20,000,000 worth of new streets and sewers and other capital improvements. To raise the money the council submitted to the people a proposal to levy a one-half-cent city sales tax. It promised to cut back the property tax and take off the vehicle license and cigarette tax. But labor viewed this as an attempt to shift the tax burden to the workingman. And the Association of Commerce objected that a city sales tax would drive shoppers out of the city. The proposal was beaten 4 to 1.

How did Peoria like their new government? Most of them liked the vice and gambling cleanup, though some felt nostalgia for the old days. They liked the housekeeping improvements in general, though many grumbled specifically about the streets. Many said they didn't know whom to complain to, now that councilmen were not elected from wards. Some said the new administration's innovations had been abrupt and arbitrary. Some said the new regime was too costly and had raised taxes; they complained about Bean's $18,000 salary and about "the outsiders" he had imported to run the city.

Organized opposition came from tavernkeepers, who felt the cleanup kept big conventions away and hurt day-to-day business, and from organized labor. The state Federation of Labor has long officially opposed the city-manager plan as not being representative government. Labor was not included in the original PCM which brought the manager plan to Peoria.

The new administration fired a city painting contractor and merely hired a painter; this antagonized the union. The administration ended "labor patronage"—took the job of sewer superintendent away from the bricklayers union, the job of building commissioner away from the carpenters union. It bought cigarette-tax stamps from a nonunion company, offending the printers union. It bought prison-made traffic signs.

Dick Estep, who speaks for the AFL, complains bitterly about PCM. "They sold the people on the idea that this type of government was going to be independent. No politics at all. But PCM has a slate, it has a treasury, it has officers—to me, it's just a political party." And Coy Lutes, of the United Auto Workers (CIO), said, "We're not against the manager form as such, but only against the way in Peoria it has been packed with management people. They are all antilabor to start out with."

The administration faced its first test in the councilmanic election of 1955. Four councilmen had to stand for re-election. Three of them originally had been supported by PCM; the fourth, a labor man, had not. This time PCM endorsed them all. The labor man promptly renounced PCM support. PCM began running ads praising him; he ran ads denouncing PCM. Otherwise the campaign was quiet until the last couple of weeks. Then all the independents began attacking PCM. An organization called Peorians for Peoria swung up to aid the independents. Its cartoons caricatured Bean. Its ads kept asking: "Who Is Mr. Syndicate?" and hinting that Bean was "Mr. Syndicate" and was involved in some devious plot of an unspecified nature. It said, "Mr. Syndicate Ordered IT for Grand Rapids and Now Peoria," not saying what "IT" was. Voters were urged to "watch tomorrow's newspapers for details" and to "Save Peoria" on April fifth.

PCM disdained to answer any of this. Its ads simply praised the incumbents and recalled the bad old days of the aldermanic system: "inefficiency," "waste," "payroll padding," "graft," "shady deals." One of the independent candidates, James J. Manning, a shrewd, genial former alderman who had become a symbol of the old regime, promptly ran an ad listing numerous members of the old regime and asking whether PCM was accusing these "distinguished Peorians" of chicanery.

Nearly everyone expected the PCM candidates to sail through. So, when the blow fell, it was a heavy one. Not a single PCM man won except the labor man who had repudiated PCM endorsement.

What had happened? Almost nobody interpreted the election as a repudiation of the city-manager plan itself. Most people, PCM and labor leaders alike, thought the election indicated resentment of "PCM domination." Mayor Morgan attributed the result to the small vote— "the aginners always get out and vote." The vote was indeed very light —only 41 per cent of the registration. But it was light all over town and one of the elected councilmen said, "If The Valley had got out and voted, we'd have beaten 'em worse." How did he account for the light vote? "It's the same all over the country. The people figure why should they vote; they got a nice big house, nice big car, they got television, they got everything they want, they got money." He found the people's mandate somewhat cloudy. "The people definitely want a change. You've got to change something." Probably, he thought, they wanted better streets and alleys and more stop signs.

After the election, many people expected that Bean would be fired forthwith. Citizens bought chances in a pool, betting on the day of the month the city manager would be fired. The night the new council was inaugurated a sizable crowd turned out. But Bean wasn't fired, and four months later he still hadn't been.

Council, however, adopted a resolution asserting its authority over the manager and its sole power to determine policy and limiting the manager's authority to administering council's policies. Council established committees to "investigate" city problems. The independents say that formerly one or two PCM councilmen, meeting secretly with Bean, made major policy decisions and presented them to council for rubber-stamp approval. They insist that they will scrutinize the city's every act and return government to the people.

They have certainly worked at it. The former council had met only twice a month, and then only briefly; the new council holds long meetings twice a week or oftener. Council voted to "adopt a policy of having windows of city buildings washed every two months." Council voted to reinstall stop signs at one intersection whence Hanson had removed them. Council spent weeks studying the comparative merits of a brass pump and a cast-iron pump on a new fire truck. As a consequence of this attention to detail, business is transacted slowly and major problems tend to pile up.

Bean appears to have adopted a strategy of asking council's guidance before making the most unimportant decision. Possibly he hopes to bore council to death, so that it will restore to him some of his duller prerogatives. Council leadership has devolved upon two holdover anti-PCM councilmen—Robert McCord, an attorney; and Myrna Harms, a young woman of considerable charm. At almost every council meeting one of them takes a pot shot from the floor at Bean or PCM. Recently, Mrs. Harms' criticism of fire-department purchasing blew up a scandal that resulted in a vitriolic dispute between Mrs. Harms and Mayor Morgan, the indictment of the fire chief, and a councilmanic vote of confidence on Manager Bean, which he survived, 6–3.

Bean, a hotheaded, upright man, has tried to avoid brawling with his critics. He said recently that the manager plan functions best in cities where the manager and council feel a mutual confidence. That this is no longer so in Peoria disturbs him, not only because he is involved but because the plan itself is involved.

Why has a government so widely acclaimed aroused so much opposition? Some has been aroused by councilmanic headline hunting. But PCM invited opposition at the outset by failing to embrace all segments of the city, including labor. PCM was blinded by its mistrust of politicians. It blamed all the city's woes on them and said that ousting them would solve all problems. It forgot that politicians perform a real service: they respond to the people's wishes. PCM leaders neglected to do this. The councilmen, enthusiastic about the plan and anxious to make progress rapidly, were too eager to hand over responsibility to the manager. The administrators reckoned too much with slide rules and too little with people. Their determination to solve the city's financial problem led them to propose the unpopular sales tax. And yet surprisingly few people in Peoria seem to think the manager plan is on the way out. Many people, however, do think the city may return to the ward system of electing councilmen, to meet the most widespread objection to the plan: people feel their government is remote.

Recently the state legislature authorized council to enact a one-half-cent city sales tax without referendum, and it did so, repealing the vehicle and cigarette taxes. The new tax solves Peoria's financial problem. It will mean better streets and sewers. But it is still an unpopular tax.

The election demoralized Bean's aides. Councilmen talked of abolishing some of their jobs. Recently, however, the staff has taken heart. One of them said, "At first the election seemed a repudiation of everything we stood for. But maybe it was good for us. We experts have a tendency to take ourselves too seriously, to think that 'papa knows best,' to just go ahead and do things. In administrative government you forget that politics underlies everything in a democracy."

PART TWO

THE TARGETS OF CORRUPTION

(3)

Nullification of
Law Enforcement

THE SELECTIONS in the first two chapters discuss the problems involved in defining corruption and describe cities in which various forms of corruption have played a major role in local political life. In this chapter we begin our more detailed examination of the process of corruption. In some cities, despite the condemnation of various activities by the criminal law, the effects of law enforcement agencies and criminal justice processes are nullified through bribery of police officers, prosecutors, and judges, leaving individuals and organizations free to ignore the law. While many of the selections in this chapter address problems that are unique to the criminal justice system, they also provide a basis for discussing the broader questions to be considered in chapters 5 and 6: What factors affect the likelihood that a particular type of governmental activity will involve corruption? How do corrupt relationships become established? What are the relationships among the involved parties? What are the consequences of corruption both for the parties involved and for others? Finally, what changes might reduce the likelihood that corruption will occur in the future?

Overcriminalization and the Use of Discretion in Law Enforcement

As portrayed in the mass media, the world of criminal law enforcement revolves around serious crimes and long dramatic trials. In television shows like "The F.B.I." or "Perry Mason," the police are constantly fighting murderers, bank robbers, and kidnappers, and the outcome is in doubt until the conclusion of an exhaustive trial or an appeal to the Supreme Court. In reality, serious offenses are but a small part of the activities of the police, and few cases are decided by trials. The day-to-day life of a policeman is largely taken up with maintaining order—settling neighborhood quarrels or barroom brawls—and handling petty offenses such as speeding, gambling, or drug abuse. Once a suspect is arrested, the question of guilt or innocence is usually discussed less often than whether the arrestee will be detained in jail, charged with a crime, or sent to prison. It is in the context of this low-level, informal handling of minor criminal matters that corruption in law enforcement is to be understood, since the processing of robbery, murder, and other "Part I crimes"[1] is almost always honest and aboveboard.

The heavy involvement of law enforcement and criminal justice agencies in relatively minor matters can be explained by the availability of the police and the vast scope of our laws and ordinances. Only policemen and firemen are available twenty-four hours a day, seven days a week, so in time of trouble we do not hesitate to ask them to quiet a noisy party, rescue cats from trees, locate missing children or spouses, or help us when we are locked out of our apartments. Furthermore, Americans have a habit of writing a law condemning anything they deem undesirable, and then asking the police and the courts to enforce that law. For example, when the mass production of automobiles led to a high accident rate, states passed criminal laws condemning speeding rather than addressing the mental health of dangerous drivers or the engineering of roads and vehicles. Failure to pay alimony is frequently treated as a criminal offense rather than simply a violation of contract. Where merchants once could deceive their customers as to the weight or quality of their products, blithely saying "caveat emptor," they are now controlled (in theory at least) by a complex system of criminal laws and ordinances governing pricing, labeling, and standards of quality. Buying a drink, once totally legal, then totally illegal, is now legal or illegal depending on who is buying it, who is selling it, and when and where the sale takes place.

The effects of this extensive use of the criminal law to regulate undesirable behavior have been debated for years. On the one hand, the practice has been defended for its supposed deterrent effects and for its symbolic role in spelling out society's values. On the other hand, overcriminalization has been blamed for taxing the resources of crim-

1. The term "Part I crimes" covers willful homicide, forcible rape, aggravated assault, robbery, burglary, larceny of $50 and over, and motor vehicle theft. See the FBI's annual *Crime in the United States*.

inal justice agencies, for assigning complex social and economic problems to agences that are unequipped to deal with them, and for blurring social priorities by declaring too many things illegal. Finally, it has been argued that if the conduct of routine business and family and other social relationships requires the constant violation of one petty regulation or another, then the legal system will lose its legitimacy and the agencies and processes of criminal justice will be viewed with suspicion or contempt.

Faced with an endless set of rules and regulations that might be invoked in almost any situation, policemen, prosecutors, and judges constantly have to decide how to allocate their resources and when to exercise discretion. Patrolmen searching out building code violations are not available to guard school crossings; prosecutors researching gambling cases cannot expedite the trial of robbery suspects. Even more critical than the loss of staff time on minor matters is the loss of other resources critical to law enforcement agencies, such as public support, the cooperation of witnesses, and access to informants. A landlord slapped with a summons for building code violations is unlikely to volunteer information about a ring of car thieves working in his neighborhood. Prosecutors must decide whether to press charges on gambling suspects or offer leniency in return for information on higher-ups. If a defendant will demand a trial on robbery charges but will plead guilty to aggravated assault, the prosecutor may accept the offer simply to save court time. Law enforcement officials' low-level decisions regarding arrest, charging, or plea bargaining are seldom overturned by higher authorities.

Social Values and the Criminal Law

In regard to the major crimes of rape, robbery, burglary, and murder, there is widespread public support for law enforcement activities. If we look, however, at the minor crimes such as gambling, loansharking, minor drug abuse, and traffic offenses, the picture changes. While precise data are unavailable, it is likely that one-third to one-half of the American public have gambled,[2] and that a substantial portion of the population under thirty have used marijuana or minor drugs. Probably as much as two-thirds of the motoring public violate a traffic law at least once a year. If these estimates are at all accurate, then there must

2. See, for example, Gerald M. Smith, "A Survey of Gambling in the United States," a report submitted to the National Institute of Law Enforcement and Criminal Justice, 1971.

be strong variations in how citizens want these laws enforced. Some citizens, whether honestly or hypocritically, will want strict enforcement of gambling, drinking, and narcotics laws, while others will want open access to these goods and services.[3] In some lower-class neighborhoods, illegal operations are the most prolific source of new capital, and it has been argued that some of the larger fortunes in America today began with racketeering and bootlegging fifty years ago.[4] As a result of these conflicting attitudes and the substantial tolerance of some forms of illegal activities, it would not be surprising to find that law enforcement officials were not certain what was expected of them. In some cities, particularly upper-middle-class suburbs, strict enforcement is the norm, and bookies are promptly hustled out of town. In other cities, including most industrial areas, the police become regulators of illegal operations, acting only to shut down *dishonest* bookies or after-hour bars that are annoying their neighbors. Frequently, then, the policies adopted by law enforcement agencies mirror the attitudes of the communities they serve, cracking down where desired, tolerating where desired, or sitting back to wait for specific complaints.

Nullification of Law Enforcement

This, then, is the setting in which corruption of law enforcement and criminal justice processes takes place. The criminal law covers a wide range of activities, only some of which are generally condemned by the public. The administration of justice depends heavily upon the exercise of discretion by low-level officials, creating many opportunities for low-visibility, corrupt abuse of authority. The market created for illegal goods and services (the National Crime Commission estimated in 1967 that the annual volume of gambling in the United States was somewhere between seven and fifty billion dollars) provides enormous financial incentives for criminals to seek nullification of the force of the criminal law. If the police can be persuaded to look the other way, whether through a free lunch for the patrolman on the beat or a regular bribe to the precinct captain, then consumers will have access to desired opportunities and suppliers can reap enormous profits. Similar

3. See John A. Gardiner, *The Politics of Corruption* (New York: Russell Sage, 1970), pp. 46–53.
4. Daniel Bell, "Crime as an American Way of Life," in *The End of Ideology* (New York: Free Press, 1960). The involvement of criminals and criminal activities in the social life of lower-class neighborhoods is discussed in William Foote Whyte, *Street Corner Society* (Chicago: University of Chicago Press, 1943), chapter 5.

arrangements can nullify the threats posed by the crusading prosecutor or the tough judge.

The readings in this chapter describe the processes which lead to the nullification of law enforcement. In the first one, a black tavern owner in Louisville tells a reporter how he paid off the local police in order to keep open his illegal gambling activities. In the second, a racketeer tries to persuade a detective to change his testimony so that a bribery case will be thrown out of court. The selection by Salerno and Tompkins paints a wide-ranging picture of the techniques which organized crime[5] uses to secure protection. The fourth one reports the results of a detailed survey of police conduct and misconduct in three cities. Next, the analysis of ticket-fixing in Massachusetts reveals an interesting situation in which minor traffic infractions were overlooked, not for money as is often the case, but as part of a system of local patronage and favoritism. Nicholas Gage's study of organized crime cases in court suggests that judges can manipulate rules of evidence or assess minor penalties so as to minimize the effects of criminal sanctions. Finally, the seventh selection offers some of the major findings of the Knapp Commission, established in 1970 to investigate allegations of corruption in the New York Police Department, the largest local police force in the nation.

5. For the past twenty-five years, discussions of organized crime in the United States have centered around the existence or nonexistence of a national cartel or confederation of crime, usually called the Mafia or La Cosa Nostra. The pro-Mafia theory began with the Kefauver Committee hearings in 1950 and 1951; the evidence supporting the theory is presented in Donald R. Cressey, *Theft of the Nation* (New York: Harper and Row, 1969) and Ralph Salerno and John S. Tompkins, *The Crime Confederation* (Garden City: Doubleday, 1969). The theory is strongly questioned in Bell, pp.138ff.; Norval Morris and Gordon Hawkins, *The Honest Politician's Guide to Crime Control* (Chicago: University of Chicago Press, 1970), pp.202–235; and Joseph L. Albini, *The American Mafia: Genesis of a Legend* (New York: Appleton-Century-Crofts, 1971).

LOUISVILLE—OPEN CITY
WHAS-TV

REPORTER: Cleve White has operated after-hours clubs on the fringe of Louisville's West End for almost a decade. His joints have featured bootlegging, gambling and prostitution. He has been raided, and city attorneys have obtained injunctions in unsuccessful attempts to shut him down. In a remarkably candid interview, White talks about how he has continued to operate outside the law over the years.

REPORTER: Can you run an after-hours joint without paying somebody?

WHITE: Uh uhh.

REPORTER: Why not?

WHITE: You can't do nothing wrong without paying somebody.

REPORTER: Why not?

WHITE: Man, people ain't goin let you breathe. If you breathe too hard they gonna make you pay. You got to pay.

REPORTER: How do they know . . . what you're doing?

WHITE: They're gonna come around. They've got these snitches going around to find out what you're doing . . . plainclothesman, you know, just getting dressed up . . . when a beat policeman gets dressed up he's gonna check an see what's goin on. Maybe they'll call you up, come around make like he's got a complaint on you, and walks through the place real slow and looks around, that means we wants to see you . . . just walk back and forth—what you got back there—what you doin in here . . . ?"

REPORTER: Does he ever ask for anything besides money?

WHITE: I don't know what more they can ask for than money.

REPORTER: Did you take it to them or did they come get it?

WHITE: They come on by and picked it up.

REPORTER: Usually in the daytime or at night?

From the transcript of a documentary entitled "Louisville—Open City," telecast February 8–9, 1971, by WHAS-TV, Channel 11, Louisville, Kentucky. Portions deleted.

136

WHITE: They'd come anytime you call them. Don't make no difference when it is . . . in front of anybody.

REPORTER: What would you say when you called? How does that work? When you telephone in what do you say when you call, you call the police station?

WHITE: Just say captain so and so, or major so and so, or lieutenant so and so, meet me over here, at ———?

REPORTER: This is at the police station?

WHITE: Yeah, meet me over here in 15 or 20 minutes.

REPORTER: On duty?

WHITE: On duty. Right.

REPORTER: Would they come in uniform?

WHITE: Come in uniform with a brass band, it don't make them no difference. (Laughter) A brass band.

REPORTER: In a marked car?

WHITE: Police car.

REPORTER: Parked out front?

WHITE: Yeah.

REPORTER: And they'd come right in?

WHITE: Come right in the place.

REPORTER: Would there be customers in the place while this happened?

WHITE: Well, sometime there would, sometime there wouldn't . . .

REPORTER: We asked White what his neighbors think about police payoffs.

WHITE: Oh they know, they know. It's routine to them. They know what's happening . . . the customers and things.

REPORTER: Does it make them mad?

WHITE: No.

REPORTER: They just accept it?

WHITE: Yeah, they accept it.

REPORTER: It's just a fact of life?

WHITE: Yeah.

REPORTER: If you run, you've got to pay?

WHITE: That's right if you run, if you play, you've got to pay. That's the deal.

REPORTER: How do you feel about that?

WHITE: Well, it don't make me no different so long as they leave me alone.

REPORTER: How long would it take if you set up a new place, with gambling and bootlegging, . . .

WHITE: For them to find you?

REPORTER: . . . for them to find you?

WHITE: The first night.

REPORTER: And then what would happen?

WHITE: They'd just come by and make like a complaint . . . come around, look around see what you doing you know . . .

REPORTER: Would they arrest you the first night?

WHITE: No no no, they not going to arrest you the first night. They gonna make you, they want you to talk to them, come in.

REPORTER: Come in to the station?

WHITE: No, come in to them, and then if you don't come in, then they they'll arrest you and raid you.

REPORTER: You mean by comin' in . . .

WHITE: Money . . .

REPORTER: Come across . . .

WHITE: Yeah, come across with some dough.

REPORTER: And is there any set rate, for this? Do you pay a certain rate for bootlegging, a certain rate for prostitution.

WHITE: Yeah, it's according to what your doin', you know, if your not doin' nothing but just bootlegging, it's not going to hurt you too much. They'll take bootlegging money, but if you go in bootlegging, gambling, prostitution, everything, then you got to come in good.

REPORTER: And what is coming in good?

WHITE: Ah around $100 a month for each one of them.

REPORTER: For each policeman?

WHITE: Well not no sergeant and beat police you know. A sergeant usually get $25 maybe $50.

REPORTER: Is that a month now?

WHITE: Yeah, a month, and the a beat police usually get $5, $10, apiece, a car.

REPORTER: Now the beat police, that's the patrolman . . .

WHITE: Yeah, the patrolman.

REPORTER: The guy that rides around in the cruiser?

WHITE: Yeah the guy that rides around in the cruiser.

REPORTER: And the sergeant would get maybe $50 or $100?

WHITE: No, the sergeant would get maybe $25 or $50, lieutenants maybe get $75, $50, or $100 . . . just cording to how it's runnin', how your business is going and what you're doing.

REPORTER: How high up does it go? Does it go past the lieutenants?

WHITE: Oh yeah. It goes all the way, it'll go all the way up to a colonel.

REPORTER: Do the colonels come by also?

WHITE: No, no. Usually the men will take their money to em, yeah, usually the captain will take it by, or maybe the major or somebody come pick it up for em.

REPORTER: What's the highest ranking officer you've ever had in your place when you were running illegally?

WHITE: A major, yeah, major.

REPORTER: Did he come by to get some money, or just to look?

WHITE: No, he came by to talk. Tip me off, when it looked like some, like there was going to be some heat.

REPORTER: How does the heat come on and off? Can it be on one day and off the next day?

WHITE: Yeah.

REPORTER: Who decides the heat?

WHITE: Well, now I think it comes down all the way just like if you was working over there and you was the captain or major or colonel, or something, and you hear something, well then you gonna run it on down and you know, and go on out there and tell him to kinda raise up tonight.

REPORTER: Raise up means . . .

WHITE: Stop. That the state police are being in town.

REPORTER: When you buy protection does part of the price include the service to be tipped off?

WHITE: Oh yeah, oh yeah.

REPORTER: When you pay protection, you expect to be tipped?

WHITE: Yeah, you expect to be tipped and everything. And well they will tip you to protect their interest, you see. Yeah, see, they got an interest in the joint.

REPORTER: The interest is just the monthly . . .

WHITE: Monthly payment. See, they're your partners.

THROWING A CASE
Michael Dorman

How does the corrupter go about trying to put a local official or
policeman "in his pocket"? A graphic description of the Mafia technique was provided in a secretly made tape recording of a racketeer's
purported attempt to bribe an officer to join forces with the Mob. The
alleged corrupter in this case was a Mafia boss—Joseph "Joey" Aiuppa,
mastermind of the rackets in Cicero, Illinois. One of Aiuppa's underlings, Casper Ciapetti (alias John Carr), had previously been accused
of offering a $500 bribe to Detective Donald Shaw of the Cook County
Sheriff's Vice Squad in an attempt to fix a case resulting from a Cicero
slot-machine raid. Shaw, after informing his superiors of Ciapetti's
offer, had accepted the $500 while other officers watched from hiding
places. Ciapetti was then arrested and indicted on bribery charges.
While Ciapetti was awaiting trial, Aiuppa was accused of making his
own attempt to corrupt Shaw—offering him money to weaken his testimony in the bribery case and to provide the Mob with warnings of future raids against gambling rackets.

Aiuppa made his approach to Shaw through an intermediary, Jacob
"Dutch" Bergbreiter, a former commanding officer of the sheriff's vice
squad. Bergbreiter, who had left the sheriff's office and opened a real-
estate business, asked Shaw to meet him and Aiuppa. Shaw agreed, notified his superiors and went to the meeting equipped with a tiny radio
transmitter strapped under his jacket. The conversation was secretly
transmitted to other officers stationed in a nearby parked car, who tape-
recorded it. Part of the conversation went this way:

> AIUPPA. Would you have any objection to helping John Carr [Ciapetti]
> get off the hook in court for a consideration and, if in doing so, it
> wouldn't hurt your position as a police officer?
> SHAW. I wouldn't mind helping if I didn't hurt myself as a police of-
> ficer and I didn't perjure myself in court.

From Michael Dorman, *Payoff: The Role of Organized Crime In American Politics*, pp.37–43. Copyright © 1972 by Michael Dorman. Published
by David McKay Company, Inc., and reprinted with its permission.

AIUPPA. You won't hurt yourself and you won't have to be in court. Just give the lawyer a loophole in our prosecution. Now, you wouldn't want to see them put him [Carr] in the pen for ten years.

SHAW. I don't know him. I heard rumors that the guy has been an assassin.

AIUPPA. What?

SHAW. An assassin.

AIUPPA. Never.

BERGBREITER. Don't believe all the stuff you hear. Who told you he was an assassin?

SHAW. I don't know. I just heard.

AIUPPA. Excuse me, do you think there's such a crime as playing a slot machine or a pinball machine?

SHAW. By the law, there is.

AIUPPA. Wait a minute. The laws are flexible, they are made to bend, just like a big tree standing there. It's made to flex. I agree with this. I am a servant of the law and a citizen. . . . Let's put it cold. This is your home town. These are your people. Do you want to let an out-of-town guy like O'Mara [Michael O'Mara, commander of the sheriff's vice squad] come in and wrap you around his finger? Like all these Negroes and these demonstrators. Is that any goal to you? To me, to our friends? To our kids? It's the law. It's not right, but it's the law.

SHAW. Like I say, it's the law. I get paid to do it.

AIUPPA. All right, all right. Fine. We understand each other. There are several ways to do things. Take this man like O'Mara. . . . He's going to try to break the syndicate. He's going to try to get with the state's attorney. He's building up his stature, you understand, on your work. He's brainwashing all you young guys. Then [after the next sheriff's election] he dumps you. [Aiuppa then assured Shaw he would take care of his interests if a new sheriff were elected.] You just can't hurt people. . . . You have to use good common sense. You really do, reasoning. Our machines aren't taking money away from children, their milk money or the money they go to school with. When you find out about me, you will see I am a pretty nice guy. All I am interested in is the gambling and night spots in Cicero. It would be different if I sold broads, if I sold junk, if I sold counterfeit money. But I can go into a bar or a drug store and someone might even sit down and have a cup of coffee with me. We have nice people here. You will find out as you travel in Cicero that it is really a nice town. I'll guarantee you that my mother, sister, my daughter, could walk down the residential streets with no problem. I've been here for forty years.

BERGBREITER. And he will still be there when others are gone. I know that he will stand up. What he says, he will do.

AIUPPA. I expect you to stand up, too. If you can't stand up, I don't want to talk to you. We're men, we're friends, we try to help each other. Do you want to go along?

SHAW. Tell me what you want me to do.

[Aiuppa then explained that Shaw could change his testimony in court to indicate that the $500 given him by Carr might have been intended for use in posting bond for a man arrested in the slot-machine raid, Edward Doyle. "Isn't it possible it could have been that way?" Aiuppa asked. But Shaw pointed out that his vice squad partner had also witnessed the payment and would testify at the trial. He said he feared a conflict between his testimony and his partner's.]

AIUPPA. Forget about Jim [the partner]. I know what you said before the grand jury and I know what Jimmy said. I know more about it than you think I do. This is yours—two big ones. [Aiuppa purportedly held up two fingers at that point, indicating he would give Shaw $2,000.] For yourself. Don't tell anybody.

BERGBREITER. Don't even tell your wife. Believe me.

AIUPPA. If you tell anybody, I want no part of it. . . . Every month I will see that there is a C-note [$100] or some worldly goods in your mailbox. You'll be on the [pay] roll.

SHAW. What do you want from me to be on the roll?

AIUPPA. All I want from you is the information [on impending gambling raids], so that they will not be kicking me with the point of the shoe but the side of the shoe. If you find something out, see something you think I should know about, I'll give you a [phone] number. You follow me?

SHAW: The thing of it is, I would suddenly be out of a job if I stopped making pinches. We can do it like you say and kick you with the side of the shoe and not the toe.

AIUPPA. You will never stop making pinches. If you haven't got an out, go ahead. I paid for these pigeons [set-up raids in which Mafia subordinates, but never Aiuppa or his high-ranking associates, were arrested].

BERGBREITER. He will give you some good ones.

AIUPPA. Do you follow me? All I'm interested in is the gambling and the night spots in Cicero. I am not interested in the residential areas. You could go anywhere outside the business district and you will find nothing but a nice area.

BERGBREITER. Shaw, can I give you a little advice, being a boss like I was out there?

SHAW. In vice and gambling?

BERGBREITER. That's right. I used to be the [sheriff's] captain in charge of vice and gambling . . . and the Outfit [the Mob] always took care of me after I got smart and got on their payroll. Do this on your own. This is between the three of us. Don't trust your partner, nobody.

[Aiuppa then explained that if Shaw ever got in trouble and faced a trial, the Mob's money would be available to help him.]

SHAW. Say the [Chicago Police Department] Intelligence Unit had a game under surveillance for a while and then gave it [information on the game] to us and suddenly it wasn't there any more. They would get wise. They would know someone blew the whistle.

AIUPPA. Fine. The tables would be there. The game would be there, but the money wouldn't be on the table [so it couldn't be seized]. Do you follow me? I'll never embarrass you, never hurt you. I can be nice to you. I can help you. I can decorate the mahogany a bit. You know what I mean? I can help with the payments on the new car. I can see that you are taken care of every month. I can see that every month there is a little worldly goods for you. . . . If you walked into a place and saw me there and your superior said, "Pinch him," I never even met you. Go ahead and pinch me. I go along with the show.

SHAW. I kick you with the side of the shoe.

AIUPPA. Now you're catching on. Are you with me now?

SHAW. I guess.

Aiuppa then said he would obtain from inside sources a transcript of Shaw's secret grand jury testimony in the John Carr bribery case, so that Shaw could study it and avoid offering contradictory testimony at the upcoming trial. Aiuppa also made arrangements for Shaw to telephone him to warn of impending gambling raids. A short time after the meeting ended, Bergbreiter appeared at Shaw's home and gave him a $500 down payment on the $2,000 bribe offered by Aiuppa. During the next few weeks, Shaw talked several more times to Bergbreiter and each time the conversation was recorded. But, about a month after Shaw's meeting with Aiuppa and Bergbreiter, it became apparent that information about the potential bribery case against Aiuppa was being leaked to him by someone on the vice squad.

Late one night, as Shaw arrived home, he was confronted by Bergbreiter. "Listen, I hear you were wired for sound when you met Joey," Bergbreiter snapped.

"You crazy?" Shaw replied. "Not me."

"Joey [Aiuppa] learned that there was a guy under your crawlspace."

"You're kidding."

"And Joey learned that a helicopter was used for surveillance on him when he met with you."

"Well, they must be watching me. They wouldn't be watching you."

"Joey don't want to see you again until he gets a chance to test you."

In view of the evident leak of information from the vice squad, Shaw's superiors instructed him to break off his dealings with Aiuppa and Bergbreiter. Meanwhile, they launched an investigation to find the source of the leak. Sheriff Richard B. Ogilvie ordered all members of the vice squad to take lie-detector tests on whether they had given information to Aiuppa. Two officers refused to submit to the tests. They were at first suspended for thirty days and later fired.

Aiuppa and Bergbreiter were indicted on charges of offering bribes to Detective Shaw. Bergbreiter was convicted and sentenced to two years in prison. But Aiuppa, whose defense relied heavily on the fact that he was not present when Bergbreiter paid Shaw the $500, was acquitted by the judge on grounds of insufficient evidence. John Carr also beat his bribery case, using strategy outlined by Aiuppa in his recorded conversation with Shaw. Carr testified that the $500 he had given Shaw was intended as bond money for Edward Doyle. This version was supported by Doyle. The trial judge, commenting that perhaps Doyle's testimony "could be counted on," found Carr not guilty.

PROTECTING ORGANIZED CRIME
Ralph Salerno and John S. Tompkins

The Democratic party in the United States is against organized crime. The Republican party in the United States is against organized crime. Organized crime is thoroughly pleased with the two-party system.

Corruption is necessary to the successful operation of the Syndicate. And to the average citizen the most offensive kind of corruption is the policeman who takes a payoff. Because he wears a uniform and is under quasi-military discipline, we are as shocked by corrupt police as we would be by an Army officer who has sold out to the enemy. The public forgets, of course, that the police are merely a part of the executive branch of government.

Law-enforcement units are organized so that most patrolmen and detectives do what their sergeants and lieutenants tell them to do.

From Ralph Salerno and John S. Tompkins, *The Crime Confederation: Cosa Nostra and Allied Operations in Organized Crime*, pp.243–248, 252–256. Copyright © 1969 by Ralph Salerno and John S. Tompkins. Published by Doubleday & Company, Inc., and reprinted with its permission. Some footnotes deleted.

Sergeants and lieutenants get their orders from captains and inspectors, who, in turn, follow the direction of the chief. The chief of police, or the commissioner, or superintendent usually serves at the pleasure of the mayor of the city. If the mayor wants traffic regulations strictly enforced, they are enforced. If the mayor wants a particular section of town to get special police attention, it will get such attention. If the mayor wants a crackdown on any particular violation of law, the police will respond to his wishes. In the same way, if the mayor thinks that any one kind of law-enforcement effort is rocking the boat, then the boat will not be rocked. The police will quickly get the message and turn their attention to less controversial crime. There is always enough to occupy their attention.

The easiest way to corrupt the police is to avoid the lower and lowest-paid levels (even though they do the investigating and make the arrests). There are just too many there to corrupt efficiently. It is very expensive, time consuming, and unreliable. This is not to say that the cop on the beat never gets paid off; simply that the payoffs to individual patrolmen are the nickel-and-dime kind that are not important in Syndicate strategy. As we pointed out in the President's Crime Commission report: "Organized crime currently is directing its efforts to corrupt law enforcement at the chief or at least middle-level supervisory officials."

Naturally, the corruption of police effort, or its nullification, can be accomplished most smoothly through political influence. In addition, political corruption can affect the entire system of justice, of which the police are only the intake. With enough political power one can also influence prosecutors, judges, probation officers, prison administrators and parole boards. All of these are run either by an elected official or by someone appointed by an elected official and responsible to him.

One of the things that makes successful corruption easy is the fact that its results are nearly invisible to the public. The reason is that the members of organized crime who come into contact with our system of justice are only a tiny fraction of the total. Even if all members of the Confederation and their employees were given immunity by the police, there would still be thousands of murderers, rapists, muggers, purse snatchers, car thieves, burglars, and other assorted amateurs to be arrested and produce an impressive record of crime-control statistics. The FBI has built an enviable reputation with just such a numbers game.

Moreover, if all the cases resulting from arrests of Syndicate men were to be fixed with a district attorney, he could still enjoy a fine batting average of successful prosecutions. And if both the police and the prosecutor were incorruptible, and every organized crime case was improperly influenced by the judge, or if his sentences were not commensurate with the facts, he could still handle the rest of his case load so sternly as to establish a reputation as a hanging judge. In short, all levels of justice can easily hide evidence of corruption by their severity and straightforwardness in handling routine crime in the streets.

As Daniel P. Moynihan has observed, electing a crime buster is not the same thing as busting crime. Time and again, sincere and incorruptible district attorneys have successfully prosecuted gangsters and ridden into office on reform tickets—only to be surprised and embarrassed a year or two later by political corruption scandals in their own administration. Part of the reason for this, of course, is that most reformers have had an oversimplified view of organized crime. The legend persists that when Mr. Big is sent to prison, the organization falls apart. Another factor, though, is that Syndicate influence in politics is very well concealed. A few arrests and well-publicized convictions of top mobsters is no more guarantee that a city is free of organized crime than the exposure of a Soviet spy ring means that Russian espionage efforts have been stopped.

Another fact that makes present-day corruption difficult to detect is its subtlety. The day when a police official or politician was bought with a satchelful of cash is largely gone. Large campaign contributions through an acceptable go-between are just as effective, and far less dangerous to both sides.

The contributions that come to light are usually those that were refused.

Richard Hatcher, the first Negro mayor of Gary, Indiana, stated in a TV interview on February 12, 1969 that he had been offered $100,000 by syndicated gambling interests to withdraw from the Democratic primary two years earlier. He said that he refused the offer, and that when he won the nomination and was given a good chance to be elected, the $100,000 was again offered, this time for an "understanding" between Hatcher and the gamblers. The money was again refused.

Several years ago, a national magazine published a story—based on information from an FBI bug—that a New England Cosa Nostra family had offered a $100,000 campaign contribution to a candidate for attorney general of Massachusetts. The man confirmed the offer to newspaper reporters, and added that when he turned the money down the men who had offered it said they would use all their resources to defeat him. Among other things, they spread the word that the candidate had taken their money, and he lost the election.

Often, the contribution is not even in cash. The economics of local politics is such that little money is allocated by party organizations for minor offices. A man running, say, for tax assessor or county clerk or assistant coroner, will have to use his own ingenuity to pay for the printing of handbills and posters. And he will not readily refuse the offer of ten loudspeaker sound trucks to broadcast his message in the neighborhoods.

Since the advent of the wealthy amateur in politics—the Kennedys, Harriman, Percy, the Rockefellers, Romney, and others—a faith has developed, and been fostered, that such men are too rich to be corrupt. Even those who oppose them concede their obvious honesty. And this is true, as far as it goes: none of the millionaires in public life need to steal or take bribes. But the logic overlooks the rich man's party, his running mates, and his entourage, all of whom may be quite desperately in need of money.

Money, of course, is not the most important thing in politics. The name of the game is to get elected, and a rich candidate needs votes just like anybody else. A well-organized bloc of votes that organized crime can deliver or withhold can be used to corrupt the wealthiest politician. A man running for office in New York City, for example, would have a hard time if a whispering campaign charged him with being anti-Italian. To avoid such a threat, his managers might well be willing to make a deal that could not be arranged for any amount of cash.

And after the man has won, and is in office, he is rarely asked to exercise blatant influence on behalf of the Syndicate. After all, the idea is to have influence without it ever being obvious enough to attract attention. As the head of the Detroit police put it a few years ago: ". . . the net result is that there is somebody close to the seat of power who at least can put in a good word—not control, but just put in a good word, and a good word at the seat of power at various and sundry times can be a very, very potent thing."

Good associations, being seen with the right people, and having important contacts are as vital to organized crime as they are to an ambitious businessman, politician, or social climber. In the political area, Syndicate men's activities are designed to secure power, or the appearance of power, which is almost as good as having it.

A man who can put in a good word, in fact, does not even need to put one in to make his influence felt. If he is friendly with someone in high office and can display his friendship at banquets or political rallies, he becomes a man with influence. Most underworld figures shy away from public association with politicians nowadays. They fear that being seen with a man in office might hurt his image, and reduce his value to them. The usual solution is to have a respectable go-between, often a lawyer, benefit from the association, knowing that perceptive and useful observers, policemen and other city employees, will understand the connection and get the message. They will be influenced without anyone ever pressuring them.

❊   ❊   ❊

The target of organized crime is always the district, ward, or county political leader, who governs not as an elected office holder, but as king of the clubhouse. Young men, entering public life, usually start out at the clubhouse level under the tutelage and control of the local leader. The friends they make and the political debts they incur at that time follow them through their careers. It is for this reason that many a Syndicate member can brag of a Senator, a Judge or a Mayor, that "I've known him for thirty years."

The phrase "I've known him for years" is a conventional way of saying that someone is an old friend who could never be guilty of any wrongdoing. Often, the statement is connected with a rough bit of sentimental reminiscence about the old slum neighborhood and how some of the boys became priests and others went to the death house.

Item—In 1967, a national magazine suggested that Senator Edward V. Long, the zealous Missouri investigator of wiretapping abuses, was using his committee to help Teamster boss James Hoffa establish that he had been improperly convicted on wire-tap evidence. The Senator was accused of taking $48,000 from a St. Louis lawyer who represented Hoffa. The Senate Ethics Committee who looked into the affair, cleared Long—and mentioned that he and the lawyer, who represented many racketeers and gamblers, had been friends for twenty-five years.

Item—In June 1967 a political rival accused August Petrollo, Republican candidate for mayor of White Plains, New York, of having been offered $10,000 by a local gambler named John (Peanuts) Manfredonia. Petrollo denied that any such offer had been made, but said he knew Manfredonia "since we grew up together."

Item—In 1952, the New York State Crime Commission took testimony from Francis X. Mancuso, a former judge and Tammany district leader. After admitting that he knew the then notorious Frank Costello, he was asked how long he had known him. "About thirty-five years or so," said Mancuso. "His people come from the same town my people come from. They know each other. I may say there is intermarriage in the family; my first cousin married his first cousin."

Lawyers whose practice is active in criminal defense bar are much more active in political clubhouses than are corporate lawyers. In the first place, they will get to meet and know the assistant district attorney who is supposed to be their adversary, because the assistant DA probably got his appointment on the recommendation of the local party leader. Similarly, they will come into contact with judges who will preside over their cases, since the designation as candidates for the bench also came from the clubhouse leader.

Later in his career, such a lawyer may get such a political plum himself in return for faithful service to the party. And when he becomes a prosecutor or a judge he will not necessarily divorce himself from old friends.

Occasionally, the easy familiarity between party leaders and Syndicate men becomes a public embarrassment. A dozen years ago, for example, an investigation by the New York District Attorney's office revealed that there had been a meeting of Democratic county leaders— a group known collectively as Tammany Hall—in the East Harlem area of Manhattan. The meeting had been attended by members of the Cosa Nostra family then headed by Frank Costello. The presence of these men at such a political meeting could not be explained by any of the party leaders. Some of them held top city offices, but they were fired by Mayor Vincent R. Impelitteri in the ensuing scandal.

The mayor himself was shortly embarrassed when it was found that he had met with Thomas Lucchese, head of another Cosa Nostra group, shortly before a new police commissioner was to be appointed. Impelitteri's explanation was that Lucchese had been introduced to him as a clothing manufacturer (which he was) and it was only in this role that they had come to meet. The appointment of a new police commissioner, said the mayor, had not been discussed.

While many of the big cities in which organized crime flourishes are Democratic party strongholds, the Confederation extends its backing to the rival party, too. It also backs prohibitionists, civil rights organizations, and even extremist groups. If the vegetarians or the retired pensioners should mount a major campaign, they too would be supported. Crime is not particular who wins at the polls—as long as it has taken care to make sure its voice is heard by the winners. To insure that it will be on the winning side, it usually backs every major candidate. After all, even the man who loses may turn out to be a winner in some future election.

When Al Capone was running Chicago, the mayor was a Republican named William Hale ("Big Bill") Thompson, who had originally run on a reform platform ("He cannot be bought, bossed, or bluffed") but who got along very well with the Syndicate. Since then, Chicago has had a succession of Democratic mayors, but the same men who ran organized crime in earlier days still run it. As late as the middle 1960s, the local chairmen of both parties "cleared" their lists of candidates with Sam ("Momo") Giancana, a successor to Capone.

The so-called "West Side Bloc," a political group put together in the days of Capone, remains a force in Chicago to this day. In 1963, a law was passed establishing the Illinois Crime Commission, and a joke went the rounds in Chicago to the effect that the bill must have been pushed through the State Legislature on the day that the West Side Bloc had its annual picnic—or it would not have passed.

In the mid-1950s a power struggle developed within New York's Tammany Hall. The details of the fight are unimportant, but the secret discussions to resolve it were held by the Democratic leaders in a hotel suite paid for by a well-known Syndicate figure. The man was then living in a nearby suburban town that happened to be a Republican stronghold, and he knew and supported three of the five city councilmen. In short, he played no partisan political favorites but took steps to insure that he would have friends in the political power structure no matter which party was in office.

The most effective and long-lasting political relationships that organized crime has developed are also the most inconspicuous. To avoid possible embarrassment to its political allies, the Syndicate has often changed its local domicile so that the incumbent can claim that his city or state is "clean." Again, Capone pioneered the technique. He moved his headquarters from Chicago to the adjacent, but unincorporated, town of Cicero. The action was taken when the city administration was under momentary pressure from a public reform movement, and Capone wanted to spare his friends at City Hall any embarrassment. With Capone in Cicero, Chicago officials could disclaim any responsibility for what went on there.*

Almost the same thing happened in Youngstown, Ohio, twenty-five years later when an aggressive police chief with the backing of the mayor began to give local Confederation men a hard time. Casino

---

* As the Illinois Crime Survey reported in 1929, the Capone forces took over Cicero "legally" by backing a handpicked slate of Republicans. "On the Monday night preceding the election gunmen invaded the office of the Democratic candidate for clerk, beat him, and shot up the place. Automobiles, filled with gunmen, paraded the streets, slugging and kidnaping election workers. Polling places were raided by armed thugs, and ballots were taken at the point of a gun from the hands of voters waiting to drop them into the box. Voters and workers were kidnaped, brought to Chicago, and held prisoners until the polls closed."

gambling was set up just beyond the jurisdiction of the Youngstown police in the village of Halls Corners (pop. 30) where the mayor was a Youngstown tavern operator. Youngstown police tried to get the cooperation of the county sheriff, but found him hostile rather than cooperative, concerned that any action against the casino might imperil his own re-election.

Cincinnati long enjoyed the reputation of having a first class police force that, somehow, was able to curb crime more efficiently than most cities its size with a lower ratio of officers per thousand citizens. This miracle was possible because the wide open towns of Covington and Newport, Kentucky, right across the Ohio River enabled Cincinnatians to sin as much as they pleased outside the city and the state.

Similar patterns have been followed successfully by relocating gambling operations outside the city of Detroit, by moving certain New York City activities across the river to New Jersey, and by headquartering Syndicate operations in the New Orleans area in Jefferson Parish or across the river in Algiers so that the Parish of Orleans could safely claim that most crime took place outside its boundaries.

POLICE VIOLATIONS
OF THE LAW

Albert J. Reiss, Jr.

The data presented in this selection are based upon direct observation by thirty-six field observers in high-crime districts in Boston, Chicago, and Washington during the summer of 1966. Additional findings from this study are contained in Albert J. Reiss, Jr., ed., *Studies in Crime and Law Enforcement in Major Metropolitan Areas*, President's Commission on Law Enforcement and Administration of Justice Field Survey III (Washington, D.C.: Government Printing Office, 1967).

Officers may be charged with violations of the law, as might ordinary citizens. Among the offenses it is commonly alleged officers com-

From Albert J. Reiss, Jr., *The Police and the Public*, pp. 156–163, 170–172. Copyright © 1971 by Yale University. Reprinted by permission of the publisher, Yale University Press. All footnotes deleted.

mit are theft of money and goods, burglary of establishments, accepting bribes, shakedowns of offenders, offering false testimony, and participation in the illegal markets and practices of syndicated crime.

Officers can violate criminal statutes when on or off duty, but we shall consider only on-duty violations since our primary data were gathered through observation of officers on duty. Each observer spent an eight-hour tour of duty either on foot or in a car with one or more officers so they could not only observe how officers handled law-enforcement matters with citizens, but also how they behaved at all other times. Some officers, in some police precincts and cities, were observed more frequently than others. The effect of observation on limiting misconduct cannot be assessed accurately. It should be noted, however, that the highest rates of misconduct occurred where officers were observed least often.

Counting all felonies and misdemeanors, except assaults on citizens, the rate of criminal violation for officers observed committing one or more violations was 23.7 in City X, 21.9 in City Y, and 16.5 in City Z per 100 officers [see table]. Excluding any participation in syndicated crime, roughly 1 in 5 officers was observed in criminal violation of the law. There was some variation among the three cities in the crime patterns of police officers and the rate of violation.

The types of opportunities and situations that give rise to officers violating criminal statutes are relatively few. Opportunities arise principally in connection with the law-enforcement roles of officers, particularly in relationships with businesses and businessmen, policing traffic violators and deviants, and controlling evidence from crimes [see table]. Obtaining money or merchandise illegally is the principal officer violation. A striking fact is that few officers were observed committing crimes against the residential property of citizens, although this may be a function of the fact that they usually were observed policing low-income residential areas. The major exception is the violation of criminal statutes by controlling evidence illegally, as by swearing false testimony or carrying additional weapons for the sole purpose of using them as evidence against citizens. These additional weapons were obtained from previous searches of the person, and are used as evidence against other citizens who were injured or killed, thereby buttressing the officer's argument that he injured or killed a citizen in self-defense.

The fact that criminal violations of the law by officers are restricted to relatively few types of offenses hints at the explanation for these offenses. The bulk of offenses committed by officers provide income supplements derived from exchange relationships. The price exacted by the officer provides something in exchange, generally exemption from the effect of the law. Given the relatively low remuneration of police officers, relative to their prestige and life style, the pressures to supplement income are considerable. Many police departments in the United States either prohibit moonlighting or severely restrict its practice to certain kinds of jobs. In any case, the "easy" money available to the officer with the low risk of sanctioning renders it a highly attractive form of income supplementation when contrasted with moonlighting. Though claims are easily exaggerated, some officers said they could earn as much from their violations as from their salary. Where either the pay-offs are regularized—as they often are for the protection offered illegal activity, or where there is considerable opportunity to exact money because the market is large, as is the case for shakedowns of traffic violators—and the pressure to balance income with expenditure is high, as it is for police officers, one should expect this pattern of violation of the criminal law. Gains are considerable relative to opportunity costs, assuming psychic income from exemplary conduct is not too great. Historically, political officials as well as police officers have been particularly vulnerable to this pattern of deviance.

Parenthetically, it might be noted that the effect of the criminal violations of officers still sanctions negatively the activity from which the financial gain is made. While the motorist who pays the police officer in exchange for exemption from official processing pays a cost below that which its sanctioning agents normally assess (the fine plus court costs and points), it nonetheless is a cost, and therefore a sanction. Indeed the police officer must make the cost of his sanction competitive.

The criminal violations of officers against the operation of the system of criminal justice is explained on altogether different grounds. The explanation of that misconduct lies in the officer subculture as a reaction to the system of punishment for police officers, a matter we shall turn to later.

A gray area of offending also exists. Many businessmen in a community engage in exchanges or practices with police officers that from the standpoint of the law could bring charges of bribery. A variety of such practices were uncovered in our observations of the police including almost daily free meals, drinks, or cigarettes, the profferment of gifts marking anniversaries and holidays, and discounts on purchases. Such practices are specifically prohibited by the rules and regulations of any police department and subject to disciplinary action if "officially" discovered.

Rate Per 100 Officers of Criminal Violations in Field Settings
of Three Cities Reported by Observers or
Officers or Alleged by Others

Type of crime or dishonest practice	City X		City Y		City Z	
	Number of Officers*	Percentage of officers observed, self-reported, alleged	Number of officers*	Percentage of officers observed, self-reported, alleged	Number of officers*	Percentage of officers observed, self-reported, alleged
Officer accepts money to alter testimony report:						
Officer reports at trial stage	2	0.9	—	—	—	—
Officer reports intent for case	1	0.5	—	—	—	—
Officer reports for altering report	1	0.5	—	—	—	—
Subtotal	(4)	(1.9)	—	—	—	—
Officer carries weapon to leave on citizen:						
Observer saw weapon and officer reports this as reason	2	0.9	2	1.4	2	0.9
Subtotal	(2)	(0.9)	(2)	(1.4)	(2)	(0.9)
Officer receives money/merchandise on return of stolen property:						
Officer reports he has done	2	0.9	4	2.7	—	—
Subtotal	(2)	(0.9)	(4)	(2.7)	—	—
Officer takes money/property from deviants:						
Observer saw	6	2.7	8	5.5	2	0.9
Officer reports he has done	4	1.8			—	—
Subtotal	(10)	(4.5)	(8)	(5.5)	(2)	(0.9)

Traffic violation: officer gives no citation and gets money:

Observer definitely saw	4	1.8	—	—	2	0.9
Observer heard solicitation	2	0.9	—	—	—	—
Officer reports he does	3	1.4	—	—	—	—
Subtotal	(9)	(4.1)	(0)	(0)	(2)	(0.9)

Officer takes merchandise from burglarized establishment:

Observer saw	3	1.4	3	2.0	—	—
Officer reports he has done	1	0.5	—	—	—	—
Alleged by merchant in observer's presence	2	0.9	—	—	—	—
Subtotal	(6)	(2.8)	(3)	(2.0)	(0)	—

Officer receives money or merchandise from a business:†

Observer saw merchandise taken and no citation or arrest	4	1.8	2	1.4	3	1.3
Observer saw only receipt of merchandise	11	5.0	6	4.1	15	6.5
Observer saw officers give special assistance for merchandise	2	0.9	6	4.1	10	4.3
Officer reports he does	2	0.9	1	0.7	4	1.7
Subtotal	(19)	(8.6)	(15)	(10.3)	(32)	(13.8)

Summary Officer Crimes/Practices:

Total officers observed	32	14.5	29	18.5	34	14.8
Total officers by self-report	18	8.3	3	3.4	4	1.7
Total alleged against officers	2	0.9	—	—	—	—
Total officers—no crimes or dishonest practices	168	76.0	115	78.0	192	83.0
Total officers observed in study	220	100.0	147	100.0	230	100.0

Source: Albert J. Reiss, Jr., Center for Research on Social Organization, University of Michigan, Project 947.
* An officer is counted only once with the offenses rank ordered in the table.
† Excluded are all free meals, discounts, small favors such as cigarettes or free drinks, and similar.

Within each of the cities, one-third (31 percent) of all businessmen in wholesale or retail trade or business and repair services in the high-crime-rate areas openly acknowledged favors to policemen. Of those giving favors, 43 percent said they gave free merchandise, food or services to all policemen; the remainder did so at discount. When observers were present with officers during their eight-hour tour of duty, for almost 1 of every 3 of the 841 tours (31 percent), the officers did not pay for their meals. For the remaining cases, small discounts were common. Similarly many officers reported large discounts on purchases of durable goods. On most occasions, free goods or discounts are not solicited, largely because officers know well which businesses offer them and which do not. The informal police networks carry such information, obviating in most cases open solicitation. Presentation of self in uniform is all that is necessary to secure many benefits. These transactions are viewed as "favors" by the line and tacitly approved by their superiors.

The fact that mobility within police departments occurs almost exclusively by promotion from the line *within* a department makes line and staff officers subject to supervision by the line. They readily overlook practices and violations that are common among patrolmen either because they, themselves, engaged in them when they served as patrolmen or many of their friends did so. Not infrequently, when superior officers investigate or hear charges in disciplinary proceedings for men in the line, their judgment is subverted because they served with them. These facts—the absence of lateral mobility across police departments and mobility within them resting on promotion from the line—are a structural feature of American police departments that renders them vulnerable to many forms of internal subversion and jeopardizes their disinterest in personnel decisions and discipline. The classic separation of recruitment into staff and line and the use of civil-service examinations is designed to temper subversion in promotion. No such safeguard is built into the typical disciplinary investigation and hearing within the police department. Businessmen regard favors to police officers as guarantees that special attention may be given their business. Most such favors, therefore, do not occur as specific exchanges, characteristic of bribery and shakedowns. Rather, as Dalton points out for American businesses, they represent "favors due" that cannot be exchanged in the course of carrying out regular duties. Although it can be argued, as he notes, that people are being persuaded to violate their official duties by accepting such favors, it can equally be argued that they contribute to the carrying out of official duties. Thus, it is the duty of the police to protect business establishments in the community. Indeed, since businesses are highly vulnerable to criminal activity in many areas, special attention may even be officially approved. In Detroit and Chicago, as in some other large American cities, the police department may even provide a police escort at closing time so that businessmen may safely deposit their daily receipts at a bank. Such attention, though not officially acknowledged by either party as payment, can be recognized through favors. For the police, then, as for workers and officials in corporations, favors often are unofficial rewards for regular duties.

Such exchanges may not afford businesses the protection anticipated. Within each of the police precincts a sample of businesses was investigated to determine whether personal relationships with police officers affects a business's capacity to cope with crime against it. Examining the businesses in 1966 and 1968, it was found that businesses with personal links to police officers in 1966 maintained them in 1968. However, these personal relationships were totally ineffective in reducing the level of crime against these businesses. Thus, the high degree of personal links that businesses have with the police cannot be explained by any added benefits to the organization in meeting its crime problems.

We have tried to show how the deviant conduct of officers may arise based on the structure and organization of police work as well as police culture. We have shown that a substantial proportion of officers have engaged in one or more forms of deviant conduct and the annual rates of offending may be high. Yet, what standard does one use to determine whether the rate of offending by officers is high or low?

This is an important question, because the police encounter in their work much pressure and opportunity from offenders as well as legitimate and illegitimate organized interests to deviate from laws and rules governing conduct. Even in such minor matters as traffic violations, the conforming citizen wants a pass, expects special consideration, and often is willing to pay an officer to ignore the matter. Businessmen wanting to violate ordinances for closing hours or serving customers or wishing profit from illegal markets are willing to offer special consideration in return for the opportunity to do business as they wish. In short, there is ample opportunity for subversion of any and all officers.

All officers are, to a large extent, exempt from law enforcement. This fact, combined with the pressures on an officer to deviate in many situations, make each crime opportunity for him a more likely criminal event. Bearing this in mind, the question is not, what makes officers violate the law, but what protects officers from deviating more often than we have observed?

The likelihood of an officer accepting illegal exchanges is increased when such practices are institutionalized and legitimated by the police subculture and organization. We found that traffic bribes were most common in the city where they had long been an institutionalized form of exchange between police and citizens. The exchange became legitimated. At the same time, however, an officer takes a certain risk in making the exchange. Thus, he generally will not do so in the presence of witnesses or when detection is likely. A further element influencing officer involvement in such exchanges is the degree to which these illegal practices are organized, as in a system of exchange with organized crime. Typical of such exchanges is that they get organized as an economy where rewards are distributed on a routine basis.

What may be most pertinent here is the legitimacy that attaches to the exchange. To deviate on one's own is to be a criminal, but where the offense is consensual, not only is there mutual implication in the offense, and therefore minimization of risk, but the offense is also easily legitimized. For an officer to share in a payment from illegal gambling is accepted, but for an officer to burglarize an establishment is to step beyond the bounds of what is legitimate. Deviation, we observe, often is *shared* with fellow officers, providing peer support to each. Furthermore, rules infractions, such as drinking or sleeping on duty, are participated in by several officers at a time, although when this is not the case, they may rely on the subculture to protect them. No doubt, image protection operates here as well, but the punishment system is important, a matter we shall turn to later. To suggest, of course, that the only pressures against deviance are these is to scant the fact that officers do commit themselves to uphold a moral order. Some psychic investment is made in exemplary conduct.

Summary

Police standards and conduct are based primarily on five sources: (1) subversion by the citizenry; (2) the input-output system, particularly where the police lack control over final outcomes; (3) the quality of citizen behavior toward the police; (4) the existence of a dispersed command that does not lend itself to close supervision; and (5) legitimation by the police subculture and shared participation in deviance. In the long run, we have had only one solution to the problem of conformity to standards for occupations that are dispersed in work situations, their professionalization. Lest anyone assume that professionalization is a uniquely satisfactory solution, he must be reminded that charges of professional malpractice are not uncommon. In our legal system, such charges can on occasion reach even to the highest levels of our appellate system, the United States Supreme Court.

░░

TICKET FIXING
John A. Gardiner

One Massachusetts legislator, invited by a local League of Women Voters to discuss the functions of a legislator, startled the ladies by beginning, "The chief function of a legislator is to fix traffic tickets for his constituents." In a state in which most public employees are under the civil-service system, fixing tickets may be one of the few services a legislator can perform for his constituents. One state senator, hearing a safety council official prpose a no-fix system, asked incredulously, "Do you really mean that I'm not going to be able to help out friends who get into trouble? There's nothing immoral about fixing minor traffic tickets." Legislators protested an earlier attempt to end fixing on the ground that it would cut down their influence, and they denied a request to increase the size of the state police force after it adopted a no-fix policy.

For the policeman as well as the legislator, requests to fix tickets may well be one of the primary bases of contact with the public. Any motorist, of course, can try to talk his way out of a ticket—"I didn't see the stop sign"; "My speedometer is broken"; "I'm late for work"; and, fairly certain to anger the patrolman, "How dare you stop me? I'm a friend of the governor (bishop, mayor, chief)." But even if a Massachusetts motorist is unable to convince the officer not to write up the offense, there is still a good chance that he can avoid punish-

From John A. Gardiner, *Traffic and the Police: Variations in Law-Enforcement Policy*, pp.118–126. Copyright © 1969 by the President and Fellows of Harvard College. Reprinted by permission of the publisher, Harvard University Press. Some footnotes deleted.

ment. (The course of action will vary from city to city, depending on whether the policeman carries the Registry ticket books or is recording the facts on a departmental ticket form. In the latter case, the motorist can erase all evidence of the violation if someone in police head-quarters rips up the form. If, on the other hand, the arresting officer fills out the Registry tickets on the road—in Cambridge and twenty-seven other cities in the state—the motorist's only hope is to persuade the chief to mark the ticket "warning," since chiefs and policemen fear that someone in the Registry will notice if a Registry form is com-pletely destroyed.)

How does the process of ticket fixing work? Although your ultimate chance for success in getting a ticket fixed (termed by all Massa-chusetts police officers, "to give consideration") varies from city to city, the list of persons to call does not. Your best bet is to know a member of the police force that stopped you. (If you knew the officer himself, you would not, of course, have received the ticket in the first place.) Other persons to call are: *any* police chief in the state, any policeman in the state, a politician from the city involved, any other politician in the state, and then "friends" of any of these persons. Once you state your case to your contact ("I wasn't going very fast," "I've never had a ticket before," "I need my license to keep my job"), the pattern of communication varies. If your contact does not come from the city in which the ticket is written, he will probably call the chief; someone within the city might have a friend lower down on the force who can take care of it more quietly.

The origins of these lines of communication are lost in antiquity, but their existence is clear. The most effective intercity line of com-munication is through the home-town police chief. Police chiefs in Massachusetts frequently said that their "constituents" call them re-garding tickets received in other towns and that they then call the other chief to ask for consideration for the motorist. The philosophy of all police chiefs seems to be this: the chief should call for his con-stituent, and the other chief should grant consideration, unless: (1) the Registry ticket has already been written and the recommendation made (if the ticket has been written but the recommendation not yet made, fixing involves a warning rather than destroying or voiding the ticket); (2) the offense is of a serious nature (no chief or politican is willing to involve himself in any situation involving alcohol, accidents, or *dangerous* speeding—"What if the guy later gets involved in an accident or kills somebody? I don't want my name mixed up with his," one city councilor said); or (3) the motorist was rude to the officer.

The logic of the last policy is interesting: the chiefs say that they will not intervene for rude motorists because "they are showing disrespect for the law"; it would seem equally likely that they refuse because a rude motorist has got an officer mad, and the cost to the chief of fixing a ticket written by an angered officer is greater than when the officer is less personally interested in the violation or violator. In all three situations, chiefs feel no obligation to their constituents or to other chiefs. Otherwise, Massachusetts chiefs generally seem to assume that consideration will be given; several chiefs said that they would be surprised if another chief did not give consideration in ordinary circumstances.

Several things should be noted about the organization of ticket fixing in Massachusetts. The first is that the general standards used in appraising requests for fixes—the violation is minor, it is a first offense, and the motorist was not rude to the officer—are known and accepted by all of the participants in the system, and few attempt to jeopardize the system by requesting fixes that do not satisfy these standards. A former mayor in one city mentioned that every politician knows at least one person on the force to call, but "if the violation *might* be regarded as 'serious,' the fix has to be cleared with the chief first. If he decides that it is serious, he won't fix it and politicians won't touch it." A councilor added, "I just leave the message with whoever answers the phone at headquarters. If the motorist gave the cop any trouble, or if he was a bad guy (had a prior record), they'll know I don't want to have anything to do with it."

A second interesting aspect of Massachusetts ticket fixing concerns the *quid pro quo* on which the system is based. Even though, according to one probably exaggerated safety-council estimate, half of all traffic tickets written in the state are fixed,[1] it seems that money is not the reason why tickets are fixed. All policemen who spoke freely about their fixing activities were indignant at any suggestion that they or their colleagues would accept money for their services. One lieutenant hotly replied, "If we found that one of our men was taking money for fixing, he'd be fired immediately!" None of the evidence collected either during my study or during the three-year investigations of the Massachusetts Crime Commission (which, though it concentrated on corruption at the state level, also investigated ticket fixing)[2] revealed any

1. "State's Safety Council Says 50% of Traffic Tickets Fixed," *Boston Herald*, March 23, 1965.
2. Interview with Alfred Gardner, Chairman of the Massachusetts Crime Commission, August 3, 1965.

instances in which money was accepted to cover up a minor traffic violation. The only explanation for this is that, since police chiefs are so willing to fix tickets on the basis of friendship or political influence, there is no reason to offer cash when stopped by an officer. If corruption in the sense of an exchange of money exists in the field of traffic-law enforcement—and there was no evidence that it does in Massachusetts at least—it would probably exist at the level of the chief rather than at the level of the arresting officer.

If money is not the basis of ticket fixing, why do policemen do it? For chiefs and men alike, fixing tickets is an easily effective form of patronage. One traffic officer described fixing as a kind of insurance. "If you take care of a ticket for a liquor dealer or salesman," he noted, "you can expect consideration when you go in to buy a suit or a bottle." Policemen distinguish sharply, it might be noted, between accepting a bribe and receiving consideration; to a policeman, accepting five dollars from a motorist is dishonest, but buying a suit for less than its list price is not. Ticket fixing also provides insurance of another sort. When asked why policemen were willing to fix tickets when called by policemen from another city, one officer replied, "Well, some day one of our men may want to take care of something in that city, so we'll fix this thing for them now."

For the police chief, fixing tickets also offers a means of maintaining cordial relationships with state and local politicians as well as with local citizens. One patrolman philosophically noted, "Fixing tickets is about the only thing that the chief can do for politicians." The chiefs in Cambridge and Malden were the statehouse lobbyists for, respectively, the Massachusetts Chiefs of Police Association and the Massachusetts Police Association; and both men appeared regularly at the statehouse to ask for legislative favors. All police chiefs must also appear before city councils and town boards of selectmen to ask for pay raises, new equipment, and so forth. Finally, since chiefs must deal with other chiefs, both socially at the monthly association meetings and professionally in conducting multicity crime investigations, they face pressure to honor fix requests from other chiefs and their friends. Some chiefs said that, unless they fixed tickets, they could not expect cooperation from other police forces on more serious matters (such intercity matters as escaped convicts or an auto-theft gang). This, of course, assumes that there is a basic feeling that chiefs *should* fix for their colleagues. A more plausible explanation involves a feeling of reciprocity—"I will not be able to fix one of *his* tickets for my friends if I don't take care of his friends who get *my* tickets. Besides, knowing the problems that I have with officials and politicians in my city, I don't want to cause him any extra problems with his officials and their friends."

Although ticket fixing is a practice generally accepted by chiefs and policemen, it is also a source of conflict between them. As the chief in one small town said, "You have to strike a balance between townspeople and the men on your force or you'll never get anything done." The fixing standards described earlier leave a gray area between violations which both the chief and the arresting officer agree are definitely fixable and those which are not. Under pressure from another chief or a local citizen or politician, a chief may be required to persuade the officer that the motorist was not too rude or that his speed was not too dangerous. Conflict about *who* will do the fixing may also be engendered, as it was by two aspects of the Massachusetts law in effect when my study was conducted. The chief had the choice of whether or not to give Registry ticket books to his men, and the decision whether to take a violator to court had to be made by the chief or by "an officer of a rank not lower than sergeant," not by the arresting officer.[3] Earlier I pointed out that only 28 of the 180 police chiefs gave Registry ticket books to their men; chiefs also varied in encouraging or even permitting their men to *suggest* the recommendations to be made on individual tickets. Patrolmen were angry that they were not given Registry books, and many cited instances in which recommendations they had suggested were ignored by the chief, who either downgraded requests for court summonses or upgraded suggested warnings.

While collecting information on ticketing in Massachusetts, I asked over one hundred chiefs for opinions regarding a bill then pending before the legislature which would (1) require every chief to give Registry books to his men and (2) allow the arresting officer to decide whether the motorist would receive a summons or a warning. About two thirds opposed the bill. Some of their arguments sounded farfetched: "It's hard to write a ticket in the rain." "Some of my men have poor penmanship." "Some tickets might get lost if they are carried around." "The ticket books are too heavy to carry around." Most of the chiefs, however, presented arguments founded on a basic distrust of their men. Back in 1960, "Police chiefs who opposed the no-fix system said the judgment of their officers in issuing tickets is not always

3. Mass. G.L. Ch. 90C §2.

good; and there are times when they have to overrule them. They feel, therefore, that this discretion should remain with department heads."[4] In 1965, the arguments were almost identical. "Some of our men have bad judgment." "If I couldn't control things in my office, those guys would be fixing tickets out on the street." "If we gave them the Registry books, they would conduct vendettas." And, finally, "If I gave them the chance, they would ticket all of my friends." The lineup of witnesses testifying on the 1965 no-fix bill showed the chief-patrolman split: the lobbyist for the Chiefs' Association opposed the bill; the secretary of the Police Association supported it.

A final note should be added on the subject of ticket fixing: from all available evidence, fixing is almost identical in all parts of Massachusetts and thus bears no relationship to the frequency with which police forces *write* tickets. Interviews with policemen and politicians in high-enforcement cities indicated that fixing there followed the same pattern as in the low-enforcement cities. Even more surprising is the fact that policemen on forces whose chiefs urged ticket writing felt no greater dislike of their chiefs' fixing preferences than patrolmen on the low-enforcement forces. Even the traffic men who wrote over a thousand tickets apiece in 1964 felt free to request fixes for their friends and relatives.

If traffic officers know that their chief fixes tickets and refuses to give them the Registry ticket books, why do they write tickets? The answer is that they seem to dissociate fixing from departmental pressures to write (or not write) tickets. From their limited contacts with policemen in other cities, they know that other chiefs fix tickets and refuse to give out the books. "Sure, the chief fixes," one traffic man said, "but I don't think he's as bad as some other chiefs." The answer to the question of why fixing does not bother the traffic men seems to be that they accept fixing as something that *all* chiefs do; as long as their chief does not fix a ticket in which they are *particularly* interested (when the motorist was offensive, say), they see no troublesome conflict—their day's work, to borrow a phrase used earlier, is over once the tickets have been written.

Ticket fixing, then, shows another dimension of the political context in which police chiefs must view traffic-law enforcement. While there are few general pressures against enforcement (other than budget restrictions), the chief must be prepared for calls to fix individual tickets. Although this gives him an opportunity to make friends and to

4. "Legislators Support No-Fix," *Boston Herald*, March 13, 1960.

build up his bargaining power when other needs arise, it can also put him in a position where he makes enemies. I quoted above the statement of a small-town police chief who had to strike a balance between townspeople and patrolmen; an order to fix a ticket falling in the "gray area" on the scale of "fixability" can antagonize members of the police force. A general willingness to fix tickets can also at times antagonize politicians. As one captain summarized his experience, "They always forget that you've fixed nine tickets for them if you have to say no to the tenth request."

ORGANIZED CRIME IN COURT

Nicholas Gage

On Sept. 8, 1967, Paul Vahio, who is listed by the Justice Department as a captain in the Mafia family of the late Thomas Luchese, pleaded guilty before Supreme Court Justice Domenic S. Rinaldi to commercial bribery of a police officer.

Vario, whose criminal record dates back to 1925 and includes a conviction for rape, could have been given up to a year in jail. Instead, Judge Rinaldi fined him $250.

On the same day Justice Rinaldi sentenced Luis Guzman, 19 years old, to up to five years at Elmira Reformatory for robbing a drugstore in Huntington, L. I.

Vario is not the only Mafioso who has fared better than ordinary defendants in New York State courts.

Last year the State Joint Legislative Committee on Crime conducted a study of 1,762 cases in state courts in the years 1960 through 1969 involving organized crime figures, including Vario.

The committee, whose chairman is Senator John H. Hughes of Syracuse, found that the rate of dismissals and acquittals for racketeers was five times that of other defendants.

In New York City, 44.7 per cent of indictments against members of

Originally published as "Study Shows Courts Lenient With Mafiosi," *The New York Times*, September 25, 1972. Copyright © 1972 by the New York Times Company. Reprinted by permission.

organized crime were dismissed by Supreme Court judges during the 10-year period. Only 11.5 per cent of indictments against all defendants were dismissed, according to the study.

In 193 instances where organized crime figures were actually convicted, the study showed that judges let the defendants off with suspended sentences or fines in 46 per cent of the cases.

In order to determine some of the factors in the wide discrepancy between the treatment of racketeers and ordinary defendants in the courts, *The New York Times* during the last six weeks has investigated the handling of several of these cases as well as more recent ones that have come before state courts in the metropolitan area.

One case in which an organized crime figure fared well in court involved an imaginative swindle that netted over $1-million during a six-week period in 1963. Counterfeit checks of Mays Department Store in Brooklyn were made out to fictional suppliers of Mays at banks where swindlers had previously established accounts for the bogus suppliers.

Seven persons were indicted in the swindle on charges of grand larceny and forgery. One of the seven, Salvatore Agro, was connected to the Mafia. According to information from investigations of the principals involved in the swindle, the person who devised the scheme, Herman Witt, borrowed $30,000 from a Mafia lieutenant to start the bank accounts used to cash the counterfeit Mays checks, and Agro was assigned to look after the investment.

In 1966, all seven defendants pleaded guilty to lesser charges before Justice Rinaldi, the same judge who had fined Vario, and he sentenced six of them to prison terms. Agro, the reputed Mafioso, was given a suspended sentence by Judge Rinaldi and walked out of the courtroom a free man.

In a telephone interview last week, Justice Rinaldi, who has been on the Supreme Court, Second District, since 1962, was asked about the sentencing of both Agro and Vario.

He said he could not remember the Vario case at all, which came before him while he was sitting in Suffolk County rather than in Brooklyn, his regular assignment. "I must have handled 200 cases for them out there that year," he said. "I don't remember any of them."

The judge said he did remember the Agro case. "There were several defendants in that one and I gave all of them but Agro time," he said. "His charge was reduced to a misdemeanor, which the prosecution went along with, and the probation report showed no previous record for him."

The assistant district attorney in charge of the case, Edward Panzarella, apparently concurred with the judge's decision. He later signed a report saying that the pleas "in each instance are recommended and the sentence will in all respects be adequate."

He said in the report that Agro was "the least culpable" of the defendants. "Salvatore Agro is 38 years old and has no prior record," Mr. Panzarella wrote.

However, during the police investigation of the case, detectives taped conversations between Witt, who devised the swindle, and Agro. In those tapes, which were made available to Mr. Panzarella, Agro stated that he was fully involved in the swindle and that he was close to leading Mafiosi in New York.

"First of all, the people, the big people in New York, knew about this score, the Mays score. . . ." Argo told Witt in one of the tapes "They financed—gave me the money—for this [obscenity] thing."

Moreover, *The Times* discovered in the course of its investigation that, contrary to what Mr. Panzarella said in his report, Agro did have a previous record.

The files of the Federal courthouse in Buffalo show that on March 6, 1953, Agro pleaded guilty to conspiracy to deal in narcotics and received a year's sentence.

Mr. Panzarella is no longer with the Brooklyn District Attorney's office. He resigned after it was disclosed that he had failed to prosecute a city correction officer arrested with more than $200,000 worth of cocaine. He could not be reached for comment.

The Agro case illustrates that in some instances lenient treatment given organized-crime figures by a judge is approved by the prosecutor involved. But even when the prosecutor resists such treatment, racketeers can wind up doing very well in the courts.

On Sept. 24, 1971, Vincent DeCicco, listed by the police as a member of the Mafia family of Carlo Gambino, was convicted of contempt of a Brooklyn grand jury for failing to testify after being given immunity.

Joseph R. Corco, a Supreme Court justice in the Second District, threw out the verdict and dismissed the indictment against DeCicco on the ground that the District Attorney had not explained properly the immunity given him before the grand jury.

Eugene Gold, the Brooklyn District Attorney since 1969, appealed Justice Corso's ruling and the Appellate Division unanimously reversed the judge, reinstating the indictment and restoring the guilty verdict.

When DeCicco came before the court for sentencing, Justice Corso had before him a written recommendation from the Probation Department that DeCicco be sentenced to a year in jail. The recommendation was based in part on DeCicco's record, which went back to 1931 and included a conviction for robbery.

The judge instead sentenced him to three months and at the time offered the following explanation for the sentence:

"On Aug. 2 of 1971 I had a discussion with one of the top men in the Probation Department and I know he did not swear me into secrecy, nor did he say that our conversation was a confidential matter, and I made a notation on Aug. 2, 1971, that this individual, high up in the Probation Department, felt that a one year sentence was entirely too rough and he made a different recommendation."

Last week Justice Corso said that after getting the original recommendation of a year from the Probation Department he "heard that other judges had given lesser sentences in similar cases" and he called the department to ask about its recommendation on DeCicco.

A probation supervisor, whose identity he said he was not at liberty to disclose, told him that one year was too much and that 30 days to three months would be adequate, Justice Corso said.

Of course judges and prosecutors are not the only factors that influence the treatment of organized-crime figures in the courts. "Obviously the skill of counsel is one reason racketeers do better," said Richard Kuh, a former assistant district attorney in Manhattan. "They can afford better lawyers."

Many organized-crime figures favor a small group of criminal lawyers who are usually busy with cases in a number of courts. They are often so busy that they request repeated postponements for their clients and judges usually grant them. Meanwhile, witnesses may develop faulty memories or change their stories or even disappear.

A classic example of such a case involved Carmine Persico, who is listed by the Justice Department as a captain in the Mafia family of Joseph A. Colombo Sr.

Persico was indicted on 37 counts of extortion, coercion, usury and conspiracy early in 1969 along with two other defendants, Joseph Winograd and his wife, Sylvia.

The star witness in the case was Samuel Lessner, an associate of the Winograds in their loan-sharking operation. Persico, the state charged, was a silent partner in the operation.

Persico was arraigned on Feb. 28, 1969, before Justice Charles Marks, a Supreme Court judge who has since retired. At that time

Samuel Yasgur, who was prosecuting the case, made a strong plea to the judge to set a target date for trial. Mr. Yasgur said that the factor of witness intimidation was great in this particular case and would increase with any delays in the trial.

Justice Marks refused to set a target date and in the next 30 months, attorneys for the defendants were granted 25 adjournments, for the most part because they were busy in other courts.

On April 30, 1969, the star witness, Samuel Lessner, disappeared. He was last seen being escorted into an automobile by Persico's bodyguard, Jerry Langella, according to the prosecution.

The trial finally started last November and the presiding judge, George Postel, became the subject of a legal debate when he barred the press from it. He was criticized later for the ruling by the Court of Appeals, which said it violated the free press guarantee of the First Amendment.

During the trial Judge Postel made a ruling that the prosecution said undermined whatever case it had left on Persico after the disappearance of Mr. Lessner.

Judge Postel quashed a subpoena served on Harry Solowey, a vice president of the newspaper *El Diario*, who had been expected to testify about a meeting he had requested with Persico to discuss a loan he had received from other lenders.

The judge acted on the ground that the detective who had served the subpoena had not given Mr. Solowey the statutory $2 witness fee. The general custom at the time was to give the witness the fee after he had testified.

When detectives next tried to serve Mr. Solowey with a subpoena and give him a fee, he had disappeared. Shortly after the trial ended he returned home.

Mr. Yasgur, the prosecutor, feels that all the witnesses would have been at the trial and would have testified accurately if it had been scheduled early. Moreover, he said that the practice of some judges giving defense lawyers adjournments stretching over several years to accommodate their schedules consistently undermined cases against organized-crime figures.

"If every racketeer in the city went to one lawyer, would we have to wait 30 years to bring them to trial?" Mr. Yasgur said. "It's absurd."

He believes defense counsels should be required by judges to commit themselves to be ready for trial within a specified period when they file a notice of appearance in a case.

Told of these comments, Maurice Edelbaum, Persico's lawyer, said that he felt "cases now move along pretty well." When delays occur, he said, "they are caused just as often by prosecutors."

In another case involving a Mafia figure, the defense counsel was granted repeated delays over an 18-month period by several judges. But the first time the prosecutor asked for a postponement, the presiding judge dismissed the indictment against the defendant.

The case involved Frank Cangiano, listed by the police as a member of the Genovese Mafia family who was indicted on April 15, 1970, for criminal possession of forged instruments.

Cangiano pleaded not guilty and in the next year and a half his trial was adjourned more than a dozen times at the request of Cangiano's lawyer.

When the case was called for trial on Oct. 12, 1971, before Justice John A. Monteleone, the prosecution asked for a short delay to handle another case about to go to trial in the same court.

Judge Monteleone refused to grant the adjournment. At that point the defense counsel made a motion to dismiss the indictment for failure to prosecute and the judge granted it.

Judge Monteleone said last week that on Oct. 4, 1971, he had told both sides that the case had dragged on too long and they had to be ready for trial on Oct. 12.

When the time arrived, the prosecution wanted another date set, he said. "Basically it was a question of who runs the calendar—the judge or the District Attorney."

The judge said he did not consider the fact that the prosecution had not asked for adjournments previously, while the defense had received a number of them, because other judges had granted those adjournments. "I made the same demands on both sides," he said.

District Attorney Gold appealed the dismissal of the indictment and the Appellate Division reinstated it unanimously. The case is pending.

The appellate court held that the judge had the power to run the calendar, but judge Monteleone "improvidently exercised" that power when he dismissed the indictment.

Even when the prosecution prevails in spite of repeated delays, the result is not always a jail sentence for those involved in organized crime.

On Feb. 2, 1965, Matthew Ianniello, listed by the police as a member of the Mafia family of the late Vito Genovese, was indicted for contempt of a grand jury in Manhattan. He pleaded not guilty and a year later the indictment was dismissed by Justice Marks.

The office of District Attorney Frank S. Hogan appealed the ruling and two years later the Court of Appeals unanimously reversed Justice Marks.

During the next three years Ianniello's counsel, the ubiquitous Mr. Edelbaum, sought and received 39 adjournments from the court. The case finally came to trial on April 16, 1971, and Ianniello was convicted.

When he came before the court for sentencing, Mr. Edelbaum pointed out that Ianniello was a good family man, had served honorably in World War II and the indictment against him was an old one. He suggested to Justice Harold Birns, who had presided at the trial, that Ianniello receive a fine for his offense.

The prosecutor, Assistant District Attorney Kenneth Conboy, pointed out that the delay in the case was entirely attributable to the defendant and his counsel.

However, Justice Birns, a former prosecutor in Mr. Hogan's office, was not swayed. "In assessing punishment of the defendant's conduct I must take into consideration the defendant's personal life, also the fact that the offense occurred seven years ago," he said. Judge Birns then gave Ianniello a one year suspended sentence.

Justice Birns said last week that he had based the sentence on a probation report on Ianniello's background, and he indicated that several members of the jury had recommended leniency after finding Ianniello guilty—a fact disclosed in the court record.

However, the record also shows that during the selection of the jury, Judge Birns himself told jurors that imposing the penalty was not to be their concern because most factors involved in sentencing were outside their competence.

A fact that emerged from the *Times* investigation is that some lawyers handling organized-crime cases are able to achieve consistently good results before certain judges. Attorney Joseph Aronstein, for example, has been particularly successful with motions and writs submitted before Justice Gerald P. Culkin.

In 1962 Justice Culkin granted a motion filed by Mr. Aronstein to dismiss gambling charges against Joseph Gentile, listed by the police as a member of the Mafia family then headed by Joseph Profaci.

In 1966, Justice Culkin granted a writ of habeas corpus filed by Mr. Aronstein for David Betillo, a lieutenant of Lucky Luciano who had been convicted of 62 counts of compulsory prostitution in 1936 and later returned to prison for violation of parole.

In 1968, Justice Culkin ordered a hearing on a writ of error filed by Mr. Aronstein on behalf of Samuel Kass, who alleged that his 1951 guilty plea to selling narcotics had been coerced. The same allegations had been raised on earlier petitions and had been turned down without a hearing.

These favorable rulings, all three of which were reversed by higher courts, are among half a dozen granted by Justice Culkin on Mr. Aronstein's cases.

The rulings aroused comment in the criminal justice community because they were based on questionable legal grounds and because of Justice Culkin's close friendship with Mr. Aronstein, who is now under indictment for allegedly offering a policeman a bribe to change his testimony against a client.

The lawyer and Justice Culkin have dined together for many years on an almost weekly basis at the Tough Club, a private social club at 343 West 14th Street. The judge is a trustee and Mr. Aronstein has served as first vice president of the club.

In 1971 District Attorney Hogan, in a rare action, publicly criticized Judge Culkin for a ruling in a case concerning the corruption of police by organized crime.

Justice Culkin had dismissed a criminal contempt indictment against Francis X. Ward, a police lieutenant, later dismissed from the force, who was cited for being evasive to a grand jury after being given immunity. The lieutenant was being questioned about his relationship with Hugh Mulligan, the reputed bookmaker and loan shark.

Justice Culkin held that the evasiveness had been the product of "apparent confusion" on the part of Mr. Ward. Mr. Hogan said the judge "either misread the record or chooses to ignore it."

Shortly afterward, Supreme Court Justice Xavier C. Riccobono dismised a criminal contempt indictment against Mulligan himself.

Both rulings were appealed by Mr. Hogan and he was successful in winning reversals in higher courts. The Ward case is still pending. Mulligan was convicted and sentenced to three years in prison by Justice Myles J. Lane.

Mulligan appealed again and he went before Justice Culkin last December to ask that he be released on bail pending the outcome. Assistant District Attorney Conboy asked that Mulligan be remanded to jail noting that the Court of Appeals already had ruled on substantive issues in the case and that the defendant had defied a grand jury on a major investigation involving police investigation.

Justice Culkin released Mulligan on $5,000 bail. "We are not going to stop corruption by putting in a fellow today," he said. "He is not running a house of some kind that is open to the public and everybody is getting corrupted."

Justice Culkin, a short, stout man with a strong interest in horticulture and politics—his father was a power in Tammany Hall for many years—is one of the most talked about judges in the city among lawyers and prosecutors.

An indication of his reputation was given several years ago in remarks made by Gussie Kleinman, a lawyer and an old friend of Justice Culkin, when she went to a Democratic district leader seeking support for the judge for a possible race for the Surrogate Court.

"Culkin has always been a party man," Miss Kleinman told the district leader, Charles Kinsolving, who taped the conversation. "If somebody from the club comes before him, he will find law to support him . . .

"Because some of his decisions look so radical, they figure he must have gotten something for it. But it's not true at all. Because he wouldn't make those decisions if he was really taking. You know what I mean?

"First of all he doesn't need the dough. But I would say this—if you come in front of him and you're a friend of his, he'll bend over backwards to find law to support you."

Justice Culkin is on vacation and could not be reached for comment.

Most state judges treat organized-crime figures leniently for certain offenses, such as gambling. While Federal courts give prison terms of up to several years when racketeers are convicted of felony gambling violations, judges in state courts give a few months in a small number of cases and fines in all the others.

For example, in the summer of 1969 Michael Yanicelli, an associate of Nicholas Rattenni, the reputed Mafia boss of Westchester County, was arrested with $36,000 in policy plays and $4,000 in cash in Eastchester, N. Y. While he was out on bail on that charge, he was arrested with $12,000 in policy plays and $6,000 in cash.

Last January he pleaded guilty to two counts of felony gambling charges for which he could have received up to eight years in prison. Instead, Judge Bruce C. Dean of Tompkins County, a visiting judge brought in to help dispose of the backlog of cases in Westchester County, sentenced Yanicelli to three months in jail and a fine of $1,000.

Judge Dean made the following statement to explain his sentence: "Gambling is a victimless crime and it cannot be claimed that gambling laws protect morals when the State of New York operates its lotteries, New York City has its horse parlors and bingo is a household word."

Prior to the sentencing, Judge Dean wrote the District Attorney of

Westchester County, Carl Verigari, stating his projected sentence for Yanicelli.

Mr. Verigari called Judge Dean and complained about the sentence. He said he requested that Judge Dean disqualify himself from the case because of his predispositions to the gambling laws.

Later Judge Dean said that Mr. Verigari accused him of taking a "payoff" in the case but Mr. Verigari denied making such a charge.

Mr. Verigari has since appealed the case to the Court of Appeals.

The incident was not the first time Yanicelli received generous treatment in court. In 1953, he was convicted of bookmaking and sentenced to five days in jail. In 1962, he was arrested for bookmaking and for assaulting a police officer. He was given a one year suspended sentence on the assault charges and sentenced to three months in jail and a $500 fine on the gambling charges.

One reason many state judges are not as tough on organized-crime figures for gambling and certain other offenses, said Mr. Conboy, is that they deal so much with violent crimes.

"After the violence and the brutality they come to know day after day in their courtrooms, they may not see the more subtle offenses of racketeers with the same seriousness as Federal judges who don't deal with many violent cases," he said.

The "contract"—fix—is not unheard of in New York courts either, according to Maurice H. Nadjari, the special prosecutor named by Governor Rockefeller to combat corruption in the criminal justice system.

He said in an interview shortly before his appointment as special prosecutor last Tuesday that political influence is more likely to be used to arrange contracts rather than money.

"Our judges come up through political organizations and build up obligations along the way," said Mr. Nadjari, who was a prosecutor in Manhattan and in Suffolk County for 18 years. "At the same time racketeers cultivate political figures and when their people get in trouble they try to use whatever influence they have.

"The influence is not going to be stopped completely until we separate justice from politics," he said.

POLICE CORRUPTION
IN NEW YORK CITY

Knapp Commission

The Extent of Police Corruption

We found corruption to be widespread. It took various forms depending upon the activity involved, appearing at its most sophisticated among plainclothesmen assigned to enforcing gambling laws. In the five plainclothes divisions where our investigations were concentrated we found a strikingly standardized pattern of corruption. Plainclothesmen, participating in what is known in police parlance as a "pad," collected regular bi-weekly or monthly payments amounting to as much as $3,500 from each of the gambling establishments in the area under their jurisdiction, and divided the take in equal shares. The monthly share per man (called the "nut") ranged from $300 and $400 in midtown Manhattan to $1,500 in Harlem. When supervisors were involved they received a share and a half. A newly assigned plainclothesman was not entitled to his share for about two months, while he was checked out for reliability, but the earnings lost by the delay were made up to him in the form of two months' severance pay when he left the division.

Evidence before us led us to the conclusion that the same pattern existed in the remaining divisions which we did not investigate in depth. This conclusion was confirmed by events occurring before and after the period of our investigation. Prior to the Commission's existence, exposures by former plainclothesman Frank Serpico had led to indictments or departmental charges against nineteen plainclothesmen in a Bronx division for involvement in a pad where the nut was $800. After our public hearings had been completed, an investigation conducted by the Kings County District Attorney and the Department's

Extracted from Commission to Investigate Allegations of Police Corruption and the City's Anti-Corruption Procedures (Knapp Commission), *Commission Report*, pp.1–7, 74–77, 81–84, 89–93, 94–97. Some footnotes deleted.

Internal Affairs Division—which investigation neither the Commission nor its staff had even known about—resulted in indictments and charges against thirty-seven Brooklyn plainclothesmen who had participated in a pad with a nut of $1,200. The manner of operation of the pad involved in each of these situations was in every detail identical to that described at the Commission hearings, and in each almost every plainclothesman in the division, including supervisory lieutenants, was implicated.

Corruption in narcotics enforcement lacked the organization of the gambling pads, but individual payments—known as "scores"—were commonly received and could be staggering in amount. Our investigation, a concurrent probe by the State Investigation Commission and prosecutions by Federal and local authorities all revealed a pattern whereby corrupt officers customarily collected scores in substantial amounts from narcotics violators. These scores were either kept by the individual officer or shared with a partner and, perhaps, a superior officer. They ranged from minor shakedowns to payments of many thousands of dollars, the largest narcotics payoff uncovered in our investigation having been $80,000. According to information developed by the S.I.C. and in recent Federal investigations, the size of this score was by no means unique.

Corruption among detectives assigned to general investigative duties also took the form of shakedowns of individual targets of opportunity. Although these scores were not in the huge amounts found in narcotics, they not infrequently came to several thousand dollars.

Uniformed patrolmen assigned to street duties were not found to receive money on nearly so grand or organized a scale, but the large number of small payments they received present an equally serious if less dramatic problem. Uniformed patrolmen, particularly those assigned to radio patrol cars, participated in gambling pads more modest in size than those received by plainclothes units and received regular payments from construction sites, bars, grocery stores and other business establishments. These payments were usually made on a regular basis to sector car patrolmen and on a haphazard basis to others. While individual payments to uniformed men were small, mostly under $20, they were often so numerous as to add substantially to a patrolman's income. Other less regular payments to uniformed patrolmen included those made by after-hours bars, bottle clubs, tow trucks, motorists, cab drivers, parking lots, prostitutes and defendants wanting to fix their cases in court. Another practice found to be widespread was the payment of gratuities by policemen to other policemen to expedite normal police procedures or to gain favorable assignments.

Sergeants and lieutenants who were so inclined participated in the same kind of corruption as the men they supervised. In addition, some sergeants had their own pads from which patrolmen were excluded.

Although the Commission was unable to develop hard evidence establishing that officers above the rank of lieutenant received payoffs, considerable circumstantial evidence and some testimony so indicated. Most often when a superior officer is corrupt, he uses a patrolman as his "bagman" who collects for him and keeps a percentage of the take. Because the bagman may keep the money for himself, although he claims to be collecting for his superior, it is extremely difficult to determine with any accuracy when the superior actually is involved.

Of course, not all policemen are corrupt. If we are to exclude such petty infractions as free meals, an appreciable number do not engage in any corrupt activities. Yet, with extremely rare exceptions, even those who themselves engage in no corrupt activities are involved in corruption in the sense that they take no steps to prevent what they know or suspect to be going on about them.

It must be made clear that—in a little over a year with a staff having as few as two and never more than twelve field investigators— we did not examine every precinct in the Department. Our conclusion that corruption is widespread throughout the Department is based on the fact that information supplied to us by hundreds of sources within and without the Department was consistently borne out by specific observations made in areas we were able to investigate in detail.

The Nature and Significance of Police Corruption

Corruption, although widespread, is by no means uniform in degree. Corrupt policemen have been described as falling into two basic categories: "meat-eaters" and "grass-eaters." As the names might suggest, the meat-eaters are those policemen who, like Patrolman William Phillips who testified at our hearings, aggressively misuse their police powers for personal gain. The grass-eaters simply accept the payoffs that the happenstances of police work throw their way. Although the meat-eaters get the huge payoffs that make the headlines, they represent a small percentage of all corrupt policemen. The truth is, the vast majoriy of policemen on the take don't deal in huge amounts of graft.

And yet, grass-eaters are the heart of the problem. Their great numbers tend to make corruption "respectable." They also tend to encourage the code of silence that brands anyone who exposes corruption a traitor. At the time our investigation began, any policeman violating the code did so at his peril. The result was described in our interim report: "The rookie who comes into the Department is faced with the situation where it is easier for him to become corrupt than to remain honest."

More importantly, although meat-eaters can and have been individually induced to make their peace with society, the grass-eaters may be more easily reformed. We believe that, given proper leadership and support, many police who have slipped into corruption would exchange their illicit income for the satisfaction of belonging to a corruption-free Department in which they could take genuine pride.

The problem of corruption is neither new, nor confined to the police. Reports of prior investigations into police corruption, testimony taken by the Commission, and opinions of informed persons both within and without the Department make it abundantly clear that police corruption has been a problem for many years. Investigations have occurred on the average of once in twenty years since before the turn of the century, and yet conditions exposed by one investigation seem substantially unchanged when the next one makes its report. This doesn't mean that the police have a monopoly on corruption. On the contrary, in every area where police corruption exists it is paralleled by corruption in other agencies of government, in industry and labor, and in the professions.

Our own mandate was limited solely to the police. There are sound reasons for such a special concern with police corruption. The police have a unique place in our society. The policeman is expected to "uphold the law" and "keep the peace." He is charged with everything from traffic control to riot control. He is expected to protect our lives and our property. As a result, society gives him special powers and prerogatives, which include the right and obligation to bear arms, along with the authority to take away our liberty by arresting us.

Symbolically, his role is even greater. For most people, the policeman is the law. To them, the law is administered by the patrolman on the beat and the captain in the station house. Little wonder that the public becomes aroused and alarmed when the police are charged with corruption or are shown to be corrupt.

Departmental Attitudes Towards Police Corruption

Although this special concern is justified, public preoccupation with police corruption as opposed to corruption in other agencies of government inevitably seems unfair to the policeman. He believes that he is unjustly blamed for the results of corruption in other parts of the criminal justice system. This sense of unfairness intensifies the sense of isolation and hostility to which the nature of police work inevitably gives rise.

Feelings of isolation and hostility are experienced by policemen not just in New York, but everywhere. To understand these feelings one must appreciate an important characteristic of any metropolitan police department, namely an extremely intense group loyalty. When properly understood, this group loyalty can be used in the fight against corruption. If misunderstood or ignored, it can undermine anti-corruption activities.

Pressures that give rise to this group loyalty include the danger to which policemen are constantly exposed and the hostility they encounter from society at large. Everyone agrees that a policeman's life is a dangerous one, and that his safety, not to mention his life, can depend on his ability to rely on a fellow officer in a moment of crisis. It is less generally realized that the policeman works in a sea of hostility. This is true, not only in high crime areas, but throughout the City. Nobody, whether a burglar or a Sunday motorist, likes to have his activities interfered with. As a result, most citizens, at one time or another, regard the police with varying degrees of hostility. The policeman feels, and naturally often returns, this hostility.

Two principal characteristics emerge from this group loyalty: suspicion and hostility directed at any outside interference with the Department, and an intense desire to be proud of the Department. This mixture of hostility and pride has created what the Commission has found to be the most serious roadblock to a rational attack upon police corruption: a stubborn refusal at all levels of the Department to acknowledge that a serious problem exists.

The interaction of stubbornness, hostility and pride has given rise to the so-called "rotten-apple" theory. According to this theory, which bordered on official Department doctrine, any policeman found to be corrupt must promptly be denounced as a rotten apple in an otherwise clean barrel. It must never be admitted that his individual corruption may be symptomatic of underlying disease.

This doctrine was bottomed on two basic premises: First, the morale of the Department requires that there be no official recognition of corruption, even though practically all members of the Department know it is in truth extensive; second, the Department's public image and effectiveness require official denial of this truth.

The rotten-apple doctrine has in many ways been a basic obstacle to meaningful reform. To begin with, it reinforced and gave respectability to the code of silence. The official view that the Department's image and morale forbade public disclosure of the extent of corruption inhibited any officer who wished to disclose corruption and justified any who preferred to remain silent. The doctrine also made difficult, if not impossible, any meaningful attempt at managerial reform. A high command unwilling to acknowledge that the problem of corruption is extensive cannot very well argue that drastic changes are necessary to deal with that problem. Thus neither the Mayor's Office nor the Police Department took adequate steps to see that such changes were made when the need for them was indicated by the charges made by Officers Frank Serpico and David Durk in 1968. This was demonstrated in the Commission's second set of public hearings in December 1971.

Finally, the doctrine made impossible the use of one of the most effective techniques for dealing with any entrenched criminal activity, namely persuading a participant to help provide evidence against his partners in crime. If a corrupt policeman is merely an isolated rotten apple, no reason can be given for not exposing him the minute he is discovered. If, on the other hand, it is acknowledged that a corrupt officer is only one part of an apparatus of corruption, common sense dictates that every effort should be made to enlist the offender's aid in providing the evidence to destroy the apparatus.

✳   ✳   ✳

The Pad

The heart of the gambling payoff system was found to be the plainclothes "pad." In a highly systemized pattern, described to the Commission by numerous sources and verified during our investigation, plainclothesmen collected regular biweekly or monthly payoffs from gamblers on the first and fifteenth of each month, often at a meeting place some distance from the gambling spot and outside the immediate police precinct or division. The pad money was picked up at designated locations by one or more bagmen who were most often police officers but who occasionally were ex-policemen or civilians. The proceeds were then pooled and divided up among all or virtually all of the division's plainclothesmen, with each plainclothes patrolman receiving an equal share. Supervisory lieutenants who were on the pad customarily received a share and a half and, although the Commission was unable to document particular instances, any commanding officer who participated reportedly received two full shares. In addition, the bag-man received a larger cut, often an extra share, to compensate him for the risk involved in making his collections. Some bagmen made extra profits by telling gamblers there were more plainclothesmen in the divi-sion than there actually were, collecting shares for these non-existent men and pocketing the proceeds. Division plainclothesmen generally met once a month to divide up the money and to discuss matters con-cerning the pad—*i.e.*, inviting plainclothesmen newly assigned to the division to join, raising or lowering the amounts paid by various gam-blers, and so forth. A man newly assigned to plainclothes duty in a division would be put on the pad after he had been with the division for a specified period, usually two months, during which time the other members would check him out and make sure he was reliable. This loss of revenue was customarily made up to him when he was transferred out of the division at which time he would receive severance pay in the form of two months' payments after his transfer. Plainclothesmen who put a new gambling operation on the pad were entitled to keep the entire first month's payment as a finder's fee.

This pattern of collection and distribution appeared to Commission investigators to be quite standardized. It was evident in the four Man-hattan divisions and the one Queens division which were the focus of the Commission's investigation. Evidence of the same patterns was also turned up in the other Manhattan division and in one division each in Brooklyn and the Bronx, for a total of eight divisions out of the sixteen divisions and Staten Island. In addition, the Commission received alle-gations of similar pads in most of the other divisions in the City.

William Phillips, then recently assigned as a plainclothesman in the division covering lower Manhattan, testified on the basis of his own ex-periences and conversations with fellow plainclothesmen that the aver-age monthly share per man ranged from $400 to $500 in midtown Manhattan divisions, to $800 on the Upper West Side, $1,100 in lower Manhattan, and $1,500 in Harlem. He stated that the reported "nut" (share per man) in two Queens divisions was $600, that in the three Bronx divisions it was $600, $800, and $900, and that in one Brooklyn division it was $800. These figures corroborated quite precisely those received by the Commission from the many sources willing to talk privately but who did not want to take the risk of public testimony, and further corroboration has come from similar sources since the Commission's hearings.

The pad was a way of life in plainclothes. According to Patrolman

Phillips, the pad was openly and endlessly discussed whenever plainclothesmen got together. The Commission found no reason to doubt
Phillips' opinion, echoing that held by other knowledgeable police officers and informants: "In every division in every area of plainclothes
in the City, the same condition exists. There is a pad in every plainclothes precinct and division in the City of New York."

Revelations made before and after the Commission's investigation
bore out the consistent nature of plainclothes gambling pads. Prior to
the Commission's existence, Patrolman Frank Serpico told about his
experience in a Bronx plainclothes division in 1967 and 1968 and described an almost identical pattern of payoffs. In May, 1972, after the
Commission's hearings, Kings County District Attorney Eugene Gold
announced the indictment of virtually an entire division plainclothes
squad in Brooklyn, which collected payments from gamblers without
interruption during the Commission's public hearings in precisely the
same fashion being described by Commission witnesses. The indictments and related departmental charges involved a total of thirty-six
current and former plainclothesmen, twenty-four of whom were indicted. According to Mr. Gold, at one time twenty-four of twenty-five
plainclothesmen in the division were on the pad. It is highly significant
that this investigation was carried out without the Commission's
knowledge, and yet, like the information given by Frank Serpico, it
revealed a pattern of share payments, severance pay, and bagmen that
matched in detail the patterns described by Patrolman Phillips and
other Commission witnesses and informants.

The corrupting influence of gambling operations is not limited to
plainclothes. Gambling pads of various sorts were also found to exist
in the uniformed patrol force.

Generally, where such pads existed among uniformed men, the
sector car had its own pad, the sergeant theirs, and the desk lieutenant
and precinct commander had their own personal pads if they were so
disposed. (Precinct commanders who received graft almost always
designated a patrolman, "the captain's man," to make their pickups,
and in some instances, when a corrupt captain was transferred out and
an honest one took over, the captain's man continued to collect payments "for the captain" and kept the money.)

At the time of the investigation, certain precincts in areas with
widespread gambling had special gambling cars (patrol cars with the
words "gambling car" painted on them) to which two uniformed patrolmen were assigned with the ostensible mission of harassing gam-

blers. According to Phillips, these patrolmen were notorious for the extensiveness of their pads.

* * *

Gamblers were found to pay policemen amounts which varied according to the nature of their operations. One ambulatory runner, who moved from place to place in Harlem collecting bets in hairdressers' shops, candy stores, and apartment house hallways, paid $200 a month to division plainclothesmen while an operator of a permanent spot paid $600 a month. Another gambler, who ran a fixed spot, told the Commission he paid $750 a month to division plainclothes and $300 to borough, as well as $196 to the detective squad, $180 to the precinct sergeants, $60 to the precinct desk officers, $60 to the precinct gambling car when there was one, and $120 a week to the local patrol car, for a total of $1,600 a month. At another Harlem spot, several police cars stopped by every morning except Sunday* at around 7:00 a.m., and the lookout gave money to the patrolmen in the car.

When borough plainclothes squads were eliminated in February, 1971, Queens division plainclothesmen reportedly demanded, in addition to their own monthly share, the entire monthly share that had been going to borough plainclothes. Queens numbers operators held a meeting to discuss the demand and present a unified front. It was agreed that they would increase the monthly payment by an average of $200 to $300. According to one source, this meeting of numbers operators to resolve a common problem was most unusual in Queens, which the source stated was the only borough where policy operators did not have some sort of unity.

Uniformed men also scored gamblers on a catch-as-catch-can basis. Patrolman Droge testified about some well-known gamblers in one precinct he worked in, who used to drive around the precinct in a car. Police officers were constantly on the lookout for them, because it was their custom to throw $8 into a police car whenever they came across one.

In Queens, one gambler operating from a fixed spot told the Commission that he paid $2,100 a month, while the operator of a smaller game without a fixed location said that he paid $1,200, split evenly between division and borough. Another Queens gambler, whose spot was said to have been found for him by the police, reportedly paid

---

* There are no horse races on Sunday, and thus no numbers.

$1,750 a month for as long as he operated the spot. He later gave up the spot and changed his operation to an ambulatory one, whereupon the police lowered the price to $1,200 a month. Gamblers who operated without a spot often escaped making pad payments at the precinct level, although they were always subject to scores by men from the precinct.

In return for these payments, gamblers were protected from all police action at precinct, division, and borough levels, with the exception of occasional token arrests. These payments did not protect them from action by the Public Morals Administrative Division (PMAD) of the First Deputy Commissioner's office, a unit which Phillips said was generally feared by corrupt police officers. If PMAD made an arrest at a gambling spot, to protect themselves division and borough plainclothesmen would then make follow-up arrests at the same spot.

But there are indications that a partial pad may also have existed in PMAD involving some members of the unit. Patrolman Phillips, while working undercover for the Commission, was told by a plainclothes patrolman that arrangements could be made with PMAD to protect a gambling operation at least partially. In addition, a former controller in a Harlem combine stated that he had been approached by a PMAD plainclothesman who sought to put him on what he said was a PMAD pad. The gambler refused even to discuss the pad with the plainclothesman until he had had him checked out by other plainclothesmen he knew, because he wanted to make sure that the PMAD plainclothesman was not setting him up for a possible bribery case. The check indicated that the plainclothesman was corrupt and he put the gambler on what he claimed was a PMAD pad for $185 a month with $25 extra for himself.

Most often, when plainclothesmen needed a token arrest to meet arrest quotas or to give the appearance of activity, they would tell the operator of a spot and arrange a time and place for the arrest. The operator would then select someone to take the arrest, who was usually either one of his employees who had a relatively clean arrest record or an addict who was paid for his trouble. Whoever took the arrest would put a handful of bogus policy slips in his pocket and meet the plainclothesman at the designated time and place, where, often as not, he would get into their car without even waiting to be asked.

Alternatively, when police needed a gambling arrest, they would pick up someone known to them as a gambler and plant phony numbers slips on him (a practice known as "flaking"), then arrest him. They were rather casual about this, sometimes flaking bookmakers with number slips or numbers runners with bookmaking records, a practice which infuriated the gamblers more than being arrested. When police decided to score gamblers, they would most often flake people with gambling slips, then demand $25 or $50 for not arresting them. Other times, they would simply threaten a flake and demand money. As mentioned above, they also scored people after arrest by offering to change their testimony at trial. When this happened, the take was higher, usually several hundred dollars.

Another method plainclothesman used to score gamblers was to arrest a gambler, then take money from him for writing up the arrest affidavit in such a way that he would be acquitted. If, for instance, the arresting officer stated he found numbers slips *near* the suspect, perhaps on a radiator or a counter, rather than on his person, defense counsel could make a motion for dismissal and the judge would have no choice but to throw out the case. At other times, officers would make their complaints sufficiently vague so that acquittal or conviction depended on their testimony at trial. One such affidavit reads, "Deponent states that the Defendant had in his possession *on a counter* [emphasis added] in the said premises a total of 118 slips of paper bearing a total of 842 plays MRHP [mutuel racehorse policy] with amounts wagered and identities." When officers had filed ambiguous affidavits like the one above, they would often score the suspect for whatever they could get, then change their testimony so that he was acquitted.

Another common method of scoring numbers operators consisted of policemen confiscating the gambler's numbers slips, which are known as "work." The police officer would then offer to sell the work back to the gambler. Such scores generally involved sizable amounts of money, because it is vitally important to the operator to have his work, so that he can know who the winners are in the day's play and pay them—and only them. If a police officer kept the work, many players would claim that they had the winning number, and the numbers operator would have to pay them all off at 600–1, or not pay any of them, which would ruin his future business since he would get a reputation for welshing on bets.

In his testimony at the public hearings, ex-Patrolman Waverly Logan described an incident in which two uniformed officers walked up to a policy bank and simply rang the bell, whereupon the operator opened the door. The two officers then arrested the banker and took him to the precinct house, where he was booked. Logan testified that

plainclothes officers at the precinct said they had known all along where
the bank was and were just waiting to raid it.

*   *   *

Comments

The most obvious effect of gambling corruption is the fact that gambling operations all over the City are allowed to operate openly and
almost completely unhindered by police action. For most people, who
do not regard gambling as a great moral evil, this in itself is not particularly alarming. What is alarming is that plainclothes units serve as
an important breeding ground for large-scale corruption in other areas
of the Department. Some officers who have managed to stay honest
before being assigned to plainclothes are initiated into corrupt practices while in plainclothes units and go on to practice what they
learned there for the rest of their tenure in the Department. Others,
who have indulged in minor corruption before assignment to plainclothes, learn how to expand their activities.

But perhaps the most important effect of corruption in the so-called
gambling control units is the incredible damage their performance
wreaks on public confidence in the law and the police. Youngsters
raised in New York ghettos, where gambling abounds, regard the law
as a joke when all their lives they have seen police officers coming and
going from gambling establishments and taking payments from gamblers. Many ghetto people who have grown up watching police performance in relation to gambling and narcotics are absolutely convinced
that all policemen are getting rich on their share of the profits of these
two illegal activities. While it is certainly not true that all police officers, or even a majority, get rich on gambling and narcotics graft, the
fact that a large number of citizens believe they do has a tremendously
damaging effect on police authority.

The Department announced in January, 1972, that, as of February
1, anti-gambling enforcement efforts would be concentrated on high-
level figures in gambling combines and that low-level runners would
no longer be arrested except when complaints were received. In another move to limit opportunities for corruption, the Department also
laid down the rule that uniformed patrolmen may no longer make
gambling arrests unless a superior officer is present.

The Commission feels that these are eminently sensible reforms
insofar as they will tend to limit corruption. However, gambling is tra-

ditional and entrenched in many neighborhoods, and it has broad public support. In view of these factors and the severe corruption hazard posed by gambling, the Commission feels that gambling—including numbers and bookmaking—should be legalized. To the extent that the legislature feels that the state should impose controls on gambling, such regulation should be by civil rather than criminal process.

Narcotics

Police officers have been involved in activities such as extortion of money and/or narcotics from narcotics violators in order to avoid arrest; they have accepted bribes; they have sold narcotics. They have known of narcotics violations and have failed to take proper enforcement action. They have entered into personal associations with narcotics criminals and in some cases have used narcotics. They have given false testimony in court in order to obtain dismissal of the charges against a defendant.
—Donald F. Cawley, Commander, Inspections Division
Testifying before the State Commission of Investigation, April, 1971.

Corruption in narcotics law enforcement has grown in recent years to the point where high-ranking police officials acknowledge it to be the most serious problem facing the Department. In the course of its investigation, the Commission became familiar with each of the practices detailed by Chief Cawley, as well as many other corrupt patterns, including:

Keeping money and/or narcotics confiscated at the time of an arrest or raid.

Selling narcotics to addict-informants in exchange for stolen goods.

Passing on confiscated drugs to police informants for sale to addicts.

"Flaking" or planting narcotics on an arrested person in order to have evidence of a law violation.

"Padding," or adding to the quantity of narcotics found on an arrested person in order to upgrade an arrest.

Storing narcotics, needles and other drug paraphernalia in police lockers.

Illegally tapping suspects' telephones to obtain incriminating evidence to be used either in making cases against the suspects, or to blackmail them.

Purporting to guarantee freedom from police wiretaps for a monthly service charge.

Accepting money or narcotics from suspected narcotics law violators as payment for the disclosure of official information.

Accepting money for registering as police informants persons who were in fact giving no information and falsely attributing leads and arrests to them, so that their "cooperation" with the police may win them amnesty for prior misconduct.

Financing heroin transactions.

In addition to these typical patterns, the Commission learned of numerous individual instances of narcotics-related corrupt conduct on the part of police officers, such as:

Determining the purity and strength of unfamiliar drugs they had seized by giving small quantities to addict-informants to test on themselves.

Introducing potential customers to narcotics pushers.

Revealing the identity of a government informant to narcotics criminals.

Kidnapping critical witnesses at the time of trial to prevent them from testifying.

Providing armed protection for narcotics dealers.

Offering to obtain "hit men" to kill potential witnesses.

There is a traditional unwritten rule among policemen that narcotics graft is "dirty" money not acceptable even to those who take "clean" money from gamblers, bar owners, and the like. However, more relaxed attitudes toward drugs, particularly among young people, and the enormous profits to be derived from drug traffic have combined to make narcotics-related payoffs more acceptable to more and more policemen. According to officers in the Narcotics Division, the widespread narcotics corruption in the unit was well known to both the men and their superiors, all of whom tolerated it at least to the extent that they took no action against those known to be corrupt.

✻   ✻   ✻

Patterns of Corruption in Narcotics Law Enforcement

The most common form of narcotics-related police corruption is not the systematic pad common in other areas such as gambling, but the individual score of money, narcotics, or both, seized at the scene of a raid or arrest.

Extortion and Bribe-Taking

In many cases police officers actively extort money and/or drugs from suspected narcotics law violators. Recently, for example, the motel room of a "dealer" (actually a federal undercover agent who was recording the conversation) was raided by two detectives and one patrolman. They found $12,000 in cash on the premises and demanded that the "dealer" surrender $10,000 to avoid arrest. The "dealer" was finally able to persuade them to leave him $4,000 as getaway money. The detectives later paid a $1,000 finder's fee to another detective who had alerted them to the "dealer's" presence in town.

In June, 1972, a dismissed plainclothesman who had been assigned to the Narcotics Division was convicted in New York County and sentenced to up to four years in prison for his part in an extortion scheme which involved six members of the Narcotics Division. According to testimony at the trial, he and two other police officers contacted a restaurant owner and demanded $6,000, threatening to arrest his daughter-in-law on a narcotics charge unless he paid them. They further theatened to send the woman's two children to a foundling home in the event of her arrest. The restaurant owner paid them what they asked.

Within a few months, the same policeman, along with some other members of the unit, again approached the man and demanded an additional $12,000. The man told them to return in a few days, and in the interim he arranged for police surveillance of the next transaction. The plainclothesman was arrested when he accepted a down payment in marked money.

Two of the Commission's informants in the narcotics area were hard-core heroin addicts who, as registered police informants, were able to witness and sometimes record many instances of police profiteering on the street level. While these informants' credibility is necessarily suspect, there is ample evidence from other sources that the extortion practices they described were common occurrences in the Narcotics Division at the time of the Commission's investigation.

They told of participation in police shakedowns of narcotics "cribs" and said that it was standard practice for an informant to find a location where drugs were being sold in large quantities, and by attempting to make a buy with a large denomination bill, to induce the seller to reveal the hiding place of his cash supply. (Sellers in stationary locations try to keep as little money as possible on their person in order to minimize losses in case of an arrest or shakedown.) On leaving, the informant would arrange to return later to make another buy. On his next visit, as the seller opened the door, the police would crash in behind the informant. If the police felt they could score without risk, they would take whatever money and narcotics were available and let the seller go. If the amount of money was small, they would usually arrest the seller but still keep most of the narcotics, turning in only the amount necessary to charge a felony or misdemeanor as the case might be.

The informants stated that three out of every four times they went out on a raid with plainclothesmen from the Narcotics Division, no arrests were made and scores ranged from a few hundred dollars to as much as $20,000 on one occasion, with the informants getting some money and quantities of drugs as compensation.

The Commission found that, even without prompting from the police, it was quite common for an apprehended suspect to offer to pay his captors for his release and for the right to keep part of his narcotics and cash. This was especially true at higher levels of distribution where the profits to be made and the penalties risked by a dealer were very high. One such case was that of a suspended Narcotics Division detective who was recently indicted in Queens County and charged with taking bribes to overlook narcotics offenses. The indictment alleged that this officer accepted $1,500 on one occasion for not arresting a suspected drug pusher who was apprehended while in possession of $15,000 worth of heroin. There is evidence that on another occasion this detective was paid $4,000 by a different narcotics pusher for agreeing not to confiscate $150,000 worth of heroin. The detective has pleaded guilty to attempting to receive a bribe, and his sentence is pending.

Even after arrest, a suspect would sometimes try to pay the arresting officer to leave him enough money for his legal expenses, or to downgrade the arrest by holding back a large part of the seized narcotics, or to make sure that his case would be a "throw-out" in court. Police officers have accomplished this favor by writing up an ambiguous complaint which did not explicitly link the evidence seized in the arrest to the defendant. For example, an officer's affidavit could aver that narcotics had been discovered not on the defendant's person, but on the ground near his feet. In such a case, of course, the evidence would be inadmissible against the defendant and the case would be thrown out.

The opportunity for an arresting officer to score does not end at the scene of an arrest. As suspended patrolman William Phillips told the Commission in the course of his testimony about similar fixed arrest affidavits in gambling cases, "It's never too late to do business." That is, a police officer who is skillful or experienced enough can write an affidavit which appears to be very strong, but is still open-ended enough to work in favor of a defendant when coupled with appropriate testimony from the arresting officer. For example, an officer could state in his complaint that the suspect threw the evidence to the ground at the approach of the police. Should that officer later testify that he lost sight of the evidence as it fell, the evidence and the case could well be dismissed. The Commission learned that it was not uncommon for defense attorneys in narcotics cases to pay policemen for such favors as lying under oath and procuring confidential police and judicial records concerning their clients' cases.

(4)

Government Contracts, Programs,

and Regulations

THE EXTENSIVE VARIETY of non-law-enforcement targets of corruption is examined in this chapter under the general headings of abusing government contracts, undermining government programs, and nullifying government regulations. City governments regularly perform a host of functions, any of which may be susceptible to corruption. Municipal authorities formulate policies and create the instruments to carry them out, enact regulations and establish the means for enforcing them, and continually contract for goods and services. Each of these activities creates opportunities for corruption. Moreover, the clear and consistent trend in the twentieth century has been for city governments to contract for ever-increasing goods and services, develop more programs with broader coverage, and regulate a myriad of activities previously thought beyond the purview of local government.[1] The duration of this century will likely witness even greater extensions of these functions with increased opportunities for corruption.

Abusing Contracts

City contracts are an appealing target for corruption. The stakes involved and the private gain to be made are sizable because the kinds of goods and services contracted for are almost limitless. Goods pur-

1. A good indicator of the amount of governmental activity is the size of local government expenditures. In 1971 it exceeded $100 billion. Bureau of the Census, *Governmental Finances in 1970–71* (Washington, D.C.: Government Printing Office, 1971), p.21.

chased by cities range from such incidentals as paper clips and pencils to major items like automobile fleets and street construction and repair materials. Contracted services similarly range from seemingly innocuous functions like stocking vending machines in city hall to vital ones like picking up trash and garbage throughout the city. City contracts additionally include the sale of used, outmoded, or surplus municipally owned materials.

Public officials have various motivations for abusing contracting procedures. Private financial gain for officeholders is one; it is commonly secured by awarding inflated contracts to firms which then kick back to the officeholder the amount by which the contract has been inflated—usually between 5 and 10 percent of the total. Or, elected officials concerned about securing future campaign contributions will award contracts to firms that will make "voluntary" contributions to party campaign coffers. These two motivations appear to be the most common; others include rewarding past friendships or encouraging future ones, nepotism, creating ill-defined debts that may later be cashed in, securing future job offers from contracting firms, and engendering support from groups within the community.

The primary motivation of firms is to insure their own economic well-being. Contracts may be obtained improperly by bribing city officials directly with cash, gifts, or other material favors; or indirectly through collusively arranging campaign contributions, inflating contracts with kickbacks to public authorities, and deliberately submitting low bids with the expectation of delivering shoddy goods and inadequate services. Additionally, a firm may attempt to obtain crucial information from public officials to enable it to submit the lowest bid and compromise the competitive bidding process.

Undermining Programs

Government programs provide a second target of corruption. Here the motivation may simply be theft from the public till. Outright stealing of funds from government programs periodically reaches scandalous proportions, discrediting the individuals involved and undermining public support for the affected programs. The communications media, prosecuting attorneys, and public officials most often direct the public's attention toward the offending individuals in cases of embezzlement, although in the long run the loss of legitimacy and support for the programs involved is more significant. The viability of government programs in this respect is dependent upon the probity of its personnel.

Government programs can be undermined by other forms of corruption with equally destructive consequences. A common device is to saturate the bureaucracy that administers the program with personnel chosen not on the formal basis of merit or technical competence but as a favor to friends, relatives, or political supporters, or to award jobs to the highest bidders. In another technique, public officials place their friends and supporters on the payrolls of private contractors responsible for carrying out publicly funded programs. While patronage employees are considerably fewer today than even ten years ago, their numbers remain significant.[2] More important, they tend to be less committed to fulfilling a program's mission than to furthering the good fortunes of particular officeholders or political parties. Programs become inefficient and ineffective when untrained and unskilled personnel are awarded jobs requiring standard levels of competence. This is most clearly the case when program funds are diverted to pay "ghost employees" or to provide for "no-show" jobs. But it also applies in the less dramatic abuses where the single criterion for appointment to the payroll is past party service. Even where minimal civil service requirements are in effect, programs may be undermined by allowing civil service jobs to go unfilled and appointing "temporary" employees who in effect become permanent by repeated reappointment.

At the highest level of governmental programs, within public policy-making boards, conflicts of interest may threaten to undermine the programs. Representatives of private interests are usually appointed to policy boards that govern programs directly affecting those interests because of their familiarity with complex and technical matters or their expressed concern and willingness to serve in positions carrying little prestige and even less direct monetary compensation. But the position of public trust can be used to private advantage. The frequency with which realtors are appointed to city planning boards, liquor retailers to city alcoholic beverage commissions, and contracting engineers to city public works boards illustrates the severity of the conflict-of-interest problem.

2. In the state of Indiana, for example, about 7,400 of the state's 12,000 employees are patronage workers, from whom the party in power extracts a mandatory two percent of their annual wages. In the presidential election year of 1972, forty-six percent (amounting to $375,000) of the total money received by the State Republican Central Committee came from patronage contributions.

Cash bribes to the municipal legislators who formulate policy or to the city administrators who implement it will guarantee that the program will service certain special interests. Policies may be purchased in less direct ways as well. Often campaign donations are given with the understanding that programs will be altered in directions favorable to the contributor's interests. Although this arrangement is not as immediate as a bribe, the program policies are effectively bought.

Nullifying Regulations

A final target of corruption considered in this chapter is regulations adopted by city governments. Officials responsible for enforcing prohibitions or strict limitations of particular goods and activities may be persuaded to ignore the restrictions, ease their application, or apply them in a discriminatory manner. Each official act represents a deviation from legal requirements and adds to the nullification of the regulations.

A host of regulations have been applied to two general areas. The first deals with questions of public morals. As was discussed in chapter 3, ordinances restricting the manufacture, sale, and use of alchohol and drugs and prohibiting prostitution and gambling are the most frequent regulations designed to preserve the moral climate of communities. But the withdrawal of these goods and activities creates unmet demands deriving from human needs and wants that are not easily satisfied. They may be fulfilled, however, by resorting to illicit means. Regulations are nullified when public officials or regulatory agencies ease restrictions, usually in return for money or other favors given by those who profit from providing the banned goods or those who partake of them.

Government regulations in a second area are intended to manage the orderly development of communities and usually deal with the physicial aspects of cities. They provide for the issuing of permits, licenses, zoning variances, and public franchises and the conducting of inspections, tax assessments, and compliance procedures. These regulations may be nullified either by totally ignoring them or by easing their enforcement. The officials or agencies responsible for enforcing them sometimes require payment of an illegal fee before they will approve permits or licenses; at other times they are approached by firms willing to purchase favorable action on their applications. Either way, in time discriminatory enforcement will create the expectation that applications will only be approved for a fee. Communities interested in rapid development may also let it be known that zoning restrictions will be easily waived and tax assessments lowered in order to attract outside firms to the city.

Even commoner than outright buying of permits, licenses, and franchises is the practice of making payments to expedite government action on applications, certifications, and compliance reviews. The responsibility for enforcing most physical regulations is lodged in municipal bureaucracies, institutions not widely esteemed for their rapidity of action. It might be argued that corruption of this variety has its advantages insofar as it provides faster service from usually lethargic municipal agencies, but expediting one application or inspection means assigning a lower priority to other (non-paying) applications or inspections. Moreover, bureaucratic personnel may deliberately slow down service after the initial payoff and create more red tape in order to establish additional inducements for others to make payments or to raise the ante.

In the first selection in this chapter, Steffens describes a case where bribery was used to secure a municipal franchise, showing how the business elite in St. Louis paid $300,000 to city councilmen to obtain rights-of-way covering the city's street railroads. Next, Costikyan's contemporary account of corruption in New York City argues that the political bosses of Steffens' day are no longer the primary agents for dispensing public largesse; rather, the locus of corruption has shifted to public officials free from machine control and to supposedly scrupulous civil servants. Dorman's selection deals with the extortion of funds in Newark, where businessmen had to kick back ten percent of the value of city contracts to city officials, and with the case of a high city administrator in New York City whose indebtedness to Mafia-linked figures led to kickbacks from and shakedowns of firms doing business with the city. In the fourth selection the Knapp Commission describes the extensive graft in New York City's construction industry, with permit and license regulations unenforced by police who have been paid off. The National Advisory Commission on Criminal Justice Standards and Goals shows how corruption affects government regulations in many more cities than just New York, and argues that if present arrangements remain in force this pattern is likely to increase in the future. The next selection deals with corruption in the poverty program. Finally, excerpts from the evidence against former Vice President Agnew show instances of corruption in construction contracts awarded in Baltimore County and the state of Maryland.

TWEED DAYS IN ST. LOUIS
Lincoln Steffens

One afternoon, late in January, 1903, a newspaper reporter, known as "Red" Galvin, called Mr. Folk's attention to a ten-line newspaper item to the effect that a large sum of money had been placed in a bank for the purpose of bribing certain Assemblymen to secure the passage of a street railroad ordinance. No names were mentioned, but Mr. Galvin surmised that the bill referred to was one introduced on behalf of the Suburban Railway Company. An hour later Mr. Folk sent the names of nearly one hundred persons to the sheriff, with instructions to subpœna them before the grand jury at once. The list included Councilmen, members of the House of Delegates, officers and directors of the Suburban Railway, bank presidents and cashiers. In three days the investigation was being pushed with vigor, but St. Louis was laughing at the "huge joke." Such things had been attempted before. The men who had been ordered to appear before the grand jury jested as they chatted in the anterooms, and newspaper accounts of these preliminary examinations were written in the spirit of burlesque.

It has developed since that Circuit Attorney Folk knew nothing, and was not able to learn much more during the first days; but he says he saw here and there puffs of smoke and he determined to find the fire. It was not an easy job. The first break into such a system is always difficult. Mr. Folk began with nothing but courage and a strong personal conviction. He caused peremptory summons to be issued, for the immediate attendance in the grand jury room of Charles H. Turner, president of the Suburban Railway, and Philip Stock, a representative of brewers' interests, who, he had reason to believe, was the legislative agent in this deal.

"Gentlemen," said Mr. Folk, "I have secured sufficient evidence to warrant the return of indictments against you for bribery, and I shall

Originally published in *The Shame of the Cities*, 1904. Reprint (New York: Doubleday, 1966), pp.27–40.

prosecute you to the full extent of the law and send you to the penitentiary unless you tell to this grand jury the complete history of the corruptionist methods employed by you to secure the passage of Ordinance No. 44. I shall give you three days to consider the matter. At the end of that time, if you have not returned here and given us the information demanded, warants will be issued for your arrest."

They looked at the audacious young prosecutor and left the Four Courts building without uttering a word. He waited. Two days later, ex-Lieutenant Governor Charles P. Johnson, the veteran criminal lawyer, called, and said that his client, Mr. Stock, was in such poor health that he would be unable to appear before the grand jury.

"I am truly sorry that Mr. Stock is ill," replied Mr. Folk, "for his presence here is imperative, and if he fails to appear he will be arrested before sundown."

That evening a conference was held in Governor Johnson's office, and the next day this story was told in the grand jury room by Charles H. Turner, millionaire president of the Suburban Railway, and corroborated by Philip Stock, man-about-town and a good fellow: The Suburban, anxious to sell out at a large profit to its only competitor, the St. Louis Transit Co., caused to be drafted the measure known as House Bill No. 44. So sweeping were its grants that Mr. Turner, who planned and executed the document, told the directors in his confidence that its enactment into law would enhance the value of the property from three to six million dollars. The bill introduced, Mr. Turner visited Colonel Butler, who had long been known as a legislative agent, and asked his price for securing the passage of the measure. "One hundred and forty-five thousand dollars will be my fee," was the reply. The railway president demurred. He would think the matter over, he said, and he hired a cheaper man, Mr. Stock. Stock conferred with the reprsentative of the combine in the House of Delegates and reported that $75,000 would be necessary in this branch of the Assembly. Mr. Turner presented a note indorsed by two of the directors whom he could trust, and secured a loan from the German American Savings Bank.

Bribe funds in pocket, the legislative agent telephoned John Murrell, at that time a representative of the House combine, to meet him in the office of the Lincoln Trust Company. There the two rented a safe-deposit box. Mr. Stock placed in the drawer the roll of $75,000, and each subscribed to an agreement that the box should not be opened unless both were present. Of course the conditions spread upon the bank's daybook made no reference to the purpose for which this fund had been deposited, but an agreement entered into by Messrs. Stock and Murrell was to the effect that the $75,000 should be given Mr. Murrell as soon as the bill became an ordinance, and by him distributed to the members of the combine. Stock turned to the Council, and upon his report a further sum of $60,000 was secured. These bills were placed in a safe-deposit box of the Mississippi Valley Trust Co., and the man who held the key as representative of the Council combine was Charles H. Kratz.

All seemed well, but a few weeks after placing these funds in escrow, Mr. Stock reported to his employer that there was an unexpected hitch due to the action of Emil Meysenburg, who, as a member of the Council Committee on Railroads, was holding up the report on the bill. Mr. Stock said that Mr. Meysenburg held some worthless shares in a defunct corporation and wanted Mr. Stock to purchase this paper at its par value of $9,000. Mr. Turner gave Mr. Stock the money with which to buy the shares.

Thus the passage of House Bill 44 promised to cost the Suburban Railway Co. $144,000, only one thousand dollars less than that originally named by the political boss to whom Mr. Turner had first applied. The bill, however, passed both houses of the Assembly. The sworn servants of the city had done their work and held out their hands for the bribe money.

Then came a court mandate which prevented the Suburban Railway Co., from reaping the benefit of the vote-buying, and Charles H. Turner, angered at the check, issued orders that the money in safe-deposit boxes should not be touched. War was declared between bribe-givers and bribe-takers, and the latter resorted to tactics which they hoped would frighten the Suburban people into submission— such as making enough of the story public to cause rumors of impending prosecution. It was that first item which Mr. Folk saw and acted upon.

When Messrs. Turner and Stock unfolded in the grand jury room the details of their bribery plot, Circuit Attorney Folk found himself in possession of verbal evidence of a great crime; he needed as material exhibits the two large sums of money in safe-deposit vaults of two of the largest banking institutions of the West. Had this money been withdrawn? Could he get it if it was there? Lock-boxes had always been considered sacred and beyond the power of the law to open. "I've always held," said Mr. Folk, "that the fact that a thing never had been done was no reason for thinking it couldn't be done." He decided in this case that the magnitude of the interests involved warranted unusual action, so he selected a committee of grand jurors and visited one of the banks. He told the president, a personal friend, the facts that had come into his possession, and asked permission to serach for the fund.

"Impossible," was the reply. "Our rules deny anyone the right."

"Mr. ———," said Mr. Folk, "a crime has been committed, and you hold concealed the principal evidence thereto. In the name of the State of Missouri I demand that you cause the box to be opened. If you refuse, I shall cause a warrant to be issued, charging you as an accessory."

For a minute not a word was spoken by anyone in the room; then the banker said in almost inaudible tones:

"Give me a little time, gentlemen. I must consult with our legal adviser before taking such a step."

"We will wait ten minutes," said the Circuit Attorney. "By that time we must have access to the vault or a warrant will be applied for."

At the expiration of that time a solemn procession wended its way from the president's office to the vaults in the sub-cellar—the president, the cashier, and the corporation's lawyer, the grand jurors, and the Circuit Attorney. All bent eagerly forward as the key was inserted in the lock. The iron drawer yielded, and a roll of something wrapped in brown paper was brought to light. The Circuit Attorney removed the rubber bands, and national bank notes of large denomination spread out flat before them. The money was counted, and the sum was $75,000!

The boodle fund was returned to its repository, officers of the bank were told they would be held responsible for it until the courts could act. The investigators visited the other financial institution. They met with more resistance there. The threat to procure a warrant had no effect until Mr. Folk left the building and set off in the direction of the Four Courts. Then a messenger called him back, and the second box was opened. In this was found $60,000. The chain of evidence was complete.

From that moment events moved rapidly. Charles Kratz and John K. Murrell, alleged representatives of Council and House combines, were arrested on bench warrants and placed under heavy bonds. Kratz was brought into court from a meeting at which plans were being formed for his election to the National Congress. Murrell was taken from his undertaking establishment. Emil Meysenburg, millionaire broker, was seated in his office when a sheriff's deputy entered and read a document that charged him with bribery. The summons reached Henry Nicolaus while he was seated at his desk, and the wealthy brewer was compelled to send for a bondsman to avoid passing a night in jail. The cable flashed the news to Cairo, Egypt, that Ellis Wainwright, many times a millionaire, proprietor of the St. Louis brewery that bears this name, had been indicted. Julius Lehmann, one of the members of the House of Delegates, who had joked while waiting in the grand jury's ante-room, had his laughter cut short by the hand of a deputy sheriff on his shoulder and the words. "You are charged with perjury." He was joined at the bar of the criminal court by Harry Faulkner, another jolly good fellow.

Consternation spread among the boodle gang. Some of the men took night trains for other States and foreign countries; the majority remained and counseled together. Within twenty-four hours after the first indictments were returned, a meeting of bribe-givers and bribe-takers was held in South St. Louis. The total wealth of those in attend-ance was $30,000,000, and their combined political influence sufficient to carry any municipal election under normal conditions.

This great power was aligned in opposition to one man, who still was alone. It was not until many indictments had been returned that a citizens' committee was formed to furnish funds, and even then most of the contributors concealed their identity. Mr. James L. Blair, the treasurer, testified in court that they were afraid to be known lest "it ruin their business."

At the meeting of corruptionists three courses were decided upon. Political leaders were to work on the Circuit Attorney by promise of future reward, or by threats. Detectives were to ferret out of the young lawyer's past anything that could be used against him. Witnesses would be sent out of town and provided with money to remain away until the adjournment of the grand jury.

Mr. Folk at once felt the pressure, and it was of a character to star-tle one. Statesmen, lawyers, merchants, clubmen, churchmen—in fact, men prominent in all walks of life—visited him at his office and at his home, and urged that he cease such activity against his fellow-towns-people. Political preferment was promised if he would yield; a political grave if he persisted. Threatening letters came, warning him of plots to murder, to disfigure, and to blackguard. Word came from Tennessee that detectives were investigating every act of his life. Mr. Folk told the politicians that he was not seeking political favors, and not looking forward to another office; the others he defied. Meantime he probed the deeper into the municipal sore. With his first successes for prestige and aided by the panic among the boodlers, he soon had them suspicious of one another, exchanging charges of betrayal, and ready to "squeal" or run at the slightest sign of danger. One member of the House of Delegates became so frightened while under the inquisitorial cross-fire that he was seized with a nervous chill; his false teeth fell to the floor, and the rattle so increased his alarm that he rushed from the room without stopping to pick up his teeth, and boarded the next train.

It was not long before Mr. Folk had dug up the intimate history of ten years of corruption, especially of the business of the North and South and the Central Traction franchise grants, the last-named being even more iniquitous than the Suburban.

Early in 1898 a "promoter" rented a bridal suite at the Planters' Hotel, and having stocked the rooms with wines, liquors, and cigars until they resembled a candidate's headquarters during a convention, sought introduction to members of the Assembly and to such political bosses as had influence with the city fathers. Two weeks after his arrival the Central Traction bill was introduced "by request" in the Council. The measure was a blanket franchise, granting rights of way which had not been given to old-established companies, and permitting the beneficiaries to parallel any track in the city. It passed both Houses despite the protests of every newspaper in the city, save one, and was vetoed by the mayor. The cost to the promoter was $145,000.

Preparations were made to pass the bill over the executive's veto. The bridal suite was restocked, larger sums of money were placed on deposit in the banks, and the services of three legislative agents were engaged. Evidence now in the possession of the St. Louis courts tells in detail the disposition of $250,000 of bribe money. Sworn statements prove that $75,000 was spent in the House of Delegates. The remainder of the $250,000 was distributed in the Council, whose members, though few in number, appraised their honor at a higher figure on account of their higher positions in the business and social world. Finally, but one vote was needed to complete the necessary two-thirds in the upper Chamber. To secure this a councilman of reputed integrity was paid $50,000 in consideration that he vote aye when the ordinance should come up for final passage. But the promoter did not dare risk all upon the vote of one man, and he made this novel proposition to another honored member, who accepted it:

"You will vote on roll call after Mr. ———. I will place $45,000 in the hands of your son, which amount will become yours, if you have to vote for the measure because of Mr. ———'s not keeping his promise. But if he stands out for it you can vote against it, and the money shall revert to me."

On the evening when the bill was read for final passage the City Hall was crowded with ward heelers and lesser politicians. These men had been engaged by the promoter, at five and ten dollars a head, to cheer on the boodling Assemblymen. The bill passed the House with a rush, and all crowded into the Council Chamber. While the roll was being called the silence was profound, for all knew that some men in the Chamber whose reputations had been free from blemish, were under promise and pay to part with honor that night. When the clerk was two-thirds down the list those who had kept count knew that but one vote was needed. One more name was called. The man addressed turned red, then white, and after a moment's hesitation he whispered "Aye"! The silence was so death-like that his vote was heard throughout the room, and those near enough heard also the sigh of relief that escaped from the member who could now vote "no" and save his reputation.

The Central Franchise bill was a law, passed over the mayor's veto. The promoter had expended nearly $300,000 in securing the legislation, but within a week he sold his rights of way to "Eastern capitalists" for $1,250,000. The United Railways Company was formed, and without owning an inch of steel rail, or a plank in a car, was able to compel every street railroad in St. Louis, with the exception of the Suburban, to part with stock and right of way and agree to a merger. Out of this grew the St. Louis Transit Company of today.

Several incidents followed this legislative session. After the Assembly had adjourned, a promoter entertained the $50,000 councilman at a downtown restaurant. During the supper the host remarked to his guest, "I wish you would lend me that $50,000 until tomorrow. There are some of the boys outside whom I haven't paid." The money changed hands. The next day, having waited in vain for the promoter, Mr. Councilman armed himself with a revolver and began a search of the hotels. The hunt in St. Louis proved fruitless, but the irate legislator kept on the trail until he came face to face with the lobbyist in the corridor of the Waldorf-Astoria. The New Yorker, seeing the danger, seized the St. Louisan by the arm and said soothingly, "There, there; don't take on so. I was called away suddenly. Come to supper with me; I will give you the money."

The invitation was accepted, and champagne soon was flowing. When the man from the West had become sufficiently maudlin the promoter passed over to him a letter, which he had dictated to a typewriter while away from the table for a few minutes. The statement denied all knowledge of bribery.

"You sign that and I will pay you $5,000. Refuse, and you don't get a cent," said the promoter. The St. Louisan returned home carrying the $5,000, and that was all.

Meanwhile the promoter had not fared so well with other spoilsmen. By the terms of the ante-legislation agreement referred to above, the son of one councilman was pledged to return $45,000 if his father was saved the necessity of voting for the bill. The next day the New Yorker sought out this young man and asked for the money.

"I am not going to give it to you," was the cool rejoinder. "My mamma says that it is bribe money and that it would be wrong to give it to either you or father, so I shall keep it myself." And he did. When summoned before the grand jury this young man asked to be relieved from answering questions. "I am afraid I might commit perjury," he said. He was advised to "Tell the truth and there will be no risk."

"It would be all right," said the son, "if Mr. Folk would tell me what the other fellows have testified to. Please have him do that."

Two indictments were found as the result of this Central Traction bill, and bench warrants were served on Robert M. Snyder and George J. Kobusch. The State charged the former with being one of the promoters of the bill, the definite allegation being bribery. Mr. Kobusch, who is president of a street car manufacturing company, was charged with perjury.

The first case tried was that of Emil Meysenburg, the millionaire who compelled the Suburban people to purchase his worthless stock. He was defended by three attorneys of high repute in criminal jurisprudence, but the young Circuit Attorney proved equal to the emergency, and a conviction was secured. Three years in the penitentiary was the sentence. Charles Kratz, the Congressional candidate, forfeited $40,000 by flight, and John K. Murrell also disappeared. Mr. Folk traced Murrell to Mexico, caused his arrest in Guadalajara, negotiated with the authorities for his surrender, and when this failed, arranged for his return home to confess, and his evidence brought about the indictment, on September 8, of eighteen members of the municipal legislature. The second case was that of Julius Lehmann. Two years at hard labor was the sentence, and the man who had led the jokers in the grand jury anteroom would have fallen when he heard it, had not a friend been standing near.

Besides the convictions of these and other men of good standing in the community, and the flight of many more, partnerships were dissolved, companies had to be reorganized, business houses were closed because their proprietors were absent, but Mr. Folk, deterred as little by success as by failure, moved right on; he was not elated; he was not sorrowful. The man proceeded with his work quickly, surely, smilingly, without fear or pity. The terror spread, and the rout was complete.

When another grand jury was sworn and proceeded to take testimony there were scores of men who threw up their hands and crying *"Mea culpa!"* begged to be permitted to tell all they knew and not be prosecuted. The inquiry broadened. The son of a former mayor was indicted for misconduct in office while serving as his father's private secretary, and the grand jury recommended that the ex-mayor be sued in the civil courts, to recover interests on public money which he had placed in his own pocket. A true bill fell on a former City Register, and more Assemblymen were arrested, charged with making illegal contracts with the city. At last the ax struck upon the trunk of the greatest oak of the forest. Colonel Butler, the boss who has controlled elections in St. Louis for many years, the millionaire who had risen from bellows-boy in a blacksmith's shop to be the maker and guide of the Governors of Missouri, one of the men who helped nominate and elect Folk—he also was indicted on two counts charging attempted bribery. That Butler has controlled legislation in St. Louis had long been known. It was generally understood that he owned Assemblymen before they ever took the oath of office, and that he did not have to pay for votes. And yet open bribery was the allegation now. Two members of the Board of Health stood ready to swear that he offered them $2,500 for their approval of a garbage contract.

THE LOCUS OF CORRUPTION
Edward N. Costikyan

Just as our ideas about good city government are largely the product of confusing a symptom of bad government with its cause, so our defenses against the symptom of bad government—corruption—are the product of the same confusion. In narrow obedience to our tradition,

From *Behind Closed Doors*, pp.296–307, copyright © 1966 by Edward Costikyan. Reprinted by permission of Harcourt Brace Jovanovich, Inc.

the principal defense against corruption continues to be an attempt to keep political leaders out of the government process. Nothing more is thought necessary to mind the store.

This defense presupposes that political leaders as a group are less honest and more likely to engage in nefarious conduct than other groups such as lawyers, businessmen, and civil servants. The evidence to support this assumption is flimsy at best. I do not have the statistics, but I suspect that the percentage of political leaders convicted of crime is far less than the percentage of political leaders in the population. It is not, for example, unusual to read in the press of businessmen or lawyers or doctors convicted of income-tax evasion or some other crime of corruption. The back pages usually suffice to carry this not unusual news. But let a charge of corruption be even leveled at a political leader and it is front-page news. Even the prominence accorded to such news is not sufficient in itself to justify the assumption that underlies our defense against government corruption: that the political leaders are the likeliest causes of the disease.

I reject this assumption.

In my experience it is not true.

That is not to say that all political leaders are honest and incorruptible. They are not, and I know they are not, but I reject the popular assumption about the frail honesty of political leaders, even though I acknowledge that they, like all human beings, are corruptible and from time to time are corrupted.

Indeed, the last thing a serious practitioner of the political process can afford is to be naïve about the possibility of corruption. There is nothing worse than having your own people stealing behind your back. If they do steal, the defect, while hardly yours at law, does not make them less your people in the public's eye. And the public—though it may forget and forgive—will not be wrong. They were your people. You put them there. That you called the police, and they were fined and their offices cleaned out as soon as possible, does not quite take the smell out of the air. For his own effectiveness, then, as well as for his own self-respect, the politician may never forget that men and women who can be corrupted are always in sufficient supply.

A serious politician allows his power to be exercised by subordinates only so long as he trusts them. The flow of power to a subordinate responds with the utmost delicacy to the eddies of disquiet which corruption—or the suspicion of it—inevitably sets in motion.

It is not a particular group of people that is the magnet which attracts corrupters. Power, and power alone, attracts. The natural locus of corruption is *always* where the discretionary power resides. It follows that in an era when political leaders exercised basic power over the government officials whom they controlled, the locus of corruption was in the offices of the political bosses—Tweed, Croker, Kelly, and the rest. But as power has shifted from the political leader to the civil servant and the public officeholder, so the locus of corruptibility and of corruption has shifted. The evidence demonstrates this clearly, and yet little attention is paid to the evidence, because the old myths and preconceptions are too strong.

Let us first put aside the few cases that invite public attention because the items involved are so easily understood. For example, an Oriental rug given to a political official is something the ordinary voter comprehends. Many millions of dollars in a Dixon-Yates contract (involving no political leaders) is not. A bathtub given to a political leader is understood. A television-antenna franchise awarded to businessmen is not. A deep-freeze given to a political leader is understood. Stocking a substantial part of a retired general's farm with cattle from wealthy friends is not. But the deep-freezes and the vicuna coats and the bathtubs and the Oriental rugs are not the great danger to honest government. It is the relationship reflected by these gifts that causes the problem.

The question of whether Sherman Adams used his public power to help his friend Bernard Goldfine is more disturbing than the hospitality enjoyed and gifts received by Adams. Indeed, these gifts are neither the stuff with which corruption is accomplished, nor the subject matter of political deals. The real corrupters rarely leave tangible evidence of where they have been and what they have sought.

Those who seek the benefit of licit and illicit government favors are nothing if not perfectly attuned to shifts in power, and they instinctively go where the power is. What needs to be made clear is that the power is no longer in the hands of political leaders. It has been transferred to the hands of public officials and civil servants long since.

So why deal through a political leader when you can go direct to the source of power? Why contribute to the party when you get more consideration by making your contribution to the candidate himself? Why deal with secondary sources when the primary source is an independent, uncontrolled civil servant?

When a parking-meter company's public relations expert sought to create a "bribe plot," in order, as it later developed, to pocket the bribe himself, the person whose name he invoked as the recipient of the bribe was a former career civil servant, then high in the city govern-

ment, not a political leader. In 1961, one newspaper, intent upon attempting to discredit the Wagner administration, ran a box-score of
"scandals" day after day; I remember that it got as high as twenty-one
or twenty-two "scandals." With *one* exception, every one of the "scandals" involved civil servants, not political leaders or appointees. By the
same token, Republican strategists, in early 1965, before Congressman
John Lindsay decided to run for mayor, were reported to be disheart-
ened at the prospects of "fusion" because fusion had never succeeded
in the absence of widespread *political* scandals.

Does the absence of political scandal mean there is no corruption?
Of course not. It means that corruption has taken new forms and found
a new locus.

By "corruption" I mean not only the use of a consideration such as
money to persuade government to do something it shouldn't, although
that is one form of corruption. There are other forms: The exercise of
discretion to award a government privilege to an old friend as against
an equally or better qualified applicant is a form of corruption. The
tender treatment of a regulated industry by a regulatory commission
whose members look to an ultimate future in private industry is a form
of it. In short, corruption is the exercise of governmental power to
achieve nongovernmental objectives.

From the point of view of the public and competing aspirants, what
difference does it make whether the consideration for such an exercise
of power is cash, or friendship, or future campaign contributions, or a
future job, or nothing?

For example, since World War II a massive government-sponsored
housing program has been carried on almost continuously in one form
or another. The essence of the slum-clearance program has been to encourage private enterprise by almost guaranteeing builders a substantial profit and perhaps a windfall. The essence of the program—"Title
I" or "urban renewal"—is for government to acquire slum properties
at market value and resell them (or make them available) to private
builders or sponsors at a lower cost. The subsidy is supposed to permit
the construction of housing that will rent—or in the case of co-opera-
tives, sell—at lower prices than would otherwise obtain.

The rule is that the sponsor is selected through the exercise of discretion among a host of applicants who are for all measurable purposes
equally qualified. Why is A selected, instead of B or C, to sponsor or
build such a development? There is no public bidding; no objective
measure of who ought to be selected is applied.

Under current practices a "project" for a given area is developed by government officials and approved. A "sponsor" of the development, who is in charge of carrying it out and controls it, is then selected by government officials. The sponsor selects a builder, an architect, a lawyer, an accountant, insurance broker, and all of the rest of the retinue needed to build a complex of buildings, hires them through a corporation organized to build the project, secures financing, and sees that the development is created.

The power to designate these participants is a valuable one. The architect, the lawyer, the insurance broker, may be prepared to share their profits with the source of business. The possibilities for profit to the sponsor are substantial. Certainly the builder, the lawyers, the architect, and the insurance broker are all well compensated.

"Title I," urban renewal's predecessor, was administered by Robert Moses, that conspicuous agent of good government. He and his varied Public Authorities, accountable to no one ("since there are no politicians involved, it must be honest, so why should it have to account?") are a monument to the anti-political good-government tradition of "keep the politicians out and it will be okay."

Moses' administration of Title I was so unsatisfactory that the program was killed. If a political leader had made one-tenth of the mistakes Moses made in that program alone, he would have been destroyed, defeated, out of business. Arbitrariness; designation of favored associates for choice patronage, high salaries, limousines, and chauffeurs; and invulnerability to any requirement of public accountability or auditing of accounts are the earmarks of an entrenched machine. Moses' Public Authorities have them all.

Moses' reward for so directing his many enterprises has been continuing editorial adulation, new jobs, constant praise, and finally the opportunity to run the greatest boondoggle of them all, the 1964–65 New York World's Fair—again, because he is politically pure and deemed to be "efficient."

The potential for abuse in such a set-up could not have escaped the attention of those who seek the pleasures of governmental favor. Who would not prefer the favors of an anonymous Public Authority, which is not subject to public accountability, to the friendship of a political boss. (Moses' critics have repeatedly suggested that his authorities should be subjected to methodical public examination. All to no avail.)

Probably the reason is Moses' accepted and undisputed personal honesty in money matters. But this begs the question. Personal honesty is the *first* requirement for public service, not the only one. And, as noted above, corruption as I have used the term does not require cash as a consideration. There are subtler and more utilitarian forms—future support, campaign contributions, honorific appointments, even ill-defined debts and obligations available for later redemption, or merely old friendships—or whim!

The irregularities in the Moses operation of Title I are well documented elsewhere. Their significance, however, as a demonstration of the new locus of corruption has been generally disregarded—except, I suspect, by the corrupters.

What of Title I's successor—urban renewal? Here again a sponsorship is a valuable asset. Anyone schooled in traditional notions about good government would expect to find the politician's heavy hand allocating sponsorships and designating builders, architects, and the like.

There were political leaders involved in the process, but as supplicants for favors, not dispensers of them. My successor as county leader, J. Raymond Jones, a Harlem political leader, was the most notable of these. Jones's dealings in urban renewal projects—he became a sponsor of at least one major project—came to light when he and Congressman Adam Clayton Powell had a falling out about one project, and a lawsuit was started in which Powell claimed that a sponsorship which was to have been awarded to a company in which they were both interested was at the last moment awarded to a company in which Jones was interested but Powell was not.

Decisions on sponsorships of these projects were made on the very highest level of city government—not by any political leaders. The political leaders, except occasionally as supplicants, played no role in the process. But I cannot believe that their absence rendered the projects $99^{44}/_{100}$ percent pure. For the discretionary power to designate sponsors carries with it all the conditions that inevitably lead to "influence" and influence-peddling. If indeed these sponsorships have value, why shouldn't they be *sold* by government to the highest bidder, instead of given away? If an FCC license to operate a television station is of great value, why not have the government *sell* it, instead of giving it to one of half a dozen equally qualified applicants?

The gift of public privileges by government officials on a discretionary basis in the absence of public bidding is the greatest source of corruption, quasi-corruption, influence-peddling, and demeaning of the governmental process in America today. That distribution of public largess is more and more nonpolitical does not make it any better. Indeed, as in so many other cases, the division of power between political leaders and public officeholders might tend to diminish the opportunities for overt corruption in the dispensation of such government favors.

But the greatest preventive would be to charge for the value of the government privileges being dispensed.

A classic example of the whole problem is the tale of the television-antenna franchise in New York City, which briefly attracted public attention in the spring of 1965. Six applicants sought the privilege of running master television antennas beneath New York City's streets, and charging residents at stipulated rates for connecting into the master antenna and thus securing first-rate reception. In some areas of the city where high buildings block reception (especially public housing projects), such a service was badly needed.

The proposed charges and rates varied from a $60 connection charge to $19.95, and from $20 a month service fee to $4.50. Some of the applicants had had extensive prior experience in operating such systems and some had not. Lo and behold, the two approved franchisers had the least experience and the highest charges of all the applicants. According to the New York *World-Telegram and Sun,* one of the two successful applicants had some unexplained connection with a former legislative representative and close confidant of the mayor. This mayoral friend had been involved in the process of securing the franchise. The other successful applicant was a firm headed by another old mayoral friend. Both had cut their proposed fees (although they were still well above those of the other applicants). What is more, according to the New York *World-Telegram and Sun,* the cuts had been made by the head of the Bureau of Franchises at the *mayor's* suggestion. No political leaders were involved in any way with the successful applicants (what a departure from the days of Boss Tweed!), so it was okay. One unsuccessful applicant was represented by the law firm to which New York County's former law chairman belonged. And one of my partners—by then I had retired as a political leader—represented another unsuccessful applicant.

If the myths were true, should not the ex-Tammany law chairman's client and the ex-county-leader's partner's client have triumphed—especially since their rates were lowest and their experience greatest?

The point, it seems to me, is clear. The pathway to government preference no longer passes through Tammany Hall or the internal political leader's office. It goes direct to the source. This phenomenon of modern urban government has hardly been noted by the theorists or the specialists in good government. They seem to be so convinced that civil service and growth of the public officeholder's independence have created such impregnable fortresses of rectitude that they have devoted all their attention when discussing corruption to looking for political leaders in the governmental process. Noting their absence, the good-government forces viewing a veritable parade of nude emperors have been satisfied that corruption has disappeared.

Indeed, not long ago this preconception so dominated the thinking of those investigating the city government that they laid a colossal egg. In 1959 the state legislature created a "Little Hoover Commission" to investigate New York City. The commission's activities were supposed to expose enough political corruption to lay the basis for a 1961 fusion movement to defeat Mayor Wagner. The Commission and its staff honestly believed, I think, that New York City was beset by the same conditions of political corruption that had laid the basis for the 1933 election of La Guardia. The staff apparently immersed itself in the literature of corruption, particularly that revealed by the Seabury Commission, which uncovered and documented the shenanigans of the political leaders of the 1930's. They had fixed judges and commissioners, sold contracts, and generally operated the city through the public office-holder nominees they controlled. (When one of their designees, Mayor O'Brien, was asked in 1933 who his police commissioner would be, he replied: "I don't know. They haven't told me yet." And he was telling the truth!) But thirty years later, the pattern wasn't there. The corruption was among civil servants—usually lowly ones—and it was minor nickels-and-dimes stuff, not the classic corruption of the Tweed era.

Yet, obsessed by their preconceptions about what *ought* to be wrong (i.e., crooked politicians, not dishonest civil servants), the investigators never realized that what had been established was a shift in the nature and locus of corruption from the socially despicable politician middle-man to the socially acceptable reform product—the civil servant, the career government servant, the elected public official who was free of domination by the machine. What had happened was that the cor-rupters, like water, had found their own level—underpaid and frustrated civil servants who yearned for a more affluent life, or ambitious public officeholders hoping to make affluent friends upon whom they could call when campaign funds were needed.

The frustrated civil servants do not represent any real threat to government. Their number is low and the graft is comparatively small, and no serious student of government would attribute to this kind of activity the manifold faults of modern urban misgovernment.

Of course, petty corruption remains a heavy burden to the person who must endure it. The construction of buildings in New York, for example, is still reported to involve substantial amounts in ten- and twenty-dollar payments to inspectors. How much of this gets to the inspector and how much is an excuse for the builder to get a little tax-free income ("petty cash" in his books) is anyone's guess.

But several things are clear. First, the supposition that such bribery exists, whether the supposition is true or not, saps popular confidence in government. Second, none of the principal defenses built up to protect government from corruption—the isolation and elimination of the politician from government—have had any success in eliminating the occasional bribery of civil servants.

My own belief is that the amount of such corruption is exaggerated, that the overwhelming bulk of civil servants are honest and that, like politicians, they have about the same percentage of corruptible people as the population at large—or less.

The real threat posed by corruption to good government is the fact that, as the form and locus of corruption has shifted from the middle-man politician to the civil servant or elected official, so has the technique of receiving discretionary governmental largess.

The corrupter seeking to lease the Brooklyn Bridge for a dollar a year in exchange for $100,000 in cash, or engaged in an effort to accomplish such misbehavior, is a political and governmental joke. Nobody pays any attention to him. Moreover, the political graft of the Tweed and post-Tweed eras—liquor, prostitution, police protection and the like—is simply nonexistent (unless it is a direct deal between criminal and civil-servant policemen).

"Graft" today, if it can be called that, is the kind described by George Washington Plunkitt as "honest graft"—only now it is more "honest" by far. In short, the political plums today are nonpolitical: urban-renewal projects, contracts to build schools and public buildings and roads and sewers, franchises to install community television antenna systems, and what have you—all involving government funds or privileges, with contracts given for value received with built-in profit of varying amounts, and all disbursed on a *discretionary* basis.

When the time comes to raise funds for the public officeholder who dispensed that favor, or this sponsorship, he has a ready-made list of potential contributors, just as Charles Murphy and Boss Tweed and their predecessors did—the recipients of discretionary public largess.

Should a portrait be painted and presented to the city? Run down the list! And before you know it a patron has hired a portraitist. The patron, moreover, has a tax-deduction. He is, of course, a public benefactor, not a political wheeler-dealer.

Sometimes the cloak of purity achieved through association with public officeholders instead of dirty political leaders reaches ridiculous proportions. For example, one prominent citizen, who, unlike the late Vice-President Alben Barkley, would far rather "sit at the feet of the mighty" than be a "servant of the Lord" is famed for his ability to move fireplugs on Park Avenue. The basis of his celebrity arises from the desire of Park Avenue building managements to have a "no parking" area near their front doors, so that tenants don't have to crawl between parked cars as they come and go. The best way to achieve this is to have a fire hydrant right next to the awning—that guarantees twelve feet of "no parking" on each side of it.

And so this scion of civic virtue specializes in securing fireplug movements in exchange for long-term retainers. He accomplishes these results (and Park Avenue's fireplugs have seen a fair amount of movement lately) not because of any relation with political leaders, but because of his nonpolitical, good-government status and his close friendships with significant public officeholders.

The locus of corruption is always where unrestrained power exists. The political leader's present function in the scheme of corruption is to be a scapegoat, who shields the self-styled public vindicator of political morality from public scrutiny. After all, so long as the "bosses" exist, their opponents, being saints, should be protected. So long as the political leaders are excluded from the process, why is it necessary to inquire why fire hydrants are moved or how urban-renewal-project sponsorships are allocated?

Of course, I am sufficiently skeptical to be unable to believe that corruption will be eliminated from the conduct of human affairs, either by eliminating the power of political leaders or by restoring their power to what it once was. But I do believe there are ways to minimize the improper exercise of governmental power—ways that would make it more difficult for the corrupter to corrupt and easier to uncover him and his activities.

The first step is to realize that the locus of corruption is where the power is. The second is to destroy the stereotypes that brand the political leader as thief and the public official as saint. The third is to eliminate the discretionary distribution of governmental privileges—Title I housing projects, urban-renewal sponsorships (and construction contracts), public architecture contracts, and so on—without competition for either quality (where the arts are involved) or quantity (where money is involved).

Is there any good reason why every architect who wants to should not submit a design for a school or a courthouse and have the winning design selected on the basis of the merit, utility, and decent cost ratios of the design, and not because of the name attached to it? Why should not an urban-renewal sponsorship, worth a million dollars to the sponsor, be awarded on the basis of price paid to the city, instead of unexplained "discretion"?

The reason why such discretion is granted to public officials—especially the "nonpolitical" ones—is the public supposition that since they are outside the traditional political structure, they, rather than the politician, should have power—and by some magic, rectitude will be achieved.

What has happened is that a new politics has been created, certainly no better and in some ways worse than the politics this "nonpolitical" politics has replaced. It is indeed time to re-examine the post-Tweed-era assumptions which have led to this new form of urban mismanagement.

The ideas I am suggesting seem at first blush to be radical, perhaps half-baked, certainly unusual. But it seems clear to me that in a city where the power is in the bureaucracy, the locus of corruption must also be there. And the discretionary exercise of power by bureaucrats is to be feared and needs to be dealt with at least as much as—probably far more than—the venality of Boss Tweed's successors.

THE CORRUPTERS
Michael Dorman

The first half of this selection deals with contract kickbacks in Newark during the administration of Mayor Hugh A. Addonizio. The second describes the relationship between syndicate figures and one of Mayor John V. Lindsay's highest administrative officials in New York City.

By the time Addonizio went to trial in mid-1970, only seven of the original fourteen codefendants were in court with him to face the

From Michael Dorman, *Payoff: The Role of Organized Crime in American Politics*, pp.54–60, 62–64, 78–90. Copyright © 1972 by Michael Dorman. Reprinted by permission of the publisher, David McKay Company, Inc.

charges. The remainder either were dead or their cases had been severed from Addonizio's because of claims of illness or other reasons. And during the course of the trial two other defendants, including Tony Boy Boiardo, had their cases severed because of what were described as heart ailments. Those whose cases were severed were scheduled to be tried separately at later dates.

When the trial began, prosecutor Lacey told the jurors in his opening summary that the government would prove a dummy bank account had been used to funnel extorted funds to Addonizio and his codefendants. He said a group headed by Boiardo had been responsible for setting up the dummy account. The Boiardo group, Lacey said, was also responsible for arranging the terms of kickbacks from contractors to city officials—so that the officials would "not have to meet the [extortion] victims except under extraordinary circumstances."

Mayor Addonizio, who had refused to relinquish his office after being indicted and was running for re-election even while standing trial, immediately issued a press release calling Lacey's opening statement "the most fantastic story I have ever heard." The release claimed: "There is not a single iota of evidence linking me with such an incredible scheme in any way and there never will be because I have never been involved with Mr. Boiardo or anybody else in any illegal manner whatsoever."

But Lacey and his chief assistant prosecutor, Herbert J. Stern, promptly set about proving otherwise. Among their first witnesses was a Newark businessman, Irving Kantor, who testified that Boiardo's group had induced him to open the dummy bank account under the name of the Kantor Supply Company. Following instructions from Boiardo and his associates, Kantor said, he then sent false bills on the supply company's stationery to contractors doing business with the city. The bills, which referred to nonexistent supplies ostensibly sold to the contractors, were made out in the exact amounts of kickbacks being made by the contractors to city officials. The contractors sent checks in the required amounts to Kantor, who testified he then deposited them in the dummy account and converted them into cash. After deducting a small percentage for his services, Kantor said, he turned the cash over to a Boiardo subordinate, Joseph Biancone, who was a defendant in the trial, or to some other agent designated by Boiardo. The cash was then divided among members of the Boiardo group and the city officials taking the kickbacks. All told, Kantor said, he funneled more than $1 million from the contractors to the politicians and racketeers.

Kantor was followed to the stand by the prosecution's chief witness,

Paul Rigo, an engineering contractor who had been identified as one of the main victims of the extortion scheme. Rigo had been kept under guard by Federal marshals and agents after reporting that his life had been threatened by Boiardo. Rigo testified that he had first met Addonizio when another contractor asked him to give the mayor his expert advice in a controversy over what kind of pipe should be used on a city sewer project. The dispute concerned the relative merits of steel and rubber-jointed pipe versus concrete and rubber-jointed pipe. Rigo said he explained to Addonizio why the steel and rubber pipe was better, but that the mayor replied that "his people thought they could get away with rubber and concrete." He said Addonizio added: "You know, I have an interest in Mario Gallo; he makes rubber and concrete pipe, and that's what we're going to use." (Gallo, a member of Tony Boy Boiardo's group, was the defendant killed in an automobile crash shortly after agreeing to cooperate with the prosecution.)

A few months later, Rigo testified, he again met with the mayor at the Newark City Hall. Also present were two other defendants in the case, City Public Works Director Anthony La Morte, who later became executive director of the Newark Municipal Utilities Authority, and Norman Schiff, then city corporation counsel. La Morte told the mayor at the meeting that he had discussed a projected emergency extension of the Newark water-main system with Boiardo and that Boiardo had "approved" the project, Rigo testified. The idea of city officials having to get the approval of a Mafia leader to undertake a municipal construction project seemed astonishing to some, but Rigo mentioned it as matter-of-factly as if it were standard procedure in Newark.

Rigo said Addonizio was "upset" because pipe manufactured by Mario Gallo was not going to be used on the new project. Steel and rubber-joined pipe provided by a company called Lockjoint would be required. Rigo quoted the mayor as saying: "Tony [Boiardo] had better figure out a way to get something [a kickback] out of Lockjoint." Corporation Counsel Schiff complained that Boiardo couldn't get "enough." But Rigo said Addonizio replied: "Tony will figure out a way to get enough."

Later, Rigo testified, he began personal dealings with Boiardo. He said Public Works Director La Morte took him to meet Boiardo after emphasizing: "This is the most important meeting you'll ever have. This is the man who really runs Newark!" Again, while the notion of a Mafia leader being described by an important city official as "the man who really runs Newark" might have seemed extraordinary, Rigo took it in stride. By the time of his first meeting with Boiardo, Rigo had obtained a city contract for work on a sewer project known as the Southside Interceptor. He said Boiardo told him at the meeting that he would have to kick back ten percent of his gross earnings on the job. He testified the following exchange then occurred:

RIGO: I can't pay ten percent.
BOIARDO: You will pay—and in cash.
RIGO: I can't. What do we get for the money?
BOIARDO: There are a lot of mouths to feed in city hall. I take care of the mayor and the city council and anybody else that needs taking care of.

Rigo testified that he tried to work the kickbacks down to five percent, but that Boiardo told him: "Look what happened to Killam [Elson T. Killam, a consulting engineer who had formerly held city contracts.] He's not in Newark [any more], and he's going to sweat a long time before he gets what the city owes him." Under Boiardo's pressure, Rigo said, he eventually agreed to pay the ten-percent kickbacks.

After receiving the first of his payments from the city, Rigo testified, he began paying the kickbacks to members of Boiardo's group and directly to Public Works Director La Morte. Later, however, payments from the city to Rigo started lagging. Rigo testified he complained about the problem to La Morte, who sent him to Addonizio. The mayor, in turn, told him to see Boiardo. Even this incredible situation—the mayor of the nation's thirteenth largest city referring a contractor to a Mafia leader about collecting debts from the city—did not faze Rigo. He dutifully went to Boiardo, who complained that Rigo's kickback payments themselves were lagging. Rigo testified he told Boiardo that he hadn't been able to keep up the kickback payments because of the city's delay in paying him. He said Boiardo told him: "Pay the ten percent or I'll break both your legs!" Anxious to keep his legs intact, Rigo scraped together $30,000—which he testified he put in a paper bag and handed to a member of the Boiardo group, codefendant Ralph Vicaro.

Rigo said he continued making kickbacks through Boiardo and his subordinates for several years, and periodically was granted new contracts by the city. Eventually, he testified, La Morte told him during a conversation at city hall that Boiardo was in a "sensitive situation" and could no longer handle distribution of the kickbacks to Addonizio and other officials. He quoted La Morte as telling him that Boiardo was "desirous of me making payments" directly to the officials involved.

At the time, Rigo was seeking a city contract for work on a new project in the city's watershed area. He testified La Morte told him that, in order to get the contract drawn and the appropriations for the work approved, he would have to pay Addonizio and the eight city councilmen $10,000 each. In addition, La Morte wanted $25,000 for himself because he was "the department head" approving the contract. La Morte felt that Corporation Counsel Schiff "should have something, too," Rigo said. Prosecutor Stern asked whether he wanted to make these payoffs. "No," Rigo replied. "But if we didn't we'd have lost God knows how much money and, in addition, there was always the fear."

He said he began making the demanded kickbacks in stages directly to the officials, and the watershed contract was awarded to him. Consulting a diary in which he had made coded entries referring to the kickbacks, Rigo ticked off a seemingly endless list of payoffs. A $5,000 payoff to La Morte, for example, was indicated with the code letter "S" —representing La Morte's nickname, "Sonny." A $2,000 payoff to Addonizio was noted in the diary as "P plus 2"—with the letter "P" standing for the mayor's code name, "the Pope." Rigo testified he had made that payoff to Addonizio in the mayor's office with nobody else present. When prosecutor Stern asked him to identify the payoff recipient, Rigo pointed across the courtroom and Addonizio rose from his seat with a faint smirk. On the same day he paid Addonizio the $2,000, Rigo said, he paid the eight city councilmen $1,000 each.

And, although Boiardo was no longer handling distribution of the kickbacks to the officials, the Mafioso and his associates continued to get a cut of the bribery proceeds. Rigo testified he handed over $10,500 to codefendant Ralph Vicaro for the Boiardo group, among other payments. Later, he said, he went to city hall with a paper sack containing additional payoffs for the public officials. He took with him his secretary, Norris Whitehead, and his bookkeeper, Charles Fallon. They counted up the money "in a little back room in the public works department" and put it in envelopes with appropriate initials, Rigo said. He and Fallon then distributed the money to the recipients— including Addonizio, La Morte, and the councilmen.

During his conversations with Addonizio, Rigo testified, Addonizio explained why he had retired from Congress and run for mayor. He said the mayor told him: "There's no money in Washington, but you can make a million dollars in Newark."

* * *

Addonizio denied all the charges of wrongdoing, claiming repeatedly that Rigo and other witnesses against him had lied. He denied that meetings in his city hall office described by Rigo and others had ever taken place. He also denied taking any kickbacks, having knowledge of any or making the statement that he had left Congress to run for mayor because "you can make a million dollars in Newark." Under cross-examination by Prosecutor Lacey, however, Addonizio conceded maintaining a long-time friendship with Mafia leader Boiardo. He admitted attending by invitation Boiardo's wedding twenty years earlier, at which the best man was Gerardo "Jerry" Catena, a member of the Mafia's national commission. He also admitted dining with Boiardo and attending parties with him in New York, Puerto Rico, and Florida during the five years preceding the trial. Addonizio never satisfactorily explained why, as a congressman and mayor, he felt justified in carrying on a friendship with a high-ranking Mafioso.

He testified that, on various trips to Puerto Rico and Florida, his hotel bills and "perhaps" some of his gambling losses had been paid by "old personal friends." Among these friends, he said, were Vincent Salerno, owner of a Newark optical firm: Herman Gering, who sold his plastics business "a few years ago for several million dollars" to Monsanto Chemical Company and had recently died; and Harold Lockheimer, a wealthy real-estate and construction executive.

Despite having such moneyed friends and despite having more than $45,000 in available cash in his bank accounts, Addonizio conceded under Lacey's questioning that he had "borrowed" $14,000 from Paul Rigo during the summer of 1968. He said he had given Rigo promissory notes for the money and had paid them off in 1969. But Lacey drew from him the admission that the promissory notes had not been given at the time of the original "loan"—that they had been drawn up some months later and backdated. Lacey contended that the notes had been a subterfuge—a belated effort to make the transaction appear normal after a grand jury had begun investigating Addonizio's dealings—but Addonizio insisted no irregularity had been involved.

Since Addonizio was the only defendant to take the stand, the presentation of the defense case was limited. The few witnesses called by the defense were unable to rebut much of the prosecution case. One, in fact, unexpectedly bolstered the government's case. The witness, Ferdinand J. Biunno, former business administrator for the city of Newark, had been called by the defense in an attempt to cast doubt on Rigo's testimony. Instead, Biunno generally supported Rigo and provided information, not covered in Rigo's testimony, that further damaged the defense cause. Biunno testified that he and former Public Works Director La Morte, while on city payroll, had allowed Rigo to pay for airline tickets, lodging and other expenses when they and their wives attended a convention in Miami. Prosecutor Lacey introduced evidence that La Morte had collected expense money from the city for the trip, even though Rigo had paid his way.

*   *   *

By September 1966 [Lindsay] decided that Marcus deserved a promotion and a salary from the city. He appointed Marcus to a $30,000-a-year job as commissioner of water supply, gas, and electricity. Moreover, he soon announced that he had even bigger things in mind for his appointee. Lindsay was in the process of reorganizing the city government, and planned to create ten super-agencies that would have enormous powers. He disclosed that Marcus was in line to head one of the super-agencies, the Environmental Protection Administration, which would include the Department of Water Supply, Gas, and Electricity, the Sanitation Department, and the Department of Air Pollution Control.

To casual observers, all seemed to be going swimmingly well for Marcus. But, unknown to such observers, Marcus was in deep trouble. His financial investments had continued to be disastrous, he was in desperate need of money, and his city salary did not begin to fill the gap in his bank account. His financial problems were compounded by the fact that he felt obligated to keep up the pretense that he was independently wealthy.

In an attempt to solve the problems, Marcus turned to several recently-found associates. One of them was a shadowy character named Herbert Itkin, a labor lawyer whom Marcus had met while seeking labor support for Lindsay's mayoral campaign. Itkin's activities went far beyond the mere practice of law. He had all sorts of mysterious connections with such assorted figures as racketeers, politicians, foreign officials, spies, and financiers. He acted as a middle-man, for a fee, in lining up borrowers who wanted to make loans from Teamster Union pension funds. He registered with the Justice Department as an agent representing such foreign clients as the government of the Dominican Republic, and an exile group calling itself the Provisional Government of Haiti. Moreover, he served as a secret informer for both the FBI and the Central Intelligence Agency.

Marcus, evidently impressed with Itkin, became embroiled in a series of business ventures with him. Among other things, they formed a company called Conestoga Investments, Ltd., while Marcus was still working on Lindsay's campaign. Conestoga was registered in London, where Itkin visited frequently on business, and used Itkin's law office as its New York address. Itkin and Marcus persuaded outsiders to invest in Conestoga, saying the firm was involved in numerous profitable operations in the underdeveloped countries of Africa. Among the projects they mentioned were a housing project in Mauritania, a power dam in Sierra Leone, and a beef distributorship in Mali. Despite the impressive talk, however, Conestoga was as unsuccessful as Marcus's other ventures. He quickly lost more than $100,000, mostly borrowed from other people.

But, through Itkin, he met other men he hoped could bail him out of his financial troubles. Itkin introduced him to Daniel Motto, president of a New York local of the Bakery and Confectionery Workers Union, and a member of the Union's seven-state Northeast District Council. During World War II, Motto had been convicted of racketeering in the black-market sale of gasoline ration coupons. His union had later been expelled from the AFL-CIO for engaging in corrupt practices. Notwithstanding this background, Motto served on the board of directors of the American-Italian Anti-Defamation League, whose main goal was to halt use of the term "Mafia" by news media and law-enforcement agencies.

Motto, in turn, introduced Marcus to Tony Ducks Corallo. After Marcus went to work at City Hall, he pleaded with Itkin for financial help. Itkin referred the problem to Motto, who then consulted Corallo. The situation was made to order for a Mafia corrupter such as Corallo —a chance to get his hooks into a city official with the power to award contracts worth millions of dollars. Corallo and Motto listened to Marcus's tale of woe and immediately offered to lend him money. The rate of interest they proposed was exorbitant—two percent a week— but the desperate Marcus snapped at the bait. At first, he took $10,000 to pay off his most pressing creditors. Corallo told him plenty more would be available if he needed it. A few days later, Marcus borrowed another $40,000. Corallo wanted the loans repaid, of course, and wanted the hefty interest payments as well. But his real interest, more than any profit he would make on the shylocking deal, was in getting a hold on Marcus. He fully expected that Marcus would be unable to keep up regular payments on the loans. And, the more Marcus fell behind, the more indebted he would become to the Mob. He would then be forced to do Corallo's bidding at city hall.

Matters developed just as Corallo had expected. While using some of the borrowed money to satisfy creditors, Marcus invested much of it in the stock market in an attempt to make a quick financial comeback. He bought 1000 shares in one company at $96 a share and, a week later, another 1000 shares at $160 a share. The purchases were made on margin, with Marcus putting up more than $40,000 in cash. Later, the stock dropped more than forty points and Marcus was pressed for more margin. Again, he borrowed money from Corallo.

The time had come for Corallo to start cashing in on his investment. Marcus was about to award a city contract for draining and cleaning the 700-million-gallon Jerome Park Reservoir in the Bronx. Since the project was considered a high-priority emergency job, city regulations empowered Marcus to give the contract to any firm he chose—without taking competitive bids. Corallo had just the firm in mind for the job. It was S. T. Grand Inc., headed by Henry Fried, who was active in politics and no stranger to New York City scandals. Nine years earlier, it had been disclosed that Fried had paid a city councilman $30,000 four days after the city agreed to use a product called "fly ash," marketed by Fried, in mixing construction concrete. During the resulting investigation, Fried resigned a state job to which he had been appointed by then-Governor W. Averell Harriman—membership on the commission that supervises New York state prisons. Two of Fried's brothers Richard and Hugo, both ex-convicts, were vice presidents of S. T. Grand Inc. Despite their records and Fried's involvement in the scandal involving the councilman, the firm did considerable work for New York City and other municipalities in the metropolitan area.

But it wanted more city work than it was getting—presenting another situation made to order for Corallo. Working with Itkin and Motto, Corallo put the squeeze on Marcus to award the reservoir-cleaning contract to the Grand firm. Although some estimates were that the job should be worth only about $500,000, Marcus agreed to pay Grand $835,000. Corollo, of course, had not acted on behalf of Grand out of the goodness of his heart. He had a kickback deal in the works. The plan called for Grand to make a payoff amounting to five percent of the total value of the contract—with two percent going to Marcus and one percent each to Corallo, Itkin, and Motto.

At first, Henry Fried balked at paying the kickback. But then he received a visit from an associate of Corallo, Joseph Pizzo, who describes himself as a labor consultant. Fried would later describe Pizzo in court somewhat differently, as follows: "He was connected with Cosa Nostra, a muscle man who wouldn't hesitate to put the arm on anybody. I know if he came up to me and gave a command, I would have to adhere. I remember forty-ton, fifty-ton cranes dropped overboard into the river." Fried said Pizzo insisted the kickback be paid and told him: "I don't want any trouble with you. . . . If I make up my mind, you know what could happen. I could slow down your drill runner, your laborers, your engineers; it could cost you $100,000." Fried agreed to pay.

There was eventual testimony that periodically, as the Grand firm received payments on the reservoir job from the city, Fried turned over kickback money to the plotters. The money was carried from Grand's office to Itkin's office by Fried's lawyer, Carl D'Angelo, a former assistant district attorney in Manhattan and the son of one of Marcus's predecessors as commissioner of water supply, gas, and electricity. At Itkin's office, the money was taken from D'Angelo by Motto, who then carried it to Corallo. After taking his cut, Corallo had the remainder of the money distributed to the others. All told, Fried paid $40,000 in kickbacks on the reservoir job. When the job was completed, Marcus and Mayor Lindsay flew to the reservoir in a helicopter amid great fanfare for a reopening ceremony. Marcus even went so far as to write an article about the efficient handling of the job for a magazine called *The American City*. The article, entitled "How to Clean a Big Reservoir," boasted: "Because of the magnitude of the job, we awarded it to an experienced and well-equipped contractor."

Corallo viewed the $8,000 he made on the reservoir deal as the mere down-payment on a potential bonanza that could be reaped through the manipulation of Commissioner Marcus. He quickly began making other demands on Marcus. Seeking a killing in real estate, he asked Marcus for inside information on property the city planned to condemn, lease, or rezone. To protect various rackets in which he was involved, he urged Marcus to use his influence with the Police Department to have certain precinct commanders transferred.

Even more important, Corallo and others involved in the reservoir-cleaning plot next concocted a scheme to extort money on construction contracts from New York's giant utility firm, Consolidated Edison Company. Commissioner Marcus, whose jurisdiction gave him broad powers over Con Ed's activities, would force the utility to award contracts to Henry Fried's S. T. Grand Inc. As in the reservoir deal, Fried would kick back a percentage of the profits to Corallo, Marcus, and Itkin. In the Con Ed case, however, there would be a prominent new figure among the conspirators—Carmine De Sapio.

Once the most powerful Democratic Party boss in New York state and an influential figure in national politics, De Sapio had given up his official party positions—but remained active as a string-puller be-hind the scenes. The other plotters called DeSapio into the affair be-cause the Con Ed scheme would be extremely complex, requiring the sort of political sophistication he could provide. To some, it seemed odd that a prominent Democrat such as De Sapio would be involved in a conspiracy capitalizing on the corruption of a prominent Republican such as Marcus—serving in Lindsay's Republican administration. But Marcus later explained: "Political influence comes from strange direc-tions." Once again, there was evidence that the Mob cares little for party lines, as long as it can get its bidding done.

The initial stages of the plot involving Con Ed as described later in a Federal court trial, centered around the utility's urgent need to pro-vide New York City with more electricity. Con Ed wanted to build a new transmission line in Westchester County, north of the city limits, over an aqueduct right-of-way owned by the city. To do so, it needed a permit from the city, and Commissioner Marcus would decide whether the permit should be issued. The conspirators planned to use Marcus's decision-making power as a lever to force Con Ed to grant construction contracts to Fried's company. Fried and DeSapio would subtly indicate to Con Ed officials that De Sapio controlled Marcus. Meanwhile, Marcus would hold up approval of the permit until Con Ed awarded Fried the desired contracts.

It was contemplated that this would be just the beginning of a long-range extortion plan. Witnesses would later testify De Sapio assured the other plotters: "There's millions to be made if you handle it right, and I know how to handle it." A luncheon meeting was set up between De Sapio and a Con Ed vice president, Max Ulrich, at Man-hattan's swanky L'Aiglon restaurant. De Sapio offered to serve as a sort of referee between Con Ed and Marcus's department. He said he "knew the department and Con Ed were two vital organizations in supplying lifeblood to the city" and had heard that relations between them were not particularly good. Since he had "a lot of experience in governmental works," De Sapio said, he might be able to help Con Ed in its troubles with the city. Ulrich replied that Con Ed would welcome all the help it could get.

Later, Marcus told Itkin that Con Ed wanted a letter from him permitting the company to start work on the Westchester transmission line. Itkin met with De Sapio to discuss the request. De Sapio cau-tioned Itkin that things had to be done "my way" and that "in this type of work we have to be very sophisticated." He said Marcus would have to "hold up that letter" until De Sapio okayed it. De Sapio feared that Marcus lacked the nerve to stick it out during the lengthy time it might take to consummate the extortion plot. Itkin explained that, despite the loans from Corallo, Marcus was still caught in a financial bind that had him "wild." In that case, De Sapio said, he could arrange a $25,000 payment to ease Marcus's crisis—but Marcus "must be patient."

Itkin, who had been serving as an FBI informer for the previous four years, secretly kept the FBI posted on all the developments concerning Marcus's involvement with Corallo, De Sapio, and the other conspirators. Using equipment provided by the FBI, Itkin covertly recorded some of his conversations with the plotters. Among them was a discussion of the Con Ed scheme with Marcus and Corallo at Itkin's apartment. The recording included numerous references to De Sapio's role in the conspiracy.

After this conversation, De Sapio and Fried had lunch with another Con Ed vice president, Gerald Hadden, who was in charge of the company's construction projects. Hadden complained that Con Ed still hadn't been able to get Marcus to approve the start of work on the transmission line. De Sapio knowing the company had already told Marcus it would settle temporarily for a letter from Marcus if the construction permit were not immediately available, asked Hadden what was needed. "Would a letter do?" Hadden replied that it depended on what sort of letter it was. "I'll see what I can do," De Sapio said.

A short time later, assured that Con Ed would come through with the contract awards for Fried's company, De Sapio telephoned Itkin and gave him a coded message to have Marcus send the letter: "You can send that insurance policy out," De Sapio said. Marcus followed the order.

Itkin visited De Sapio's apartment four days later and De Sapio gave him an initial payment of $5,000 in cash. The following week, at De Sapio's office, Itkin received another $2,500. "Let's just see and make sure everything goes right," De Sapio told Itkin. "I have to get it all back from Henry Fried before I pay any more out." When Itkin returned to De Sapio's office for still another payment, De Sapio complained that Marcus had written Con Ed a "terrible letter." As a result, he said, "Henry decided we are only going to get $20,000." De Sapio planned to keep $7,500 of the $20,000 for "all the work" he had done, but turned the remainder over to Itkin. All told, Itkin received $12,500 from De Sapio—which he shared with his confederates. The assumption was that these were merely the first installments on what would eventually be enormous payoffs from a continuing plot to shake down Con Ed.

But the fact was that the conspiracy had just about reached the end of its road. The FBI apparently intended to encourage Itkin to continue playing along with his confederates while it gathered additional evidence, but an unexpected development forced the Federal men to move ahead of schedule. Two men who had invested money in the firm operated by Marcus and Itkin, Conestoga Investments, Ltd., filed a complaint with Manhattan District Attorney Frank Hogan about Marcus's handling of the company's funds. Hogan took the complaint before a grand jury and notified Mayor Lindsay that Marcus was under investigation. Lindsay questioned Marcus, who assured him that Hogan's investigation stemmed from a dispute with a former partner about expense accounts in Conestoga and had nothing to do with city business. Nonetheless, Lindsay instructed his investigations commissioner, Arnold Fraiman, to begin checking on Marcus's affairs.

With three investigations of Marcus being conducted simultaneously, the FBI and Federal prosecutors decided to act quickly before the waters became muddied. Evidence concerning Marcus's involvement with Corallo, Itkin, and others in the reservoir-cleaning case was immediately presented to a Federal grand jury. Meanwhile, Marcus resigned his city job—still insisting to Lindsay that he had done nothing wrong.

Six days after Marcus's resignation, the Federal grand jury indicted him with Corallo, Fried, Motto, and Itkin on charges of violating the anti-racketeering laws in the reservoir scheme. (Itkin's inclusion in the indictment was intended to prevent the other defendants from suspecting that he was an FBI informer.) News of the indictment hit the Lindsay administration like a thunderbolt. Marcus was the highest-ranking New York City official in decades to be involved in a scandal. And his involvement with a Mafioso such as Corallo struck some officials as virtually unbelievable. The indictment was all the more sensational because Lindsay and his aides had tried to create the impression that they had lifted city government high above the image of dirty politics that had long pervaded New York.

Mayor Lindsay, clearly jolted by the scandal, commented: "If the charge in the Federal indictment is true, then it's clear that Mr. Marcus lied to me, lied to Commissioner Fraiman, and lied to District Attorney

Hogan. To say that in that event I have been ill-served and the public also is an understatement, obviously. I consider this a betrayal of a personal and a public trust."

Marcus, after briefly contemplating suicide, decided to tell all to the FBI, plead guilty, become a government witness and throw himself on the mercy of the court. Meanwhile, word leaked out that Herbert Itkin was actually an FBI informer. Less than a month after the return of the indictment, FBI agents arrested two men—one of them a lawyer —on charges of plotting to murder Itkin. The defendants in the murder-conspiracy case were Robert Schwartz, an attorney who was also under indictment in a stock-fraud case, and Robert Roden, an ex-convict who had formerly been a professional light-heavyweight boxer. Schwartz conceded he had been involved in financial dealings with Itkin, but both he and Roden denied knowing anything about a murder plot. Federal authorities charged, however, that the two men had tried to hire someone to kill Itkin to prevent him from testifying in the Marcus case. A court complaint filed by the authorities said that Roden had met several times with a man who turned out to be another government informer and had offered the man money to murder Itkin. The first offer was $1,500, but the bounty was later raised to $2,500. The informer told FBI agents about the offer and was instructed to play along with the plot until the arrests were made. Assistant United States Attorney Michael Fawer charged at a preliminary hearing in the case that the murder conspiracy was so "well plotted" and so far along that "all that had to be done was the pulling of the trigger." Schwartz and Roden pleaded not guilty and the case is still pending at this writing. In the stock-fraud case, Schwartz was found guilty of using stock he did not own as collateral for a loan. He was fined $2,500, but is currently appealing the conviction.

The sensation created by the indictment in the city reservoir case and the arrests in the murder-conspiracy case was further compounded by a later indictment charging De Sapio, Corallo, and Fried with conspiracy in the Con Ed case. De Sapio was an even better-known figure than Marcus, both in New York and on the national scene. Moreover, his involvement with Corallo, coming on the heels of Marcus's indictment with Corallo, pointed up the Mob's ability to do business with both top-echelon Democrats and Republicans in New York. Other indictments followed, charging Marcus in the state courts with conspiracy and taking bribes.

Marcus and Itkin became the government's chief witnesses against the other conspirators in both the reservoir case and the Con Ed case. Both prosecutions were successful. In the reservoir case, Corallo was sentenced to three years in prison, Fried to two years and Marcus to fifteen months. In the state court cases, Marcus was sentenced to three concurrent one-year terms. In the Con Ed case, De Sapio got two years and Corallo got four and a half years. (Fried was found to be too ill to stand trial in the Con Ed case.)

During the Con Ed trial, Assistant U.S. Attorney Paul Rooney emphasized that the kickback scheme involving the transmission line was "peanuts" compared with more grandiose plans concocted by the conspirators—plans that were foiled by the revelation of the Marcus scandal. Next, Rooney charged, the De Sapio-Corallo combine intended to get its hooks into a $100 million nuclear power plant that Con Ed planned to build on Storm King Mountain near Cornwall, New York. The kickback projected on that job was $5 million, Rooney said, and the transmission-line deal was intended simply to set the "ground rules" for the bigger caper. "This is a case of big-time corruption," Rooney said. "This is corruption at the highest level. This is sophisticated corruption. This isn't four guys sitting in the back of the bar, plotting."

CORRUPTION IN THE
CONSTRUCTION INDUSTRY
Knapp Commission

It is virtually impossible for a builder to erect a building within the City of New York and comply with every statute and ordinance in connection with the work. In short, many of the statutes and rules and regulations are not only unrealistic but lead to the temptation for corruption.

So said H. Earl Fullilove, Chairman of the Board of Governors of the Building Trades Employers Association of the City of New York,

From Commission to Investigate Allegations of Police Corruption and the City's Anti-Corruption Procedures (Knapp Commission), *Commission Report*, pp.123-131.

in testimony before the Commission on October 29, 1971, summing up a situation which has led to extensive graft in the construction industry. The Commission found that payments to the police by contractors and subcontractors were the rule rather than exceptions and constituted a major source of graft to the uniformed police. It must be noted that policemen were not alone in receiving payoffs from contractors. Much larger payoffs were made to inspectors and permit-granting personnel from other agencies.

The Investigation

In its initial investigation into corruption in the construction industry, the Commission came up against a stone wall. Sixteen veteran job superintendents and two project managers interviewed at construction sites solemnly denied that they had ever paid off the police or known anyone who had. Similar denials were made under oath by other construction people and by three patrolmen and their precinct commander, who were subpoenaed by the Commission. Later, in private talks with members of the construction industry, quite a different story began to emerge. From information obtained in these lengthy, off-the-record interviews, the Commission was able to piece together a detailed picture of corruption in the construction industry.

Although several of these sources were unusually helpful to the Commission in private talks, only one agreed to testify extensively in executive session (and then only under the cloak of anonymity) and none would testify at the public hearings. Their testimony could at no time be compelled, because the Commission lacked the power to obviate claims of Fifth Amendment privileges by conferring immunity. However, it was arranged that the construction industry would be represented at the public hearings by Mr. Fullilove, whose association is made up of 800 contractors and subcontractors, including industry giants as well as smaller companies.

Speaking for his membership, Mr. Fullilove said, "Many—if not most—people in the industry are reluctant to appear at an open hearing and to testify on these matters. Our members feel that unless the entire situation can be remedied in one fell swoop, it's a tremendous burden on a member to become a hero for a day and then suffer the consequential individual harassment." He then went on to detail the laws and ordinances leading to police harassment and consequent graft. This information was corroborated and buttressed by the testimony of Patrolmen William Phillips and Waverly Logan.

Reasons for Police Corruption
in Relation to Construction

Corruption is a fact of life in the construction industry. In addition to extensive payoffs contractors make to police and others in regulatory agencies, there is evidence of considerable corruption within the industry itself. Contractors have been known to pay owners' agents to get an inside track on upcoming jobs; subcontractors pay contractors' purchasing agents to receive projects or to get information helpful in competitive bidding; sub-subcontractors pay subcontractors; dump-truck drivers exact a per-load payment for taking out extra loads they don't report to their bosses; and hoist engineers get money from various subcontractors to insure that materials are lifted to high floors without loss or damage. In this climate, it is only natural that contractors also pay the police.

The heart of the problem of police corruption in the construction industry is the dizzying array of laws, ordinances, and regulations governing construction in the City. To put up a building in New York, a builder is required to get a minimum of forty to fifty different permits and licenses from various City departments. For a very large project, the total number of permits needed may soar to 120, 130 or more. These permits range in importance from the initial building permit down through permits required for erecting fences, wooden walkways and construction shanties, to seemingly petty ones like that required whenever a track vehicle is moved across a sidewalk. "This [latter] regulation is often violated," Mr. Fullilove told the Commission, "because it is tremendous inconvenience to obtain a one-shot permit to move a bulldozer over a five-foot stretch of sidewalk." In practice, most builders don't bother to get all the permits required by law. Instead, they apply for a handful of the more important ones (often making a payoff to personnel at the appropriate agency to insure prompt issuance of the permit). Payments to the police and inspectors from other departments insure that builders won't be hounded for not having other permits.

Of the City ordinances enforced by the police which affect construction, most relate to use of the streets and sidewalks and to excessive dust and noise. Ordinances most troublesome to contractors are those which prohibit double-parking, flying dust, obstructing the sidewalk, or leaving it strewn with piles of sand and rubble, and beginning work before 7:00 a.m. or continuing after 6:00 p.m. (This last is for the protection of neighborhood residents already subject to eleven legal hours a day of construction noise.)

Most large contractors seem to regard all of the ordinances mentioned above and many of the permit requirements simply as nuisances which interfere with efficient construction work. Thus, they are willing parties to a system which frees them from strict adherence to the regulations.

Police Enforcement of Laws
Regulating Construction

Although building inspectors are responsible for enforcement of regulations concerning construction techniques, the responsibility for inspecting certain permits and enforcing the ordinances outlined above lies with the police. The police officers charged with this responsibility have always been faced with a particularly tempting opportunity for corruption. The Department has attempted, since the Commission hearings, to lessen the opportunities by cutting back on enforcement. It has ordered its men to stop enforcing all laws pertaining to construction, unless pedestrians are endangered or traffic is impeded. If a patrolman observes a condition which affects pedestrians or traffic, he is to call his superior to come to the site and take whatever action is needed. Nevertheless, pending a revision of the laws to make them more realistic, they cannot go entirely unenforced and whoever is given the job will meet the same pressures found by the Commission.

Traditionally, construction enforcement was the function of one foot patrolman in each precinct called the "conditions man" who concentrated on construction enforcement. At the time of the investigation, a growing number of precincts had abolished the post, leaving the responsibility for construction enforcement to other officers, such as "summons men" who had broader responsibilities for issuing summonses in other areas. Foot patrolmen and those in patrol cars were also empowered to go onto any site in their sectors to check for violations. In any case, the patrolman whose duty it was to enforce construction laws was, at the time of the investigation, required to make periodic checks of all construction sites in the precinct to make sure that they 1) had the proper permits, 2) conformed to the limitations of those permits, and 3) adhered to all City ordinances not covered by the permits. If he found any violations, he was supposed to issue a summons. Department regulations provided that he make a notation in his memo book whenever he visited a construction site and maintain a file at the precinct with a folder for each construction job in his jurisdiction, containing copies of all permit numbers for the site and a record of all civil summonses it had received.

In practice, the Commission found, officers responsible for enforcing ordinances relating to construction simply kept pro forma files and pretty much let the job go at that. Examination of conditions men's memo books in the Twentieth Precinct, where there were between twenty and fifty construction projects underway at one time, indicated that a grand total of thirty-nine visits were reported to have been made to construction sites over the two-year period from March, 1969, to March, 1971, with over half those visits recorded as having been for the purpose of copying down permit numbers. The patrolmen whose notebooks were examined admitted under oath that they did not follow Department regulations in getting permit numbers from new sites or in making entries in their memo books every time they entered a site. In short, the Commission found that these patrolmen had not been doing their jobs properly, were aware that they weren't, and knew that their work would not be reviewed by senior officers.

These rules were designed to facilitate control of corruption. Where the rules were ignored by supervisors, the spread of corruption was almost inevitable.

Patterns of Police Corruption in Construction

The most common pattern of police payoffs in the construction industry, as described to the Commission by police officers and by contractors and their employees, involved payment to the sector car of a fixed monthly or weekly fee, which varied according to the size of the construction job. Occasionally, the sergeants would also have a pad, and in larger jobs, the precinct captain sometimes had one of his own. In addition, all construction sites, no matter how small, were found to be vulnerable to overtures from local foot patrolmen.*

In a small job like the renovation of a brownstone, the general contractor was likely to pay the police between $50 and $150 a month,

---

* One small contractor told how it's done: "Put a five dollar bill in one pocket, a ten in the other. Fold it up real small. Size up the situation and pay accordingly. You can pass it in a handshake if necessary. It really isn't. You know the touch is on as soon as he . . . walks on the job to see your permit and questions it."

and the fee ascended sharply for larger jobs. An excavator on a small job paid $50 to $100 a week for the duration of exacavation to avoid summonses for dirt spillage, flying dust, double-parked dump trucks, or for running vehicles over the sidewalk without a permit. A concrete company pouring a foundation paid another $50 to $100 a week to avoid summonses for double-parking its trucks or for running them across a sidewalk without a curb cut. (Concrete contractors are especially vulnerable, as it is essential that foundation-pouring be carried on continuously. This means that one or more trucks must be kept standing by while one is actually pouring.) Steel erectors paid a weekly fee to keep steel delivery trucks standing by; masons paid; the crane company paid. In addition, all construction sites were approached by police for contributions at Christmas, and a significant number paid extra for additional police patrols in the hope of obtaining protection from vandalism of building materials and equipment.

In small contracting companies, payments were generally negotiated and made by the owner; larger firms often had an employee whose sole job was to handle negotiations with agencies which regulate construction. This man, called an expeditor, negotiated and made all such payments, both to the police and to inspectors and permit-granting personnel from other agencies. In either case, when work was started on a new site, arrangements were made with the local police.

One contractor, whose experiences were fairly typical, spoke at length with Commission investigators and later—with promise of anonymity—testified before the Commission in executive session. He was a small general contractor who worked on jobs of less than one million dollars. He started his own company in the early sixties with a contract for a small job in Brooklyn. During the first week of construction, a sector car pulled up to the construction site and a patrolman came onto the site, asking to see the permits for demolition, sidewalk construction, etc. He looked over the various permits and left. The following day, another sector car came by, and one of the patrolmen issued a summons for obstruction of the sidewalk. The contractor protested that he had the necessary permit and was in no way violating the law. "If we don't work together," the patrolman told him, "there will be a ticket every day." When the contractor asked how much "working together" would cost, he was told, "$50 a week." The contractor testified that he balked at this, claiming that his was a small operation and that he couldn't afford such payments. He said he would prefer to operate within the limitations of his permits and go to court to answer any summonses he might receive.

The following day, the contractor received another summons for $100. Two days later, he was approached again and told that it would be cheaper to pay off the police than to accumulate summonses. "We decided for our own good to make that $50 payment and not maintain our hero status," he said. He continued to make payments of $50 a week to a patrolman from the sector car for the duration of the construction work, which lasted about one year. His site was never again inspected by the police and he received no more summonses.

This contractor further testified that he was approached by the police, and paid them, on all the jobs he did in various City precincts. On none of these was he ever served with a summons. On his last job, in 1970, when he was in financial difficulties which eventually led to bankruptcy proceedings, he was, as usual, approached by the police for payoffs. Pleading insolvency, he refused to pay and used various ruses to avoid payment. He again began receiving summonses for violations—the first that had been served on him since he started paying the police.

This contractor stated that in addition to paying the police he has also made payments to personnel from the Department of Buildings, other divisions of the Housing and Development Administration, the Department of Highways, and such federal agencies as the Department of Housing and Urban Affairs and the Federal Housing Administration.

Another builder, the owner of a medium-sized contracting company which does work for such clients as Consolidated Edison, the New York Telephone Company and the Catholic Dioceses of New York and Brooklyn, told Commission investigators that his company had paid off the police on every construction job it had done in the City, including the six or eight jobs in progress at the time of the interview. He told the Commission that he paid the police from $50 to $100 a week for each job he had in progress, and that payments were made by his expeditor, whose job it was to obtain permits and pay off police and others. He went on to say that his company frequently negotiated the amount of payment with the precinct commander either at the building site or at the local precinct.

A reliable informant who was intimately connected with this builder told the Commission that the builder's payoffs were in fact much larger than the $50 to $100 he claimed. The informant also reported that the expeditor handled all negotiations for payoffs, then reported to officers of the company, who gave him the appropriate amount out of petty cash. At a later date, the expeditor submitted covering expense vouchers indicating travel or entertainment expenses. During the time this informant was giving information to the Commission, he observed a sergeant approach a foreman at one of the company's construction sites in Queens and threaten to write out a summons for burning refuse. The foreman then told the sergeant that he couldn't see going to court over it and would give him $20 to forget about it. The sergeant said he would have to discuss it with his boss and left the site. That afternoon, the sergeant returned to the construction site with his precinct captain, who advised the foreman that there were "a lot of violations around." He said he wanted to speak to someone about "taking care of it" (a clear reference to the expeditor), and would return on the Tuesday afternoon following. At this point, the informant's role was discovered and the Commission was not able to find out how big a payoff the captain had in mind, although a three installment $2,500 payoff which the informant said was arranged with a building inspector a few days earlier indicates that it would have been sizable.

INTEGRITY IN GOVERNMENT
Standards and Goals Commission

The Target Areas

In 1968 the National Commission on Urban Problems wrote:

> In some communities, there is a very real problem of corruption in zoning decisions. A property owner who could build a shopping center or a high-rise apartment suddenly discovers that his property is worth many times as much as the property owner who is relegated to low-density development. The values at stake are enormous, so it is not surprising, therefore, that the zoning system is subject to enormous pressures by landowners and developers and that outright corruption is more than simply an occasional exception.[1]

From National Advisory Commission on Criminal Justice Standards and Goals, *Community Crime Prevention* (Washington, D.C.: Government Printing Office, 1973), pp.254–258. Some footnotes deleted.

1. *Building the American City*, Final Report of the National Commission on Urban Problems (1968), p.19.

In 1973, the problem not only remains but shows every prospect of growing. The Commission on Urban Problems estimated that more than 18 million acres of land would come into new urban use between 1970 and 2000. The land, now in farm and randomly owned semiurban parcels, will be subjected to increasingly attractive purchase options by developers speculating against future urban growth. In fact, the race is already on in many major urban areas. In 1968, farmland in Frederick County, Md.—more than 30 miles from Washington, D.C.— was selling for as little as $100 per acre and seldom for more than $1,000 per acre. In 1971, Frederick County acreage having reasonable access to Interstate 70S was selling for $2,000 per acre and more.

Most of this new land use will require rezoning (from farm to nonfarm uses). Purchase options contingent upon successful rezoning decisions are becoming the norm in many areas. Assuming very conservative transaction values, more than $20 billion will be involved in the initial land sales associated with projected urbanization. Initial investments in improvements and debt service in this growth easily will equal twice that amount and might well be greater as skilled labor and sophisticated plant costs rise. In short, residential and commercial developers, and businesses building for themselves, will be facing more than $60 billion in investments over the next 30 years, keeping pace with expanded urban markets. The financial pressures on developers for quick and favorable zoning are staggering and put a premium on finding ways to obtain those decisions.

In 1968, more than 18,000 jurisdictions in the United States had one or more kinds of zoning, planning, or building ordinances. More than half of these jurisdictions were outside Standard Metropolitan Statistical Areas (smsa). Almost 90 percent of the jurisdictions with populations in excess of 5,000 had planning boards or commissions and nearly 80 percent had, in addition, zoning boards of appeals. The average membership on planning boards is seven or eight persons and on zoning boards, five or six. In the more than 3,300 governments involved, nearly 50,000 people sit on these boards. Most are political appointees who have little or no technical experience in the areas they are supposed to regulate.

In 1967, expenditures and employment for these activities totaled less than $300 million and involved over 50,000 full- and part-time employees. Local governments within smsas accounted for 86 percent of total expenditures and 72 percent of total personnel. Salaries for planning and zone boards and their staffs tend to be significantly lower than those paid to persons in the private sector with whom the boards deal. Average salaries for professional and technical public employees range from less than $7,000 a year to just over $9,000, depending on the size and location of the jurisdiction. Private sector salaries, depending on the firm and region, range from 25 percent to 150 percent greater than comparable government positions. Only 2 percent of the jurisdictions reported top salaries of $15,000 or more a year in these activities.

This disparity has two implications for the integrity of government operations in these areas. First, public employees with salaries significantly lower than their private sector counterparts are under more pressure than most to opt for illegal profit. As one observer stated, ". . . it just isn't reasonable to expect a $4,000 a year building inspector to remain honest for altruistic reasons." Second, government cannot compete effectively for high-caliber staff. The best trained and most ambitious potential recruits go to the highest bidders in the employment pool. Governments rarely head that list.

Pressures on zoning officials as well as on private sector groups involved in the urbanization process are enormous. While zoning does not create land values, it determines whether landowners—and which landowners—will reap the benefit of increased values. It does this by setting up development goals, presumably in the public interest, that take precedence over the real estate market as the arbiter of land uses. It follows, therefore, that those who control the zoning decision control the land values.

Zoning, however, is only the first element of concern to urban developers. Building and construction codes and tax assessment policies of local jurisdictions affect costs and are integral parts of corporate and development planning. Favorable regulatory and tax environments are as important as favorable purchase arrangements, and developers tend to seek out jurisdictions responsive to their interest for the best arrangement possible on taxes and services.

Some Examples

Corruption in regulatory operations is not new, but the probability of corruption is increasing significantly and the gigantic costs already are being borne by overburdened homeowners and taxpayers. The situation in New York, N.Y., is reputed to be so bad that one observer has said it is impossible to get a building or occupancy permit honestly there.

The Commission to Investigate Alleged Police Corruption in New York City (Knapp Commission) heard testimony in October 1971 that as much as 5 percent of the total construction costs in the city are attributable to graft paid to city employees. Five percent of the estimated $1.5 billion annual construction bill amounts to $75 million in that city alone, or just slightly less than the expected 1972 general fund revenues of Cleveland, Ohio. The contractors pay—and through various "budgetary arrangements" pass the costs on to tenants—because there are at least 40 licenses or permits required to construct a new building in the city. A construction delay of several days resulting from a pending permit would cost contractors substantially more than they lose in payoffs.

In Chicago, the Justice Department and the Internal Revenue Service are investigating reported cash payoffs for city zoning changes. Cash payments for as much as $3,000 allegedly have been made to "officials" for allowing specific variances to the city's code. In 1966 in one large eastern county, the outgoing County Council—in its final 48 hours of life—made several hundred changes in the county's carefully developed master plan. Although no collusion was ever proven between the outgoing council members and the land developers in whose favor the changes were made, over 5 years and thousands of dollars in court costs were required to reverse those decisions.

Property Tax Abuse

The most sensational abuses and perhaps the most complex ones occur in the area of property taxation. The prevention of corruption in tax assessments is more than a legal or moral issue—it involves the financial solvency of already hard-pressed cities.

In 1966, property taxes and revenues from local user charges (licenses, permits, etc.) accounted for more than 51 percent of the general revenue of America's 25 largest cities.[2] For all American cities in 1968-69, the amount was just under 70 percent. A "reasonable" tax break on one or two principal commercial locations can cost individual taxpayers tremendous sums either in increased taxes or lost services. When the assessor of Cook County, Ill. (which includes the city of Chicago), discovered he was being investigated by a local citizens' group for "arbitrary and manipulative" operation of his office he "reassessed" nine high-rise properties in the city. The reassessment of those nine buildings alone added $34 million to the city's tax base.

Occasionally, violations of tax laws and their consequent effects are allowed by local officials—usually, but not always, under pressure

2. Bureau of the Census, *Census of Governments* (1970).

from local business and industrial groups—in the name of "progress and development." In September 1970, a group of Richmond County, Ga., taxpayers, responding to tax concessions granted by local officials, took the county to court contending that most of the new industries in the community were paying less than their fair share of local property taxes. When, as a result of a court order, the properties were reassessed according to State law, one firm's tax bill increased 1,100 percent. Four companies alone accounted for over $200,000 in direct revenue increases to the county.

Unfortunately, while the industrial assessments were being challenged, assessments on some individually held land were not. Thus a 26-acre parcel purchased by two local political leaders in 1968 for $33,000 was listed on the county books as worth $1,190. In 1969, the book value on the entire parcel dropped to $300 while the owners were selling two of the 26 acres for $14,000.

Corruption, or the nonlegal and illegal administration of government regulatory powers, occurs at all levels of government administration, from field inspectors to senior review board members and elected officials.[3]

A good deal of it is the result of outright, but sophisticated, theft and collusion; an equal amount, however, is the result of badly designed public programs operated by a staff that is too small, poorly trained, and underpaid.

Avenues of Corruption

The types of corruption that occur in the regulatory areas of government are varied.

One kind of relationship exists when the crimes committed by corrupt government officials are perpetrated in order to facilitate other

3. No reliable statistics exist on which to estimate the number of corruption incidents in the United States. The nearest thing to an estimate resulted from work done for the President's Commission on Law Enforcement and Administration of Justice by the National Opinion Research Center (NORC) in 1966. The NORC study was based on a 10,000 family nationwide survey of victimization. More than 33,000 people were involved. A result of that survey was the calculation of incident rates per 100,000 population for various classes of crime. Two crimes, soliciting bribes and building violations, relevant to this study were detailed. Bribes were shown to occur three times as often as murder, with an incident rate of 9.1 occurrences per 100,000 population. Building violations occurred about half as often as robbery, with 42.5 incidents per 100,000 population. See: Philip H. Ennis, *Criminal Victimization in The United States: A Report of a National Survey* (1967), pp.8, 11, and 108.

crimes committed by the corruptors and their allies. A corrupt member of a permit review board might, for a fee, issue a license to another criminal to operate an illegal liquor establishment under the guise of a special exception to local codes.

Another relationship exists when public officials accept or demand bribes for doing their ordinary duty. A lawyer sitting on a zoning appeals board sees a developer at a cocktail party the weekend before a hearing; he lets the developer know that his law firm is interested in acquiring a few new clients. When the word gets back to the lawyer that his partner has been approached about representing the developer's firm, he calls the developer to assure him that he looks favorably on a variance request. The damage from this kind of corruption is much greater today than it was in the past because of government's increasing regulatory role. Government officials guilty of such malfeasance are not likely to prosecute when, if the applicant is also a criminal, the variance or permit is used illegally. Effective nullification of government functions is the result and all Americans pay the cost.

A third situation occurs when a government official conspires with a businessman or labor leader to cheat the public. The former commissioner of streets in a midwest city, was convicted recently of taking kickbacks on truck rental contracts let by the city during past summer paving seasons. In this case, the private sector criminal gets legitimate work—but at greater than competitive rates—and the official gets paid a commission on the profits.

Finally, there is a situation in which two corrupt individuals interact but one of them is also a victim. In this case, a construction superintendent whose project violates city codes is harassed by a building inspector into paying a fee for a clean inspection report. The superintendent is both the corruptor and the victim.

The above examples are only a portion of the possible victim-criminal interactions. There also are numerous circumstances under which citizen-government interactions in the target areas may appear to be corrupt but are in fact completely honest. Both corrupt, and honest but corrupt-appearing, transactions are possible, mainly because of the nature of the operating system.

How Corruption Occurs

Government zoning, licensing, and tax assessment processes share several characteristics that contribute to the occurrence of corruption.

Many of them have been detailed by the National Commission on Urban Problems.

A fundamental factor contributing to abuse in these areas is the lack of clearly stated public purposes and goals. Most jurisdictions define the actions that may be taken in these target areas and may even do so with some precision. There is considerable difference, however, between what action may be taken and why it is to be taken.

The rationale for zoning and licensing actions generally is defined in terms of the government's police power to protect the health, safety, and welfare of its citizens. Broadly drawn master plans are compiled by the city or by firms working for the city, and these plans purport to show proper and reasonable patterns for the area. Land uses are identified in terms of some desired future position. Occupancy and building use permits and licenses presumably insure reasonable distribution of carefully screened services that are compatible with the community in which they are located; they also serve as the bases for tax assessment valuations. As a matter of practical fact, however, the objectives of these programs are not based on measured change or growth goals.

Although property taxation is a slightly different program, it suffers essentially the same shortcoming. The planning of local government expenditures for particular services is carried out—if at all—after the probable tax revenues are calculated. Inventories of needed services do not exist. Hence, the expenditure for street surfacing, parks and recreation facilities, police and fire protection, and water, sewer, and other governmental services are internally negotiated pieces of an uncontrolled fiscal pie. Citizens have little or no say about which services will be provided in what order. It never occurs to most citizens, or to their political leaders, that tax rates can be established rationally, providing the purposes of the tax program are spelled out carefully.

An obvious and immediate consequence of the lack of planning and management goals is substantial arbitrariness in day-to-day governmental decisions. The legislative criterion for granting zoning variances, for example, may well read like the Standard State Zoning Enabling Act, which permits variances if they:

> . . . will not be contrary to the public interest, where, owing to special conditions, a literal enforcement of the provisions of the ordinance will result in unnecessary hardship, and so that the spirit of the ordinance shall be observed and substantial justice done.[4]

4. *Building the American City*, p. 226.

Language this broad not only makes the work of honest zoning boards difficult, it actually invites abuse. In view of the value implications of many zoning exception decisions, the time pressures under which zoning boards often work, and the lack of technical expertise held by members, it is not surprising that large numbers of patently illegal variances are granted every year. In studies done for the Commission on Urban Problems, for example, it was found that in only 15 of 284 variance approval studies in Alameda, Calif., was there any showing of special circumstances or hardship.

The same applies to property tax assessment and administration. Preferential exemptions for certain types of property owners open legal loopholes that contribute significantly to abuse. The Advisory Commission on Intergovernmental Relations, writing in 1963, observed that: " . . . the extent to which some personal property tax laws have become legal fictions is notorious. Evasions and the condoning of evasion are so widespread as to make such laws a tax on integrity . . ."[5]

A Case Study

An example of the degree to which a tax assessment system, allowing loopholes and failing to spell out administrative criteria, is subject to abuse is detailed in the brief filed by the Campaign Against Pollution against the Cook County assessor. Having established the legal framework in which the injunction was sought, the plaintiffs went on to raise questions, the remedies to which constitute a real public-interest-related standard for operation of a tax assessment office. The list of complaints included assertion that:

1. The assessor had not prescribed a standard method of assessment and the assessor's office was operated without appropriate rules and regulations.

2. The office was inadequately staffed and ". . . positions requiring technical skills are instead filled with patronage employees not qualified or trained to serve in . . . " the positions they held.

3. There existed no system for assessing formerly exempt property, and holders of exempt property were not required to file annual statements of exemption.

4. There existed no system for assessing properties previously omit-

5. *Ibid.*, p.368.

ted or for reassessing upon first improvement or expansion of improvements. Specifically, the plaintiffs charged that:

> The Assessor either ignores building permit applications made to the
> various building departments within the county, and fails to pick up
> improvements, or the Assessor knowingly relies on the amounts repre-
> sented as the value of the improvement set out in such applications,
> knowing such representations to be false and understated for the pur-
> pose of obtaining an unwarranted and low assessment.

1. The assessor not only did not bring suit against property owners
misrepresenting improvement values on permit requests, but condoned
the practice.

2. Real estate tax transfer declarations were not reviewed.

3. No system existed for examining appropriate records of other
public agencies where land improvements would be identified, and no
routine reporting by those agencies had been requested.

4. The assessor assessed property below its fair cash value as required by law and " . . . purposefully maintained an irrational and
random system solely because such a system is subject to manipulation
and preference."

5. Without statutory authority, a system of allowing lower assessments on commercial properties on the basis of economic hardship,
called "objection one," was instituted whereby a ". . . random and
arbitrary 'condition factor,' [was used] to give preference and lower
assessments to persons who supported his political activities . . . "

6. As a part of the objection one process, the assessor did not require sworn or certified statements and did not maintain copies of
which documents were used in objection one proceedings.

Although not exhaustive, the list is illustrative of the real or potential abuses arising in badly managed programs where significant
discretion in decision making is allowed. However, even when good
guidance is available to government employees, if the administrative
procedures themselves are poorly supervised or excessively decentralized, abuses will still occur. For example, few cities control applications
for permits and licenses. Private citizens and agencies otherwise satisfying the legal and administrative requirements for a building or other
license stand a good chance of being victimized by corrupt public officials, or of having to bribe officials to get action, when they submit
their application to Rube Goldberg bureaucracies. The situation today

is no better than it was 4 years ago, when the Commission on Urban Problems wrote:

> In many jurisdictions developers must navigate their way through a maze of officialdom, with different officials reviewing the plan for street layout, sanitary facilities, building location and so on. Intentional delays are not uncommon . . . and the disapproval of a single official along the way, based perhaps on personal whim, can destroy the proposal entirely or set it back for months.[6]

Under these circumstances, public regulation of proposed private activities degenerates into a bargaining process in which bribes and payoffs are likely to result. Developers themselves, however, are not blameless. Aside from outright dishonesty, applicants often seek special exceptions or approval of regulation variances that are illegal, or of questionable legality. In fact, a good deal of public red tape has come into being in response to earlier misrepresentations and substandard performance by private agencies and groups.

Much of this problem could be prevented through the simple expedient of sound management. Applications should be centrally controlled with review deadlines specified for the various evaluations; evaluations (specific review element approval/disapproval) should be required in writing from the reviewing official; and the application pipeline should be audited regularly by an external agency, particularly field inspection reports.

The need for external audits is critical. Public surveillance of zoning, licensing, and tax decisions is hampered by secrecy, technical obfuscation of both regulations and decisions, and a too-frequent unwillingness of public officials to relinquish their "flexibility" by publicizing detailed decision criteria. Regular audits by external agencies would go a long way toward protecting the public from venal public officials and their private corruptors.

Summary

There is no doubt that corruption exists in the areas of zoning, licensing, and tax assessment. The extent and cost of this corruption can only be estimated, however, because little has been done to document known occurrences. Conditions contributing to corrupt practices exist in governmental jurisdictions of all sizes. Moreover, probable ur-

6. Ibid., p.227.

banization in the near future is going to involve increasingly complex financial operations of enormous magnitude. Pressures on both private groups and public officials to achieve special ends are going to intensify. The need for administrative reforms, already great, can be expected to grow still greater as the pace and complexity of government planning, regulatory, and revenue requirements increase.

The administrative standards that follow are not intended as all-inclusive solutions to public corruption. In the final analysis, only honest people can insure honest government operation. What the standards do, however, is remove from ill-equipped public employees the burden of administering difficult functions with poor guidance in a high-pressure environment. They place the burden and responsibility of decision where it should be—with elected and publicly accountable officials.

THEFT AND INEFFICIENCY IN THE POVERTY PROGRAM

Richard Reeves, Barnard L. Collier, Richard Phallon, and Richard Severo

Multiple investigations of the city's $122-million-a-year antipoverty program are disclosing chronic corruption and administrative chaos that have already cheated New York's poor of uncounted millions of dollars.

"It's so bad that it will take 10 years to find out what's really been going on inside the Human Resources Administration," said an assistant

Originally entitled "Millions in City Poverty Funds Lost by Fraud and Inefficiency," prepared by Richard Reeves, Barnard L. Collier, Richard Phallon, and Richard Severo, *The New York Times*, January 12, 1969. Copyright © 1969 by the New York Times Company. Reprinted by permission.

district attorney who has spent the last four months studying the super-agency. It was formed 27 months ago to run the city's antipoverty and welfare programs.

More than 100 investigators—from the office of District Attorney Frank S. Hogan, the city's Department of Investigation and Federal agencies—have discovered that the mismanagement and internal dishonesty still exist; that while auditors and detectives were studying the H.R.A. in the last two months, some persons were carrying out a $1-million embezzlement plot.

As late as last Dec. 19 a confidential survey by the United States Department of Labor—which largely finances H.R.A.'s Neighborhood Youth Corps—reported:

"Unless vast changes are made, it is the opinion of this office that H.R.A. cannot possibly cope with the many additional problems that will be brought about by the substantial increase in enrollees under the summer programs."

An inside evaluation—a staff memorandum last May to Mitchell I. Ginsberg, the superagency's administrator—warned that in some cases management failures had "more than negated the impact of the anti-poverty program in local communities."

Investigators from Washington and Mr. Hogan's office have charged that some city officials are destroying important H.R.A. records and are reluctant to cooperate. The city has informed the investigators that less than $1.5-million has been stolen from H.R.A., but independent investigators say the actual figure will be much higher.

For the last three months reporters of *The New York Times* have interviewed dozens of former and present city officials, investigators and some of the men and women under investigation.

Those interviews have disclosed cases of apparent corruption either compounded or encouraged by chaotic administrative practices.

The cases which follow appear at this time to be unrelated, except that they indicate problems in the H.R.A.

¶A complex plot was discovered three weeks ago by suspicious bankers, to transfer four checks totaling more than $1-million from H.R.A. accounts to a secret bank account in Zurich, Switzerland.

¶Two former officials of the agency and a high-ranking official still on the job are being investigated on suspicion that they embezzled funds and took kickbacks.

¶The theft of at least $1.75-million in nine months was charged to a group of young H.R.A. employes from Durham, N. C., who call themselves "the Durham Mob"—suspected of rigging city computers to produce fraudulent paychecks.

¶The District Attorney and Department of Investigation are looking into the disappearance of Social Security payments withheld from thousands of Neighborhood Youth Corps paychecks, but never forwarded to the Federal Government.

¶One city fiscal officer "intercepted" Federal checks intended for the City Controller and, without authorization, deposited more than $6-million in an H.R.A. account. The officer then made cash withdrawals to pay overtime salaries, records of which never appeared on the payroll records or in the records of the Internal Revenue Service.

¶A bizarre scheme was hatched five weeks ago, to steal $52,000 in H.R.A. funds by the purchase of a Los Angeles house with a check made out to an apparently fictitious man who "identified" himself by writing a false license plate number and the unlisted phone number of a movie star on the back of a stolen H.R.A. check.

¶A plan submitted to the Labor Department to "safeguard" Neighborhood Youth Corps Funds was developed last August by two H.R.A. officials who were arrested a month later and charged with Youth Corps thefts.

These situations are only a sampling of the problems of the Human Resources Administration—problems that could multiply as more Federal investigators come into the city and produce reports such as the April 24, 1968, document produced by Labor Department auditors. That was titled "Absence of Fiscal Responsibility in the Human Resources Administration, City of New York."

And the problems of New York are in many ways those of the nation, not only because internal corruption is now being investigated in the antipoverty programs of other cities, including Los Angeles and Detroit, but because that corruption could influence the attitude of the new Nixon Administration toward all programs to aid poor people.

Mr. Ginsberg, former associate dean of the School of Social Work at Columbia University, is aware of that danger.

"Even with all the inefficiencies and mistakes coming to light—and they are serious—the [Youth Corps] and other programs like it have made an important difference to the poor and they must not be destroyed," he said recently.

"We are a fantastically big business," he said yesterday during an interview in his office at 40 Worth Street, in which he was asked about information turned up by *The Times's* investigation. "We improvise and hope we will get through," he said.

In the interview he said: "I'm not suggesting there was no dishonesty. But I don't think it is a massive problem."

He said he had ordered full cooperation with investigators, but conceded there might have been occasions when lower-ranking officials at first resisted supplying information and records.

After the interview Mr. Ginsberg informed Mayor Lindsay of *The Times* investigation, according to Harry J. O'Donnell, the mayor's press secretary. Mr. O'Donnell said last night that Mr. Lindsay would not comment on the investigation until today.

H.R.A., in fact, has problems—gigantic size, explosive growth and inexperience.

The superagency was established by Mayor Lindsay on Aug. 15, 1966, to combine the old Department of Welfare and the two antipoverty agencies: the Manpower and Career Development Agency, which manages job training programs and the Youth Corps, and the Community Development Agency, which coordinates the varied programs of community corporations.

Both confusion and corruption were a problem in city antipoverty agencies before the Lindsay administration took office.

Mr. Ginsberg made it clear yesterday that his major interest was in getting programs moving, not in building rigid financial controls.

"If we had better controls," he said, "we wouldn't have had the programs."

That point of view got the city in trouble with the United States Department of Labor, which reported that Youth Corps irregularities in New York were made possible "because all payroll safeguards used in the past were disregarded."

The Labor Department added that high city officials had given instructions to payroll and fiscal personnel to disregard all controls "to get the enrollees paid."

The city's reason for paying quickly, according to members of Mayor Lindsay's staff, was that there appeared to be danger of race riots if slum-area teen-agers were not put to work and paid.

The Labor Department, on the other hand, was worried about the $19.9-million it had provided for the Youth Corps, and other Federal agencies are worried about the money flowing from Washington to 100 Church Street, the H.R.A. headquarters.

Last September the Labor Department threatened to cancel the city's sponsorship of the program because of fiscal irregularities that led to the intensive scrutiny of the Manpower and Career Development Agency.

Most of the disclosures to date have concerned the Youth Corps, according to one Federal investigator, "simply because that's where we're looking at the moment."

A Federal decision last week to extend city sponsorship of the corps for five more months was interpreted by Mr. Ginsberg as a "vote of confidence" in the Human Resources Administration.

But Labor Department memorandums on the decision reveal that city sponsorship was continued because "of the inherent difficulties in securing new sponsorship."

In fact, the Federal investigators studying city sponsorship concluded last Dec. 18:

"The present staffs of the H.R.A. fiscal office, Manpower Career Development Agency and Neighborhood Youth Corps Fiscal Office do not possess the qualifications to implement a management system, however well designed."

Federal investigators had concluded three months earlier that:

"There is substantial evidence to indicate that employes of New York, staff employes of delegate agencies and even NYC [Neighborhood Youth Corps] enrollees have either conspired or engaged in wholesale larceny, theft through fraud or embezzlement of funds advanced to New York City by the United States Department of Labor."

Those reports are evidence of the cloud of corruption that plagues the Human Resources Administration. Whether they are well informed or not, employes of the agency tend to say such things as "Oh, yes, he's stealing, too."

Dishonesty in neighborhood antipoverty offices also taints the entire agency. Bronx District Attorney Burton B. Roberts found "ghosts" on the payroll of the Hunts Point Community Corporation in 1966.

A Federal auditor in a written report has said that when he informed Robert Shrank, who was Youth Corps director in 1967, of irregularities, "Mr. Shrank informed this auditor that he was a liar and destroyed the report."

Mr. Shrank, who is now an urban-affairs consultant to the Ford Foundation, said yesterday that he did not destroy any report and had only accused the auditor of "exaggerations."

A confidential report by Federal auditors to United States Attorney Robert M. Morgenthau asserts that Mr. Shrank reacted to information that stop-payment orders would be issued on a batch of stolen checks by calling his staff together "to tell them that if any of them had the stolen checks they should not cash them since a 'stop-payment' had been issued."

"I did warn anybody who attempted to cash the checks," Mr. Shrank said yesterday when informed about the report. "After all, we were paying $42,000 a week in checks. I'm not saying it's forgivable, but I don't know how you can ever stop the stolen-check problem."

In another area of investigation the charge of destroying records was heard often in the last three months. But a more common complaint by Federal and District Attorney investigators was that city officials refused to volunteer information or were tardy in providing requested material.

The one official who generally escaped that kind of criticism was Mr. Ginsberg, who was praised by both Federal and local investigators for his sincerity and cooperation.

One aspect of corruption in H.R.A. that has not been mentioned in any report but is often discussed by employees is that the persons arrested to date have all been black. Most employes of the poverty program are Negroes who have been brought into the mainstream of city government.

And the mainstream, in the words of a man who has been at City Hall for 30 years, "has always included taking a little now and then."

"Boss Tweed was a WASP [white Anglo-Saxon Protestant] and the Irish and the Jews followed him," he said. "Now the Negroes are getting their chance and everyone thinks it's a new thing."

"Yes," agreed a Negro who has been arrested, "it looks like some of us have moved up to the white man's thing."

The four fraudulent H.R.A. checks that found their way into a Swiss bank were dated Oct. 9, 1968—the same day that the Rev. H. Carl McCall, then an H.R.A. deputy administrator, told a meeting of Federal and city investigators about new fiscal controls that had been devised to keep antipoverty money from illegally draining out of the agency into private pockets.

Seemingly undisturbed by scores of Federal and city investigators looking into agency books and records, someone—investigators do not yet know who—stole seven blank checks from the back of a brand new H.R.A. checkbook.

All the checks bore the stamped signature, in faded black ink, of Mitchell I. Ginsberg, the H.R.A. administrator. The stamp was either stolen or duplicated.

Three of the checks are still missing, but had the plan to convert the four checks worked out as planned, the H.R.A.'s Manpower and Career Development Agency (from whose checkbook the checks were torn) would have been out precisely $1,017,615.01.

What investigation by *The Times* and the District Attorney into the Swiss bank caper shows is this:

Sometime last November, the four checks were made out—on two different typewriters—jointly to the city's Department of Finance and a concern called Pagliuca Associates. Both names appear as the payees on all the checks and were separated by three asterisks, a slash mark and three more asterisks.

The checks—for $340,063.38; for $105,366.80; for $106,005.59 and $466,179.24—were then mailed or personally carried to Europe, where they were deposited for collection to the private account of one George José Mendoza Müller in the Zurich office of the Banque Populaire Suisse, a relatively small institution with no affiliation to an American bank.

Bank officials interviewed by *The New York Times* in Switzerland say that the checks arrived there simultaneously and that, because of the large amounts involved, they were immediately suspected. Thus, though the checks were accepted for collection purposes, no money was paid out for them.

The Swiss bankers refuse to disclose anything more about the checks, and therefore the identity of Mr. Mendoza Müller remains a mystery.

Nothing was seen of these checks in New York until two days before Christmas, when all four turned up at the Chase Manhattan Bank for payment.

There is some dispute about who first spotted the checks as frauds. The Banque Populaire maintains that it cabled Chase Manhattan immediately after the attempt to deposit them was made in Zurich. Chase Manhattan, however, says that the Swiss routinely forwarded the checks for collection and that it was Chase's people who ordered payment stopped on them. And Mr. Ginsberg said yesterday that his office was the first to spot the theft.

In any case, neither bank seems to have paid out any money on them and the city lost nothing in the transactions. It is not known, however, if the persons who wrote the checks sold them at a discount to intermediaries or attempted to cash them on their own.

The police in Zurich say they are looking for two men who apparently tried to make the deposit at the Banque Populaire office.

After Chase Manhattan stopped the checks, Mr. Hogan's office was notified by the bank and began an investigation.

One of the questions being studied by the District attorney is whether similar forged checks were cashed before the four recent ones. Chase Manhattan says it is also alert for possible new checks turning up.

It is clear that some degree of sophistication was involved in the attempted check-cashing coup. The Swiss bank route is one that has been heavily traveled by big-time swindlers. The Mafia, too, has used the cloak of absolute secrecy, guaranteed by Swiss law, that shields depositors in Swiss banks from any scrutiny by the Federal Bureau of Investigation and the Treasury Department.

One lead checked out by Mr. Hogan's staff was the name of the second payee—Pagliuca Associates. Its principal turned out to be Angel Pagliuca, an elderly Argentine of little means and many debts who maintained a tiny office at 80 Wall Street which he used to "watch over my investments."

Mr. Pagliuca has disclaimed any knowledge of the checks and maintains that his name was used without his permission. The District Attorney's office has made no move aginst him.

The two former officials of the Human Resources Administration and the present official under investigation have not been identified by the District Attorney's office. Although *New York Times* reporters originally uncovered some of the reported details of their activities, names are not being published pending further investigation.

Informants have said that the three officials received kickbacks— or helped others to receive kickbacks—on the millions of dollars in contracts that are awarded each year to local antipoverty agencies in New York City.

No indictments have been prepared against the suspects. Assistant District Attorney Jeffrey M. Atlas, who is handling the case for Mr. Hogan's office under the direction of Leonard Newman, chief of the Frauds Bureau, declined last night to comment.

The most extensive conspiracy that investigators believe they have discovered within the Human Resources Administration is the so-called "Durham Mob," a group of flamboyant young men who grew up together in the Negro poverty of Durham, N.C., came to New York to be together again in H.R.A., and, according to the investigators, conspired to steal at least $1.75-million and possibly much more.

When asked if he had ever heard of a group calling itself "the Durham mob," Mr. Ginsberg replied: "The Durham mob? I never heard of it."

According to sources within the District Attorney's office and other

investigatory agencies, the alleged conspiracy may have been discovered only because one young man happened to park a rented car
in a bus stop on West 42d Street last Aug. 26.

The policeman ticketing the car that night saw—from a notice previously sent out by the rental company—that the car was overdue, and
when he looked into it he found a briefcase that contained 105 Youth
Corps checks.

The four men who returned to the car—Charles Clinton, payroll
director of the corps, and three men who worked under him, Sidney
Hall, Wakefield Thompson and Oscar Williams—were charged with
grand larceny.

The four men had come North from Durham. Coy D. Smith, formerly the Youth Corps' chief fiscal officer and also from Durham, was
arrested with them.

Mr. Smith, who had been considered one of H.R.A.'s brightest
young men, is a former auditor-investigator on the staff of State Attorney General Louis J. Lefkowitz, a former cost analyst for *The
New York Herald Tribune* and the holder of a master's degree in
accounting.

None of the men, whose ages range from 23 to 30, have been indicted, but investigators have assembled a picture of their life style.

"They're the black Lavender Hill mob starring in 'Hot Millions,' "
said one man who knows them.

The investigators believe they are linked to the systematic, massive
looting of Youth Corps checks during the first nine months of 1968.

The mob, according to investigation records, was formally organized one night in September, 1967, at a meeting of 8 to 10 people in a
Harlem apartment.

During that meeting, plans were made to defeat the computers that
printed out some 6,000 corps checks 42 weeks a year and 40,000 checks
during the 10 weeks of summer.

The plans completed and the assignments made, one informant relates, a young man leaped on a chair and shouted. "What do we want?"

"Money!" the others shouted back.

"How are we going to get it?"

"Steal!"

If the District Attorney's office is right, the mob did just that, taking
a minimum of $750,000 between last January and June and at least
$1-million more during the summer.

Their reported operation involved creating an army of fictitious
Youth Corps members, identified by false Social Security numbers,

which would produce a $38.80 weekly paycheck when fed into the right computer at the right time. Many of the make-believe teen-agers "worked" at job sites that never existed.

For example, if the computers were fed the code FA-12, and 102 numbers that looked like Social Security numbers, they produced 102 checks each week for summer workers cleaning up vacant lots under the sponsorship of Haryou-Act, the community corporation serving Harlem.

The computers, of course, could not know that there were no workers, no vacant lots and no one at Haryou-Act who knew anything about the matter.

There was only an unidentified young man picking up 102 checks each week and taking them to two-day-long parties in expensive apartments, where the revelers would endorse the checks and fill out time cards for the following week's haul.

Perhaps 30 persons were involved in the operation, about the number of young men and women who might drift in and out of the party action in a Riverdale apartment with a living room dominated by a long leather-cushioned bar under a monogrammed canopy.

"They lived," said a man who was there. "Flashy cars, flashier women—if they had been born white they might be running the country. Beautiful people."

Last summer the Federal Government discovered serious irregularities in H.R.A.'s payment, or nonpayment, of Social Security taxes on paychecks to Youth Corps enrollees.

In a memorandum dated Aug. 20, 1968—from Sidney L. Pollock, the Federal Government's audit manager for the New York region, to the Labor Department's regional manpower administrator, Terrell J. Whitsitt, the following explanation of the apparent fraud was given:

"It was disclosed to us by an official of the Social Security Administration that in one quarter alone the Form No. 941 filed by NYC (Neighborhood Youth Corps) lists 8,000 impossible Social Security numbers.

"The Forms No. 941 were filed only two quarters, from the dates that the contracts [with the Department of Labor] were consummated. The Social Security Administration made repeated attempts to obtain voluntary compliance by the NYC to file delinquent Forms No. 941 and to submit corrective Social Security numbers in the forms previously submitted but without any success.

"These requests were completely ignored. No adequate accounting was made of NYC FICA tax and it appears there is substantial liability to the U. S. Government for unpaid FICA taxes.

"The Department of Investigations [the city's] is presently engaged in determining the extent of such liability."

The "interception" of Federal checks was discovered by the Labor Department last April and Mr. Ginsberg received another in a series of complaining letters from Mr. Whitsitt.

"In violation of contractual agreements," Mr. Whitsitt wrote, "monies forwarded by the Department of Labor were intercepted prior to delivery to the Office of the Controller of the City of New York and were deposited directly in the Neighborhood Youth Corps bank account by staff."

The intercepter, according to a department report, was Irving Roberts, an H.R.A. fiscal officer. Asked yesterday why he had circumvented Controller Mario A. Procaccino, who normally disburses Federal money, Mr. Roberts answered: "I have been instructed by my superiors not to talk about this to reporters."

Federal auditors said that Mr. Roberts intercepted a total of $6,092,299 between Nov. 20, 1967, and April 1, 1968.

'"In violation of law and [Labor Department] regulations," the auditors reported, "overtime salaries were paid in cash to New York City employes. Tabulating-machine operators employed by the City of New York Social Services Agency are frequently used by the Neighborhood Youth Corps on an overtime basis.

"Irving Roberts paid these persons in cash by first drawing an NYC check to himself, cashing it and paying the people involved. These amounts have never been reported to the Internal Revenue Service for proper reporting and payment of taxes, nor have they been entered to the payroll records."

The attempt to convert the $52,000 check—drawn as in the case of the Swiss bank checks against the account of the H.R.A.'s Manpower and Career Development Agency—apparently began in Las Vegas, Nev., in early December.

The story of that stolen check comes from a Los Angeles real-estate broker, Allen C. Woodard, who was interviewed at his office early last week. It goes this way:

Mr. Woodard and his wife visited Las Vegas's Castaways Motel for a vacation on Dec. 4 and 5, and he met several strangers at the bar there.

Eventually, Mr. Woodard said, they told him they had a friend who was looking for a house in Los Angeles, and promised to see that the two got together.

The man's name, Mr. Woodard said, was Saul Belinsky—"a charming man, who was very distinguished and had a slight British accent."

Mr. Woodard says he was told to meet Mr. Belinsky at a hotel—the name of which Mr. Woodard no longer remembers—on a street called Hillcrest Drive in Los Angeles. "He came out to the car as I drove up," Mr. Woodard said. "I guess he recognized me because I was the only black face around."

The two then went to the house Mr. Woodard was trying to sell, which was not far away, at 4266 Hillcrest Drive. Mr. Belinsky was immediately interested in buying, according to Mr. Woodard, and after brief negotiations, Mr. Woodard says, he asked $50,000 in cash for the house.

Mr. Belinsky signed over to Mr. Woodard the $52,000 check, which bore the signature stamp of Mr. Ginsberg, the H.R.A. director.

Mr. Woodard said Mr. Belinsky gave him a telephone number at which he could be reached, and under his signature wrote a California driver's license number for purposes of identification.

Apparently anxious to close the sale, Mr. Belinsky tried to reach Mr. Woodard by telephone. "I couldn't call him," said Mr. Woodard, "because the number he gave me wasn't right. And the address he gave me doesn't exist."

Mr. Woodard said that after a week of waiting, because of a hitch in the title search, Mr. Belinsky telephoned him and told him to call off the sale and get the money back, in cash.

Mr. Woodard then called the escrow company, only to find that the New York District Attorney had advised one of its officers that the check was a forgery.

"When Belinsky called back," said Mr. Woodard, "I told him his check was no good and that the deal was really off. What he said was, 'Okay, we'll do business another time.'"

That, said Mr. Woodard, was the last he has heard of Mr. Belinsky. A subsequent investigation by the New York and Los Angeles district attorneys' offices revealed that the California license number did not exist, and that the phone number that was not Mr. Belinsky's actually was the private line of Mary Tyler Moore, the actress who of course knew nothing of the affair.

The Human Resources Administration informed Federal officials last Aug. 19 of a plan to "safeguard" Youth Corps funds from the thievery that had plagued the corps for two summers.

The two H.R.A. officers credited with developing the plan were

Mrs. Helynn Lewis, the agency's chief fiscal officer, and Charles Clinton, chief payroll officer of the corps.

Within a month, both Mrs. Lewis and Mr. Clinton had been arrested on charges of grand larceny. Mrs. Lewis was accused of having embezzled $22,000 and Mr. Clinton was held because of his involvement with his friends from Durham.

Mrs. Lewis on Aug. 19 reported to the Labor Department the procedures that had been developed to correct "procedural difficulties" in H.R.A.

"Your statement, 'Disbursements have been made without proper documentation,' was in some cases in the past correct," she wrote in answer to earlier letters of inquiry in May and August.

"But," she continued, "based on a memorandum sent to your office by Mr. Charles Clinton you can see that safeguards have been improved, strengthened and are operating on a current basis."

KICKBACKS ON ENGINEERING CONTRACTS IN MARYLAND

George Beall

On October 10, 1973 former Vice President Spiro T. Agnew pleaded *nolo contendere* (no contest) to a single count of income tax evasion. He was placed on probation for three years and fined $10,000. The evidence submitted to the grand jury concerned relationships between Mr. Agnew, when he was Baltimore County Executive and Governor of Maryland, and engineers seeking consulting contracts with the county or state. I. H. Hammerman II was a highly successful real estate developer, mortgage banker, and close Agnew associate. Jerome B. Wolff was an engineer, attorney, president of Greiner Environmental Systems, Inc., and an aide to Agnew. George Beall was the government's prosecutor in the case.

Excerpted from "Exposition of the Evidence against Spiro T. Agnew accumulated by the Investigation in the Office of the United States Attorney for the District of Maryland as of October 10, 1973," submitted by U.S. Attorney George Beall (dated October 10, 1973).

Hammerman has known Spiro T. Agnew for many years. When Mr. Agnew ran for Baltimore County Executive in 1962, however, Hammerman actively supported his opponent. The day after the election, Hammerman called to congratulate Mr. Agnew and asked to see him. They met in Hammerman's office and again Hammerman congratulated Mr. Agnew on his victory. Hammerman told Mr. Agnew that he knew all campaigns had deficits, and he offered Mr. Agnew a post-election contribution of $10,000. Mr. Agnew refused, but he told Hammerman that he would expect a contribution three times as large when he ran for office again.

Between 1963 and 1966, while Mr. Agnew was the Baltimore County Executive, he and Hammerman developed a close, personal friendship. During this period and continuing up until early 1973, they often discussed Mr. Agnew's personal financial situation. Mr. Agnew complained about it, and told Hammerman that he had not accumulated any wealth before he assumed public office, had no inheritance, and as a public official received what he considered a small salary. Mr. Agnew believed, moreover, that his public position required him to adopt a standard of living beyond his means and that his political ambitions required him to build a financially strong political organization. During the period when he was County Executive, Hammerman entertained him, introduced him to substantial political contributors, and gave him substantial gifts. . . .

In the late 1950's, while Wolff was Deputy Chief Engineer and later Assistant Director of Public Works for Baltimore County, Mr. Agnew became a member of the Baltimore County Board of Zoning Appeals. Mr. Agnew and Wolff became acquainted as a result of Wolff's appearances as a witness before the Board.

Wolff left employment with the County approximately six months after Mr. Agnew took office as County Executive. Mr. Agnew and he became good friends between 1963 and 1967 while Wolff was in business as a consulting engineer, and Wolff became an unofficial advisor to him. Mr. Agnew arranged for him to receive contracts from the County. Wolff greatly admired Mr. Agnew, and believed that Mr. Agnew was sincerely attempting, with considerable success, to do a good job as County Executive.

Friends in the consulting business asked Wolff, while Mr. Agnew was County Executive, how much Wolff was paying for the engineering work that he was receiving from Baltimore County. They seemed to assume that he was paying, as it was well known in the business community that engineers generally, and the smaller engineering firms in particular, had to pay in order to obtain contracts from the County in those days. Only a few of the larger and well established firms were generally considered to be immune from this requirement.

It is Wolff's belief, based upon his experience and his understanding of the experience of others, that engineering firms generally have to struggle for 10 to 15 years in order to become established. During this period, and for some time thereafter, they generally make payments—sometimes through middlemen—to public officials at various levels of government throughout Maryland in order to receive public work. Sometimes they reach a point where they are sufficiently established as qualified engineers that they do not generally have to make illegal payments in order to obtain a fair share of the public work.

It was Wolff's belief that a certain close associate of Mr. Agnew's (referred to hereafter as "the close associate" or "the middleman") was his principal middleman in Baltimore County. The close associate courted engineers, developers, and others and bragged a great deal about his relationship with Mr. Agnew. Although Wolff was in a favored position with Mr. Agnew, on two or more occasions while Mr. Agnew was County Executive, the close associate requested money from Wolff in return for contracts Wolff wanted or had obtained from the County. Wolff paid him $1,250 in cash in April 1966, and in addition made a payment to another associate of Mr. Agnew's, ostensibly as legal fees. Wolff's present recollection is that he also made one or two other payments to the close associate.

It was Wolff's belief that another individual also acted as a middleman for Mr. Agnew. Wolff learned from others that a certain Baltimore engineer was paying for work through that other individual. It is Wolff's recollection that in his office, Mr. Agnew once remarked to Wolff that the engineer in question was paying 10% for the work that he received from the County. Wolff inferred from Mr. Agnew's comment that Mr. Agnew was surprised that that engineer was paying as much as 10%, in view of the fact that the going rate was generally 5%. Through conversations with still another engineer, Wolff learned that he also was making payments for County work.

During Mr. Agnew's 1966 campaign for Governor, Wolff gave him $1,000 in cash as a campaign contribution. Wolff also worked in Mr. Agnew's campaign. Wolff knew that he had a potential personal stake in Mr. Agnew's candidacy, as Mr. Agnew had sometime earlier indicated to him the possibility that he might appoint Wolff as Chairman-Director of the State Roads Commission if Mr. Agnew were elected Governor.

Wolff had first become acquainted with Hammerman during the period when Wolff had been an assistant engineer employed by the Baltimore County Public Works Department. Hammerman considered Wolff to be a brilliant engineer, and Wolff had handled in an efficient manner various problems that Hammerman had had with County agencies in connection with Hammerman's building ventures. A close personal friendship had developed between them. Hammerman had been so impressed with Wolff that he had advised him that if he ever decided to leave County government, Hammerman would retain him as the engineer for his building projects. After Wolff had left County government in 1963 and established his own engineering business, he had done virtually all of Hammerman's engineering work.

After his election as Governor, Mr. Agnew told Hammerman that he intended to appoint Wolff Chairman-Director of the Maryland State Roads Commission. Hammerman objected strenuously because he wanted to retain Wolff's engineering services. Mr. Agnew responded, however, that Hammerman should not be too upset about Wolff's appointment because, Mr. Agnew told Hammerman, "You won't lose by it."

On or about March 1, 1967, Wolff took office as Governor Agnew's appointee as the Chairman-Director of the State Roads Commission. Governor Agnew had Wolff monitor every consulting engineering and construction contract that came through the State. It became obvious to Wolff that, in view of the provisions of State Roads Commission legislation, he would in effect control the selection of engineers and architects for contracts to be awarded by the State Roads Commission, subject only to the ultimate decision-making authority of Governor Agnew.

Shortly after Wolff took office, Governor Agnew asked Hammerman to come to his office in Annapolis, Maryland. At this meeting, Governor Agnew advised Hammerman that there was in Maryland a long-standing "system," as he called it, under which engineers made substantial "cash contributions" in return for State contracts awarded through the State Roads Commission. Governor Agnew referred to the substantial political financial demands that would be made on both himself and Hammerman, and said, in effect, that those who were benefitting (the engineers) should do their share. Governor Agnew said that Hammerman could help him by collecting cash payments from the engineers, and told him to meet with Wolff to set things up.

Hammerman subsequently met with Wolff and told him of the discussion he had had with Governor Agnew. Wolff readily agreed to participate, and suggested that the payments be equally divided among the Governor, Hammerman, and Wolff. Hammerman then met again with the Governor and told him of the suggested division of the payments. Governor Agnew at first replied that he did not see why Wolff should receive any share of the money, but he agreed to a division as long as he received 50% of the total payments. He told Hammerman that he didn't care what Hammerman did with his share.

Hammerman went back to Wolff and told him that Mr. Agnew insisted on 50% of the money and that Hammerman and Wolff should equally divide the rest between themselves. Wolff agreed.

Over the course of the subsequent 18 or 20 months that Mr. Agnew served as Governor of Maryland, the scheme agreed to by Mr. Agnew, Hammerman, and Wolff was fully implemented. Wolff kept Hammerman informed as to which engineers were to receive state contracts and Hammerman kept Wolff informed as to which engineers were making cash payments. It was soon generally understood among engineers that Hammerman was the person to see in connection with State Roads engineering contracts. As a result Hammerman soon found himself meeting with individual representatives of certain engineering firms. They would inform Hammerman of their interest in obtaining state work, and Hammerman would reply that he would see what he could do. In some cases an engineer would specify the particular work in which he was interested; in most cases, the engineer would not specify any job. There was no need for Hammerman to make coarse demands or to issue threats because the engineers clearly indicated that they knew what was expected of them. The discussions were generally about "political contributions," but the conversations left no doubt that the engineers understood exactly how the system worked—that is, that cash payments to the Governor through Hammerman were necessary in order for their companies to receive substantial state contracts. The "contributions" were almost always in cash, and many of them were made when there was no campaign in progress. Although Wolff had told Hammerman that "contributions" should average between 3% and 5% of the contract amount, Hammerman did not specify any exact amount to be paid, and accepted any reasonable sum. Sometimes the "contribution" was made when the contract was awarded, sometimes as the engineer received payments on the contract. Sometimes the "contribution" was made in one payment, sometimes in several. When a contract was about to be awarded to one of the engineers who was known to be willing to make payments, Wolff would advise

Hammerman that the engineer had been selected for a certain job. Hammerman would then contact the engineer and congratulate him. These congratulations were intended as signals that a cash "contribution" was due, and the engineer would then meet with Hammerman and bring the money.

Pursuant to his understanding with Mr. Agnew and Wolff, Hammerman retained 25% of the payments and delivered to Wolff his 25% share. Hammerman generally held Mr. Agnew's 50% share in a safe-deposit box until Mr. Agnew called for it. From time to time, Mr. Agnew would call Hammerman and ask how many "papers" Hammerman had for him. It was understood between Mr. Agnew and Hammerman that the term "paper" referred to $1,000 in cash. Hammerman would tell Mr. Agnew how many "papers" he had, and Mr. Agnew would ask Hammerman to bring the "papers" to him. Hammerman would then collect the cash from his safe-deposit box and personally deliver it to Mr. Agnew in his office in Annapolis or in Baltimore or wherever else Mr. Agnew would designate.

The cash which Wolff received from Hammerman was initially kept in Wolff's home. It was then transferred to two, and later, three safe-deposit boxes, two in Baltimore, and one in Washington. Most of the money was spent on ordinary personal expenses over a period of more than four years. A small portion of it was used by Wolff to make payments to other public officials in order to obtain work for the two consulting firms which he had sold before he had become Chairman of the State Roads Commission, but in which he still had a financial interest. Wolff kept detailed contemporaneous documents on which he recorded the dates, amounts, and engineering firm sources of the monies that he received from Hammerman as his share of the proceeds of the scheme. These records are among a large volume of corroborative documents that Wolff has turned over to the United States Attorney's Office.

The selection process for state roads contracts generally worked in the following manner: usually, based upon previous discussions with Governor Agnew, Wolff would make preliminary decisions with regard to the consulting engineering and architectural firms to be awarded contracts. He would then obtain the approval of the State Roads Commission. Governor Agnew would then make the final decision.

During Mr. Agnew's tenure as Governor of Maryland, Wolff met with him from time to time to discuss the status of various projects and the decisions which had to be made with respect to engineering, management, and sometimes architectural contracts. Wolff generally prepared agendas for these meetings in advance. Governor Agnew appeared to have confidence in Wolff's technical ability and generally accorded substantial weight to Wolff's preliminary decisions as to which consulting firms should be awarded contracts, generally concurring with Wolff's selection. Where important or unique projects were involved, Wolff would present Governor Agnew with a list of several possible firms from which Governor Agnew would select the firm to be awarded the contract. Governor Agnew always had and from time to time exercised the power to make all final decisions.

Several factors influenced Wolff in his own decision-making in the selection process outlined above:

1) It was a basic premise of Wolff's selection process that an engineering firm had to be competent to do the work before it could even be considered for a contract. Any engineering firm which, in Wolff's judgment, was competent to perform a certain assignment might be given consideration.

2) Both Governor Agnew and Hammerman would from time to time ask Wolff to give special consideration to a particular engineering firm, which might or might not be making cash payments, and he would then try to do so. He remembers, for example, that the Governor on one or more occasions asked him to give work to two specific engineering firms. Hammerman also recommended to Wolff presumably because of Hammerman's friendship with one or more particular engineers, that work be given to at least one company that, according to Wolff's understanding, had not made any cash payments.

3) Wolff's decision-making (and he recalls that this was a matter that he discussed with Hammerman in particular) was intended to avoid substantial and noticeable deviations from general fairness— that is, he tried to avoid a situation in which any firm received more or less work than could be justified on a purely legitimate basis. Wolff always viewed the process as one of accomplishing competent public work for the State of Maryland, very similar to that which would have been accomplished if all the selections had been made strictly on their merits, while at the same time serving the mutual ends of Mr. Agnew, Hammerman, and himself.

Wolff believed it was important not to deviate too obviously from the appearance of fairness and even-handedness in his selections of engineers. For example, he became aware—he believes initially as a result of a conversation he had with Governor Agnew—that Hammerman had apparently approached a certain engineer to solicit cash payments in connection with potential state work, and that the engineer had complained to Governor Agnew that state contracts should not be awarded on this basis. The Governor was very upset, as Wolff understood it, because Hammerman had apparently been especially heavy-handed with the engineer, and apparently because the Governor felt that the engineer might make his complaint public. For these reasons, Wolff continued thereafter to give the engineer's firm some work.

The investigation has also established that the same engineer also complained to his attorney, a close personal friend of Mr. Agnew's, about Hammerman's solicitation. Shortly after the engineer had complained to his attorney, and several months before the engineer complained directly to Mr. Agnew, the attorney met with Mr. Agnew and gave him a detailed account of Hammerman's solicitation and of his client's outrage. He warned Mr. Agnew that Hammerman's activities could undermine all that the attorney believed Governor Agnew was attempting to accomplish. Although he indicated that he would look into the matter, Mr. Agnew never reported back to the attorney. He did several months later meet personally with the engineer, at the attorney's insistence, but the investigation has established that Mr. Agnew did nothing whatever to stop Mr. Hammerman's continuing solicitations of cash payments from engineers in return for state work and that he (Mr. Agnew) continued for several years thereafter to accept his 50% share of those cash payments.

4) The fact that a certain firm was making cash payments was a definite factor in that firm's favor. It was, therefore, accorded special consideration in the decision-making process. Wolff believes that a comparison of the amounts of work given to certain firms before, during and after Governor Agnew's Administration would confirm this.

On the other hand, there were times when a firm was selected for a specific job without regard to whether or not that firm was making cash payments. Some local Maryland firms had outstanding expertise in certain fields of engineering. This made them obvious choices for certain jobs, whether or not they were making cash payments. Even such firms, however, could never be completely sure that such considerations would be decisive in the decision-making process, so that even some of those companies were vulnerable to solicitations for cash payments.

5) Various other factors worked for or against particular firms or individuals in the selection process. For example, Wolff definitely favored Lester Matz and Allen Green, and their companies, not only because he understood they were making cash payments directly to the Governor, but also because Wolff was receiving money from certain

illegal dealings that he had with Matz and Green that did not involve Governor Agnew. Conversely, one engineering firm was disfavored by Wolff because in his view that firm had taken positions contrary to the best interests of the Commission.

The evidence accumulated to date, both testimonial and documentary, establishes that Hammerman obtained, and split with Mr. Agnew and Wolff, cash payments from seven different engineering firms in return for State engineering contracts, and from one financial institution in return for a lucrative arrangement with the State involving the financing of certain State bonds. Those seven engineering firms and the one financial institution will not be named in this statement in order to avoid possible prejudice to several presently anticipated prosecutions. It is worth noting, however, that Hammerman specifically recalls discussing with Mr. Agnew whether or not the particular financial institution would be awarded the lucrative State bond business, and that during that discussion Mr. Agnew commented that the principals at the particular financial institution in question were "a cheap bunch" who "don't give you any money." Mr. Agnew informed Hammerman that he did not intend to award that institution the bond business in question unless a substantial "contribution" were made. Hammerman carried that message to the appropriate person; a substantial cash "contribution" was made; the institution got the bond business.

Hammerman also remembers that, while Mr. Agnew was Governor, Hammerman observed that Allen Green and Lester Matz, two engineers whom he had known for some time, were receiving very substantial amounts of State Roads work. Hammerman mentioned that fact to Wolff and, since he had not received any money from Green and Matz, asked Wolff if he should approach them. Both Green and Matz had indicated to Wolff that they were making their payments directly to the Governor. Wolff therefore told Hammerman that both Green and Matz were making "contributions" and that Hammerman should "stay away." Hammerman did so. . . .

Allen Green is the President and one of the principal owners of Green Associates, Inc., a Maryland engineering company which has, over the years, performed various types of engineering work. . . .

Green has been an engineer in Maryland for 21 years. During this period, he has often made cash payments on behalf of his company in return for various State and local consulting contracts and in order to remain eligible for further contracts. He used cash for the simple reason that checks could have been traced and might have led to the discovery of these illegal payments. These payments formed a pattern over the years and reflected his understanding, based upon experience, of the system in which a firm such as his had to participate in order to insure its survival and growth in the State of Maryland. This system had developed long ago in Maryland and in other States as well. Engineering contracts have not been awarded on the basis of public bids in Maryland. Instead, the selection of engineers for State Roads contracts has rested exclusively in the discretion of public officials—in Maryland, the Governor and the members of the State Roads Commission. They have had virtually absolute control. There are many engineering companies which seek contracts, but price competition was not allowed under the ethical standards of this profession until October of 1971. Therefore, engineers are very vulnerable to pressure from public officials for both legal and illegal payments. An engineer who refuses to pay can be deprived of substantial public work without effective recourse, and one who pays can safely expect that he will be rewarded.

A few companies developed in time a size, expertise, and stature that insulated them to some extent from this system. One or two developed an expertise, for example, in large bridge design, that other local companies could not match. One or two grew so large and had been awarded so many substantial contracts that the State could not do without their services unless out-of-state consultants were employed. In these ways, a few companies in effect "graduated" in time from the system to a position of lesser vulnerability, and they could afford to resist and perhaps in some instances, refuse to participate. In fact, Green believed that his own company was in recent years in the process of moving into this class.

It was seldom necessary, in Green's experience, for there to be any express prior agreement between an engineer and a public official in Maryland. Under this system, which each State administration perpetuated, the connection between payments and contracts rested on a largely tacit understanding under which enginers knew that if they did not pay, they would not receive very many contracts and that if they did pay, they would receive favored treatment. Therefore, when a politician requested a payment or when an engineer offered one, it was not necessary for anyone expressly to refer to the connection between payments and contracts because everyone understood the system, and could rely upon it without actually talking about it.

Green came to know Spiro T. Agnew in mid-1963 when Mr. Agnew was the County Executive for Baltimore County, Maryland. Although his company received some engineering contracts from the County, Green does not recall making any cash payments to Mr. Agnew or to anyone in his administration during these years. Green cultivated his relationship with Mr. Agnew and occasionally had lunch with him. By 1966, they had developed a closer relationship.

In connection with Mr. Agnew's successful 1966 campaign for Governor, Green gave him approximately $8,000 to $10,000 in campaign contributions. He did so in part because he genuinely admired Mr. Agnew and believed that he would make an excellent Governor. He also knew, however, that Mr. Agnew would be grateful for his support, and he anticipated that Mr. Agnew would express his gratitude by giving the Green company State work if he were elected.

After the inauguration, Green met with Governor Agnew on several occasions in his new offices, usually in Baltimore, but sometimes in Annapolis. At one of these meetings Governor Agnew expressed his concern about the substantial financial obligations and requirements imposed upon him by virtue of his new position. He told Green that as the titular leader of the Republican Party in Maryland, he would need substantial funds in order to support his own political organization. In addition, he believed that he would be called upon to provide financial assistance to other Republican candidates around the State. Furthermore, he complained that it was extremely difficult for a person in his limited financial situation to bear the personal expenses of high public office, in the sense that his new position would require him, he believed, to adopt and maintain a life style that was beyond his means. He said that he had served as County Executive at substantial financial sacrifice because of the small salary and that, although the Governor's salary represented an increase in income, it would still be insufficient to meet the additional demands that he believed his new position would impose upon him. This was neither the first nor the last occasion upon which Mr. Agnew mentioned to Green his concern about his personal financial difficulties. He had voiced similar complaints while County Executive, and he continued from time to time to mention his personal financial difficulties thereafter.

Green inferred from what Mr. Agnew said, the manner in which he said it, and their respective positions that he was being invited in a subtle but clear way to make payments. He, therefore, replied that he recognized Mr. Agnew's financial problems and realized he was not a wealthy man. Green told him that his company had experienced successful growth and would probably continue to benefit from public work under the Agnew Administration. He, therefore, offered to make periodic cash payments to Governor Agnew, who replied that he would appreciate such assistance very much.

On the basis of Green's experience, he had developed a policy that, where required, he would make payments in amounts that did not exceed an average of one per cent of the fees that his company received on public engineering contracts. This informal calculation included legitimate political contributions as well as cash payments. He knew that many politicians believed that engineers were wealthy and often demanded payments in much greater amounts, frequently five per cent and sometimes higher. Although he believed that some engineers made payments in these amounts, he knew that such percentages were unrealistic, given the economics of the engineering industry. An engineering firm could not, in his judgment, make a profit on public work if payments in these excessive percentages were made. He had come to the conclusion that his company could not afford to pay more than one per cent and, in areas where more was demanded, he had simply refused to pay and had sought work elsewhere.

Therefore, Green calculated, largely in his head, that it would be appropriate for him to make approximately six payments a year to Mr. Agnew in amounts of $2,000, $2,500, or $3,000 each. The exact amount of each payment to Mr. Agnew depended upon the amount of cash available to Green for such purposes at the time of the payment. After the meeting at which this subject had first been discussed, Green scheduled appointments with Governor Agnew approximately six times a year. At the first such meeting, he handed an envelope to Governor Agnew that contained between $2,000 and $3,000 in cash. Green told the Governor that he was aware of his financial problems and wished to be of assistance to him. Governor Agnew accepted the envelope, placed it in either his desk drawer or his coat pocket, and expressed his gratitude. Over the next two years, they gradually said less and less to each other about each payment; Green would merely hand him an envelope and Governor Agnew would place it in either his desk drawer or his coat pocket with little or no discussion about it.

During these meetings, Green and Governor Agnew would discuss a number of matters, but Green almost always made it a point to discuss State Roads contracts with him. Indeed, Green's principal purpose in meeting with him was always to increase the amount of work that his company received from the State. They would discuss State contracts in general, and frequently, specific upcoming road and bridge contracts in particular. Green would express his desire that his company receive consideration for proposed work and would occasionally ask for specific contracts that he knew were scheduled to be awarded by the State Roads Commission. Green knew from experience and from what he learned from Wolff that Governor Agnew played a substantial role in the selection of engineers for State Roads Commission work. Governor Agnew would often tell him in these meetings that his company could expect to receive substantial work generally, and on occasion, he promised Green specific contracts. On other occasions, however, Governor Agnew would tell Green that a contract had already been or was to be committed to another company.

Green admits that his principal purpose in making payments to Governor Agnew was to influence him to select the Green Company for as many State Roads contracts as possible. Based upon his many years of experience, it was his belief that such payments would probably be necessary and certainly helpful in obtaining substantial amounts of State Roads Commission work.

With one exception (to be related later in this statement), Mr. Agnew never expressly stated to Green that there was any connection between the payments and the selection of the Green company for State contracts. According to Green, the understanding was a tacit one, based upon their respective positions and their mutual recognition of the realities of the system; their relationship was such that it was unnecessary for them to discuss openly the understanding under which these payments were given and received. The circumstances were that Green gave Governor Agnew cash payments in substantial amounts and asked for contracts, and from time to time, Governor Agnew told him that contracts would be awarded to the Green company.

Green paid Governor Agnew approximately $11,000 in each of the years he served as Governor of Maryland (1967 and 1968). Green generated the necessary cash to make these payments through his company by various means that violated the Internal Revenue Code and that were designed to obscure the purpose for which the cash was used.

Green also recalls that during the early part of the Agnew Administration, the Governor occasionally asked him to evaluate the competency of certain engineering companies which he was considering for State Roads Commission work. On at least one occasion, the Governor also asked him if certain companies could be counted upon to provide financial assistance if State work were received.

Under the Agnew Administration, the Green company received substantial work from the Maryland State Roads Commission. It was awarded approximately 10 contracts, with fees approximating $3,000,000 to $4,000,000.

On a few occasions during these years, Green was asked by Jerome B. Wolff if he was taking care of his "obligations" with respect to the substantial State work that the Green company was receiving and Green replied that he was. . . .

Lester Matz has been an engineer in Maryland for approximately 24 years. He is the President of Matz, Childs and Associates, Inc., and Matz, Childs and Associates of Rockville, Inc., two Maryland engineering companies. John C. Childs is his principal business associate in these two companies. . . .

Between 1956 and 1963, Matz and Childs supplied various engineering services to private developers, principally in the metropolitan Baltimore area. Although they wanted to do as much public work as possible for the Baltimore County Government, they found it extremely difficult to receive any substantial amount of county work. They observed that a relatively small number of engineering companies received most of the substantial county engineering work during these years, and that most, if not all, of these companies were closely associated with County Administration or public officials. They simply could not break into this group, despite their repeated efforts to do so.

They, therefore, welcomed Mr. Agnew's candidacy for Baltimore County Executive in 1962 because they believed that his election would present their company with an opportunity to be one of the few engineering companies that, they believed, would inevitably form around his administration and receive most of the substantial county engineering work. Matz had known Mr. Agnew casually for possibly two years, and during the 1962 campaign, he and Childs made a $500 cash contribution directly to Mr. Agnew.

Prior to the 1962 election, Matz had also worked professionally with one of Mr. Agnew's close associates. Indeed, by this time the three of them (Mr. Agnew, Matz and the close associate) had already begun to develop what would in the next four years become a close personal friendship. Very shortly after Mr. Agnew assumed office as County Executive for Baltimore County, Matz was contacted by the close associate. During this conversation the close associate told Matz that the two of them were going to make a lot of money under the Agnew administration. Although he did not elaborate on this comment, Matz inferred from what he said during this conversation that under the Agnew administration, the two of them could expect substantial favors from the Baltimore County Government.

Shortly thereafter Matz was invited by the close associate to meet with Mr. Agnew. At this meeting there was no specific discussion about payments for county work, but Mr. Agnew told Matz that he had a lot of "confidence" in his close associate. Matz inferred from what Mr. Agnew said during this meeting that he should work through the close associate and make any payments through him.

After Mr. Agnew became County Executive, the close associate contacted Matz and asked him to prepare a chart which would set forth the amounts of money that could reasonably be expected from engineers on the various kinds and sizes of consulting contracts that the county generally awarded. Matz calculated the profits that could generally be anticipated under the various types of contracts, and he determined that, on the average, 5% of the fee was not unreasonable, although the precentage varied depending on the size and nature of the contract. He gave a copy of the chart to the close associate. The chart showed the expected profit on each type of contract and the percentage that engineers could reasonably afford to pay on it. Matz later showed his retained copy of this schedule to Mr. Agnew in his office and told him that he had given a copy to the close associate. Mr. Agnew looked at the chart and thanked Matz for his effort on the matter. Matz cannot recall today whether Mr. Agnew returned the copy to him.

When Matz gave a copy of this schedule to the close associate, he was told that he would be expected to make payments to the close associate for county contracts. The close associate said that as Matz's company received fees from the County, payments were to be made to him in the appropriate percentages, 5% on engineering contracts and 2½% on surveying contracts. He led Matz to believe that this money would be given to Mr. Agnew. These payments were not described by the close associate as "political contributions"; they were payments made in return for contracts.

Thereafter, Matz discussed this proposition with Childs. They were not surprised that payments would be necessary because it was generally understood that engineers had been making such payments for consulting work in a number of Maryland jurisdictions. They agreed that this would be a satisfactory arrangement. In fact, they were delighted that they would be among the small group of engineers who would be close to the Agnew administration and that they would, therefore, receive their share of the substantial county engineering consulting work. Although the 5% payments were not insubstantial, the company could afford to make them, and Matz and Childs both believed that the payments would make a substantial difference in the amount of work that their company would receive from the county.

During the balance of Mr. Agnew's tenure as County Executive,

Matz and Childs would find out what contracts were coming up in the county, and Matz would then contact the close associate to ask him for as many of these contracts as possible. The close associate always seemed well aware of the work to be let, and from time to time, he would advise Matz that his company had been awarded a particular contract. Matz then knew that, under their arrangement, the necessary payments were due, and he would therefore deliver the required cash payments personally to the close associate in the latter's office. On most occasions, Matz placed the necessary cash in plain white envelopes. Usually he paid in installments rather than in one total payment in advance. Matz and Childs believed that even if they had refused to make these payments their company would have received some county contracts, but that, as before, the company would not have received any substantial amount of work. In short, they believed that the payments made a great difference in the amount of work they received.

PART THREE

CAUSES AND CONSEQUENCES
OF CORRUPTION

(5)

Rotten Apples and Rotten Barrels: Explanations of Corruption and Prescriptions for Reform

WE NOW TURN to the theoretical issues raised by the descriptions of local corruption presented in the preceding chapters. How and why do patterns of corruption develop? Are some individuals, types of governmental activity, or community settings more prone to corruption than others? What avenues to reform are most likely to minimize future corruption? Finally, to be considered in chapter 6, what can be said of the costs and benefits of corruption, both to the parties involved and to the social and political systems in which corruption takes place?

Analyses of these issues are difficult, for corruption is often so thoroughly hidden from sight that the few instances that are revealed suggest more of the ineptness of the perpetrators than of the nature of the problem. Even more difficult are the problems of viewing corruption apart from the environment in which it occurs and of estimating alternatives—what would have happened in a given situation if there had been no corruption. Hard as these tasks may be, we must attempt to face them if we are to move beyond a view of corruption as a series of isolated, picturesque incidents filled with stereotyped characters from *The Godfather* or the works of Damon Runyan.

Three sets of questions emerge: (1) What can be learned from the *acts* of corruption? Do they suggest unique responses to specific situations or systematically planned activities? (2) What are the characteristics of the *persons* participating in corruption? Are they simply "rotten apples"—the few misfits who might be expected to show up in any large collection of people—or are they representative of the societies from which they come? (3) Do *settings* affect the frequency or nature of corruption? Is the problem of corruption a manifestation of the environments in which local governments conduct their activities? While the significance of each of these factors will vary from case to case, they provide starting points in the search for explanations and recommendations for change.

Corruption: Premeditated Rapacity or Crime of Opportunity?

For many years, criminologists and psychologists have searched for explanations of criminality in the family background, medical and psychological histories, educational and vocational skills, peer associations, and other characteristics of offenders. Recently, attention has focused on the nature of the crimes committed, and a theory is developing that distinguishes between planned or premeditated crimes and crimes of opportunity. To provide a simple example, a bank robbery is almost always planned, with careful thinking about timing, weapons, the getaway, and so forth, while the theft of a car may occur simply because a juvenile sees the keys in the ignition. While there are a number of problems inherent in the theory (Wasn't the juvenile *predisposed* to look for an unprotected car? Would the robber have changed his mind if the guard were armed?), it provides a means for distinguishing among several types of corruption. George Washington Plunkitt, in the first selection of this volume, concluded, "I seen my opportunities and I took 'em." The materials on organized crime, however, show an elaborate system for neutralizing the threat of law enforcement agencies. Opportunistic corruption, presumably, could be reduced by minimizing opportunities (if cash is not left lying around, no one will steal it); reduction of planned corruption requires more complicated steps to rearrange potential offenders' estimates of the costs and benefits involved.

What factors affect the availability of opportunities for corruption? Among the most obvious are:

Legal constraints. Are government employees hired and fired at the pleasure of the party, or are they covered by a civil service system whose guidelines might constrain local officials in recruiting and supervising employees? Are government purchases made at the discretion of purchasing agents, or are they controlled by laws requiring competitive bidding, open disclosure, and independent auditing of costs? Are crimes left to interpretation by policemen, prosecutors, and judges, or are they spelled out in the statute books? Are the threats posed by criminal statutes limited to token fines and short sentences, or are they substantial? While formal regulations of any of these factors can be circumvented to facilitate corruption, their existence tends to increase the possibility of discovery and thus the risks involved.

Surveillance and supervision. There are great variations in how often potentially corrupt activities are reviewed by supervisors, auditors, the mass media, and interest groups. Even if they uncover corruption they are sometimes not in a position to do anything about it. The use of informants, internal investigations units, auditors, and formal reporting and disclosure requirements can at least convince potential violators that they might be discovered. Massachusetts, for example, adopted a multi-copy system of recording traffic violations, which led police chiefs and patrolmen to fear that state officials would demand explanations for canceled tickets . (Unbeknownst to the policemen, however, the state's copies were dumped, unread, into file cabinets in Boston).[1]

Market demand. Corruption often depends on the demand for the goods and services controlled by officials: funds, jobs, privileges, and restrictions. To the extent that these are things of value to potential corrupters, an opportunity will be created. If a contract to supply paper clips to City Hall is no more profitable than other business available to a stationery wholesaler, he has no reason to offer a bribe to get the contract; if, however, the contract promised exceptionally high profits, or business was slow, he might view the bribe as a good investment. In some situations, including many discussed in this book, opportunities for corruption are *created* by laws: a city ordinance forbidding sales on Sunday or limiting the number of taxicabs, for example, provides an opportunity for corrupt city officials to extort payoffs or accept bribes from people who wish to evade the restrictions.

Corruption and Individual Value Systems

During the 1973 Senate hearings on the Watergate scandals, a former college teacher of one of the witnesses remarked, "He is proof

1. See John A. Gardiner, *Traffic and the Police* (Cambridge: Harvard University Press, 1969), pp.25–28.

that to do evil in this world, you don't have to be a Bengal tiger. It's sufficient to be a tame tabby. It's sad to see how vulnerable to the corruption of power these bright young men are."[2] Whether or not the characterization "tame tabby" was accurate, the statement illustrates a basic problem involved in trying to relate corruption to the value systems of people involved in it. While simple greed motivates some grafters, others turn to corruption to attain power or prestige, or sometimes merely to advance the interests of their friends. Although little research has been done on the factors that foster corrupt value systems, two issues have been raised:

Background. One of the most frequently offered explanations of propensities to corruption is that certain races, classes, or ethnic groups place a low value on ethics and integrity in government, at least when they stand in the way of personal gain. As a former Boston politician put it, they want "help, not justice." While there is some evidence that ethnic groups vary in their allegiance to the official norms of American society,[3] we must also remember that charges of corruption have been leveled at WASPs as well as blacks, German-Americans as well as Sicilian-Americans. Perhaps all that can be safely said is that some officials genuinely regard a public office as a public trust, while others, like Plunkitt, see it simply as another opportunity for honest (or dishonest) graft.

Socialization. As individuals move into new roles, whether they be mayors or low-ranking patrolmen, they become aware of the expectations of their superiors, the attitudes of their peers, and the demands of clients and others with whom they must deal. In some cases, this socialization process presents clear job norms and expectations that become internalized by the officeholder. In others, the employee does not grasp, or consciously rejects, the values imposed on him. In the situation where there are no clear norms, the new employee has a vague feeling that he will be praised if he does some things and censured if he does others; a large grey area in between is left undefined. There have been few studies of the impact of the socialization process on tendencies toward corruption. Perhaps we should ask two questions: Does the public bureaucracy actively stress to its employees the importance of integrity in office? Is there a clear and attainable mission

2. Quoted in William Greider, "The Lost Sheep: Magruder's Sincerity Praised," *Washington Post,* June 15, 1973.

3. See, e.g., James Q. Wilson and Edward C. Banfield, "Public-Regardingness as a Value Premise in Voting Behavior," *American Political Science Review,* LVIII (December 1964), pp.876–887.

for the organization? If the organization is able to instill a sense of purpose in its members, it will provide psychological ammunition against temptation; those who feel that their work is unvalued or meaningless may well ask, "Why not take the money, since no one really cares what I do."

Corruption as a Manifestation of System Dysfunction

In elementary civics textbooks, democratic government is often described as a straightforward process leading from public desires and values through the legislative and executive systems to the implementation of programs and policies. In fact, however, "the public" is rarely of one mind about major issues, and the dynamics of legislative bodies and executive agencies often provide an inertia that retards the adaptation of public policy to changes in public attitudes. While some gap between public expectations and official policies is probably inevitable in heterogeneous societies, it has been argued that corruption will arise if the gap becomes too wide or endures too long. Just as black markets will be created to satisfy wants unfulfilled by the economic system, political corruption will make available goods and services that the political system either forbids or delivers inefficiently. Under this view, then, widespread corruption is an indicator of a dysfunctional element of the system (whether economic, social, or political), and will only fade away if the system begins to function more effectively.

Some of the selections in this chapter focus on the factors that influence the individual participants in corruption, while the others stress the opportunities offered by the structure of government. The first article, by James Q. Wilson, provides a brief overview of the various theories that have been offered to explain corruption in America. In the second selection, muckraker Lincoln Steffens engages in a debate with leading citizens of Los Angeles on the sources of municipal corruption. The next two explore the underlying motivations of corrupt officials: Rogow and Lasswell examine the backgrounds of political bosses, identifying "game politicians" and "gain politicians," while the Knapp Commission distinguishes between policemen who actively seek out opportunities to steal ("meat-eaters") and those who simply take what comes their way ("grass-eaters"). Following are two readings that consider the problem of corruption in the context of the

value patterns and working environment of the police: Jonathan Rubinstein details the moralizing and unrealistic advice offered police recruits in the training academy, describes the temptations that face them
as soon as they go out on the street, and illustrates how citizens
purchase special services from the police; and James Q. Wilson sees
corruption (and other police problems) as inherent in the frequently
adversary relationship between the police and the public and in the
incompatible ends the police are asked to serve. Going beyond Wilson's
analysis, V. O. Key attributes political graft to the values and power
relationships that exist in the environment surrounding government,
and concludes that widespread graft exists only if the most powerful
elements in the community desire it. Rogow and Lasswell then ask how
conflicts between official behavior and popular norms are resolved,
attributing readjustments in norms to the arousal of "an active sense
of outrage." Finally, John A. Gardiner presents a detailed examination
of public attitudes toward law enforcement and corruption, showing
that citizens are sharply divided as to the goals of law enforcement
although they react strongly whenever corruption is brought to light.

THREE THEORIES OF CORRUPTION
James Q. Wilson

Why should so many state governments seem so bad? The Massachusetts Crime Commission did not try to answer that question (it
said it did not know whether corruption was worse in its state than in
others), nor did it address itself to the more fundamental questions,
"What is corruption?" "Why does it occur?" In short, the Commission
did not develop a theory of corruption. This is not simply an academic
deficiency (I am not trying to grade the Commission's report as if it
were a term paper in a political science seminar); rather, it is a prac-

From James Q. Wilson, "Corruption: The Shame of the States," *The
Public Interest*, no. 2 (Winter 1966), pp.30–32. Copyright © by National
Affairs Inc., 1966.

tical problem of the greatest importance, for without a theory of corruption there cannot be a remedy for corruption unless by happy accident.

There are at least three major theories of government corruption. The first holds that there is a particular political ethos or style which attaches a relatively low value to probity and impersonal efficiency and relatively high value to favors, personal loyalty, and private gain. Lower-class immigrant voters, faced with the problems of accommodation to an unfamiliar and perhaps hostile environment, are likely to want, in the words of Martin Lomasney, "help, not justice." If such groups come—as have the Irish and the Sicilians—from a culture in which they experienced a long period of domination by foreign rulers the immigrant will already be experienced in the ways of creating an informal and illegal (and therefore "corrupt") covert government as a way of dealing with the—to them—illegitimate formal government. The values of such groups are radically incompatible with the values of (for example) old-stock Anglo-Saxon Protestant Americans, and particularly with those members of the latter culture who serve on crime commissions. Whatever the formal arrangements, the needs and values of those citizens sharing the immigrant ethos will produce irresistible demands for favoritism and thus for corruption.

The second theory is that corruption is the result of ordinary men facing extraordinary temptations. Lincoln Steffens argued that corruption was not the result of any defect in character (or, by implication, in cultural values); rather, it was the inevitable consequence of a social system which holds out to men great prizes—power, wealth, status—if only they are bold enough to seize them. Politicians are corrupt because businessmen bribe them; this, in turn, occurs because businessmen are judged solely in terms of worldly success. The form of government makes little difference; the only way to abolish corruption is to change the economic and social system which rewards it. (Steffens admired Soviet communism because it was a system without privilege: "There was none but petty political corruption in Russia," he wrote after visiting there. "The dictator was never asked to do wrong.") A less Marxist variation of this theory is more familiar: men steal when there is a lot of money lying around loose and no one is watching. Public officials are only human. They will resist minor temptation, particularly if everyone else does and someone is checking up. They are not angels, however, and cannot be expected to be honest when others are stealing (no one wants to be thought a fink) and superiors are indifferent. The Catholic Church, having known this for several centuries, counsels the young in its catechisms to "avoid the occasion of sin." The solution to this sort of corruption is, obviously, to inspect, audit, check, and double-check.

The third theory is more explicitly political and has the advantage of seeking to explain why governmental corruption appears to be more common in America than in Europe. Henry Jones Ford, writing in 1904, observed that in this country, unlike in those whose institutions follow the British or French models, the executive and legislative branches are separated by constitutional checks and balances. What the Founders have put asunder, the politicians must join together if anything is to be accomplished. Because each branch can —and sometimes does—paralyze the other, American goverment "is so constituted that it cannot be carried on without corruption." The boss, the machine, the political party, the bagmen—all these operate, in Ford's view, to concert the action of legally independent branches of government through the exchange of favors. The solution to corruption, if this is its cause, is to bring these various departments together formally and constitutionally. This, of course, is precisely what the National Civic League and other reform groups have attempted by their espousal of the council manager plan for municipal government, and what advocates of strong and responsible political parties have sought with respect to state and national government. If the chief executive, by virtue of either his constitutional position or his control of a disciplined majority party, is strong enough to rule without the consent of subordinate or the intervention of legislators, then no one will bribe subordinates or legislators—they will have nothing to sell. The leader himself will rarely be bribed, because his power will be sufficiently great that few, if any, groups can afford his price. (This is how Ford explained the lesser incidence of corruption in American national government: the president is strong enough to get his way and visible enough to make bribe-taking too hazardous.)

LOS ANGELES AND THE APPLE
Lincoln Steffens

Lincoln Steffens was an outstanding "muckraking" journalist who exposed local graft and corruption at the turn of the century. His *The
Shame of the Cities* (1904) contained exposés of many of America's
more graft-ridden cities. This chapter from his *Autobiography*, written
at the close of his career, describes an incident that took place shortly
after he exposed corruption in San Francisco.

San Francisco learned nothing from the graft prosecution, nothing
but facts—no lessons that were applied either economically or politically. The fighting passion persisted. Francis J. Heney was hated and
admired as a fighter and highly respected as a lawyer, but his practice
was so damaged by the fear of the prejudice of the courts against him
that he had to remove his office to Los Angeles. Fremont Older
was punished by business men through his paper. The circulation had
gone up and continued to grow as his change of policy from righteous
wrath to mercy for the underdog became clear. Its advertising suffered, and his personal standing as an editor was attacked privately
by the business men who finally drove the owners to get rid of him.
Hearst called Older to his rival evening paper, the *Call*, which immediately began to rise till it passed and finally absorbed the *Bulletin*.
William J. Burns had proved himself to the men he called sons of
bitches so that when he organized a national detective bureau they
joined it as subscribers. Hiram Johnson, as governor, put the raiload
out of power for a while; he gave one of the most efficient administrations any State has ever had, was re-elected, and then went to the U.S.
Senate as the political reform boss of California. But there was no
fundamental reform in the city or the State.

Were exposures useless? I could not at that time believe this. I went
back to my theory that it was the threat of punishment which, by forc-

From *The Autobiography of Lincoln Steffens*, pp.570–574, copyright,
1931, by Harcourt Brace Jovanovich, Inc.; renewed, 1959, by Peter
Steffens. Reprinted by permission of the publisher.

ing men to defend themselves, put them in a state of mind where they could not see straight and learn. I wrote an article entitled "An Apology for Graft," showing that our economic system, which held up riches, power and acclaim as prizes to men bold enough and able enough to buy corruptly timber, mines, oil fields, and franchises and "get away with it," was at fault, and that San Francisco's graft trials showed that; and showed that we should change the system and meanwhile let the crooks go, who would confess and tell us the truth. The only reaction I got from this article was the wonder of good citizens and liberals whether I had sold out and gone back on reform!

Then it occurred to me to go to Los Angeles to see if that city had learned anything from the sight of San Francisco exposed. No one down there had been threatened with punishment; they had only to look on and see themselves in the fix of the San Franciscans. I called on Dr. John R. Haynes, a rich, very kind veteran reformer, who understands economics and men pretty well. He took me into the swell Jonathan Club, introduced me to some public service corporation men; others that I knew came up, and soon there was a group of "knowing" Los Angeles business leaders deploring the conditions of politics and business in San Francisco. They were cheerful about it. There was a self-congratulatory note in their grief at the shame of San Francisco, poor San Francisco. Los Angeles was, fortunately, not like that. I thought they were joking.

"Wait a moment," I said. "You have been having your sport with me, a San Franciscan. It's my turn now. You know, don't you; I know that you know, and you know that I know, that Los Angeles is in the same condition as San Francisco. The only difference is that San Francisco has been, and Los Angeles has not been, shown up."

Silence. Uneasiness, but no denial. I waited for the street railway or gas men to think, and one of them did mutter something about "another difference, San Francisco had a Labor government."

"Labor government!" I exclaimed, and I reminded them that that Labor government had sold out to capital and represented business.

Again no denial, only silence. They knew. They had forgotten. They wished to forget, to ignore what they knew. They had no fear of punishment, but they had learned no more from the experience of San Francisco than the San Franciscans had.

"I'll tell you what I'll do," I said into their silence. "If you will call a closed meeting somewhere soon and invite only yourselves, and your wives, and your associates, fellow directors, managers, attorneys, and—and your priests and their wives—no outsiders at all—I will show you that you yourselves should want, at the least, the public ownership of all public utilities and natural resources."

They laughed; it was partly the laugh of relief. The tension of my accusations had been unclublike. They laughed and we broke up, but they accepted my challenge. They would have a little dinner and eat me up.

Dr. Haynes managed the affair very well. He had the right kind of people there, some hundred or more. No outsiders. Nobody to enjoy and spoil the debate by making us conscious of a contest. It was a conversation. The arrangement was that I was to state my thesis and argument in a short twenty minutes, after which any one of the company might challenge any point of mine, preferably in the form of a question. But I asked leave to answer each question before another spoke. No objections.

I restated my thesis. My argument was a narrative, my own story. I had gone forth, thinking what they thought, that bad men caused bad government, especially politicians. Having to see them for information, I found politicians to be not bad men; they were pretty good fellows. They blamed the bad business men who, they said, bribed them.

Who, then, were those bad business men? They named them, each in his city, and as I saw them they were not bad, but they were always in the same business. Regardless of character, education, and station, the people in these businesses were in the corruption of politics and the resistance to reform. This suggested that it was these businesses, not the men in them, that were the cause of our evil. And that's what they told me. They did not like or wish or mean, they said they "had to" do evil. I could not for a long time believe this. It sounded like a weak excuse when a big, powerful captain of industry declared that the bad politicians "held him up" and struck him for a bribe or a contribution to a campaign fund. It was only after going through many cities and States and hearing always the same plea of compulsion that I was persuaded at last that it is true.

"You cannot build or operate a railroad," I said, "or a street railway, gas, water, or power company, develop and operate a mine, or get forests and cut timber on a large scale, or run any privileged business, without corrupting or joining in the corruption of the government. You tell me privately that you must, and here I am telling you semi-publicly that you must. And that is so all over the country. And that means that we have an organization of society in which, for some reason, you and your kind, the ablest, most intelligent, most imaginative, daring, and resourceful leaders of society, are and must be against society and its laws and its all-around growth."

My conclusion was that we, all of us, they as well as I—they more than I—should seek to rid all individuals of those things that make them work against the greater, common welfare.

The first question from that company, and the last, was, "Who started the evil?" I reminded them that the question should be what, not who, and that everything they believed would be brought together by the answer. If it was some Thing that hurt us we could be Christians and forgive sinners; we could cease from punishing men and develop an environment in which men would be tempted to be good. No use; those business men wanted me to admit that the politicians made the conditions that business men were subject to. I related how the San Francisco banker, William H. Crocker, had argued that he had to do business under conditions as he found them, and I had reminded him that his father and the rest of the Big Four who built the Central Pacific Railroad were blamed by the politicians for corrupting the State and making the conditions he, the son and successor, "had to" continue.

Somebody mentioned the fear that government operation was always inefficient. I cited Seattle, where a publicly owned power plant was breaking down so often that there was an investigation, and they learned that the private competitors had paid certain political employees to sabotage the city's plant.

Another voice asked if the public operation of utilities would not put them into politics. To answer that, I turned to William Mulholland, the popular, highly respected engineer, who was the manager of the city's water system. He had been the manager when the water company was a private corporation, and it was notorious that he was then a very active and efficient politician. Everybody in that room knew that Mr. Mulholland had said over and over again that the change from private to public operation had got him and the business out of politics. When I passed the question of politics to him he did not have to answer. The whole company burst into laughter.

There were other questions, other arguments against business in politics, which I learned in college. But the ever-recurring question that night was Who? Who started it? Who is to be blamed and— punished? And at last, the Episcopal bishop of that diocese stated it in a form that suggested an answer. I was emphasizing the point that society really offers a prize for evil-doing: money, position, power.

"Let's take down the offer of a reward," I said. "Let's abolish—privileges."

The bishop rose and very kindly, very courteously said that he felt that I was not meeting the minds of my hearers. "What we want to know," he said, "is who founded this system, who started it, not only in San Francisco and Los Angeles, in this or the last generation, but back, 'way back, in the beginning."

"Oh, I think I see," I said. "You want me to fix the fault at the very start of things. Maybe we can, Bishop. Most people, you know, say it was Adam. But Adam, you remember, he said that it was Eve, the woman; she did it. And Eve said no, no, it wasn't she; it was the serpent. And that's where you clergy have stuck ever since. You blame that serpent, Satan. Now I come and I am trying to show you that it was, it is, the apple."

The bishop sat down. You could hear him sit down. For there was silence, a long moment, and in that silence the meeting adjourned.

GAME POLITICIANS AND GAIN POLITICIANS

Arnold A. Rogow and Harold D. Lasswell

Analysis of the careers of thirty of these politicians suggests that, broadly speaking, there have been two conspicuous types of political boss in the United States and that neither type lends itself to the Acton generality. The typologies which follow are composite creations based on representative figures—the identifying characteristics of each type are not wholly those of any one individual—and we shall here distinguish them by the terms *game politician* and *gain politician*.

Our first type of boss, the *game politician,* was of early American

From Arnold A. Rogow and Harold D. Lasswell, *Power, Corruption, and Rectitude,* © 1963, pp.45–54. Reprinted by permission of Prentice-Hall, Inc., Englewood Cliffs, New Jersey. One footnote deleted.

stock and upper-class background. His father was important in business circles in the community and active in civic affairs. A Puritan in morals and a conservative in politics, the father had a strong sense of family position, and he impressed upon his son at an early age his own conviction that the best traditions of America, which the family represented, were being engulfed by a rising tide of immigration and radicalism. The father was also convinced that discipline produced moral virtue, and he was firm and unyielding in meting out punishment for youthful infractions. Since the home rules were rather strict, the boy was never certain when he was called to his father's study whether his father was to administer a sermon, a scolding, or both.

Timid, frail, and ill a good part of the time, the boy's mother played a relatively minor role in his life. Although she loved the boy (who was an only child) and longed to comfort him after an especially painful session in the study, she rarely interfered, knowing that any intercession from her was apt to increase her husband's wrath rather than reduce it. She was not passive by nature, but her role as wife had always been passive in accordance with her husband's wishes. There were few expressions of affection in the family circle, and the boy's mother, especially in her later years, became increasingly occupied with an intensely personal type of religion. It is probable that her various illnesses served as expressions of acute inner distress.

Looking back from a later vantage point, the *game politician* could not remember a time as a boy when he had been happy, and he often remarked that his life had really begun when he left home for college. He was a student leader and led an active campus life at college; he also earned sufficiently good grades to be admitted to an eminent law school. Following graduation he became attached to a well-known law firm in his home city, but the practice of law was never his foremost interest. His legal work brought him into close contact with local politicians, and within a short time he was one of them.

By the time he was thirty the *game politician* had held a variety of posts in the local government and majority party, and by the age of forty he was serving in the state legislature. During his middle years he was firmly in control of the state party organization with the power to appoint, or influence the appointment of, mayors, governors, United States senators, and other public officials; frequently he himself held one or the other of these offices. At the national level he was influential in nominating the presidential candidates of his party, and he was active, on occasion, in promoting his own chances. Frequent charges of corruption and the occasional success of reform movements threatened his career only intermittently. For most of his forty years of active political life he exercised effective control or was "the power behind the scenes."

In the course of after-dinner speeches at political banquets he was apt to make reference to "the great game of politics," and for him this expression was no mere cliché. A man of independent means, he did not exploit politics primarily, if at all, for personal gain, although he was privy to innumerable "deals" which involved the buying and selling of political favors. He regarded the uses and abuses of money in politics as legitimate, and he was always willing to arrange matters, if at all possible, to promote the financial interests of friends.

For the *game politician* politics functioned as the principal mode of self-expression and self-realization. He enjoyed "the game" for the ego rewards it offered, which were chiefly power, prestige, adulation, and a sense of importance. The manipulation of men and events, in which he excelled, served less his convictions, which were few, than as an exercise in strategy, which he valued for its own sake. Viewing the outcome as always more important than the issue, he derived great satisfaction from political victories of large and small consequence, no matter how obtained.

It was often said of our *game politician* that "he had many acquaintances and few friends." In reality he had many associates—most of them political dependents—few acquaintances, and no friends. He permitted himself a number of physical pleasures, respectable or otherwise, and on these occasions several cronies were usually to be found in his company. But his confidences in them were confined to political topics, and his association with them was based on a reciprocal exchange of various services. His relations with his immediate family were not close; indeed his wife and children saw less of him during his active life than certain key individuals in his political organization. As a result he is remembered less by his family than by the state which he dominated for so many years. His grave in the family plot is unattended, but his statue stands in front of the state capitol building.

Between 1870 and 1920 the *game politician*—to whom we shall return shortly—shared the national stage with another type of political boss, whom we shall here style the *gain politician*. Unlike his confrere in politics the second composite figure was the eldest of six children of an impoverished Irish immigrant family. The boy's father, an amiable if ineffectual man, was a bricklayer, but his earnings were too meager to support the family. The boy left school and worked at a variety of low-paid industrial jobs even before his father's death;

after his death, which occurred when the boy was twelve years of age, the full burden of the family fell on the boy and his mother.

The mother lavished on the family all the love and attention of which she was capable, and the boy was her special favorite. Long after the other children were in bed, she and the boy would sit at the kitchen table discussing family affairs and exchanging gossip of the neighborhood. She occasionally would reminisce about the Ireland of her youth, and she often expressed a desire to make a stylish return someday to the Irish village in which she had lived as a young girl (she was later to realize this dream several times over). The boy confided his own ambitions and plans, and it became his practice over the years never to make any important decision without consulting her.

He meanwhile was fighting his way to power in the neighborhood gang. In the process he became quite skilled in fighting with fist or club, and he later was to put these methods to practical use in the rough-and-tumble ward politics of his day. The gang specialized in disrupting the political rallies of the minority party in the area, and it eventually became the nucleus of his own political machine. His good looks, stature, and powerful physique—as a young man he was able to lift a barrel of beer to shoulder height—endowed him with a certain physical magnetism which was of benefit throughout his career.

While still an adolescent he was entrusted with various missions by the long-time political boss in his section of the city. He and the boss became rather friendly, and eventually, on his own authority, he was able to distribute minor political favors and small amounts of patronage. In a few years he had created a machine within a machine, and he was then capable of dealing with rivals for the boss's favor from a position of strength. When the boss died, he moved quickly to consolidate his power, and within a short period he established himself as the head of the organization.

By this time he was approaching thirty years of age and had married. He had long since learned to turn political favors to his own financial interest; and with the proceeds derived from politics he had become the owner of one retail store and part-owner of several others. He also invested in various services which the city government patronized, the operations of which he could influence in his own favor. Meanwhile his political advancement was rapid, although it was confined to local party posts and municipal offices. He served as councilman, city treasurer, and mayor, and for many years was especially popular in the role of the latter. As city treasurer he was able to extend his power in the party, and long before he was mayor, he had become the most powerful political boss in the city's history.

He had also become one of the wealthiest. His opponents believed —and correctly—that in the city no contract was let, no tax collected, no post filled, and no facility established without his extracting a commission. It was revealed after his death that he was worth considerably more than one million dollars and that he had lived in lavish circumstances for a number of years. While his children were still young, he moved his family to a large mansion in the most fashionable part of town, and he also established his mother in a comfortable home, which was staffed by several servants. All seven children, with the exception of one daughter, who became a nun, attended expensive colleges. It was his wife's custom, on shopping trips, to be accompanied by her liveried personal chauffeur.

The *gain politician*, unlike the first type of political boss we have considered, had only a minor interest in state and national politics. He twice declined to be nominated for any higher office than mayor, and while he insisted upon being consulted, especially with regard to patronage, by governors and senators, he was primarily concerned to maintain good relations with "higher-ups." He was consistently opposed to, as he put it, "rocking the boat," and he dealt wrathfully with occasional mavericks, bolters, and would-be reformers within the party. Placing enormous importance on loyalty to the organization, he prided himself on the fact that he had never deserted a party stalwart, no matter what his personal or political difficulties.

Although the *gain politician* was firmly attached to few principles, he thought of himself as a "friend of the people," and indeed in a sense he was. He put innumerable relatives and friends on the city payroll and befriended countless others with gifts or loans of money. Widows, orphans, derelicts, the sick, the unemployed, the aged, the struggling, and the fallen—all of them received a hearing from him or his lieutenants and almost all of them received some tangible help. He donated large amounts of money to churches and synagogues, schools, hospitals, and orphanages and found time to sit at sickbeds and attend funerals. Radiating warmth, fellowship, and generosity, he earned a citywide personal following that was sufficiently large and loyal to maintain him in power through several damaging investigations of his political machine.

His marriage was a happy one, and no breath of domestic scandal touched him during his entire career. He derived much satisfaction from the achievements of his children, almost all of whom were successfully established in a business or profession at the time of his death. He also had a number of close personal friends, in whom he was in the habit of confiding his innermost thoughts. Several of these friends have written eulogistic biographies of his life; others have named their children after him. And for many citizens in the city he remains, many years after his death, a vital, almost living figure.

It is common to treat the *game politician* and *gain politician* not as cousins and not even as brothers in corruption, but as identical twins. The case histories, however, suggest that the term "corrupt boss" covers a multitude of sinners whose relations to each other are limited to a common involvement in political *flagrante delicto*. The fact of corruption may constitute only the weakest link between personality types as distinct from political careers. Moreover in the cases examined here, of which the *game* and *gain politicians* serve as archetypes, the variety of motivations is as diverse as the variety of acts.

Although psychological detail in the relevant biographical materials is, on the whole, sparse, the available data indicate that severe deprivation in early life is a key factor in the background of the corrupt boss. But it is the character of the deprivation, rather than deprivation as such, which is crucial for future behavior. Our *game politician*, for example, was deprived of love and emotional security during his formative years. It is clear that the cold and withdrawn personality of his later years was essentially developed in childhood as a protective response to a punitive environment. His inability as an adult to initiate and sustain close relations with family or friends is another derivative of the early period.

But a hostile environment may be made friendly and safe through manipulation, and we may infer that manipulative skills of various types were brought into play during the frequent sessions in the father's study. The study "game"—his boast in later life was that he was often able to "get around" his father on such occasions—was the early form of the political "game," and the deviousness, evasiveness, and capacity for intrigue of the mature politician also described the behavior pattern of the boy. In other essentials of personality development, however, the boy did not succeed in "getting around" his father. His repressed hatred of his father generated in adult life an hostility to others which created unnecessary difficulties in his political relationships. It is also true that his convictions were dominated by the rigid and outmoded conservative views with which he had been indoctrinated as a child. Although he was careful to avoid taking positions, he was generally understood to favor principles rather similar to those which had been espoused by his father. His arrogance and superciliousness, which were also qualities shared with his father, were added handicaps to his ambition for political preferment beyond the state level.

Unlike his father, however, the *game politician* was never attached to moral virtue, family honor, or a conscious, if misdirected, sense of tradition. His principal attachment was to the political "game" as such, to which all other considerations related as mere expedients. Self-realization and political realization were simple equivalents; indeed the personality system did not function well outside the political arena. But the stakes of the "game" were not confined to power as such. The demands of the self upon the environment largely related to deference values, and as Table I indicates, the "game" indulged a number of demands which had been blocked or frustrated elsewhere.

TABLE I

Personality System

Deprivation	*Demand*	*Indulgence*
Parental acceptance	Power	Office, bossism
Parental recognition	Respect	Votes, elections
Parental approval	Rectitude	Self-righteousness, moral superiority
Parental love	Affection	Following, clique, cronies

The major point, however, is that politics afforded our *game politician* a control of environment which facilitated the indulgence of demands. Relative to other arenas (home, business, profession) the political world was more indulgent of demands of the self upon the environment, and it also was capable of providing a greater variety of indulgences.

Viewed from this perspective, corruption was less an indulgence than a method by which the *game politician* maintained the necessary control of environment. While corruption served the end of power, power itself mainly functioned as the means of enforcing demands generated throughout the entire personality system. Put another way, power *and* corruption were the agencies by which the personality system sought to establish and support itself. The political man represented by the *game politician* was merely an older and more successful version of the emotionally deprived and rejected child.

For the *gain politician,* on the other hand, power and corruption were also functional, but functional in a different context of demands. The early environment, except in its material aspect, was largely indulgent, and throughout his life he was supported by various emotionally satisfying relationships. His ambitions for office never extended beyond the local level, despite opportunities afforded to play a major role in state and national politics. Although he could be ruthless in dealing with opponents, his personal success owed much more to a genial disposition and warm manner than to coercive tactics. Although he consistently exploited politics for gain, it was a fact of his long career that he had won over many political enemies and never lost a friend.

The character of early deprivation largely related to the welfare values of well-being, wealth, skill, and enlightenment. But the demands of the self upon the environment, which were generated by such deprivation, were of a different order from those which developed in the personality system of the *game politician.* To begin with, the "self" was an aggregate rather than a single entity, a "we" rather than an "I." It initially included his mother, brothers, and sisters, and it later incorporated his wife and children. In a sense the collective self also embraced distant relatives, friends, and associates, because they too were beneficiaries of corrupt acts. In the second place, the demands of the self upon the environment were mainly confined to the wealth value; although other welfare values were important, the control of environment largely was exploited for material advantage. Finally the demands which were indulged, unlike demands related to deference values, rarely involved or affected interpersonal relations. Our *gain politician* did not need to dominate others; nor did he require their psychological submission. Indeed his success as a corruptionist owed much to the fact that he was never arrogant in his relations with peers or subordinates. In cheating the business leaders and taxpayers of their money, he was careful to avoid cheating them of their self-esteem.

It is also important that the *gain politician* was less cynical than indifferent to rectitude standards. Such standards had been absent in his early political training, and youthful experience had favored the view that politics essentially was a variety or form of commercial enterprise. In the context of prevailing political morality he would have considered it foolish *not* to exploit politics for gain and irresponsible to retire poor from office.

But the significant fact is that the *gain politician* employed corruption not in behalf of power, but in behalf of welfare values. As

Table II illustrates, the political arena was indulgent of demands of the environment which related to early deprivation.

Tᴀʙʟᴇ II

Personality System

Deprivation	*Demand*	*Indulgence*
Comfort	Well-being	"Rich" living
Income	Wealth	"Pay-offs," graft, "commissions"
Opportunity	Skill	"Deals," manipulations, promotions, combinations
Education	Enlightenment	"Inside" information, foreknowledge, "tips"

Again, as in the case of the *game politician,* power *and* corruption were directed toward specific ends which were generated in the personality system.

The analysis of composite "boss" types, therefore, does not support the Acton formula that "power tends to corrupt. . . ." The biographical test in general suggests, on the contrary, that corruption is a function of the relations among a number of variables in the personality system. The propositional form of such relations may be stated as follows:

1. Corruption may ensue when the early environment of the personality system promotes severe deprivation.
2. A background of severe deprivation may encourage the use of power in corrupt forms as a means of acquiring and maintaining environmental control.
3. The character of the early deprivation affects the purposes for which power is employed.
4. If the deprivation has been experienced mainly with reference to deference values, power in corrupt form will be employed in behalf of self-aggrandizement (*game politician*).
5. If the deprivation has been experienced mainly with reference to welfare values, power in corrupt form will be employed in behalf of material advantage (*gain politician*).
6. Power in and of itself neither expresses nor promotes any tendency, whether to corrupt or to ennoble.

GRASS-EATERS
AND MEAT-EATERS
Knapp Commission

Corrupt policemen have been informally described as being either "grass-eaters" or "meat-eaters." The overwhelming majority of those who do take payoffs are grass-eaters, who accept gratuities and solicit five- and ten- and twenty-dollar payments from contractors, tow-truck operators, gamblers, and the like, but do not aggressively pursue corruption payments. "Meat-eaters," probably only a small percentage of the force, spend a good deal of their working hours aggressively seeking out situations they can exploit for financial gain, including gambling, narcotics, and other serious offenses which can yield payments of thousands of dollars. Patrolman William Phillips was certainly an example of this latter category.

One strong impetus encouraging grass-eaters to continue to accept relatively petty graft is, ironically, their feeling of loyalty to their fellow officers. Accepting payoff money is one way for an officer to prove that he is one of the boys and that he can be trusted. In the climate which existed in the Department during the Commission's investigation, at least at the precinct level, these numerous but relatively small payoffs were a fact of life, and those officers who made a point of refusing them were not accepted closely into the fellowship of policemen. Corruption among grass-eaters obviously cannot be met by attempting to arrest them all and will probably diminish only if Commissioner Murphy is successful in his efforts to change the rank and file attitude toward corruption.

No change in attitude, however, is likely to affect a meat-eater, whose yearly income in graft amounts to many thousands of dollars and who may take payoffs of $5,000 or even $50,000 in one fell swoop

From Commission to Investigate Allegations of Police Corruption and the City's Anti-Corruption Procedures (Knapp Commission), *Commission Report,* pp.65–68.

(former Assistant Chief Inspector Sydney Cooper, who had been active in anti-corruption work for years, recently stated that the largest score of which he had heard—although he was unable to verify it—was a narcotics payoff involving $250,000). Such men are willing to take considerable risks as long as the potential profit remains so large. Probably the only way to deal with them will be to ferret them out individually and get them off the force, and, hopefully, into prisons.

Pads, Scores and Gratuities

Corruption payments made to the police may be divided into "pad" payments and "scores," two police slang terms which make an important distinction.

The "pad" refers to regular weekly, biweekly, or monthly payments, usually picked up by a police bagman and divided among fellow officers. Those who make such payments as well as policemen who receive them are referred to as being "on the pad."

A "score" is a one-time payment that an officer might solicit from, for example, a motorist or a narcotics violator. The term is also used as a verb, as in "I scored him for $1,500."

A third category of payments to the police is that of gratuities, which the Commission feels cannot in the strictest sense be considered a matter of police corruption, but which has been included here because it is a related—and ethically borderline—practice, which is prohibited by Department regulations, and which often leads to corruption.

Operations on the pad are generally those which operate illegally in a fixed location day in and day out. Illegal gambling is probably the single largest source of pad payments. The most important legitimate enterprises on the pad at the time of the investigation were those like construction, licensed premises, and businesses employing large numbers of vehicles, all of which operate from fixed locations and are subject to summonses from the police for myriad violations.

Scores, on the other hand, are made whenever the opportunity arises—most often when an officer happens to spot someone engaging in an illegal activity like pushing narcotics, which doesn't involve a fixed location. Those whose activities are generally legal but who break the law occasionally, like motorists or tow-truck operators, are also subject to scores. By far the most lucrative source of scores is the City's multimillion-dollar narcotics business.

Factors Influencing Corruption

There are at least five major factors which influence how much or how little graft an officer receives, and also what his major sources are. The most important of these is, of course, the character of the officer in question, which will determine whether he bucks the system and refuses all corruption money; goes along with the system and accepts what comes his way; or outdoes the system, and aggressively seeks corruption-prone situations and exploits them to the extent that it seriously cuts into the time available for doing his job. His character will also determine what kind of graft he accepts. Some officers, who don't think twice about accepting money from gamblers, refuse to have anything at all to do with narcotics pushers. They make a distinction between what they call "clean money" and "dirty money."

The second factor is the branch of the Department to which an officer is assigned. A plainclothesman, for example, has more—and different—opportunities than a uniformed patrolman.

The third factor is the area to which an officer is assigned. At the time of the investigation certain precincts in Harlem, for instance, comprised what police officers called "the Gold Coast" because they contained so many payoff-prone activities, numbers and narcotics being the biggest. In contrast, the Twenty-Second Precinct, which is Central Park, has clearly limited payoff opportunities. As Patrolman Phillips remarked, "What can you do, shake down the squirrels?" The area also determines the major sources of corruption payments. For instance, in midtown Manhattan precincts businessmen and motorists were major sources; on the Upper East Side, bars and construction; in the ghetto precincts, narcotics, and numbers.

The fourth factor is the officer's assignment. For uniformed men, a seat in a sector car was considered fairly lucrative in most precincts, while assignment to stand guard duty outside City Hall obviously was not, and assignment to one sector of a precinct could mean lots of payoffs from construction sites while in another sector bar owners were the big givers.

The fifth factor is rank. For those who do receive payoffs, the amount generally ascends with the rank. A bar may give $5 to patrolmen, $10 to sergeants, and considerably more to a captain's bagman. Moreover, corrupt supervisors have the opportunity to cut into much of the graft normally collected by those under them.

TAKING

Jonathan Rubinstein

In 1969–70, Dr. Rubinstein, a historian, reporter, and ethnographer, spent a year as a member of the Philadelphia Police Department, graduating from its police academy and spending six months on patrol. *City Police* reports his observations of the working life and value patterns of policemen.

There is no way to prepare a policeman for the situation he discovers on the street. There are some open discussions at the police academy about the possibilities for graft, but most instructors restrict themselves to repeating the traditional homilies about "not selling your soul for a bowl of porridge." The men are told by some that they will be offered free food, which is the beginning of their slide into corruption. "They'll try to buy you with a ham sandwich; don't take it. Put your money on the counter, and if the guy won't take it, leave it for the waitress. You'll see when you go out on the beat. Maybe you don't have much money in your pocket, and when you finish your hamburger, the guy says to forget it. So you do it once, and then you go down the street and the next guy wants to put a little cheese on the burger for you. Now you're gettin' to like the job. Don't do it." From the back of the room another instructor called out, "Say, John, where is this beat you're talkin' about?" and the earnest moment dissolved in mirth.

The "bad apple" theory has been the traditional explanation of corruption and scandal in an organization that is required by its nature to appear honest and "neutral" in every possible way. This idea allows the career policeman to explain to himself as well as to the public the persistence of a problem whose solution is beyond his control. For the corrupt or the compromised, too, the idea of a few bad men having succumbed to the temptations of a wicked society is a comfort that allows them to conceal the political character of most scandals. Every revelation brings with it a flood of sermons, all with the same moral—a weak man is tempted by his position and gradually slides into the ranks of the dishonest. After the Knapp Commission revealed that some New York City policemen were involved in payoffs, the reporter who broke the story wrote of their corruption:

> Police corruption begins with the notion that policemen by some peculiar divine right are entitled to free meals, free movies, and cut-rate prices on virtually everything they buy. This is known as "getting a break." "Even when I was in the Police Academy," a Tactical Patrol Force sergeant recalled, "I heard guys talking about getting a break." While almost all cops take free meals—it is so widely accepted it is impossible not to—the idea of getting a break is the platform, the launching pad, from which the bad guys spring.[1]

While this notion reaffirms our belief in the Christian idea of guilt and sin being personal and individual, it is a notion that offers the recruit no hope of coping with the real situation on the street. A policeman who becomes a thief does so for the same reasons that others are thieves—inclination and opportunity.

There are some instructors who try to give their students a more realistic picture of what to expect, but nobody can tell them how to avoid the web of collusions and compromises that makes everyone guilty. One day a lecturer was talking about the patrolman's freedom in issuing traffic tickets. "You mean we can give a guy a warning rather than give him a ticket if he makes a wrong turn?" someone asked. "That's right. Listen, fellas, let me tell you something you should know, since it's gonna come up as soon as you get on the street. We ain't supposed to talk this way, but it's important for you to know. Don't fuck with a motorist. Don't take a note from him. He's not like a prostitute or a number writer. If he complains, you are gonna be in real trouble. If you pull a guy over for something and he cops a plea about not knowin' the neighborhood, you can go with that. If he offers you a little something for a cup of coffee or lunch, well, that's your business. But don't you go out there and pinch him for a note. That's a stupid fuckin' note and there's no sense blowin' a good job for a nickel or dime. You understand me?"

A few days later a lieutenant was discussing the policeman's obligation to remain honest and report all wrongdoings. "I know there are

1. David Burnham, "How Corruption Is Built into the System—and a Few Ideas for What to Do about It," *New York Magazine* (September 21, 1970).

men out there in uniforms breaking the law. You will see some of them. If you refuse to take anything but do not report it, you are as guilty as they are, and you are not any better either. When I came into this department, I worked with the biggest bunch of crooks I ever saw. You have to refuse to go along. You have to . . ."

"Excuse me, sir, can I ask you something?" a recruit said. "I got a friend who's been on the street awhile. He told me that one night he went on a burglary call, and his partner and a few other guys stole some liquor from this place and offered him some. Now I ain't sayin' he wasn't wrong for takin' it and he's so fucked up about it he's thinkin' of quittin', but what do you expect a guy to do? It's like in the army. Everyone is checkin' out the new guy to see how he will act. O.K., there's no question you can refuse to take and they don't trust you no more. Well, you can handle that and still get along, but if you think that anyone is gonna drop a dime, you must be kiddin'. You do that once and you got a reputation that will follow you around. You're a rat and everyone will know it. Who's gonna work with you? Who will come to you if you call an assist?" Everyone in the room was noisily agreeing with their classmate.

"What's your name, son? Right. Listen, Jason, I ain't sayin' it's easy. I'm not telling you it don't take balls to do it. I was a lonely guy for a long time. Nobody to talk to, all the shit details, workin' the worst sectors in the district where there were no people around. They put me at the end of nowhere. But you see these bars? I made it. And now there are a lot of guys who dive for a fuckin' hole when they see me comin'. You gotta decide from the start in this job whether you're gonna be clean or whether you're gonna take. There are guys in this room, I know, who are comin' on the job with the idea of makin' a buck. I wish you would quit and save us the trouble of having to find you and lock you up. There are guys here who are already thinking about how they're gonna flash their tin and get this and that. Well, I'm tellin' you those days are gone in this department, and if you do it we'll get your ass."

The moralizing to which the recruit is subjected in the academy mercifully stops when he gets to the district, but he quickly discovers that even the frank advice of helpful teachers has not prepared him for what he finds. Although his experience depends greatly on the kind of district he is sent to, one thing he finds everywhere is bribery. Almost immediately people are trying to give him money, mostly motorists who are trying to get out of a ticket. He also hears rumors about things that suggest the involvement of some of his colleagues in obscure dealings, but since he is informally segregated from much of the squad's work, he does not know what is actually going on. All he is told in his first few weeks is where he can get his clothes cleaned for the "police price" and which restaurants will give him a break on his lunch check. These are gratuities the patrolman knows he receives only because he is a policeman, but he does not try to conceal them or disguise what they are since he is not doing anything illicit for them. He sees these as expressions of gratitude and friendship which mirror within his circle of influence the policies and attitudes that he sees operating at a higher level within the department and the city government.

In most American cities there are restaurant chains that feed policemen free or at a special rate. This is not the informal policy of some branch managers but a centrally organized decision. Cashiers keep a record of how many free meals they give away each day, and these tabulations are used to demonstrate the company's goodwill toward the department and the city. The patrolman does not know what kind of favors are given and received in return for this consideration, but he understands it is not done out of simple kindness. There are also restaurants and diners throughout the city known for their kindness to anyone in uniform. A radio call announced a holdup in a restaurant in a distant part of the city, causing a lieutenant to comment. "A lot of cars are gonna go in on that. They treat a cop real good in there. You can get a whole basket of chicken and they don't even give you a bill." The district patrolmen do not know where the "big bosses" dine, but they know that the considerations given to them differ only in the quality of the food and the accommodations offered to people in higher places.

Every patrolman has one or two places on his sector or nearby where he is welcome to eat for a reduced price. There are very few men who regularly eat for nothing and probably no one ever pays a full price all the time. The district police are not welcome in all restaurants; those that insist on charging the full price usually do not get their trade. But since the policeman spends a great deal of his life at all hours on the streets of places he knows well but where he is not "at home," it is hardly a surprise that he should seek out places where he is welcomed in a friendly manner. He is not supposed to eat in places where beer or liquor are served (and he usually does not), limiting him mainly to diners and luncheonettes, which are small, personal businesses. Some of these places welcome any district policemen because their presence is viewed as a guarantee against trouble and disorder, while others have special arrangements with one or two men which reflect personal associations that extend beyond the obvious bond between the policeman and the businessman.

In one district there was a restaurant that gave patrolmen a small break on meals but reserved special consideration for the sector man, who had eaten there regularly for ten years. When he was late for lunch, the owner often called the station to see if he was all right. He never ordered his meals, since the cooks simply prepared whatever was best that day. He paid a flat price weekly. When he entered the restaurant, he gave the appearance of a man about to dine in his own house.

The personal connections that dominate police eating arrangements can lead to some curious accommodations between the district men and their hosts. In one restaurant the owner was known for his dislike of the men, and he insisted that his waitresses, who were known for quite the opposite sentiments, charge them full price. When he was not there, the girls gave them a police price. Some men would check the place out before entering and, if the owner was about, would go down the street to another place, where the food was not as good but the welcome warmer. The veteran men in the squad refused to eat in the better diner because of the owner's attitude, settling for the other place, where they were guaranteed a reduced price. But the younger men, who enjoyed the company of the waitresses along with their meals, were often willing to pay the full price for their pleasure.

In another district there was a sleazy diner that opened at 4 A.M. and was a welcome haven in the dreary hours of last out. The owner, who disliked and feared being alone, welcomed the patrolmen. The restaurant was located in a ghetto, and although the owner was white, his clientele was integrated; both white and black policemen frequented the place. All of the men first-named him, and he gave them free coffee and cheap breakfasts. They provided him with a sense of security and always kept an eye on his place when they drove past. His wife, however, refused to give anyone wholesale prices and whenever she worked the men did not stop by. At one point, she worked regularly during the afternoons and on daywork the men transferred their business to another place, where they also had to pay the full price but where the food was worth the money. However, they returned on last out.

There are restaurants and diners that encourage police patronage in an effort to assure special consideration. In one district a diner had serious problems with a teenage gang that constantly threatened to wreck the place. The owner offered free meals to the sergeant, the sector car, and the wagon only for stopping in. Any patrolman could get free coffee just by appearing. In almost every district there is one place that offers the sector man and the wagon special considerations that are not extended to anyone else. Often a patrolman off his sector will stop in at a place to get a soda and be taken aback when the owner asks him for the money. The policeman does not walk in and just take something, but he asks and allows the owner the opportunity to decline payment. If the person refuses, the patrolman is confronted with the choice of paying or putting back what he has taken. He rarely returns the item, since it is an embarrassment as well as a revelation of wrongful intent. "Shit, I ain't goin' back in that place no more. I had to pay for this soda. I'm stayin' on my sector," the patrolman muttered. The considerations given the sector man over others are well understood by all. One time, during riot duty, a captain stopped a sector car as it was passing and asked the man about places to eat in the district. The options did not sound promising, and he asked the man whether a certain sandwich shop was still operating. When he was told it was, the captain said jokingly, "It's on your sector, huh? Listen, why don't you go down there and tell the guy to give you some sandwiches for you and the other guys working the sector—all four hundred of us."

The patrolman understands that he is given consideration partly because of the security he represents to the small businessmen who run the places he frequents. He is not being paid off to overlook parking violations or given special consideration to protect something in the back room (although a hostile businessman might get a few more parking tickets than a friendly person). He is given a break just for his presence. But these regular associations arouse in the patrolman a preference for one over another and encourage him to do little favors for one person, requiring him to neglect someone else. At closing time he may park his car while the owner counts his receipts and then accompany him to the bank. This is not an illegal favor, since any businessman in the city may request a money escort, but the department does not encourage the use of a service that it would have to discontinue if it were widely demanded. The sector man informally agrees to give consideration to a friend in exchange for kindnesses shown him throughout the year. He does not feel he is doing anything wrong since nobody can demonstrate to him that there is something else he might be doing that is socially more useful in these moments. If pressed to defend himself, he argues that he is only doing what the department does for big businessmen at a higher level.

There are some arrangements, however, between the police and businessmen that can be described only as organized protection. Whether these reflect departmental policy or secret arrangements within a district or a division is not clear, but since they require an illegal allocation of manpower and the faking of official departmental records, which no patrolman or sergeant can safely engineer alone, they must be conspiracies embracing commanding officers at least to the level of captain. In a number of districts some branches of a restaurant chain have a policeman assigned to sit inside during the four-to-twelve shift. This chain has an established policy of giving free food to patrolmen during certain times of the day and each branch keeps a careful record of what is given away. But the beatman's services are not offered in exchange for these favors; he is rented for a fee. It is against departmental policy to assign men fixed posts in commercial establishments; the men who do this work are officially listed as working on a sector car or a beat. In one district the man who handled the assignment on the four-to-twelve shift said that he was paid $20 a week for acting as a private guard. Since the arrangement required the permission of his sergeant and possibly his captain, it can be assumed that they, too, were being paid. The man had the additional responsibility of bringing extra food back to the station when he was picked up by the sector car at the end of his tour.

A new branch of this chain was opening in another district, and the manager, who was very concerned about the possibilities of being held up, was eager to negotiate an arrangement with the district police. A patrolman stopped by shortly before the place was to open and suggested to the manager that he speak with the sergeant, who could drop by if the man would call the district. Negotiations proceeded quickly and a bargain was struck. On the four-to-twelve shift a man would be stationed inside the restaurant, and every Saturday night the sergeant or his bagman would collect $100. The money was distributed among all the men who contributed to maintaining the arrangement. The beatman got $25, and lesser amounts were paid to the sector car, which was operated by the man's partner, and to the wagon crew that serviced the area. In addition, the sergeant, lieutenant, and captain were also given a cut. After about a month, the deal was suddenly canceled. Another restaurateur had complained about the special consideration being given to his competitor, and a phone call from downtown to the captain immediately terminated the agreement. The patrolman who initiated the negotiations regretted the passing of "a good, clean note with nothing on paper," but the police and the manager were able to salvage something. The manager continued to give out free food to patrolmen and supervisors whenever they stopped by to look the place over. This assured the restaurant of some additional protection and aided the manager's sense of security.

Although any arrangement that places a policeman in the role of a paid watchman is illegal and the payment of money for the granting of favors cannot be described as anything but bribery and graft, these transactions do not differ in character from others that are constantly forced on the police by direct political pressure. This goes on constantly in little ways—by assigning a patrolman to watch someone's house during a party, or giving a judge and his family special consideration in parking their family car—and also in more important matters. A large bakery in one district was having serious problems with gangs of teenagers, who were vandalizing trucks and terrorizing workers around the plant. The company was paying protection money to several gangs to police the area for them, but the disorders continued and culminated in the stabbing of one worker on the loading platform. The next day the district captain was ordered to assign a beatman to the plant on all tours; the sergeants were to instruct the sector cars and wagons to patrol the area intensively. The captain claimed that the order from the commissioner's office had been initiated in the office of the governor. The owner of the bakery was known to be an important contributor to the governor's party. There was no special deal made that benefited the policemen performing the service, although after a few weeks on the job, they had made informal arrangements with workers to get free bread and they were also allowed to buy quantities at wholesale prices for squad parties and picnics. In many parts of the city major business streets have beatmen who act as informal watchmen for the important merchants of their areas. Most of these beats are established at the department level and are the consequence of political pressure of one kind or another being applied directly to the department through the mayor's office or the city council.

The police are also obliged to use their authority over street traffic to favor politically influential people and to punish those who are out of favor. "When I came to this district, I was really gonna do a job, you know," a captain said. "No favors and no deals. Well, I found out. You know that place over on Elm Street? All the trucks parked everywhere during the day. It's really dangerous during rush hour. Well, I told my supervisors that I wanted it cleaned up, to ticket all the trucks and force them off the street. Lieutenant Johnson just laughed at me; he said I was kidding. I told him I wasn't, and they started putting on the tickets. Well, it went on for a few days, and then I got a call from downtown, you know, and I was told to lay off. There's plenty of people who think I'm gettin' a note out of it, maybe you do, but it just ain't true. And those trucks are gonna be parked there until someone burns down the terminal."

"Goddamn it, the captain calls me at home last night and tells me that the heat is on Jason, you know, the beer distributor. He tells me to be sure to be here early in the morning and to go directly there and make sure everything is tagged." The place in question was that of a major beer distributor in the city whose facilities were centralized at one location. In addition to maintaining its own parking lots, the company routinely left its trucks on the streets while they were being loaded. This violation of city ordinance and state law was regularly ignored until the captain was called by his inspector and told the company had become involved in a political dispute with the mayor and the order was out to enforce every regulation to the letter.

"Shit, I know my men don't have anything to do with that guy. Sure a cop goes in now and again and gets a case of beer wholesale, but nobody is taking a note out of the place. Now they're asking me if I have anything to do with the guy. Sure, I know him; sure, I know he fronts for some racket guys, but I didn't give him a distributor's license. I met him at a couple of charity functions; he gives money to aid the kids in the district and stuff like that. I could get my ass kicked over this and I don't even know what the fuck it's about," a very nervous captain said.

The sergeant personally supervised the area, while his own men and a traffic officer put tickets on all trucks and private cars in the area. The company owner's private car was ticketed three times for different violations, while he stood silently on the pavement. By 9:30 A.M. every truck was off the street. The sergeant parked his car and looked at the empty street. A young woman approached the car and said, "Excuse me, Sergeant, I've been looking for a policeman all week to complain about the trucks that always park here and now I've found a policeman, but there are no more trucks." The sergeant smiled and told her that there would be no more illegal parking allowed and he was personally supervising the effort to clean up the streets. She thanked him and left. "Sure, lady. How long do you think it'll be before they get the trucks back on the street? We write maybe fifty or sixty tickets today and keep 'em off the street a week; you wanna bet they make up with the mayor?"

The influence of powerful business interests and merchants' associations on official police policy is mirrored at all levels in the department by semiformal and informal arrangements made by captains, street supervisors, and patrolmen. Many of these are illegal in a formal sense, but often they are no more than accommodations that would be imposed from above if they were not made by the district. They are essentially exchanges of services for favors, which are negotiated in a spirit of mutual advantage. Sometimes they are initiated by the police but more frequently by business people anxious to gain special favor. There is no evidence that the district police seek to compel favors by harassment or the withdrawal of services, although a decision to enforce parking regulations, for example, in an area where they had previously been neglected, might be viewed by some as an effort to extract a consideration. Many businessmen have no special contacts with the police, do not give them anything, do not offer them wholesale prices, and get the same level of service anyone else receives when he makes a request for a policeman or directs an inquiry to the district captain.

The granting of special considerations to influential business people at the department level and the slightly less formal adjustments made at the divisional and district level to fulfill the desires of powerful commanders make it very difficult for the department to control the initiatives of patrolmen in their sectors. If a captain and a sergeant receive some kind of consideration for extending a commercial beat or allowing people on some blocks to park illegally, how can they discourage their own men from exploiting a few opportunities? Even if the captain is unwilling to take a payoff, if he has the reputation among his men of being "clean," he will not decline little favors and Christmas gifts. One captain recalled, "Christmas time is when a lot of money comes to the police. Last Christmas I received $50 from a bank. I wish they had never sent it, but I didn't return it."

Christmas money is an almost universal practice in American cities. The police themselves honor the tradition. Patrolmen give gifts to their operations crews; squads that hold their supervisors in esteem frequently honor them with a present or with cash; and the radio crew is also given money. In their turn, the patrolmen make the rounds of the merchants and small businessmen who appreciate their efforts.

Nobody wants to be away from his district at Christmas, when "jingle bells" are in the air. Even if a man does not take money, there are bottles of whiskey and free food to be had. Some commanders warn their men that anyone who solicits gifts will be punished, but nobody is told that he cannot accept a consideration if it is freely offered. However, the line between the two is very thin and most policemen exploit the possibilities available to them. Each patrolman is responsible for his own sector, concentrating on the small stores and shops that he services regularly. Nobody gives him a lot, a "nickel" or a "dime" ($5 or $10) is considered a quite decent tip. Anything less than $5 is considered an insult. (The abolition of the $2 bill has probably benefited those policemen who seek money from motorists and tips from business people.) But there are many stores the patrolman does not go to, places where he knows that he is not welcome, places he does not frequent during the year. He is being paid for a service, just like the mailman and the newsboy. The most generous rewards come from the liquor stores, bars, and clubs that frequently require the services of the police. Usually the supervisors concentrate on these places, although some businesses do not wait for a policeman to come around but send money and bottles directly to the station.

In some places the patrolman does his own collecting, while in other squads the supervisors make the collections and split the money among their men. However, there is always some individual initiative being pursued, regardless of what kind of control the supervisors exert. Even if there were a ban on any kind of solicitation, it would not be possible to stop the men from getting something. They might take home less than they do now, but business people would stop them in the streets and give them packages of food and liquor, offers of wholesale prices on goods, and invitations to drop by, "to stop back," another time. These petty rewards—they rarely amount to $100, although a corrupted policeman who is on the take will make considerably more —are part of city life; to eliminate them would require a transformation of social relationships among city people. They are expressions of thanks for services rendered and claims on continuing service—some are extortions—made to men who are seen as useful servants, although the police do not like to think of themselves in this fashion. But how else can the gift of a few dollars to a man be described?

A problem with all of these arrangements, of course, is that they are illegitimate. If a sergeant chooses to make an arrangement with a garage owner or a shopkeeper allowing him to park cars without worrying about tickets, he is only doing what the department orders him to do on occasion for others. If he accepts money for doing this, he is committing a crime, but if he accepts a consideration only at Christmas or some special service—like free maintenance on his car—he is operating within the bounds of decorum. Nobody in the department can point a finger at him and say he is doing something wrong, although, of course, he is.

These arrangements exist in every district. Often they involve only a sergeant and the sector car, sometimes they extend to all squads; but they are informal arrangements that reflect the kinds of services policemen are constantly being urged to perform whether they receive a consideration or not. In one district, there was an auto-parts supply store that was losing money to vandals and shoplifters. The manager became friendly with a sergeant, who offered to drive him to the bank. The officer also encouraged his men to keep an eye on the place. The other squads did not share the sergeant's concern or his personal connection, but after months of urging, the other supervisors were convinced that it was desirable to give the store "some consideration." In return for this, the manager willingly sold the men goods at reduced prices and made even more favorable arrangements with the sergeants and the lieutenants.

Favors that require systematic attention or prompt responses can be guaranteed only by a sergeant or a lieutenant. A policeman can collect a few dollars from a construction site to keep an eye on the equipment, but if the builders want to work on Sunday, which is forbidden by law, they must see the sergeant. The extent to which a supervisor exploits his opportunities to make special arrangements depends on his personal style and the attitude of the captain toward him. There are some men who will not take anything for free, although they gladly accept wholesale prices. Some men have reputations in the department for being "good shoppers," and occasionally middle-ranking commanders show up in a district to ask a sergeant or lieutenant to have their cars repaired or their children outfitted for school. Many offers of favors and bargains come to a sergeant or a lieutenant without his asking, but there are men who do not leave to chance any opportunity to turn a dollar.

A lieutenant noticed that the front door of a closed supermarket was open and stopped his car to investigate. Inside he found the building filled with cartons and used restaurant equipment. A man was holding a clipboard and checking the numbers on a sheet of paper. He had a pistol stuck in his belt. The lieutenant said hello and commented that he had noticed the open door as he drove past and had stopped to investigate. The man nodded and told him that he had taken over the building to store his merchandise. The lieutenant asked him if there was anything he could do for him. "I don't think so." The officer stressed how dangerous the neighborhood was, and the man patted his gun and said he had just chased a bunch of kids away. "I guess you got it under control, then," the lieutenant replied, "but if you need anything, don't hesitate to call the district and ask for me." Before he left, the lieutenant had carefully examined every corner of the hall. The businessman smiled, invited the lieutenant to stop back and chat, and returned to his work. A few days later, driving past the building, the lieutenant said, "A real nice guy, that Jew; but he won't go for nothing—yet."

In departments where the police are openly involved in protecting illegal operations it is impossible to prevent the patrolmen from exploiting the opportunities available to them. But where payoffs are restricted and the department is known for vigorously investigating complaints, it is possible for the supervisors (if they are not on the take) to limit the patrolmen's activities to what are generally considered legitimate initiatives. A supervisor may get his groceries wholesale, but he does not have to let his men make the rounds, and if he is in control of them, he will limit their acquisitiveness to keep public attention away from their operations. But if a store owner expresses a willingness to sell at police prices to the men, he will not be discouraged, nor will an effort be made to disguise that it is happening, since it is a voluntary arrangement that does not involve any special considerations. In one district, for example, there was an egg wholesaler who was happy to sell at reduced prices to all policemen. On daywork, usually on Friday, one man would take all the orders and pick up several crates of eggs for distribution in the station house. Eggs were bought for the captain as well as the detectives, and each man came by and picked up his order.

Even if supervisors prevent their men from seeking considerations and favors, they cannot prevent businessmen from making offers of gifts to encourage good service. Most often a policeman does not have to ask for anything, all he has to do is wait to be offered. A patrolman who answers a call of vandalism at a factory is met by the foreman, who seeks advice on how to protect his windows. They have a brief and friendly conservation. After a few moments there is nothing more to talk about, but the patrolman does not leave. The foreman asks him if he is the regular sector man, and when he replies affirmatively, the officer is invited to stop back later and pick up a bottle. More often than not the patrolman is not offered anything, and if he suggests something be offered him, he risks a complaint and a reprimand. But if a patrolman does a favor for a garage owner, suggesting to a stranded motorist that he call one place rather than another, who is going to complain if the man returns the favor? Maybe he keeps a can of paint around, and if the officer has a minor accident with his patrol car, the damage can be quickly remedied without a lot of paper work having to be filed.

Many of these connections between policemen and business people are highly personal. Because a man is willing to do a favor for one person it does not follow that he is available to others for the same consideration. "You want to take a ride? I gotta go over and pick up some money from a florist," the sergeant said. "Hey Sarge, not so loud, please," the corporal retorted. "No, it ain't like that." On the way over, the sergeant said he had asked his wagon crew to pick up some flowers for him and they had overpaid. In fact, as the sergeant discovered, they had not overpaid but had been obliged to pay the regular retail price. The florist, an ex-policeman, was no fool, and he was not taking any chances. "I'm sorry, Fred, but I wasn't sure they were really for you. I don't know them guys and I figured maybe it was just a private thing and I'm not gonna give 'em all a break. You know, if I start that, those guys'll put me right out of business." The sergeant nodded sympathetically, pocketing the five dollars. "I guess he should know. He was a big fuckin' crook when he was in the business," the sergeant said, as they drove away.

Many people are angered by the police exploiting their position to gain favors and special prices that are denied to others. There are police supervisors who personally refuse to indulge in these favors but allow their men to do it because they feel it prevents them from committing more serious violations. "Look, I'd rather they go in there and get the stuff wholesale from Thomas instead of him getting up a couple of bucks every week for their helping him out. They're still paying for what they get, and they ain't taking it out of his flesh," one sergeant said. Some businessmen have a real interest in encouraging the favor of the police and they will continue to exploit whatever opportunities are available to them. The police administrators cannot discourage the men, since few see anything wrong with accepting appreciations, and more importantly, they expect the men to provide informal services on occasion to members of the business community.

Objection to the police receiving special considerations should not rest on the argument that it makes them corrupt—which it does not—but rather on the effect these arrangements have on the manner in which police services are distributed in the community. The police, like every agency, have limited resources that must be deployed in response to the pressures and demands made upon them. They are under public pressures from the newspapers, city council, business and community organizations; they respond to internal pressures created by commanders who are interested in pursuing their own ideas about how the department should function, and pressures from special interests represented by city government, commercial and social organizations delivered privately and informally. Many of the things the police do for the city government are masked from public attention because they are either illegal or highly controversial.

The questionable character of many enforcement policies—gambling, liquor, traffic—requires that the elected politicians allow only the most loyal and tested men to rise to the top. They may be absolutely honest men, but they must be able to keep their mouths closed. Frequently they are given wide latitude in operating the department because many politicians do not want to know the details of some of the things they ask the police to do. The autonomy required to run the department is enlarged at the top by this discreet distancing; it also runs right down to the bottom. The collusive nature of so many administrative arrangements discourages constant and careful scrutiny of all decisions and actions in the district. Even the most ruthless administrator cannot control his commanders entirely. If he is ordering them to move against someone or to do a favor for another, he cannot expect them to ignore similar requests made directly to their offices. "I could make between $10,000 and $15,000 per year in addition to my salary and never leave my desk. Offers come in all the time in roundabout ways," one captain said. Each of these offers is a request for a favor, an appeal to prevent a policeman from doing something, or a bid for services that will deprive others in the district of a policeman's time and attention. All the captain's superiors can do is limit his inclinations to exploit opportunities by punishing those who are caught when they exceed the bounds of what is considered legitimate. It is the same attitude a patrolman expresses when he makes the distinction between good and bad notes.

The exchange of favors for services is only one aspect of the private bargaining for police attention that goes on incessantly in every city. The local businessman who offers favors in exchange for some service he feels is necessary or desirable for the success of his enterprise is doing the same thing that the chamber of commerce does when it pressures the police, through the mayor's office, to stop them from ticketing cars in certain business areas. The objection to all these efforts, at whatever level they are conducted, is that they occur outside the formal political process. Frequently decisions are made for reasons that are more private than public, but this does not mean they were made for personal reasons. When a police official accedes to the requests of a large company, he is making a decision that is ratified within the complex political system that dominates city life, but it is not a decision reached by weighing the general interests of the people who finance the city. Even if the policeman "gets something" for his trouble, often enough whatever he gets is not the cause for his decision.

The petty rewards available to policemen probably add very little to the aggregate cost of operating the city. They do not affect the fundamental character of business or commerce in the city or the direction of their development. Their rewards are the *quid pro quo* allowed policemen and their supervisors for handling the dirty work of the social system. Policemen in some cities and a few policemen strategically located in almost every department have a chance to make considerably more money than the average patrolman is ever likely to see, even if he avidly exploited every opportunity available to him. But even the disclosure of payoffs to some New York City plainclothesmen of as much as $1,500 monthly cannot disguise the fact that in economic terms the total impact of police graft is insignificant. The real cost is the degradation of the job, the destruction of morale, the erosion of discipline and supervision, and the breakdown of clear standards of what constitutes "good work" which allows some policemen to become criminals in every sense of the word.

The dilemmas every city policeman faces are well understood by all of them, but they are in no position to explain them. How can a man explain to people that his is a job that obliges some men to break the law regularly, thereby allowing others to do so if they wish to take the risks? Much of what people call corruption among the police is supported actively by large sections of the population, while the things that are despised are most frequently directed against the part of the city population that is too weak to protest effectively (and when they protest are not believed or supported). This distinction was succinctly made by a former New York police commissioner in an interview he gave shortly before his resignation under fire. He commented:

> In the ghetto, the one who is hurt the most by police corruption is the ghetto resident; for the most part he is getting little or nothing. In fact, he's being hurt tremendously because of the corruption. The considera- tion, even the courtesy extended him is less. Now, when you move from the ghetto and you consider corruption in the middle class and the busi- ness community, they are only paying for some service or product and they're getting some worth, so it's really with the poor that corruption makes the greatest impact and hurts the most.[2]

A district policeman who considers himself to be an honest cop knows that he cannot entirely escape involvement in illicit activity. He understands that he cannot explain to people who have never been on the street the difference between a good and a bad note, but having seen the opportunities available, he "knows" that there is nothing wrong with accepting a few dollars from someone who wishes to ex- press gratitude to him for getting his wife to the hospital or for finding his stolen car. If there are a few dollars coming for watching a bar or an offer of some consideration for capturing a burglar, no harm is done.

"He was a good fuckin' cop. You know I was the first guy to find him. He was slumped over the wheel with the phone still in his hand," a patrolman said to his friend. "It's a crazy, fuckin' job. He'd see some- thing, you know, something not quite right, he'd look into it. And you know, he wasn't even supposed to be workin' that night. But it was Friday night and he had a note from a bar, you know, so he'd asked the sergeant if he could work because he wanted the few bucks. So he worked. But he was out there and he musta seen something, because nobody usually patrols down that road. But he seen something and he went lookin'. He found it, and now there are six kids with no father."

The policeman cannot escape the contradictions imposed upon him by his obligations. He knows that there are many people in the city who think him just a crook in a uniform. He knows that poor people who see gamblers, pushers, hookers on the streets of their neighbor- hoods think every cop is on the take. He cannot tell them it is not true. He cannot explain to them that even if every cop were as honest as the day is long, drug addiction would not stop, gambling would per- sist, and the bars would still operate after hours. He cannot explain to

2. *The New York Times* (June 8, 1970).

them that if he really were allowed to enforce the law, everyone would be screaming at the cops for invading their privacy and destroying their opportunities to do the things which they want to do and which middle-class people can do freely and openly. Tracks were allowed to operate because horse racing was the sporting pastime of the rich and powerful; today nobody questions the money politicians make by selling franchises to open new tracks to encourage the people to gamble. Private clubs are allowed to operate high-stake card games, while plainclothesmen are out hustling crap games for a few dollars; churches sponsor bingo nights and get the police to watch the front door, even when the game violates state law; and while some policemen are trying to lock up a clean-living number writer who always pays an honest count, the state is telling his clients to put their money into a lottery ticket. The state orders them to do their drinking in bars owned by people they do not know and possibly do not care to patronize, and forbids them to pay for a drink in someone's parlor. How can a policeman explain to the people who look at him a little funny that he isn't on the take when they see the evidence of corruption all about them? How can he explain to them that if he were to enforce the law, he would have to violate their rights and the laws which are supposed to protect them even more than he already does?

THE POLICE AND
THEIR PROBLEMS
James Q. Wilson

It is noteworthy that a leading treatise on American police begins with a chapter, not on the "crime problem," but on the "police problem."[1] It begins, in other words, with a discussion, not of how many

From James Q. Wilson, "The Police and Their Problems: A Theory," *Public Policy* vol. XII (1963), pp.190–199, 214–216. Copyright © 1963 by the President and Fellows of Harvard College. Reprinted by permission of *Public Policy*. Some footnotes deleted.

1. Bruce Smith, *Police Systems in the United States* (2nd rev. ed.; New York, 1960).

crooks there are to be caught, but of how many policemen there are who seem unwilling or unable to catch them. The author cites the many and familiar charges brought against American city police departments and notes that, although no one force is guilty of all these wrongs, "at various times and places each has been convincingly proved" giving rise to the "widely held belief that even the unproved charges rest upon secure foundations of fact and that our entire police organism is rotten from top to bottom, and from periphery to core." Although he does not himself make such a sweeping indictment, he admits that "there is as yet no conclusive evidence that this gloomy view is unfounded."[2]

The police problem has many aspects, not all of which will be treated here. Corruption—i.e., accepting bribes—is one problem. Criminality—i.e., illegally using public office for private gain without the inducement of a bribe—is another. A third is brutality—mistreating civilians or otherwise infringing their civil liberties. A fourth is incompetence—inefficiency or ineffectiveness in preventing crime and apprehending criminals. There is no necessary reason why these problems should co-exist. A corrupt force may not be "criminal," and vice versa. And some would go so far as to say that a "brutal" force is the price we pay for a competent force.

There are also several possible explanations for various aspects of the police problem. Part of the problem may be the result of political meddling which is facilitated by local control of police forces. Part may be the result of poor standards and procedures in the recruitment, training, and supervision of officers. A great deal may be the consequence of the huge stakes the entrepreneurs of popular although illegal activities (such as gambling and vice) have in purchasing police protection. And some part of the problem is no doubt explainable by the influence of a few wicked men—the rotten apples.

Without prejudice to the value of these explanations, most of which are thoroughly discussed in the standard texts on police administration, a somewhat different one will be set forth here. In attempting to account for the police problem and the relative failure of reforms, we

2. Ibid., pp.2–3. Most reform efforts, Smith believes, "have proved futile and quite without effect upon the ills they were intended to cure" (pp.5–6). The major improvements in local police work have come about, he argues, largely in the area of technical and mechanical developments, not in the area of organization, discipline, or conduct. Indeed, one of the best accounts of American police work was written over forty years ago but is still accurate today: Arthur Woods, *Policeman and Public* (New Haven, 1919).

will begin, not at the top, with an account of the political system and the administrative apparatus, but at the bottom, with a discussion of the nature of the big-city police role as it is seen and experienced by the policemen themselves. After describing the police role and the peculiar problems to which it gives rise, we will indicate two major adaptative responses which policemen make to these problems. Finally, we shall indicate some of the implications of these responses for police administration and city government.

To the individual officer, the police problem is largely a morale problem. Stated more exactly, the problem for him is to find some consistent and satisfactory basis for his self-conception. This, as we shall later suggest, is not a problem for all policemen in all cities nor does it have the same character for all policemen in any one city. For the moment, let us consider the elements of this problem in the extreme case.

The problem of morale, or of self-respect, is created by at least two aspects of the policeman's role. First, the policeman is frequently in an adversary relation with his public. Unlike firemen (who save homes, rescue babies, and retrieve treed cats), the policeman in the *routine* case is often (though not always) dealing with his clientele as an antagonist: he issues summonses, makes arrests, conducts inquiries, searches homes, stops cars, testifies in court, and keeps a jail.

Second, powerful demands are made on the policeman to serve incompatible ends. This happens both because his public cannot make up its mind what it wants and because it wants certain ends to be only symbolically served (e.g., "the community shall not tolerate gambling") while other, contradictory, ends are actually served ("citizens should be allowed to place bets with honest bookies"). The officer is confronted with many such dilemmas. Formally, the policeman is expected to enforce all laws; actually, he is expected to ignore some laws and many lawbreakers. In theory, he is entitled to full information from citizens regarding their neighbors, friends, and associates; in reality, people feel that one ought not to "tell" on others. Some persons feel strongly that crime among minority groups ought to be stamped out even at a high cost in the violation of civil liberties; others feel that civil liberties ought to be safeguarded even at a high cost in crime.

The awareness that he is viewed with hostility and judged in terms of inconsistent standards can, unless other factors intervene, lead a policeman to believe that he has chosen an occupation which sets him apart from others. Even during off-duty hours, he is rarely allowed to forget that he is a policeman—even if by nothing more than the joking remarks of his friends. To live with himself and with others, he must develop some acceptable and consistent standards by which to evaluate himself. In the extreme case of which we are here speaking, such standards cannot be found in the expectations of others. In adapting to this situation, the policeman comes to be governed by norms different from, and sometimes in conflict with, those which govern the persons with whom he comes in contact.

To the extent that the policeman feels the need to develop a police "sub-culture" or "code" different from that of civilians he can be said to be "alienated." This familiar piece of jargon is used here with misgivings, for the frequency with which it is employed as an explanatory term in social science seems to be in inverse proportion to the precision with which its meaning is specified. Nonetheless, the two major causes of the morale problem for policemen seem analogous to two of the many meanings of alienation. First, the "pariah feeling" implies not only that the individual (or his occupation) is given low esteem, but more particularly that the esteem accorded is much lower than the ostensible importance of the goals he is to serve. The individual (in this case, the policeman) is obliged to perform a social function of the highest importance but is told that he will not be given an appropriately high status even if he is successful. Second, the problem of serving incompatible ends implies that society has so defined the policeman's situation that he can never act in accord with that definition. Stated another way, the inconsistent expectations of society imply that the policeman will be called upon either to use socially unapproved behavior to attain socially approved goals or vice versa.

Recent cases of police criminality accord very well with this interpretation. These have involved not bribery, but petty and not-so-petty thieving by policemen, usually working in small teams. At least this is what has come to light in Chicago, Denver, and Burlington; we cannot, of course, be certain that we know the full story. Anti-social acts which yield little material gain but which involve banding together to express not only cupidity but also a kind of collective contempt for the norms of the community are just what one might expect from members of a subculture which is in constant conflict with the community.

In one of the few published studies done on the sociology of the police, William A. Westley describes what he found to be the "culture" [my term] of a force in a midwestern city of about 150,000 population:

> [The policeman] regards the public as his enemy, feels his occupation to be in conflict with the community, and regards himself to be a pariah. The experience and the feeling give rise to a collective emphasis on

secrecy, an attempt to coerce respect from the public, and a belief that almost any means are legitimate in completing an important arrest.[3]

One of the policemen implicated in the Burlington, Vermont, scandal told newspaper reporters that he stole only small things and then only "to be one of the boys." He apparently did not approve of stealing but he did not want to risk alienating himself from his colleagues. His was the plight of many city policemen: their self-respect requires that they conform to the expectations of a group which does not have, and feels that it can never obtain, the respect of society. August Vollmer, for many years America's leading police reformer, once said:

> The policeman is denounced by the public, criticized by the preachers, ridiculed in the movies, berated by the newspapers and unsupported by prosecuting officers and judges. He is shunned by the respectables, hated by criminals, deceived by everyone, kicked around like a football by brainless or crooked politicians. He is exposed to countless temptations and dangers, condemned when he enforces the law and dismissed when he doesn't. He is supposed to possess the qualifications of a soldier, doctor, lawyer, diplomat, and educator, with remuneration less than of a daily laborer.[4]

Factors Affecting the Morale Problem

The morale problem has thus far been depicted in its most acute form. In reality, of course, it varies considerably in extent and intensity. Some hypotheses can be suggested which may account for this variation.

1. Rural and small-town policemen are probably less affected by feelings of separateness than are big-city policemen. In small communities and in thinly-settled country, a policeman does not patrol, he is summoned by complaints. Most of the people he sees have sought his aid on their own volition; his contacts thus are less likely to be of an adversary nature. In the big city, by contrast, the policeman patrols (either on foot or in a car); this puts him in a position to *initiate* complaints, to interfere with and regulate the behavior of persons who would not have summoned his aid (e.g., quarreling families or rowdy juveniles), and in general to make his (often unwanted) presence felt.

3. William A. Westley, "Violence and the Police," *American Journal of Sociology*, LIX, July, 1953, p.35. See also Westley, "Secrecy and the Police," *Social Forces*, XXXIV, March, 1956, pp. 254-7, and Westley, "The Police: A Sociological Study of Law, Custom, and Morality," Ph.D. thesis, Department of Sociology, University of Chicago, 1951.
4. Quoted in Deutsch, *op. cit.*, p.126.

2. In the most overcrowded parts of the central city, hostile police-citizen contacts are more frequent than in less densely populated areas. In a slum neighborhood, personal and family privacy is at a premium. The doors, walls, windows, and locks which provide for most of us the legally-defined privacy which it is the policeman's duty to protect are much less meaningful to people who must share their rooms with other persons and their apartments with other families. Particularly in warm weather, such people move outside, sit on their front steps, lean out their windows, and loiter in the streets. The street is, in effect, every man's front room. Such streets are often in areas where crime rates are high and therefore they are heavily patrolled by the police. The very appearance of an officer on such a street is often regarded as an intrusion. Where the middle class family sees the policeman walking in front of its home as a welcome protector of its privacy, the lower-class family is likely to see the same officer as an unwelcome invader of its privacy. In New York City recently, policemen entering streets in congested neighborhoods were issued helmets to protect them from rocks thrown from roof tops.

3. Police-citizen hostility varies with police duties. The activities of policemen vary considerably; consequently, they come into contact with different parts of the public under different circumstances and with different degrees of discretion. Detectives engaged in investigative work—particularly men assigned to the vice squad and to other units charged with apprehending people who are *willingly* participating in illegitimate or subversive activities—are probably most exposed to potential hostility. By contrast, officers assigned to directing traffic—a largely mechanical task in which the problem is to relieve "structural" disorder which is the product of individually innocent actions—are perhaps least exposed. An interesting question is the extent to which a police force as a whole takes on the characteristic attitudes of those officers assigned to that duty with the highest hostility potential.

4. The class structure of the city probably affects the extent to which the officer feels isolated or alien. In a small, middle-class residential suburb, where standards of appropriate conduct are widely shared, where the privacy of the residents is assured, and where there are no illegal enterprises, the police may exist largely to protect the community from outsiders and to offer assistance to citizens who have lost their dogs, stalled their cars, or drunk too much at parties. In such communities, police-public relations may be very congenial. In the bigger cities with a large lower-class population, the situation is altogether different. Standards of conduct are not widely shared and

resentment of authority is much greater. Illegal businesses—gambling, illegal liquor sales, and prostitution—may flourish. The stakes in organized crime, and therefore the incentives to bribe policemen, are likely to be high. In many of these cities, opportunities to frustrate the law by court delays, legal maneuvers, and even the corruption of judges are numerous.

5. The pariah-like feeling of the big-city policeman is likely to increase as the rewards of a police career, relative to other careers open to a police officer, decline. Most policemen interviewed have said that the most important of the incentives which induced them to become and remain policemen were the security of the job and the prospect of a pension. During the twenty to thirty years it takes to earn the pension, however, a policeman comes to regard the terms of employment as onerous. Police officers must often provide out of their own pockets essential equipment and out of their own labor the maintenance of that equipment.[5] Most policemen remain patrolmen—the lowest rank—all their lives, and the wage differential between the newest recruits and the oldest veterans is usually small.[6] Policemen often come to regard a niggardly salary and inadequate facilities as another sign of society's hostility toward them.

Further, being a policeman is a less attractive career than it once was. At one time police departments provided a major avenue of upward mobility for recent immigrants, particularly the Irish, and a secure occupation during times of depression. Other jobs are now equally or more attractive in both prestige and security. This is probably especially galling to younger officers who joined their forces after discharge from the armed services at the end of World War II when it was widely believed that unemployment would be a national problem. To their chagrin, the economy prospered and they found themselves committed to an occupation whose advantages were rapidly being eclipsed by those of jobs which they could have had in construction work, sales, or the professions.

Because Negroes are excluded from many other occupations that are more advantageous, the Negro populations of most large cities pro-

5. One survey indicated that most of New York City's two thousand or so detectives used, without reimbursement, their own cars for police work because of a shortage of police cars in operating condition. See *New York Times,* March 14, 1960.

6. In 1960, the range of patrolmen's salaries for all cities of 500,000 population and over was $3,780 to $5,955. The median salary was $4,800. *Municipal Yearbook,* 1960, p.394.

vide a substantial reservoir of eager and able potential police recruits. The Negro, however, is often regarded as a threat by white policemen; his presence on the force in large numbers would, they fear, lower the status of police work even further—the job would be defined, by white officers and civilians, as a "Negro job." When being a policeman was regarded as—and was in fact—a way of rising in the world, the policeman's pariah-like feeling was powerfully counteracted. Today, policemen in one big city (for example) speak bitterly of the fact that not long ago the Department advertised for recruits by putting signs on the sides of garbage trucks. "When we joined," the older officers remark, "there were thousands of good men applying. Now, you almost have to take whoever you can get."

Factors Affecting the Problem of Incompatible Ends

Generally speaking, the extent to which a policeman has a consistent set of ends depends on whether the values or ethos of the community supports one or the other of the major sets of alternatives confronting him. There are undoubtedly many communities in which it is objectively possible for a policeman to serve a consistent set of goals. In middle-class suburbs are usually found people who do their gambling elsewhere (at the race track or with bookies in the central-city office buildings where the suburbanites are employed) and who thus do not make inconsistent demands on police about enforcing anti-gambling statutes. Similarly, where there is no lower class among whom crimes of violence and a disrespect for authority are common, there is no necessity of trying to serve (empirically if not logically) incompatible goals of apprehending all lawbreakers and respecting all civil liberties.

By the same token, in communities where gambling and vice are openly tolerated, petty criminals are treated roughly by the police, and minority groups receive little or no protection against a hostile majority, policemen are not subject to inconsistent demands either.

In most big cities, however, it is unlikely that either one or the other set of ends will be consistently upheld. Rather, the police for various reasons will be expected both to enforce the law and not to enforce it at the same time. Law enforcement will present a perpetual dilemma.

One reason is that the very heterogeneity of the large city means that different social classes—with different conceptions of the public interest—will live side by side. Property owners, for example, may want maximum protection of their property and of their privacy; slum dwellers, however, may not like the amount of police activity necessary to attain the property owners' ends. Negroes and urban liberals may unite in seeking to end "police brutality"; lower-middle-class home-owners whose neighborhoods are "threatened" with Negro invasion may want the police to deal harshly with Negroes or to look the other way while the homeowners themselves deal harshly with them. The good government and church groups may want all anti-gambling laws enforced; the gamblers and their clients will want only token enforcement.

There is, however, another reason why police ends are likely to be inconsistent. This is what one might call the "problem of the crusade." Even if the force has but one set of consistent ends specified for it by the commissioner or superintendent, and even if adherence to those ends is enforced as far as possible, it is almost inevitable that there will come a time when the commissioner will decide that something must be done "at all costs"—that some civic goal justifies any police means. This might be the case when a commissioner is hard pressed by the newspapers to solve some particularly heinous crime (say, the rape and murder of a little girl). A "crusade" is launched. Policemen who have been trained to act in accord with one set of rules ("Use no violence." "Respect civil liberties." "Avoid becoming involved with criminal informants.") are suddenly told to act in accord with another rule—"catch the murderer"—no matter what it costs in terms of the normal rules.

A police department need not be told this very often before the officers will realize that they cannot take the formal rules too seriously —they *must* maintain good relations with criminal informants, they *must* know how to extract information with rough methods, they *must* resort to wire-tapping and other measures. When Fiorello La Guardia became mayor of New York City he is said to have instructed his police force to adopt a "muss 'em up" policy toward racketeers, to the considerable consternation of groups interested in protecting civil liberties. The effort to instill one set of procedural rules in the force was at cross-purposes with the effort to attain a certain substantive end.

*   *   *

Some Implications

If this theory of some of the causes of the police problem and of the adaptive responses to it is correct, certain policy implications seem to follow.

First, the prospects for a high level of professionalism in the police forces of many—if not most—large American cities seem dim. There are not in these cities either the governmental arrangements or the institutionalized political ethos necessary to support professionalism against the opposing forces represented by the conditions of the central city. As many large cities fill up with lower-income people—Negroes, Puerto Ricans, or rural whites—the police problem may grow worse. The incidence of hostile police-citizen contacts will likely increase rather than decrease. Further, if there is a continued migration of middle-class homeowners and business firms to the suburbs, the tax resources necessary to support police work may decline at the same time that the cost of law enforcement rises.[7]

This is not to argue that increased revenues, by providing higher salaries, would attract more "able" men into police work and thus solve the "police problem." Far from it, for incompetence—in the sense of the technical ability to do police work—is not the problem. Low salaries, along with inadequate equipment, run-down buildings, poor uniform allowances, and depressing squad rooms are obstacles in the way of effective police work mainly because they are interpreted by policemen as palpable evidence of the contempt in which the police are held by the public and the politicians. The police are starved for facilities and money, many policemen feel, because the public does not respect either law or law men.

Second, eliminating the wholesale corruption of police forces by gamblers and syndicate hoodlums may be a necessary, but it is not a sufficient, condition for the growth of professionalism. Wholesale corruption is not the direct or the sole cause of those police failings—such as neglect, brutality, inefficiency, and unreliability—which are of most immediate concern to the citizen. Indeed, the citizen, in so far as he indulges in gambling while supporting laws outlawing gambling, is acting as if he believed that the existence of illegal gambling, which invariably requires police corruption, does not or should not affect the quality of traffic control or the protection of life and property. In logic, this may be true. But in fact the existence of large-scale corruption is

7. Harvey E. Brazer has shown that the per capita cost of police protection, as well as of other municipal services, increases the greater the population density of the central city and the greater the percentage of the metropolitan area's population which lives outside the central city. Thus, Boston, with a very high density and a very small percentage of its metropolitan population inside the city limits, has one of the highest per capita police costs. *City Expenditures in the United States,* National Bureau of Economic Research, Occasional Paper No. 66 (1959).

a further source of demoralization for any policeman not part of the system and thus not sharing in the proceeds. Such corruption affects the entire department by bringing formal rules into contempt, providing a powerful inducement for participating in the system, and encouraging the officer to view the public as cynical and hypocritical. Valuable (and unlikely) as eliminating this corruption may be, however, doing so will not remove all the obstacles to professionalism.

Third, if a professionalized police force can only exist in large cities as part of a set of political and civic institutions of a certain character, the desirability of professionalism cannot be considered apart from the desirability of these institutions as a set. It is possible, then, that the benefits of police professionalism might be outweighed by the costs of other, necessarily related institutions. For example, professionalism may depend on giving over the government to nonpartisan officials sustained by nonpolitical elites, but these arrangements may be held objectionable because they deprive the lower classes and ethnic minorities of political representation and access to the public bureaucracy. Police professionalism is part of a "package"; its advantages and disadvantages cannot be assessed apart from those of the package as a whole.

It is even possible that a professionalized police force itself is not always, under all circumstances, superior to its alternative. Considering that professionalism has rarely lasted very long in most large, heavily lower-class immigrant-settled central cities in the United States, one must at least suspect that a police force run according to the system has served some useful social functions—some of the same ones, possibly, that have been served by the political machine. Although both the police system and the machine have disadvantages for those who are ruled by them, they have offered some benefits as well—a chance for upward social mobility without the restrictions imposed by professional entrance tests; an opportunity for rapid capital formation due to the system's permissive attitude toward gambling and other activities which are *male ad prohibitum;* and an openness to personal intervention which allows one to bend the law of the Yankee to suit the conditions of the jungle.

THE CAUSES OF GRAFT

V. O. Key, Jr.

In the light of the point of view of this study—that what is usually described as graft and corruption is, in general, power techniques employed to establish certain control relationships—any discussion of the causes of graft might be considered irrelevant. It is as if the author of a treatise on military strategy or the methods of artillery warfare should add as an afterthought a discussion of the causes of war. Or could we ask what are the "causes" of propaganda? Certain hypotheses and tentative conclusions may be submitted, however, for whatever they are worth.

It is almost futile to speak of causal relationships in the sphere of social phenomena. Single causes, direct effects are almost impossible of isolation with certainty. In ascertaining the "causes" of graft, if one wanted to search out "universal" generalizations, it would be necessary to examine a fair sampling of all cases in all countries at all times, and even then the quest might be futile. At any rate such an inquiry is beyond the range of the single investigator. Then is one to search for the "causes" of graft in the United States, in New York City, in Illinois? Or does one want to know why John Doe bribed Police Lieutenant Richard Roe to let him run a crap game in Chicago's levee district in October, 1910? It is important to define precisely the phenomenon which is being explained, and to distinguish carefully between remote and proximate causes. Glib explanations on the basis of economic "forces" are to be avoided. What are these mystic forces which emanate from locomotives, street car lines, breweries to influence politicians? The question is absurd. Political phenomena are social, human, relations.

The phenomenon to be explained is in general the abuse of the control of the power and resources of the state for personal or party

From V. O. Key, Jr., "The Techniques of Political Graft in the United States." Chicago, Ill.: University of Chicago Libraries, 1936, pp.401–413. Some footnotes deleted.

profit. These abuses, as has been shown, involve relationships of bribery, favors for political support, state-bribery, etc. Why do individuals offer bribes? Why are they accepted? Why is patronage distributed to strengthen the political machine? These and similar questions must be answered. Why are these techniques used instead of some other method? The political technique employed to achieve a given end may be a function of the situation in which it is employed. The method of attack is molded by the surrounding circumstances. When propaganda is most effective, it will be used. If force is necessary and applicable it may be employed. If bribes only will serve, they may be offered. The real problem is what are the conditions that evoke war and violence? When are bribery and other similar techniques employed?

In American legislative bodies the type of question in which bribery and allegations of bribery have been made appears to possess certain relatively definite characteristics. The gain to be secured by bribing the legislature has been immediate and often quite great. The party to be benefited by such action has usually been an individual or a group interest, such as a corporation or association, which could act as an individual. It is obvious that a vague class such as capitalists, farmers, or laborers cannot bribe a legislature or anybody else. The person to be bribed must have the power, *de jure* or *de facto,* to grant the desired action. Often the interests injured by action achieved by bribery are poorly organized or have little consciousness of injury, as when a city council is bribed to vacate a portion of a street in an obscure and little frequented part of the city. The injured interest may be relatively inconsequential in the entire social set-up. Usually the ends sought by bribery are such that they cannot be readily secured by any other method. They could hardly be secured in an open and frank manner; or publicly reconciled with the prevailing concepts of the general welfare or of fair play. A fundamental prerequisite for bribery, as well as for state-bribery and allied abuses, is the existence of agency relationships. Presumably a principal cannot be bribed to act contrary to his own interests. Where power, law making or administration, is concerned the function cannot be assimilated completely to the agency relationship, but in the proprietary activities this may be done.

A more detailed consideration of these characteristic conditions may make their nature more apparent and throw some light upon the problem of bribery in general. The nature of the decisions involved when legislative agencies are bribed, it has been noted, usually involve an immediate and substantial gain. It was either to secure a new value or to prevent the loss of one currently enjoyed. Vast land grants, mineral and timber rights, rights of an intangible character such as utility franchises, rights granting monopolies such as the "baking powder" legislation, permits to construct switch tracks, licenses or permits for certain types of business, subsidies to private enterprise, indemnification of various sorts, legislative regulation of railroad rates, insurance legislation, questions of taxation of specialized types of economic activity are examples of the sorts of questions in which legislative bribery has been proved outright or circumstantially indicated. In cases where legislatures were bribed to elect a man as United States senator intense personal conflicts often were involved which at times were merely the facade for deeper struggles between competing interests within the community. It seems that in most cases where bribery is employed on legislatures there is an immediate gain of considerable value.

Moreover, the parties which bribed legislative bodies or purchased their souls in far more subtle ways have been individuals or social aggregations with the capacity to behave as individuals. Since every relative gain of position in the social hierarchy must be secured at the expense of others, some class or group is injured by such action. It seems that as a rule the interests injured by legislative action resulting from bribery have possessed but slight feeling of a community of interest, have been weakly organized, or at least have possessed a relatively weak cohesion with reference to the question at issue, and were on the whole perhaps dimly conscious of their loss.

The relevance of these facts to an explanation of bribery is clearer if the instance is cited of a court of law deciding a case between two parties of similar strength, both provided with able counsel and equally endowed with this world's goods. Under such conditions there is not likely to be gross favoritism. It is not likely that the jury will be bribed or that the judge will accept an opportunity to sell some of his worthless real estate at a fancy price. When legislatures passed acts granting an immediate benefit to a small and definite set of individuals to the loss of the vague general public, bribery was likely to occur. All of which is another way of saying that when there are well organized pressure groups possessed of equal or nearly equal power the legislative decision on an issue between them is not likely to be influenced by bribery on behalf of one of the parties.

It may be that bribery in the sorts of questions usually decided by legislative agencies may occur on a large scale only in a relatively chaotic society in which new interests are forging upward, rapid realignments of wealth are being formed, the introduction of new inventions and new technological devices is rapidly upsetting the old economic order, society is relatively unstratified or old class alignments are being shifted and reformed. Under such conditions individuals rather than broad groups or classes are the dynamic factors. It will be remembered that bribery of legislatures usually involves action by such individualistic rather than class interests. In a relatively democratic and individualistic society under the chaotic conditions described it seems that bribery is about the only effective way in which new interests of the types mentioned may achieve power rapidly. Other techniques are not practically available. When, however, the atomistic society becomes stratified and there is a consolidation and integration of ruling economic and social interests on a fairly stable basis, there is usually not so much to be gained by bribery. The new ruling class becomes hallowed and receives popular deference. Then the more common and less censured types of political techniques are usually employed, although privilege may be as prevalent as when bribery is frequently used. Taking a shorter run view, when a strong pressure group or counter-pressure group arises, the legislative agency is not so likely to be bribed as when the briber is practically unchallenged.

Before passing to a consideration of graft in the administration of law, it should be observed that in graft in legislation the interests which aggressively bribe legislative bodies have been often involved in new sorts of questions to which there is no ready solution. No pattern or category exists into which the new situation can be conveniently applied. Government tends to become government by favor, or by grace, rather than by rule. In some instances it must be so because of the very fact that at the moment there may be one or a very few persons in like situations. If one is granted a favor by royal dispensation, why not pay for it? These considerations seem to have considerable bearing on graft in the administration of laws or rules which are verbalistic crystallizations of inter-group power relationships.

When a given set of rules, regulations, or ordinances is not generally accepted, no longer fits the requirements of the affected interests, or, as happens at times, becomes virtually unenforceable, there is likely to be favoritism in its application and it has been concluded tentatively that under such conditions bribery and extortion are likely to prevail in connection with official action. Or when a law, such as the general property tax or the laws against gambling, becomes completely unenforceable in a part of the jurisdiction at least, a new, unwritten rule may develop under which nobody has any legal rights and which may be applied in a discriminatory fashion. The general rule may embrace in its application individual cases to which its application would work great hardship and injustice or, on the other hand, it may not be sufficiently wide in its application and may discriminate by exclusion. As in legislation it appears that the interests injured by discriminatory applications of the general rule which no longer possesses any vitality are often but slightly aware of their loss or may be actually uninjured.

It appears that in some cases economic competition is an additional factor of influence in efforts to secure discriminatory enforcement of regulations applying to a given class. Failure to abide by a given rule governing working conditions, say, may result in a lowering of costs and an improved position within the market. Perhaps most of the members of the class affected by the rule would be willing to abide, but to meet the competition they too must seek similar concessions. The workers may be able to compel uniform enforcement or under some conditions the persons to whom the rule applies may unite and compel the appropriate administrative authority to apply the rule uniformly. Or, if the rule is "unreasonable," it may be reformulated. At times of preoccupation with profit-making it may be cheaper to postpone the latter alternative and make provisional adjustments by bribery. A reformulation of the rules of the particular game comes only slowly or mayhap after some disastrous incident which vitally affects and arouses from its lethargy the group for whose protection a given rule is designed.[1] In some types of matters the formulation of principles to govern the administration may be virtually impossible. Laws and regulations capable of application in actual practice with the greatest degree of equity to all individuals within the affected class in a more or less mechanical way are sometimes held out as the remedy. But this is Plato's problem—what is justice? Equity?

Many instances of discriminatory administration of ordinances, regulations, services are encouraged by an ineffective administrative control within a particular unit of governmental organization. Subordinate officials are able to accept graft and gratuities in return for favors without the knowledge of a well-meaning head of the bureau or department. The creation of effective devices of control, fundamentally an

---

1. This suggests that possibly to eliminate graft of certain types in the administration of law the best technique to employ is to follow a policy of piece-meal reform, making appeals to and organizing pressure from the interests vitally and immediately injured by a specific abuse rather than by vague mass appeals to "throw the rascals out" or other similar techniques. In some instances it might be discovered that there were no such groups to which appeals might be made. The obvious remedy is to repeal the law and legalize what has been accomplished by favoritism, bribery.

effective system of espionage and discipline, puts the fear of God into the hearts of such individuals and gives them a more rigid determination to walk the paths of rectitude. When an administrative organization is hastily improvised or expanded, as in times of war and demobilization, time is often lacking for the establishment of routinized procedures of administrative control and the careful selection of personnel, with the result that graft is more likely to occur than would otherwise be the case.

It is said that the lack of an *esprit de corps*, of a code of ethics, and of effective group opinion among public officials as a class which would vigorously reprobate the acceptance of bribes and various types of maladministration explains graft. The existence of such factors would undoubtedly hinder graft, but why have we not had such a governing group? Furthermore, it may be as important and probably more difficult to explain the absence of graft than its presence. As particular interests become less individualistic and more corporate, i.e., "group-istic," and when workable and acceptable formulae for governing their particular relationships are evolved, the personnel administering the particular rule is likely to improve because of the compelling desire to implement the consensus effectively. The cause of graft, by and large, is outside rather than within the formal governmental mechanism. The men who want a certain function administered ineffectively will try to see that it is in the hands of an incompetent personnel.

The presence of unassimilated immigrant groups has often been put forth as a cause of widespread graft. The presence of such groups which may be exploited electorally and sold out by their leaders undoubtedly has facilitated the operation of a graft system in some cases. These groups could be conveniently manipulated and utilized in the formation of a corrupt power constellation. It was not the fact of their immigrant character which made this possible, of course. Various native groups have served equally well the same purposes.

What has been said may be about the equivalent of saying that individuals buy and bribe and secure various tangible and intangible privileges and deferences under two conditions: (1) when such rights are available and valuable, and (2) when they can get away with it. Bribery has been the means of securing these ends. But a bribe may be an end in itself for the person receiving it as well as a means for the actor in the situation. As war is not an end in itself except perhaps for the generals. Similarly, state-bribery is a means of making cohesive the political organization, but it is also an end for the job-holders, the crooked contractors, and other individuals receiving unwarranted privileges directly or indirectly from the public treasury.

These beneficiary interests may be considered in the same light as groups or persons securing abstract and intangible privileges of great value as well as some tangible ones through legislative or administrative action. Such beneficiaries are willing to combine with others in order to secure the benefits which they desire. So the beneficiaries of state-bribery are willing to combine with the seekers of privilege, high and low, to get what they want at the expense of the weaker opposing interests. Job-seekers lobby for positions, contractors bring pressure to bear to secure contracts, just as do pressure groups seeking legislation and administrative action involving the exercise of a power not calling for an immediate direct public expenditure. In fact, clarification of the process may result from viewing the solicitors of state-bribes as pressure groups along with the other groups generally recognized as such. Thus, by a combination of those seeking abstract and intangible privileges as well as those wanting to divide the patronage and other perquisites, a powerful social combination is built up. When graft prevails on a wide scale this is the strongest combination. Nakedly, when a jurisdiction is thoroughly graft ridden, it is merely because the most powerful combination in the community wills that it be so.[2]

2. Many particular instances of sporadic, rather than systematic graft, cannot, of course, be differentiated either in function or nature from common thievery. In the foregoing pages little attention has been paid to this type of graft. In this sort of case the grafter acts much as a burglar or a highwayman would, and perhaps for the same "causes." They operate at times and under circumstances when the likelihood of immediate detection is not as great as at others. For example, during and immediately after wars when the nation is exultant and the government beyond criticism the vultures are likely to feed.

THE ACTIVE SENSE
OF OUTRAGE

Arnold A. Rogow and
Harold D. Lasswell

Since the American system of public order is perpetually faced by problems that result from less than universal norms—in phraseology and deed—models that guide inquiry must explore conditions of readjustment. At the moment we shall only comment upon the *active sense of outrage* that so often preconditions readjustment among norms or between articulate standards and overt action. When a collective adjustment is precipitated by a sense of outrage, few alternatives are open: either the minority norm or the inclusive norm must be changed; either the articulated norm or the pattern of deed must change. In the United States we recall many such crises; for instance the prohibition of the manufacture and sale of alcoholic beverages.

The sense of outrage is a perspective related to rectitude in which the dominant note is moral indignation. The sense of outrage may or may not be consciously perceived as justified by the violation of an explicit rule of conduct. One may in fact be seized by convictions that appear obvious; vehement affirmation, not justification, is the result. How do we relate this pattern of conduct to the maximization postulate?

The postulate does not imply that conscious processes are invariably detached, cool, and calculating; nor does it imply that the individual is explicitly aware of the value outcomes or expectations that merge in his judgment. Typically he may assume, rather than formulate, a degree of identification with other human beings, including the body politic or the legal order. The maximization postulate is a guide to the observer-analyst, leading him to probe representative cases for the purpose of uncovering the determining factors. Thus research may show that in a

From Arnold A. Rogow and Harold D. Lasswell, *Power, Corruption, and Rectitude,* © 1963, pp.72–75. Reprinted by permission of Prentice-Hall, Inc., Englewood Cliffs, New Jersey. Footnotes deleted.

"housing dispute" many value outcomes are at stake; for example the reputation of the party in power, land values in particular areas, or the permeation of the community by "low-class" elements. It may be found by appropriate investigation that a particular individual is chiefly concerned about the morals of his teen-age daughter or the resale price of his home. Or a citizen may not perceive a specific, immediate stake in the situation, becoming involved in the dispute on the basis of his identification with the ideal image of a clean and decent community. In the latter case the citizen is exhibiting "disinterested moral indignation."

If the observer-analyst prefers, the maximization postulate may be exclusively applied to conscious perspectives. Unconscious factors are then classified as conditions affecting the "capability" of the individual to think and act. For instance conscious indignation may be unconsciously motivated and spring from a revived childhood sense of guilt which has been remobilized in the current adult context by an allegation that police officers are seducing young girls.

Unconscious conflicts are present to some degree in all personality systems, and a sense of outrage points to deep, "whole person" involvement. In general a "sense of outrage" is aroused by disappointed expectations, such as when a norm that is expected to be lived up to is violated. Since all disappointed expectations do not evoke feelings of outrage, when does this happen?

Evidently a key factor is the *betrayal of confidence*. The original expectation about the behavior of an "other" fostered the "legitimate" assumption that the other person shared common expectations of future conduct. He promised to act in a particular way and presumably demanded of himself that he live up to shared expectations. Thus if A agrees to dispose of B's car for a 10 per cent commission and it later appears that he took 20 per cent, B presumably will feel outraged (in addition to noting and regretting the loss). In many cases there is no special understanding; for example individuals share general community expectations about the conduct of police officers. If police officers deviate, there is a sense of outrage; and the demand for sanction may be especially intense, since betrayal by public authority often reactivates traumatic episodes involving early experiences with family authority.

Corruption, we have said, is conditioned by "capability" as well as by "perspectives." Hence a basic hypothesis about corruption is that it is *limited by the extent to which a sense of outrage is aroused among people who are capable of making corruption more costly than correct-*

ness. Capability depends upon the degree of control exercised over all values and is indicated by an upper, middle, or lower position in the community's distribution of power, wealth, respect, enlightenment, and other values. It is not too much to say that American society has been characterized by an endemic and occasionally acute level of largely impotent outrage.

At the level of adult relationships the sense of outrage has been generated by conflicting expectations that develop outside the centers of urban civilization. Nonurban cultures include rather extended kin groups; also rural and small-town communities. Modern urban civilization is a culture of rapidly subdividing operations that create somewhat distinctive foci of attention, demands, expectations, and identifications. Perpetual revisions of perspective set the participants off from many contemporaries, whether the contemporaries are in new circumstances or continue in earlier-type environments. As a first approximation it can be asserted that: (1) All nonurbanites are susceptible to outrage resulting from falsified expectations about urban conduct; and (2) all urbanites who develop a relatively stable subculture in a neighborhood are prone to rages that are generated by the false expectations they project upon central authorities.

We speak of impotent outrage. Declining social formations have been unable to bring about wholesale transformations of conduct on behalf of earlier norms, partly because of poor skill and insufficiently enlightened knowledge of where to concentrate; largely, perhaps, because of the vague and sweeping, almost fantasy-form, character of the image of the corrupt dragon they have sought to slay. Many of the allegedly corrupt do not perceive themselves as corrupt; they believe that they are misinterpreted by the rustic and ignorant, who they think are often misled by truly corrupt labor leaders, politicians, and politically minded clericals.

Whether we have groups or individuals in mind, the role of corruption can be grasped in its fullness only when the entire context of value and practice is considered. Any cross section in the career line of groups or individuals must be examined systematically in reference to all values and to all impotant patterns of practice.

PUBLIC ATTITUDES
TOWARD CORRUPTION

John A. Gardiner

The Politics of Corruption is an analysis of organized crime and corruption in "Wincanton," a middle-sized eastern industrial city. For most of the past fifty years, Wincanton political life was controlled by a local crime syndicate headed by a man named Irv Stern.

The phenomenon of systematic nonenforcement of criminal laws due to official corruption raises a number of questions about the process by which public policies are made. On the one hand, public policies might be viewed as manifestations of the expressed or latent values of community residents, or at least of those who are politically active; nonenforcement might thus reflect community hostility to the official laws. An alternative interpretation might be that local residents know little or nothing about the policies being followed by official agencies; a policy of nonenforcement could therefore arise through the secret machinations of corrupt officials while residents assumed that strict enforcement was being practiced.

Underlying these two views are conflicting assumptions about the direction of public attitudes toward law-enforcement policy and the importance of such attitudes in policy-making. With regard to the direction of public attitudes, one might ask whether there is strong support for antigambling legislation, open hostility, or some mixture of the two? With regard to the importance of these attitudes (regardless of direction), do local residents know what their police are doing? Do they communicate their wishes to policy-makers? A number of recent studies have concluded that few citizens know what policies (e.g., strict or lax enforcement) are being followed; the law-enforcement

Excerpted from Chapter Four of *The Politics of Corruption: Organized Crime in an American City,* by John A. Gardiner, © 1970 by Russell Sage Foundation, New York. Pp.32–35, 46–51, 52, 54–56. All footnotes deleted.

"decision center," rather than acting upon pressures from a wide segment of the community, usually considers only the values of the governmental agencies charged with setting and implementing law-enforcement policies, the groups and individuals who have a particular interest in enforcement issues, and (at times) the criminals whose conduct is (or is not) to be regulated. Thus, unless some unusual event publicizes the policies followed by enforcement agencies and makes them particularly salient to the mass public, the attitudes of the average citizen may not be particularly relevant to the process of law-enforcement policy-making.

These questions concerning the direction and relevance of public attitudes toward law enforcement suggest several possible interpretations of the forty years of corruption which Wincanton has known. One possibility might be that Wincantonites wanted the wide-open gambling and prostitution which the Stern and Braun syndicates provided. Another might be that no one knew much about them (except for those who were going out of their way to find them). . . .

In the following discussion of public attitudes toward gambling and corruption, four hypotheses will be examined:

1. Most residents know little about the specific policies followed by law-enforcement agencies or about the presence or absence of gambling and corruption. Information about law-enforcement policies and official activities, like information about other aspects of politics and public policy, will be highest among high-status residents, those who are most likely to read the newspapers and participate in politics.

2. Residents of the city are sharply divided in their attitudes toward gambling. Some view gambling as harmless recreation, while others see it as immoral or illegal. Most residents, however, support law-enforcement agencies and activities. Gambling is most tolerated or desired by women, long-term residents, and members of orthodox religious groups.

3. Mass attitudes toward corruption are unrelated to attitudes toward gambling. Hostility toward corruption is felt most strongly by upper-status residents, possibly as a result of longer exposure to public norms through longer schooling.

4. . . . Attitudes toward gambling and corruption will be affected by the length of residence in Wincanton. Long-term residents are more tolerant of gambling but less tolerant of corruption, since they have been exposed to more instances of official wrongdoing.

One *caveat* must be noted before presenting survey data related to these hypotheses. For a variety of reasons, answers given to interviewers may not be accurate reflections of the respondent's attitudes, particularly when topics such as gambling and corruption are involved. In a series of questions requiring identification of Wincanton officials and racketeers, interviewers felt that perhaps 10 percent of the respondents falsely professed ignorance in order "to keep out of trouble." In some cases, an answer will be given even though the respondent knows nothing or doesn't care about the question, simply because he wishes to avoid looking stupid or else wants to speed the interviewer on her way. In other cases, the response may be deliberately misleading in order to present what is assumed to be "the right answer," one which conforms to social norms or the presumed biases of the interviewer. Some responses may be misleading in other ways: hypothetical questions designed to test attitudes toward corruption may instead be testing the ability to recognize a norm violation in the stated facts, while questions aimed at identifying the overall frequency of gambling in the city may in fact test whether the respondent or his friends gamble. While these limitations and ambiguities are unavoidable, they will be noted as each set of data is presented and interpreted.

✿   ✿   ✿

Attitudes toward Law-Enforcement Policy

In considering earlier questions concerning the level of public awareness of law-enforcement policies, it was necessary to recognize that a respondent might be lying about his familiarity with racketeers or gambling, that his information might be derived from reading the newspapers rather than from personal experience, and so forth. Analysis of questions designed to test attitudes toward enforcement policies presents further problems. For one thing, respondents vary in the degree to which an issue is salient to them. A woman whose husband has just squandered his pay check playing cards will consider a question about gambling in a different light than the minister's wife who has only heard of gambling as something which sinful people do. Moreover, respondents will vary in their interpretation of questions. One person asked about gambling may perceive symbolic issues ("Should the state condone games of chance?"), while others may think only of specific personal experiences ("Last night I bet my buddy a dollar that he couldn't finish a bottle of gin," or "The kids next door haven't eaten since their father lost his paycheck in a poker game at the Elks' Club"). Among individuals with generally similar values, the response to a particular question may depend upon whether symbolic or specific ideas come to mind; even those who, on an abstract basis, grant the state the right to regulate games of chance may also defend the right of friends to gather for a kitchen-table poker game. Even when a symbol of "law enforcement" is perceived, it may conflict with symbols of "friendship" ("It's just a bunch of buddies having a night out"), "charity" or "religion" ("The church needs to raise money through bingo games"), or "the right of privacy" ("The cops shouldn't go busting into people's houses").

This tension between symbolic and specific attitudes toward law-enforcement policy pervades responses to questions in the Wincanton survey dealing with gambling and corruption. When questions were phrased solely in terms of gambling, the respondents were quite tolerant, but tolerance diminished or disappeared when issues of non-enforcement or corruption appeared. Table 4.8 shows the frequency of tolerant responses to a series of questions dealing with gambling and other prohibited activities. It is clear that gambling (questions 1 through 5) is tolerated far more than narcotics, pornography, or prostitution (questions 10 through 12).

Despite the fairly high degree of tolerance shown in the first five questions in Table 4.8, questions 6 through 9 show that tolerance diminishes when symbols of law enforcement (the police or district attorney) are introduced. Although 81 percent had favored the legalization of bingo, for example, only 24 percent felt that it should be tolerated if the legislature did *not* legalize it. This support for enforcement activities has appeared in a number of other surveys. In 1966, the National Opinion Research Corporation asked a nationwide sample of 5,300 the following question: "In some places, vice and gambling bring a considerable amount of money to the community, even though they might give it a bad name. Do you think the police in such places should generally not interfere with vice and gambling at all, should act only on complaints, or should make every effort to stop the vice and gambling?" Seventy-three percent of the respondents felt that the police should try to stop the vice and gambling, 21 percent felt that they should only act on complaints, and only 2 percent thought they should not interfere. (Four percent didn't know.) Seventy percent of the 875 respondents in a 1947 Minnesota survey approved of "Governor Youngdahl's campaign to wipe out all gambling devices, such as slot

TABLE 4.8

Tolerance of Gambling and Corruption

Question	Tolerant Response	% Toler-ant	% Intol-erant	% "Don't Know" or "Un-decided"
1. "How do you feel . . . do you think bingo should be allowed here, or not?"	"Allowed"	81	10	9
2. "Churches and other charitable organizations should be allowed to hold bingo games."	"Agree"	64	31	4
3. "The State of New Hampshire recently set up a lottery, and the proceeds are used to support public schools. Do you think (this state) should have a state lottery, or not?"	"Yes"	59	21	20
4. "Some people feel (this state) should legalize gambling. Others disagree. Do you think this should be done, or not?"	"Yes"	55	30	15
5. "Gambling is all right so long as local people, not outsiders, run the game."	"Agree"	50	36	14
6. "The police should not break up a friendly poker game, even if there is betting."	"Agree"	47	37	16
7. "If nobody has been hurt, a policeman should give a speeder a warning instead of a ticket."	"Agree"	34	56	9
8. "If the legislature does *not* legalize bingo, do you think the mayor and district attorney should continue to enforce the law against bingo, or not?"	"No"	24	67	9
9. "The Wincanton police today are concentrating on gambling too much."	"Agree"	18	56	27
10. "England now has legalized the use of narcotics in that drug addicts can get prescriptions for narcotics from doctors. Do you think this idea should be adopted in the United States or not?"	"Yes"	18	66	16

TABLE 4.8—*Continued*

Question	Tolerant Response	% Tolerant	% Intolerant	% "Don't Know" or "Undecided"
11. "There is way too much obscene literature in Wincanton today."	"Disagree"	17	57	27
12. "Some people say that the state should legalize prostitution. "Would you agree or disagree?"*	"Agree"	14	82	4

* Question 12, dealing with prostitution, was given in a pretest interview schedule administered to a *nonrandom* sample of twenty-eight Wincanton residents, four of whom favored legalization. The pretest sample was strongly biased toward middle- and upper-middle-class residents. This question was dropped from the final interview schedule for reasons of time and fear that its subject matter would disturb respondents.

machines, in the state." When asked, "If most of the people of Minnesota wanted lotteries and raffles, do you think state officials should let them go on, even though they are not legal, or do you think the people should observe the law now and ask the legislature to change it at the next session?", 85 percent of the respondents in a 1947 survey favored enforcement, while only 10 percent favored the continued operation of the games; 5 percent were undecided. Finally, 1,000 respondents in a 1959 Texas survey were asked to choose between two hypothetical gubernatorial candidates, one of whom while serving as attorney general had closed down gambling joints in Galveston while the other had ignored them. Seventy-three percent were inclined to favor the reformer, while 12 percent favored his opponent; 15 percent were undecided. (Significantly, however, 60 percent of the respondents felt that the gambling issue alone was not a significant basis for choosing a candidate, feeling that other issues might be more important to them.)

If the Wincanton respondents were not always thinking about "law-enforcement" issues when answering questions about gambling, what values were involved? Those who favored legalization of gambling or lotteries generally cited the current loss of revenues to other states: "A lottery helped New Hampshire and I think it could help us. If people can't gamble here, they just go to another place." "If you legalized gambling, there wouldn't be as much going around the corner. You should see all the license plates [from this state] at out-of-state race-tracks." Others noted the value of gambling to churches and charitable organizations: "Fire companies and churches made money [from bingo] for good causes." "We could use the money [from a lottery] for our schools." Those who wanted bingo to be legalized noted its function as a social event for the elderly: "It's a place for them to go and enjoy themselves." "My mother loved to play bingo; she would have died if they took it away while she was living. It was the only enjoyment she ever had." Those who *opposed* legalization of gambling occasionally gave a moral reason ("It degrades the morals of the people," or "It promotes a 'something for nothing' attitude"), but the most frequent argument was that gambling endangered the family income: "Husbands would spend money instead of using it for their families." "A man could lose his whole paycheck if there were no limits." "There would be a lot of children going hungry." While many advocated legalization as a means of taking gambling out of the control of the rackets, a few respondents felt that racketeers would control even legalized gambling activities.

When questions in the Wincanton survey turned from gambling or gambling mixed with law enforcement to questions dealing specifically with official corruption, the tolerance of the respondents dropped markedly. Table 4.9 shows that as the implication of official wrongdoing becomes clear (as when cash rather than "presents" are involved), tolerance almost disappears.

TABLE 4.9

Tolerance of Official Corruption

Question	Tolerant Response	% Tolerant	% Intolerant	% "Don't Know" or "Undecided"
1. "It's all right for a city official to accept presents from companies as long as the taxpayers don't suffer."	"Agree"	35	48	17
2. "It's all right for the mayor of a city to make a profit when that city buys some land so long as only a fair price is charged."	"Agree"	27	62	11
3. "A city official who receives $10 in cash from a company that does business with the city should *not* be prosecuted."	"Agree"	13	73	14

It might be pointed out that question 2 in Table 4.9 is somewhat ambiguous; a number of persons who agreed with that statement specified
that the mayor had to *own* the land; he could not make a profit if
someone else was selling it to the city. The intensity of the respondents' hostility toward corruption was brought out most strongly when
the respondents were asked about the thirty-day jail sentences imposed on Irv Stern and Bob Walasek for extorting $10,500 on city
purchases of parking meters. Eighty-six percent felt that the sentences
were too light. When asked why they felt as they did, 32 percent felt
that Walasek had "betrayed a public trust"; 18 percent gave an answer
such as, "If it had been a little guy like me instead of a guy with pull
like Walasek, I'd still be in jail."

* * *

Tolerance of Corruption

Table 4.9 shows that as indications of official corruption became
clearer (as when cash presents to officials were involved), the tolerance

TABLE 4.13

Low Tolerance of Corruption, by Age and Education*

	Education							
	0–8 years		9–12 years		More than 12 years		Total	
Age	%	N	%	N	%	N	%	N
21–35	43	7	51	37	89	9	57	53
36–59	38	16	20	41	64	11	31	68
60 and over	9	32	25	20	40	5	18	57
Total	22	55	33	98	68	25	34	178

* This table shows the percentage of persons in each category who had a *low* tolerance of corruption (scores of 1–5 on the Tolerance of Corruption Index); thus a
high score on this table indicates a low tolerance of corruption. Forty-three percent
of the seven young, poorly educated respondents, for example, had low tolerance of
corruption. Pooling the chi-squares between tolerance of corruption and age in
three education categories produced a chi-square of 24.47; with 12 degrees of freedom, it was significant at the .02 level. The Kendall's tau correlations between tolerance of corruption and education in three age categories were −.24, −.10 and −.19.
The Kendall's tau correlations between tolerance of corruption and age in three
education categories were .24, .24, and .33.

of the respondents diminished. Tolerance decreased at different rates, however; some respondents became indignant at *any* indication of improper official activities, while others only rebelled when an exchange of money was specified. On the basis of four questions involving possible corruption (cancelling parking and speeding tickets, accepting presents, making a profit on the purchase of land, and a gift of $10 in cash), an Index of Tolerance of Corruption was constructed for the 180 respondents. . . . As anticipated, Table 4.13 shows that tolerance decreases as social status (education) increases. In addition, tolerance increases with age; regardless of education levels, older residents are more tolerant than respondents from other age groups. Furthermore, Table 4.14 shows that respondents who had spent most of their lives in Wincanton were less tolerant than the newcomers. Support for the laws (low tolerance of corruption) thus appears to be related to high social status, youth and long residence in the city. It may be that longer formal education gives upper-status residents greater contact with and reinforcement for official norms of public morality, and that the impact of education decreases as one gets older and further removed from formal schooling. Citizen demands for official honesty are increased by exposure to the gross malfeasance that Wincanton has known; hardly becoming fatalistic or resigned to corruption, long-term residents of the city seem to have a heightened sensitivity to situations possibly involving misconduct.

TABLE 4.14

Low Tolerance of Corruption, by Education and
Percentage of Life in Wincanton*

Percentage of Life in Wincanton

Education	Less than 80%		80% or More		Total	
	%	N	%	N	%	N
0–11 years	20	55	33	54	27	109
12 years or more	43	28	51	41	48	69
Total	28	83	41	95	35	178

* This table shows the percentage of persons in each category with low tolerance of corruption (scores of 1–5 on the Tolerance of Corruption Index); thus a high score on this table indicates a low tolerance of corruption. Twenty percent of the 55 poorly educated newcomers, for example, had a low tolerance of corruption. Pooling the chi-squares between tolerance of corruption and education in the two residence categories produced a chi-square of 7.9; with two degrees of freedom, it was significant at the .02 level. The Kendall's tau correlations between tolerance of corruption and education in the two residence categories were –.20 and –.18.

Conclusions

Earlier, it was asked whether widespread local corruption should be attributed to the values and attitudes of city residents. The evidence suggests that the answer is both yes and no. As an abstract issue, most people in Wincanton see little wrong with gambling. They believe that many forms of petty gambling are locally popular and seldom criticize those who indulge in them. They question the wisdom of the state's antigambling laws and would support the legalization of most forms of gambling.

As anticipated, upper-status residents of Wincanton were better informed about politics and corruption (although their information probably came from reading the newspapers rather than from actual contact with gamblers or official corruption) and were less tolerant of official corruption. Also as expected, those who gambled and those who had spent most of their lives in the city were most tolerant of gambling. However, those who had spent most of their lives in Wincanton were less tolerant of corruption than were those who had lived elsewhere.

While the Wincantonites' rejection of current gambling laws provides support for the thesis that corruption facilitates the realization of popular values—that the Stern-bribed mayors and policemen were simply giving Wincantonites the gambling they wanted—the survey clearly shows that the residents of Wincanton did not tolerate corruption per se. Whenever symbols of law enforcement and official morality were brought into survey questions, most respondents opted for public norms of morality. While some of the survey respondents were slow to perceive that corruption might arise from relationships between officials and persons doing business with the city, they clearly chose honesty and law enforcement when they recognized the nature of the relationship.

(6)

The Costs and Benefits
of Corruption

As must be obvious by now, local corruption affects many types of activities. In some cities, it means only a $5 payment to avoid a speeding ticket or to secure a building permit. In other cities, the entire political process seems dominated by corruption: massive election frauds determine who will hold public office, government jobs go to the highest bidder, every contract involves a kickback, and no one with the right connections and finances need wind up in jail. Patterns of corruption are also uneven within cities: the police may be corrupt and the tax assessors honest, or vice versa, and corrupt opportunities may be available to everyone or restricted to the friends of the party in power.

When all is said and done, what difference does it make? In large part, evaluations of corruption must depend on the questions used in making the assessment. At the simplest level, of course, there is the fact that official laws, regulations, or agency policies have been violated. Second, corrupt activities have a number of direct consequences, both positive and negative, for the people involved. Third, corruption may have indirect consequences for other people and for other parts of local political systems. Finally, in evaluating corruption, it may be necessary to look at the end results of particular transactions to see whether they are more or less reprehensible than what would have happened had city officials followed the rules.

Let us look at a set of hypothetical examples:

1. City Hall needs 10,000 pencils this year. The city purchasing agent could pick them up anywhere for $1,000. Instead, he awards the contract to a friend. The supplier is paid $1,000 from the city treasury, and kicks back $100 to the purchasing agent.

2. At 1:00 A.M. on a Sunday a man is driving at 60 miles per hour along a deserted highway. A policeman pulls him over, notifies him that the speed limit is 50 m.p.h., and starts to write out a ticket carrying a $15 fine. The driver says, "I haven't got time to go to court tomorrow morning; here's $15—will you pay the fine for me?" The driver leaves, and the policeman tears up the ticket and pockets the $15.

3. Under a state statute giving municipalities control over the sale of liquor, the residents of Suburbia vote to prohibit the sale of liquor by the drink. Every Saturday night, Mr. and Mrs. Smith hold an "Open House" in their recreation room. They invite their neighbors in and sell drinks for $1.00 (a profit of about $.50 per drink). Although the Smiths have been holding their "Open Houses" for years, the Suburbia police do not arrest them for violating the liquor laws.

4. A large tract of land on the edge of the city lies vacant, still zoned as farmland. One group of working-class residents, worried about soaring property tax rates, petitions the city council to rezone the land for high-rise apartments, which will add substantially to the city's tax base. Instead, the council members, who live in wealthier neighborhoods, condemn the land for a city park.

5. A city's sanitary landfill capacity will be exhausted within six months, and the city council decides to build an incinerator. The owner of the only suitable land refuses to sell unless he receives an extra, secret $50,000 in addition to the fair market value of his land. Otherwise, as is permitted by state law, he threatens to go to court, which will delay construction of the incinerator by at least two years. The city council approves the extra payment.

How should these five cases be evaluated? First, did they involve violations of laws or agency regulations? In the case of the pencils, it would depend on whether the city had a requirement of open and competitive procurement on all city purchases or a conflict-of-interest regulation that covered all actions taken by city officials. (Under common-law principles the city could probably recover the $100 kickback, since the purchasing agent was acting as a representative of the city.) In the case of the speeding ticket, the officer would have been within his discretionary authority not to write a ticket at all; his taking the $15, however, probably violated both departmental policies on the handling of offenses and city or state statutes covering corruption. *If* it could be proved that he knew the officer would pocket the money rather than turning it over to the department, the driver might also have violated bribery statutes. The case of the Smiths' open houses involved clear violations of the liquor ordinance by the Smiths; unless there was some sign that payoffs were involved, the inaction of the Suburbia police would not generally be regarded as a crime. The city council's decision to condemn the vacant land for a park, rather than to yield to pressures for tax-generating high-rise apartments, involved no violations of law; we would simply conclude that the council members selected one definition of public interest over another, and that those residents who disagreed with them should try to vote them out of office in the next election. Finally, in the case of the incinerator, the city council violated city and state provisions covering land acquisition, and the landowner would violate the income tax laws if he failed to report the $50,000 secret payment.

Direct Costs and Benefits

If we set aside the fact that laws or other regulations were violated, what can be said of the impact of these events on the parties directly involved? In the pencil case, the city got its pencils at the usual price, the purchasing agent received $100, and the supplier received the contract with profits reduced by $100 (although his sales costs were also reduced by whatever amount he would have spent seeking the contract through legitimate channels). Other suppliers who might have received the pencil contract were also directly injured by the purchasing agent's corruption. In the speeding ticket case, the city treasury was cheated out of a $15 fine, the police department and the state department of motor vehicles were deprived of information about a possibly dangerous driver, the policeman received $15, and the driver was saved a trip to court and an offense on his record. The directly affected parties in the Smiths' sales of liquor to their neighbors were the Smiths, who received several hundred dollars each year in profits from their parties, the neighbors who gained an opportunity for social drinking in a town which forbade bars and taverns, and the city treasury, which lost any fines that might have been assessed if the Smiths were hauled into court. Tax-conscious citizens in the vacant property case lost an opportunity to relieve tax burdens, developers lost access to scarce vacant land, and local residents received the recreational and aesthetic benefits of a new park. Finally, in the incinerator case, the landowner received an extra $50,000 for his land, and the city got its incinerator in time to meet its waste-disposal crisis, although it had to pay the extra $50,000.

Indirect Consequences

Should the evaluation of corruption stop at this point, restricting consideration to the parties directly involved? In many cases, no one else is affected, and analysis of direct consequences is sufficient. In other cases, however, it is necessary to consider a wider range of consequences of corruption. While it is impossible to detail all the possible indirect consequences of corruption, the following issues should be considered:

1. Was corruption an isolated incident or a widespread pattern? Presumably, the more widespread the pattern of corruption, the more people would be affected by it.

2. Was the existence of corruption known to the public? If it is known that laws are not being obeyed, then presumably the public's respect for and confidence in the integrity of government will decrease.

3. To what extent did corruption detract from other city goals? We expect city governments to work for the health, welfare, and safety of their citizens. If corruption takes away from city efforts directed at these goals, its effects become more widespread. A bribe to a building inspector to overlook fire and sanitation hazards would thus be considered more damaging to the community as a whole than the $15 payoff on the speeding ticket.

4. How are the costs and benefits of corruption distributed? Does corruption reinforce existing distributions of power and wealth, or does it provide an opportunity for the have-nots to move upwards? Are the costs of corruption born by the parties involved or passed on to innocent third parties, as when a landlord covers the cost of bribes to building inspectors by raising rents or when, as in the case of the incinerator, payoffs and kickbacks led to higher taxes.[1]

Were the Results Good or Bad?

As the final step in evaluating corruption, it is necessary to look at the results. Did corruption lead to governmental actions and policies that were better or worse than the results that would have followed from a decision that did not involve corruption? In the pencil case, the net result of the purchasing agent's corruption was the same as if he had selected the supplier honestly, i.e., the city got its pencils at the usual price. If the police officer took a bribe to overlook a sale of heroin

1. For a theoretical analysis of the costs of corruption, see Brian Loveman, "The Logic of Political Corruption" (Bloomington: Indiana University Studies in Political Theory and Policy Analysis, 1972).

rather than a minor speeding offense, our conclusion would probably be that hard drugs involve so many dangers that the result of the pay-off was socially harmful. In the case of the Smiths' illegal open house parties, however, we might question the wisdom or value of the local ordinance and conclude that it was a net good that people could find a place to gather for social drinking. The incinerator case poses difficult trade-off issues: was the $50,000 bonus a reasonable price to get the incinerator built in time to meet the city's waste-disposal deadline? We obviously cannot reach definitive conclusions on any of these cases, but the point is simple: in some cases, the policies made possible through corruption are on balance more desirable than those produced by legitimate political processes.

Building on the materials that have already been presented (particularly those in chapters 1 and 5), the selections that follow deal with various aspects of these issues. In the first selection in this chapter, the National Crime Commission adds up the individual violations of gambling and other laws made possible by corruption and tries to assess the overall scope of organized crime in the United States. Then, New York Police Sergeant David Durk portrays the costs of corruption both to policemen trying to do their job and to the public, who lose confidence in law enforcement. The next two selections depict the specific impact of corruption on black communities. McCord explains the power of ghetto "exploiters" in terms of black exclusion from legitimate opportunities for economic and social advancement. The New York Legislature's Crime Committee then details the costs of organized narcotics, gambling, and loansharking in ghetto neighborhoods. The fifth selection attempts to identify each of the costs and benefits of corruption in a city in which it has been common for almost fifty years. The last three selections tie their analyses of graft and corruption to certain assumptions about the governmental process: Henry Jones Ford, reviewing the works of Lincoln Steffens, asks whether Steffens ignored the beneficial role of corruption in facilitating urban progress; in a classic statement of functional analysis in social research, Robert K. Merton reviews the history of political machines, citing their ability to compensate for the deficiencies of formal governmental mechanisms; and Theodore J. Lowi concludes with a comparison of New York and Chicago, assessing the contributions of machines and reform governments to local administration.

ORGANIZED CRIME
President's Crime Commission

Organized crime is a society that seeks to operate outside the control of the American people and their governments. It involves thousands of criminals, working within structures as complex as those of any large corporation, subject to laws more rigidly enforced than those of legitimate governments. Its actions are not impulsive but rather the result of intricate conspiracies, carried on over many years and aimed at gaining control over whole fields of activity in order to amass huge profits.

The core of organized crime activity is the supplying of illegal goods and services—gambling, loan sharking, narcotics, and other forms of vice—to countless numbers of citizen customers. But organized crime is also extensively and deeply involved in legitimate business and in labor unions. Here it employs illegitimate methods—monopolization, terrorism, extortion, tax evasion—to drive out or control lawful ownership and leadership and to exact illegal profits from the public. And to carry on its many activities secure from governmental interference, organized crime corrupts public officials.

Former Attorney General Robert F. Kennedy illustrated its power simply and vividly. He testified before a Senate subcommittee in 1963 that the physical protection of witnesses who had cooperated with the Federal Government in organized crime cases often required that those witnesses change their appearances, change their names, or even leave the country. When the government of a powerful country is unable to protect its friends from its enemies by means less extreme than obliterating their identities surely it is being seriously challenged, if not threatened.

What organized crime wants is money and power. What makes it different from law-abiding organizations and individuals with those

From President's Commission on Law Enforcement and Administration of Justice, *Task Force Report: Organized Crime* (Washington, D.C.: Government Printing Office, 1967), pp.1–5. Some footnotes deleted.

same objectives is that the ethical and moral standards the criminals adhere to, the laws and regulations they obey, the procedures they use are private and secret ones that they devise themselves, change when they see fit, and administer summarily and invisibly. Organized crime affects the lives of millions of Americans, but because it desperately preserves its invisibility many, perhaps most, Americans are not aware how they are affected, or even that they are affected at all. The price of a loaf of bread may go up one cent as the result of an organized crime conspiracy, but a housewife has no way of knowing why she is paying more. If organized criminals paid income tax on every cent of their vast earnings everybody's tax bill would go down, but no one knows how much.

But to discuss the impact of organized crime in terms of whatever direct, personal, everyday effect it has on individuals is to miss most of the point. Most individuals are not affected, in this sense, very much. Much of the money organized crime accumulates comes from innumerable petty transactions: 50-cent bets, $3-a-month private garbage collection services, quarters dropped into racketeer-owned jukeboxes, or small price rises resulting from protection rackets. A one-cent-a-loaf rise in bread may annoy housewives, but it certainly does not impoverish them.

Sometimes organized crime's activities do not directly affect individuals at all. Smuggled cigarettes in a vending machine cost consumers no more than tax-paid cigarettes, but they enrich the leaders of organized crime. Sometimes these activities actually reduce prices for a short period of time, as can happen when organized crime, in an attempt to take over an industry, starts a price war against legitimate businessmen. Even when organized crime engages in a large transaction, individuals may not be directly affected. A large sum of money may be diverted from a union pension fund to finance a business venture without immediate and direct effect upon the individual members of the union.

It is organized crime's accumulation of money, not the individual transactions by which the money is accumulated, that has a great and threatening impact on America. A quarter in a jukebox means nothing and results in nothing. But millions of quarters in thousands of jukeboxes can provide both a strong motive for murder and the means to commit murder with impunity. Organized crime exists by virtue of the power it purchases with its money. The millions of dollars it can invest in narcotics or use for layoff money give it power over the lives of thousands of people and over the quality of life in whole neighborhoods.

The millions of dollars it can throw into the legitimate economic system give it power to manipulate the price of shares on the stock market, to raise or lower the price of retail merchandise, to determine whether entire industries are union or nonunion, to make it easier or harder for businessmen to continue in business.

The millions of dollars it can spend on corrupting public officials may give it power to maim or murder people inside or outside the organization with impunity; to extort money from businessmen; to conduct businesses in such fields as liquor, meat, or drugs without regard to administrative regulations; to avoid payment of income taxes or to secure public works contracts without competitive bidding.

The purpose of organized crime is not competition with visible, legal government but nullification of it. When organized crime places an official in public office, it nullifies the political process. When it bribes a police official, it nullifies law enforcement.

There is another, more subtle way in which organized crime has an impact on American life. Consider the former way of life of Frank Costello, a man who has repeatedly been called a leader of organized crime. He lived in an expensive apartment on the corner of 72d Street and Central Park West in New York. He was often seen dining in well-known restaurants in the company of judges, public officials, and prominent businessmen. Every morning he was shaved in the barbershop of the Waldorf Astoria Hotel. On many weekends he played golf at a country club on the fashionable North Shore of Long Island. In short, though his reputation was common knowledge, he moved around New York conspicuously and unashamedly, perhaps ostracized by some people but more often accepted, greeted by journalists, recognized by children, accorded all the freedoms of a prosperous and successful man. On a society that treats such a man in such a manner, organized crime has had an impact.

And yet the public remains indifferent. Few Americans seem to comprehend how the phenomenon of organized crime affects their lives. They do not see how gambling with bookmakers, or borrowing money from loan sharks, forwards the interests of great criminal cartels. Businessmen looking for labor harmony or nonunion status through irregular channels rationalize away any suspicions that organized crime is thereby spreading its influence. When an ambitious political candidate accepts substantial cash contributions from unknown sources, he suspects but dismisses the fact that organized crime will dictate some of his actions when he assumes office.

President Johnson asked the Commission to determine why organized crime has been expanding despite the Nation's best efforts to prevent it. The Commission drew upon the small group of enforcement personnel and other knowledgeable persons who deal with organized crime. Federal agencies provided extensive material. But because so little study and research have been done in this field, we also secured the assistance of sociologists, systems analysts, political scientists, economists, and lawyers. America's limited response to organized crime is illustrated by the fact that, for several of these disciplines, our call for assistance resulted in their first concentrated examination of organized crime.

The Types of Organized Criminal Activities

Catering to Public Demands

Organized criminal groups participate in any illegal activity that offers maximum profit at minimum risk of law enforcement interference. They offer goods and services that millions of Americans desire even though declared illegal by their legislatures.

Gambling. Law enforcement officials agree almost unanimously that gambling is the greatest source of revenue for organized crime. It ranges from lotteries, such as "numbers" or "bolita," to off-track horse betting, bets on sporting events, large dice games and illegal casinos. In large cities where organized criminal groups exist, very few of the gambling operators are independent of a large organization. Anyone whose independent operation becomes successful is likely to receive a visit from an organization representative who convinces the independent, through fear or promise of greater profit, to share his revenue with the organization.

Most large-city gambling is established or controlled by organized crime members through elaborate hierarchies. Money is filtered from the small operator who takes the customer's bet, through persons who pick up money and slips, to second-echelon figures in charge of particular districts, and then into one of several main offices. The profits that eventually accrue to organization leaders move through channels so complex that even persons who work in the betting operation do not know or cannot prove the identity of the leader. Increasing use of the telephone for lottery and sports betting has facilitated systems in which the bookmaker may not know the identity of the second-echelon person to whom he calls in the day's bets. Organization not only creates greater efficiency and enlarges markets,[1] it also provides a systematized method of corrupting the law enforcement process by centralizing procedures for the payment of graft.[2]

Organization is also necessary to prevent severe losses. More money may be bet on one horse or one number with a small operator than he could pay off if that horse or that number should win. The operator will have to hedge by betting some money himself on that horse or that number. This so-called "layoff" betting is accomplished through a network of local, regional and national layoff men, who takes bets from gambling operations.

There is no accurate way of ascertaining organized crime's gross revenue from gambling in the United States. Estimates of the annual intake have varied from $7 to $50 billion. Legal betting at racetracks reaches a gross annual figure of almost $5 billion, and most enforcement officials believe that illegal wagering on horse races, lotteries, and sporting events totals at least $20 billion each year. Analysis of organized criminal betting operations indicates that the profit is as high as one-third of gross revenue—or $6 to $7 billion each year. While the Commission cannot judge the accuracy of these figures, even the most conservative estimates place substantial capital in the hands of organized crime leaders.

Loan Sharking. In the view of most law enforcement officials loan sharking, the lending of money at higher rates than the legally pre-

1. In his statement to the Temporary Commission of Investigation of the State of New York on Apr. 22, 1960, Charles R. Thom, Comm'r of Police of Suffolk County (Eastern Long Island), N.Y., said: "The *advantages* of syndicate operation to the previously independent bookie included: (1) unlimited resources with absolute backing which eliminated the need to lay off, thus permitting vast expansion, and the average bookie quickly discovered he was making a bigger net on a 50–50 basis than he formerly made when he controlled the entire operation; (2) New York City telephone numbers could be passed along to regular bettors and players, which made the bookie merely a collector of money, credited on the books of the syndicate through an efficient bookkeeping system, and adding the tremendous factor that use of telephones was thus changed, greatly reducing the efficiency of telephone taps; and (3) the syndicate agreed to provide 'stand-up men' where feasible." Mimeo, p.2.

2. "It is somewhat startling to learn that the syndicates are particularly happy with the consolidation of the nine police departments into the Suffolk County Police Department, as they feel that protection is easier to arrange through one agency than through many. The intensive campaign against gamblers instituted by this Department commencing January 1st had the astounding side effect in solving the recruitment problem of the syndicate, as our drive successfully stampeded the independents into the arms of the syndicate for protection and the syndicate can now pick and choose those operators which they wish to admit." *Ibid.*

scribed limit, is the second largest source of revenue for organized crime. Gambling profits provide the initial capital for loan-shark operations.

No comprehensive analysis has ever been made of what kinds of customers loan sharks have, or of how much or how often each kind borrows. Enforcement officials and other investigators do have some information. Gamblers borrow to pay gambling losses;[3] narcotics users borrow to purchase heroin. Some small businessmen borrow from loan sharks when legitimate credit channels are closed. The same men who take bets from employees in mass employment industries also serve at times as loan sharks, whose money enables the employees to pay off their gambling debts or meet household needs.

Interest rates vary from 1 to 150 percent a week, according to the relationship between the lender and borrower, the intended use of the money, the size of the loan, and the repayment potential. The classic "6-for-5" loan, 20 percent a week, is common with small borrowers. Payments may be due by a certain hour on a certain day, and even a few minutes' default may result in a rise in interest rates. The lender is more interested in perpetuating interest payments than collecting principal; and force, or threats of force of the most brutal kind, are

3. In his statement to the Temporary Commission of Investigation of the state of New York on Apr. 22, 1960, Comm'r Charles R. Thom described how loan sharking provided the means for organizing previously independent bookmakers:
"Speaking generally, prior to 1958, professional gambling in Suffolk County was conducted primarily by independent operators. There was no known pattern of organized gambling beyond the usual facilities for laying off, and no reported rackets or collateral criminal activities.
"About two years ago, representatives of one or more syndicates began approaching these independent gambling operators with a view to incorporating them into syndicated operations. By and large, these independent gamblers refused to be so organized, and the syndicates withdrew their efforts without resort to rough tactics. The syndicates then commenced an insidious campaign of infiltration, wherein the principal M.O. was *finance*. With open pocketbook, the syndicate recruited a number of independent operators, by financing their operations until these bookies were hooked. Part of this system included the notorious 6 for 5 plus 5 percent per week, which meant simply that they financed the bookies on the basis that the gambling operator had to return $6.00 for every $5.00 borrowed, plus the staggering interest of 5 per cent per week. It follows that a bookie who had a couple of bad weeks was completely hooked and fell under the control of the syndicate. Most of these independent bookies were small businessmen, including the typical barber, candy store operator and the like, without the financial resources to withstand this squeeze, which was effectively accomplished by the money men of the syndicate. Once hooked, the bookies now worked for the syndicate on a 50–50 basis."

used to effect interest collection, eliminate protest when interest rates are raised, and prevent the beleaguered borrower from reporting the activity to enforcement officials. No reliable estimates exist of the gross revenue from organized loan sharking, but profit margins are higher than for gambling operations, and many officials classify the business in the multi-billion-dollar range.

Narcotics. The sale of narcotics is organized like a legitimate importing-wholesaling-retailing business. The distribution of heroin, for example, requires movement of the drug through four or five levels between the importer and the street peddler. Many enforcement officials believe that the severity of mandatory Federal narcotics penalties has caused organized criminals to restrict their activities to importing and wholesale distribution. They stay away from smaller-scale wholesale transactions or dealing at the retail level. Transactions with addicts are handled by independent narcotics pushers using drugs imported by organized crime.

The large amounts of cash and the international connections necessary for large, long-term heroin supplies can be provided only by organized crime. Conservative estimates of the number of addicts in the Nation and the average daily expenditure for heroin indicate that the gross heroin trade is $350 million annually, of which $21 million are probably profits to the importer and distributor. Most of this profit goes to organized crime groups in those few cities in which almost all heroin consumption occurs.

Other Goods and Services. Prostitution and bootlegging play a small and declining role in organized crime's operations. Production of illegal alcohol is a risky business. The destruction of stills and supplies by law enforcement officers during the initial stages means the loss of heavy initial investment capital. Prostitution is difficult to organize and discipline is hard to maintain. Several important convictions of organized crime figures in prostitution cases in the 1930's and 1940's made the criminal executives wary of further participation.

Business and Labor Interests

Infiltration of Legitimate Business. A legitimate business enables the racket executive to acquire respectability in the community and to establish a source of funds that appears legal and upon which just enough taxes may be paid to avoid income tax prosecution. Organized crime invests the profit it has made from illegal service activities in a variety of businesses throughout the country. To succeed in such ventures, it uses accountants, attorneys, and business consultants, who in some instances work exclusively on its affairs. Too often, because of the reciprocal benefits involved in organized crime's dealings with the business world, or because of fear, the legitimate sector of society helps the illegitimate sector. The Illinois Crime Commission, after investigating one service industry in Chicago, stated:

> There is a disturbing lack of interest on the part of some legitimate business concerns regarding the identity of the persons with whom they deal. This lackadaisical attitude is conducive to the perpetration of frauds and the infiltration and subversion of legitimate businesses by the organized criminal element.

Because business ownership is so easily concealed, it is difficult to determine all the types of businesses that organized crime has penetrated. Of the 75 or so racket leaders who met at Apalachin, N.Y., in 1957, at least 9 were in the coin-operated machine industry, 16 were in the garment industry, 10 owned grocery stores, 17 owned bars or restaurants, 11 were in the olive oil and cheese business, and 9 were in the construction business. Others were involved in automobile agencies, coal companies, entertainment, funeral homes, ownership of horses and race tracks, linen and laundry enterprises, trucking, waterfront activities, and bakeries.

Today, the kinds of production and service industries and businesses that organized crime controls or has invested in range from accounting firms to yeast manufacturing. One criminal syndicate alone has real estate interests with an estimated value of $300 million. In a few instances, racketeers control nationwide manufacturing and service industries with known and respected brand names.

Control of business concerns has usually been acquired through one of four methods: (1) investing concealed profits acquired from gambling and other illegal activities; (2) accepting business interests in payment of the owner's gambling debts; (3) foreclosing on usurious loans; and (4) using various forms of extortion.

Acquisition of legitimate business is also accomplished in more sophisticated ways. One organized crime group offered to lend money to a business on condition that a racketeer be appointed to the company's board of directors and that a nominee for the lenders be given first option to purchase if there were any outside sale of the company's stock. Control of certain brokerage houses was secured through foreclosure of usurious loans, and the businesses then used to promote the sale of fraudulent stock, involving losses of more than $2 million to the public.

Criminal groups also satisfy defaulted loans by taking over business, hiring professional arsonists to burn buildings and contents, and collecting on the fire insurance. Another tactic was illustrated in the recent bankruptcy of a meatpacking firm in which control was secured as payment for gambling debts. With the original owners remaining in nominal management positions, extensive product orders were placed through established lines of credit, and the goods were immediately sold at low prices before the suppliers were paid. The organized criminal group made a quick profit of three-quarters of a million dollars by pocketing the receipts from sale of the products ordered and placing the firm in bankruptcy without paying the suppliers.

Too little is known about the effects on the economy of organized crime's entry into the business world, but the examples above indicate the harm done to the public and at least suggest how criminal cartels can undermine free competition. The ordinary businessman is hard pressed to compete with a syndicate enterprise. From its gambling and other illegal revenue—on most of which no taxes are paid—the criminal group always has a ready source of cash with which to enter any business. Through union connections, the business run by organized crime either prevents unionization or secures "sweetheart" contracts from existing unions. These tactics are used effectively in combination. In one city, organized crime gained a monopoly in garbage collection by preserving the business's nonunion status and by using cash reserves to offset temporary losses incurred when the criminal group lowered prices to drive competitors out of business.

Strong-arm tactics are used to enforce unfair business policy and to obtain customers. A restaurant chain controlled by organized crime used the guise of "quality control" to insure that individual restaurant franchise holders bought products only from other syndicate-owned businesses. In one city, every business with a particular kind of waste product useful in another line of industry sold that product to a syndicate-controlled business at one-third the price offered by legitimate business.

The cumulative effect of the infiltration of legitimate business in America cannot be measured. Law enforcement officials agree that entry into legitimate business is continually increasing and that it has not decreased organized crime's control over gambling, usury and other profitable, low-risk criminal enterprises.

BEING A COP MEANS BELIEVING IN THE RULE OF LAW

David Durk

Revelations of corruption offered by Sergeant Durk and Officer Frank Serpico of the New York Police Department led to the formation in 1970 of the Commission to Investigate Allegations of Police Corruption (The Knapp Commission), portions of whose *Report* are presented elsewhere in this volume. This selection is taken from testimony by Sergeant Durk before the Knapp Commission.

At the very beginning, the most important fact to understand is that I had and have no special knowledge of police corruption. We (police officers) knew these things because we were involved in law enforcement in New York City and anyone else who says he didn't know had to be blind, either by choice or incompetence. The facts have been there waiting to be exposed.

This commission, to its enormous credit, has exposed them in a period of six months. We simply cannot believe, as we do not believe today, that those with authority and responsibility in the area, whether the district attorneys, the police commanders or those in power in city hall, couldn't also have exposed them in six months, or at least in six years—that is, if they wanted to do it.

Let me be explicit. I'm not saying that all those who ignored the corruption were themselves corrupt. Whether or not they were is almost immaterial in any case. The fact is that the corruption was ignored. . . .

These are very tough things to believe if you're a cop because for me, being a cop means believing in the rule of law. It means believing in a system of government that makes fair and just rules and then enforces them.

Being a cop also means serving, helping others. If it's not too corny, to be a cop is to help an old lady walk the street safely, to help a 12-year-old girl reach her next birthday without being gang raped, to help the storekeeper make a living without keeping a shotgun under his cash register, to help a boy grow up without needles in his arm.

And, therefore, to me, being a cop is not just a job but a way to live a life. Some people say that cops live with the worst side of humanity in the middle of all the lying and cheating, the violence and hate, and I suppose that, in some sense, it's true.

But being a cop also means being engaged with life. It means that our concern for others is not abstract, that that we don't just write a letter The Times or give $10 to the United Fund once a year.

It means that we put something on the line from the moment we hit the street every morning of every day of our lives. In this sense, police corruption is not about money at all. Because there is no amount of money that you can pay a cop to risk his life 365 days a year. Being a cop is a vocation or it is nothing at all.

And that's what I saw being destroyed by the corruption in the New York City Police Department, destroyed for me and for thousands of others like me.

We wanted to believe in the rule of law. We wanted to believe in a system of responsibility. But those in high places everywhere, in the police department, in the D.A.'s office, in city hall, were determined not to enforce the law and they turned their heads when law and justice were being sold on every streetcorner.

We wanted to serve others, but the department was a home for the drug dealers and thieves. The force that was supposed to be protecting people was selling poison to their children. And there could be no life, no real life for me or anyone else on the force when, every day, we had to face the facts of our own terrible corruption.

I saw that happening to men all around me, men who could have been good officers, men of decent impulse, men of ideals, but men who were without decent leadership, men who were told in a hundred ways every day go along, forget the law, don't make waves, and shut up.

So they did shut up, They did go along. They did learn the unwritten code of the department. They went along and they lost something very precious: they weren't cops any more. They were a long way towards not being men any more.

And all the time I saw the other victims, too, especially the children, children of 14, 15, and 16, wasted by heroin, turned into streetcorner thugs and whores, ready to mug their own mother for the price of a fix.

That was the price of going along. The real price of police corruption, not free meals or broken regulations but broken dreams and dying neighborhoods and a whole generation of children being lost.

That was what I joined the department to stop, so that was why I went to The New York Times, because attention had to be paid, in our last desperate hope that, if the facts were known, someone must respond.

Now it's up to you.

I speak to you now as nothing more and nothing less than a cop, a cop who's lived on this force and who's staying on this force and therefore as a cop who needs your help.

I and my fellow policemen, we didn't appoint you and you don't report to us. But all the same, there are some things as policemen we must have from you.

First, we need you to fix responsibility for the rottenness that was allowed to fester. It must be fixed both inside and outside the department.

Inside the department, responsibility has to be fixed against those top commanders who allowed or helped the situation to develop. Responsibility has to be fixed because no patrolman will believe that he should care about corruption if his superiors can get away with not caring.

Responsibility also has to be fixed because commanders themselves have to be told again and again, and not only by the police commissioner, that the entire state of the department is up to them.

And most of all, responsibility has to be fixed because it's the first step toward recovering our simple but necessary conviction that right will be rewarded and wrongdoing punished.

Responsibility must also be fixed outside the police department, on all the men and agencies that have helped bring us to our present pass, against all those who could have exposed this corruption but never did.

Like it or not, the policeman is convinced that he lives and works in the middle of a corrupt society, that everyone else is getting theirs and why shouldn't he and that if anyone really cared about corruption something would have been done about it a long time ago.

We are not animals. We're not stupid, and we know very well, we policemen, that corruption does not begin with a few patrolmen. And that responsibility for corruption does not end with one aide to the mayor or one investigations commissioner. . . . We know that there are many people beyond the police department who share in the corruption and its rewards.

So your report has to tell us about the district attorneys, and the courts, and the bar, and the mayor and the governor, and what they have done and what they have failed to do, and how great a measure of responsibility they also bear.

Otherwise, if you suggest, or allow others to suggest, that the responsibility belongs only to the police, then for the patrolmen on the beat and in the radio cars, this commission will be just another part of the swindle.

This is a harsh statement, and an impolite and a brutal statement, but it's also a statement of the truth.

Second, you have to speak to the conscience of this city. Speak for all of those without a voice, all those who are not here to be heard today, although they know the price of police corruption more intimately than anyone here.

The people of the ghetto and all the other victims, those broken in mind and spirit and hope, perhaps more than any other people in this city, they depend upon the police and the law to protect not just their pocketbooks, but their very lives and the lives and welfare of their children.

Tow truck operators can write off bribes on their income tax. The expense account executive can afford a prostitute. But no one can pay a mother for the pain of seeing her children hooked on heroin.

This commission, for what I am sure are good reasons, has not invited testimony from the communities of suffering of New York City, but this commission must remind the force, as it must tell the rest of the city, that there are human lives at stake, that when the police protect the narcotics traffic, that we're participating in the destruction of a generation of children.

It is this terrible crime for which you are fixing the responsibility, and it is this terrible crime against which you must speak with the full outrage of the community's conscience.

Third, as a corollary, you must help to give us a sense of priorities, to remind us that corruption, like sin, has its gradations and classifications.

Of course, all corruption is bad, but we cannot fall into the trap of pretending that all corruption is equally bad. There is a difference between accepting free meals and selling narcotics. And if we are unable to make that distinction, then we are saying to the police that the life of a child in the South Bronx is the same moral value as a cup of coffee. And that cannot be true for this society, or for its police force. So you must show us the difference.

Finally, in your deliberations, you must speak to the policemen of this city for the best that is in them, for what most of them wanted to be, for what most of them will be. If we try.

Once, I arrested a landlord's agent . . . who offered to pay me if I would lock up a tenant who was organizing other tenants in the building. As I put the cuffs on the agent and led him away, a crowd of people really were around and actually said, "Viva la policia."

Of course it was not just me, or even the police that they were cheering, they were cheering because they had glimpsed, in that one arrest, the possibility of a system of justice that could work to protect them, too.

They were cheering because if that agent could get arrested, then that meant that they had rights, that they were citizens, that maybe one day life would really be different for their children.

For me, that moment is what police work is all about. But there have been far too few moments like that, and far too many times when I looked into the faces of the city and saw not hope and trust but resentment and hate and fear.

Far too many of my fellow officers have seen only hate. Far too many of them have seen their dreams of service and justice frustrated and abandoned by a corrupt system—superiors and politicians who just didn't care enough.

It took five years of Frank Serpico's life [Durk's partner] and five years of mine to help bring this commission about.

It has taken the lives and dedication of thousands of others to preserve as much of a police force as we have.

It has taken many months of effort by all of you to help show this city the truth.

What I ask of you now is to help make us clean again, to help give us some leadership we can look to, to make it possible for all the men on the force to walk at ease with their better nature and with their fellow citizens and, perhaps one day, on a long summer night, hear again the shout, "Viva la policia."

PORTRAIT OF AN "EXPLOITER"

William McCord, John Howard, Bernard Friedberg, and Edwin Harwood

The contemporary Negro exploiter tends to accept the status quo and, for economic reasons, prefers society in its present form. While he claims to favor more speed in civil rights and at least gives lip service to religion, he in fact thrives on a segregated system. Compelled by circumstances or his own character, such a person truly leads a double life. Clifford Vaughn illustrates this particular dilemma. On the one hand, he is supposedly head of the numbers racket in Houston, owns several Negro tenements, runs a mortuary, and is a "loan shark." On the other, he serves as a deacon of his church, contributes large sums to the NAACP, and calls the governor by his first name.

A rather corpulent man of fifty-six, Clifford Vaughn directs his varied activities from the paneled study of his $80,000 home. He officially lists himself as "self-employed" and is naturally reticent about describing his business operations. Police sources, however, provide some idea of the nature of one of Mr. Vaughn's presumed activities, the "numbers" or "policy" racket. The business is quite simple. Cards are distributed in the Negro districts bearing twenty-five numbers (or symbols). A person bets any amount from ten cents to $21 that the number he picks will be chosen in a lottery held each week. Theoretically the winnings can be as much as $15,000. There are various "fronts"—small stores throughout Houston—where one may place a bet. About 25 per cent of the profits go to the front owners who, in turn, must pay various employees. According to some Houston Negroes, another slice of the profits goes to policemen or sheriff's deputies in the form of "protection." The remaining profit goes to "The Company" which, according to police and to general Negro opinion, is essentially Clifford Vaughn.

Reprinted from *Life Styles in the Black Ghetto* by William McCord, John Howard, Bernard Friedberg, and Edwin Harwood. By permission of W.W. Norton & Company, Inc. Copyright © 1969 by W.W. Norton & Company, Inc. Pp.189–193. Some footnotes deleted.

He in turn has other expenses since he admits openly that he contributes a great deal of money to various politicians. No one knows how much Vaughn actually keeps after everyone else has been paid off, but he owns an expensive home, a Rolls-Royce, a Jaguar, and a forty-foot cabin cruiser. While he will not acknowledge any connection with the numbers racket, he was willing to comment generally about it during an interview. "As a religious man, I suppose I should condemn the numbers," he said, "but, frankly, I see little harm if a man wants to play the game. He gets some fun out of it, never loses very much, and —if he wins—can take it easy for a year."

Vaughn was equally tight-lipped about his other businesses. He owns property in the Fifth Ward, but refused to specify the extent of his holdings. His mortuary is apparently one of the most successful in Houston; around 300 Negro families a year chose to have their funerals handled there. (The cost of a Vaughn funeral, according to our survey, averages 14 per cent higher than that charged by ten morticians who serve whites.) Reputedly, Vaughn also owns a number of apartments used by prostitutes in Houston's well-known red-light district. We were able to establish that he does own at least one apartment building frequented by prostitutes and their pimps. Clearly, Vaughn's operations skirt the boundaries of legitimate business, yet he has never been convicted of a felony and has not been publicly rebuked by an organization such as the Houston Better Business Bureau.

Outwardly he seems to be a model of respectability. He has been elected president of various Negro business groups in Houston and he says he is well received at city hall and is listened to attentively at the state capital. He plays an active political role and, he claims, exercises power in the Negro "Council of Organizations," a Houston grouping of civic clubs that either supports or condemns various political candidates.

He is also apparently a model husband and father. He has been married to the same woman for thirty years and she seems to be happy. Although Vaughn himself had only one year of college, his three children have successfully graduated from several institutions of higher learning.

Vaughn is active in certain community causes. In addition to serving on a local NAACP board, he participates in Negro lodges, a fraternity, and charitable causes. The center of his life, he claims, is his local Methodist Episcopal Church. "I enjoy stately, dignified religious services," he says; "it gives me comfort to know that I am in touch with the Lord."

He believes that the civil rights movement is moving at "about the right pace." "Many of these hot-heads like Stokely Carmichael just stir things up," he says. "The way to achieve progress is to work with the system. I have done more to advance my race by just talking with the right officials than 100 demonstrations could have accomplished." His proudest moment, he claims, occurred in 1963 when a local civil rights group was demonstrating for school integration. "Why, those people could have gone on for days and nothing would have happened. All I had to do was pick up the telephone and call a good white friend of mine who heads————[a prominent department store]. We got the Negro leaders together in a hotel with the school board members. At first they wouldn't be in the same room, but after I talked to the Negroes, they agreed to negotiate. As a result, we won more integration."

Vaughn attributes his success to "hard work, careful planning, and keeping my nose to the grindstone." He believes that many Negroes "are just plain lazy" and that their salvation lies in "pulling themselves up by their bootstraps."

In a completely free and open society, Clifford Vaughn might have been a successful businessman without having to resort to questionable methods to obtain his high income. We must always remember that Negro exploiters exist because the ghetto exists, and that American whites have created the ghetto. In a perceptive discussion of "blockbusting" (another activity in which Clifford Vaughn reputedly engages), Eunice and George Grier have observed:

> Technically speaking, blockbusters represent an unscrupulous minority of the real estate industry—"outlaws" in a moral if not a legal sense. However, their activities would not prove profitable if racial restrictions on place of residence were not accepted and enforced by the large majority of builders, brokers, and lenders, backed by the supporting opinion of a large segment of the white public.
>
> By restraining the Negro market and permitting its housing needs to be satisfied only on a waiting-list basis, "reputable" members of the banking and housing industries have helped perpetuate the conditions under which their less-scrupulous colleagues can flourish.[1]

The Clifford Vaughns of this world can exist, in other words, only so long as "reputable" white businessmen allow them to, only so long

1. Eunice and George Grier, "Equality and Beyond: Housing Segregation in the Great Society," in *The Negro American,* Talcott Parsons and Kenneth Clark, eds. (New York: Houghton Mifflin, 1966), p.534.

as white policemen close their eyes to the existence of prostitution, and only so long as white politicians lend their "protection" to such exploitive activities as the numbers racket.

What can Negroes do about "blockbusting," or other forms of exploitation? In Houston, at least, several fairly effective measures have been employed. The Houston Legal Foundation (a group of volunteer lawyers serving poor people) has, for example, exposed fraudulent house-buying operations and brought their perpetrators to justice. The Houston Civic Association (an organization of Negro and white home owners) has vigorously fought the attempts of blockbusters to ruin a particular neighborhood by joining together to prevent unscrupulous real estate practices. They did not try to keep Negroes out of the area, but worked to create a truly integrated neighborhood. Those whites who did not want to leave their old, well-established neighborhood put signs on their lawns saying, "This house is *not* for sale. It is our home." This refusal to panic in the face of rumors circulated by blockbusters has resulted in Negroes and whites working together to establish a harmonious community.

Perhaps the most effective weapon against exploitation by local merchants, Negro or white, is the economic boycott, or "selective buying," which, if properly conducted, can bring enough pressure to bear to cause a store owner or manager to make him give up his unfair practices.

Exploitation can be reduced, if not eliminated, within the Negro community, then, by educating consumers, by the use of such legal measures as tough prosecution of the numbers game, and, particularly, by selective-buying campaigns, even though the Clifford Vaughns of this world—and their more numerous white colleagues—can be eliminated only when poverty and the ghetto itself are eliminated.

ORGANIZED CRIME
IN THE GHETTO

New York State
Crime Committee

Organized crime is a major contributor to and profits handsomely from the debilitation of our inner cities. At the same time that this lecherous cartel is siphoning off millions of dollars from the ghetto as a result of its policy, loansharking and other illicit operations, it is spewing back into the same ghetto a reign of misery and death in the form of traffic in heroin. The government, both state and federal, is an unwitting supporter of organized crime through the vast sums of welfare and other remedial funds pumped into the ghetto. As one group of United States Congressmen reported:

> The victims of organized crime are the urban poor. A society concerned about poverty must be concerned about organized crime—for while [welfare] money is poured into the urban poverty areas, organized crime siphons money out of the same areas. Badly needed funds from welfare programs go to the urban poor and organized crime takes money from the urban poor. Continued indifference to organized crime threatens to turn government welfare and anti-poverty programs into a subsidy for society's most notorious predator.—Statement of 22 U.S. Congressmen, Congressional Record, Aug. 29, 1967, p. H. 11431.

This declaration reflects a growing realization that the ghetto problems of poverty and crime, particularly organized crime, are inextricably bound up, and that no anti-poverty program can be expected to ameliorate the deprivation of the ghetto resident unless the crime problem is simultaneously attacked. Indeed there is a direct relationship between civil disorders in the ghettos and crime, due primarily to the mounting anger of the ghetto resident at the society that fails to protect him from the depredations of organized crime.

From New York State Joint Legislative Committee on Crime, Its Causes, Control, and Effect on Society, *Organized Crime in the Ghetto*, (Legislative Document, 1969), pp.108–113. All footnotes deleted.

In 1968, this Committee invited an Advisory Council, comprised of leading citizens of this state, to assist it in a major investigation into the twin phenomena of violence and civil disorder now threatening the fabric of our society. In the course of these hearings, many of the witnesses pointed to the inter-relationship of civil disorder and crime in the ghetto. The witnesses testified that the prevalence of crime, especially violent and narcotics-related crime, in ghetto areas had produced a pervasive feeling of fear and helplessness in the ghetto resident which was then transformed into the alienation and rage that exploded into civil disorder. It was then decided to explore the question whether our failure to reduce crime to reasonably tolerable limits within ghetto areas was a major factor in the explosions of mass rage that we now denominate civil disorder. Subsequent investigations by the Committee indicated that there is, indeed, a direct relationship between crime in the ghetto (especially crime attributable to organized criminal operations) and the appalling conditions of basic public disorder and instability that the ghetto communities have had to endure. ...

Organized Crime and Narcotics

The most vicious activity of organized crime in the ghetto is traffic in narcotics, specifically heroin. New York City has an estimated 65,000 to 75,000 heroin addicts located mainly within the ghetto areas. About one half of these addicts are Negro, twenty-five per cent are Puerto Rican and twenty-five percent are divided among the remainder of the population. Besides the number of addicts significantly increasing from year to year, the proportion of Negro addicts to the whole is also increasing. The statistics on death are just as ugly as those on the upsurge in addiction: in 1968 there were 735 deaths which were attributable to heroin addiction. In 1969 the figure jumped to over 850.

Most alarming is the increase in the number of addicts under 20 years of age. Today there are 20,000 to 25,000, or more, teenage heroin addicts. This trend is also reflected in more somber statistics. Thus there has been a marked decrease in the average age of addicts at death, from 34 years of age in 1960 to 27 years in 1968. Indeed in 1968 almost 15% of the total deaths were of persons under 20 years old and unfortunately that figure too is on the upswing—out of the 850 addict deaths for 1969, slightly more than 25% or 220, were teenagers. Projections are that deaths attributable to heroin will reach over 1000 in 1970. Certainly if 1000 or more deaths were recorded from any other poisonous substance or disease New York City would undoubtedly mobilize all its resources on an emergency basis to combat the epidemic.

This burgeoning death rate due to narcotics coupled with the fact that addiction brings with it muggings, armed robberies, burglaries and other varieties of theft by which the addict pays for his drugs, effectively prevents anyone in the ghetto from leading a decent life. It explains why the rate of crime per 100,000 population in New York City is twice the national average, and the fact that approximately 50% of the street crimes are attributable to narcotics addicts.

Narcotics addiction is thus the central problem in the ghetto. It causes the conditions that have torn the very fabric of society apart for the ghetto resident and it is organized crime which is in a large part responsible for the situation while profiting from it to the tune of millions of dollars annually.

The President's Commission estimated that the nationwide gross heroin trade amounts to $350,000,000 annually, of which $21,000,000 constitutes profits to the importer and the distributor. This profit goes directly to organized crime groups in those few cities in which most heroin consumption occurs. This Committee surveyed the economics of the heroin traffic in just three ghetto areas and found the President's Commission's estimates were on the conservative side. The Committee took the hard data released in the Central Narcotics Register of the New York City Board of Health and applied to it certain known rates of expenditure by the average addict. For example, taking the Narcotics Register's figure for the number of known addicts under 21 years of age located within the three ghetto communities studied (Central Harlem, South Bronx and Bedford-Stuyvesant), and estimating rather conservatively that each spends $25 per day to purchase the narcotics required to satisfy his habit, the result is a total annual expenditure of over $22,000,000 on heroin by hardcore addicts under 21 years of age. Again taking the Narcotics Register's figures for identified adult heroin addicts located in the ghetto area and estimating that each adult spent $25 a day on narcotics to supply his habit, the Committee estimated that adult heroin addicts in the three ghetto areas spent over $93,700,-000 annually on narcotics. These figures should again be increased by a factor of about 50%, since a $25 a day habit is a minimum habit. Thus, the gross revenue of the narcotics traffic in Central Harlem, South Bronx and Bedford-Stuyvesant at a conservative estimate, ranges from a minimum of $122,000,000 annually to $238,000,000 annually. . . .

In contrast, the amount of welfare monies annually funnelled into these same areas is $272,525,000. It can readily be seen that gross criminal revenues extracted from the ghetto by the traffic in narcotics comes to more than 50% of the government's welfare expenditures in the same area. No one can say what percentage of welfare expenditures is diverted to the narcotics traffic, yet no one can deny that welfare monies represent a substantial portion of the money spent for narcotics in New York.

These statistics tell only part of the story. Although it is impossible to estimate the amount of legitimate income used by drug addicts to finance their habits, it is clear that limited employment opportunities and the general unreliability of addicts would tend to minimize this source. The money used to purchase heroin is largely obtained through crimes committed primarily upon the ghetto resident. The addict, of necessity, must steal, rob, mug or burgle to obtain the large amounts of funds necessary to purchase heroin. That he is robbing from the needy is clear from the vast number of welfare and social security checks which are stolen and cashed each month. Stolen property, other than negotiable instruments, is resold in the ghetto at an 80% discount, the standard resale of stolen property. Thus, the total value of the property stolen from the ghetto residents by the narcotic addict could be double or triple the amount actually spent on heroin. Indeed some authorities estimate it to be as high as several billion dollars. The narcotics traffic has thus engendered a huge and thriving black market to supply the cash requirements of the narcotics traffic. In addition to theft offenses a leading source of income for addicts is the sale of narcotics to others —indeed witnesses suggested that this is one of the most likely sources and the one most able to raise the kind of money needed to support habits costing $25 or more per day.

What effect do these criminal activities have on living conditions in the ghetto? Testimony before the Committee revealed that the ghetto resident has become a prisoner in his own home, where he must remain in order to protect whatever worldly possessions he has from theft by the addict-burglar. Similarly, the welfare recipient, whose property usually consists solely of his clothing and home furnishings, fears to leave his residence to undertake job training or rehabilitation programs because he knows that any prolonged absence from his home inevitably means it will be burglarized and looted. The ghetto resident cannot venture out at night except on emergency errands lest he be victimized by the army of addicts made desperate by the necessity to obtain funds to purchase the next "fix" before withdrawal sets in. Doctors and dentists fear to practice in the ghetto since they become a prime target of the narcotics addict seeking either drugs or the money to purchase them. The absence of the private practitioner in the ghetto means that medical attention must be obtained from a municipal hospital which is inevitably overwhelmed at having to meet the medical needs of so many ghetto residents. The hospital in the ghetto is also plagued by an inability to hire nurses or other personnel for the evening shifts since they fear the risks entailed in the trip between the hospital and their homes.

This Committee has concluded that no meaningful progress can be made in the anti-poverty effort, or in the general effort to improve conditions in the ghetto, unless the narcotics traffic is suppressed. Indeed, a solution to the narcotics problem is a prerequisite to meaningful reforms in the welfare and anti-poverty areas. Achievement of these purposes, however, necessarily requires the destruction of the organized criminal operation that imports and distributes the narcotics to the ghetto resident.

Organized Crime and the Policy Racket

The largest source of cash for organized crime in the ghetto is gambling in the form of "policy" or "numbers." With the exception of some small independent operations, the numbers racket is monopolized by organized crime, which skims off huge profits from it. The overriding evil of the numbers racket is, however, the operating capital it provides organized crime for exploitive use in other illicit enterprises. Law enforcement intelligence personnel have established that the profits accruing to organized crime from the policy racket are reinvested, in large part, to finance the importation of narcotics from abroad and loansharking operations.

Committee investigators have established a fairly firm basis for estimating the illegal income attributable to policy or numbers. It was found that approximately 75% of the adult population in the ghetto wager an average of $3 per week on policy. Based on 1969 population figures for the three ghetto areas, it can be estimated that the policy racket take is in excess of $105,000,000 annually in Central Harlem, South Bronx and Bedford-Stuyvesant combined.

The Committee's investigators have also identified six separate policy banks operating in Central Harlem. Four are controlled by members of the Genovese family: one each by Raymond (Spic Raymond) Marquez and Louis (Louis the Gimp) Avitable and two by Anthony (Fat Tony) Salerno. The two other banks are controlled by Negro policy bankers. The South Bronx has five separate policy banks operating in its area, all of which are controlled by the Genovese family. The Bedford-Stuyvesant area has nine policy banks operating within its borders, two of which are controlled by the Colombo family, one by the Genovese family, and two each controlled by three different independent operators.

The policy operation could not function in the ghetto without official tolerance induced by corruption. Every major study of organized crime from the Kefauver investigation, through the investigations by the McClellan Committee, to the most recent pronouncement of the President's Commission on Crime has concluded that organized crime and its illegal gambling operations could not flourish without official corruption. The fuel for such corruption readily comes from the gambling revenue itself. Testimony at hearings before this Committee clearly reveals that the ghetto residents are perfectly aware of the corrupt relationship between the policy racketeers and certain elements in the Police Department, and, for this reason, have a deep cynicism concerning the integrity of the police in maintaining law and order in the community. On the other hand, the same witnesses that decried this corruption provided an insight into the pervasive character of numbers gambling in the ghetto. In the midst of such squalor and deprivation, a ghetto resident's hope is always raised by the prospect of an immediate and grand scale winning which his small money bet affords. Indeed among a large segment of the community, numbers gambling is viewed as a socially acceptable practice, or at least as an inevitable phenomenon.

Organized Crime and Loansharking in the Ghetto

Another of the large scale criminal operations conducted by organized crime in the ghetto is loansharking. The President's Commission estimated loansharking to be the second largest source of revenue for organized crime. Certainly the profit margins on loansharking are higher than those of the gambling operation. Although exact estimates in this area are impossible, the President's Commission has estimated that loansharking takes over a billion dollars a year from America's poor.

The welfare recipient cannot borrow from a bank or other lending institution. If his funds run out before the receipt of the welfare payment, there is no one to turn to but the loansharks. The exorbitant interest charged by these criminals comes out of the next check, which means that the already low standard of living of the welfare recipient must be cut back further to meet the interest payment owed to the loanshark. If the welfare recipient falls too far behind in his payments, he has no alternative but to engage in crime to obtain the funds to pay off the loansharks. For a woman, this means shoplifting or prostitution. For a man, it means any one of a number of criminal activities, such as mugging, burglary or armed robbery. One of the inherent difficulties which confronts law enforcement in this area is the reluctance of loanshark victims to report the usurious transactions or to identify the criminal lenders. This can be attributed partly to ignorance of the illegality of usurious loans, but primarily to the borrower's realistic fear that if one member of the organized crime family does not "get him" another one surely will.

The Message from the Ghetto

A part of this report is a digest of the testimony taken by this Committee in three days of hearings in Central Harlem on February 20, 27 and 28, 1969. . . . Twenty-three witnesses, including several well known community leaders, stated in stark and dramatic terms the social and personal implications inherent in the cold statistics recounted in the foregoing part of this report. The witnesses from Central Harlem unanimously condemned the appalling conditions that prevail in their community and which are attributable to organized crime's operations. There is no reason to doubt that the witnesses have accurately and trenchantly reflected the distress of the ghetto resident. The inescapable conclusion from the three days of testimony taken by this Committee is that the citizens of Harlem believe they are under siege by the forces of organized crime and as citizens they angrily invoke their right to demand protection by their government. The following excerpts from the digest of testimony of these hearings will serve to exemplify the message from the ghetto.

Vincent Baker, Chairman of the Anti-Crime Committee of the New York City Branch of the National Association for the Advancement of Colored People, urged that all-out war be declared on crime. He stated that the crisis of public order in Harlem called for the emergency measures normally associated with wartime. He noted that his Committee had seriously considered recommending the quartering of units of the National Guard in Harlem to protect the residents against the criminals loose in that community. The witness declared that a reign of criminal terror prevailed in Harlem, and that the political leadership of the City had misread the attitudes of the Harlem community by equating the call for law and order with racism. The primary complaint of the Harlem community is not that the police over-react, but that the law is not being enforced either because of indifference or corruption, or because the police had been ordered to "take it easy."

Other witnesses, such as Rev. Oberiah Dempsey, Assemblyman Hulan Jack and State Sen. Basil Paterson, testified to the disintegration of community life because of the crime situation. They stated that more than 500 churches in Harlem have curtailed evening worship because of harassment of worshippers by narcotics addicts.

Drug stores throughout the Harlem community are also closing up because of the constant danger of armed robbery. Locked churches are victimized, items are even stolen from the altar. Since worshippers have been attacked on church steps, services have been curtailed. Because people fear to attend them at night, civic meetings have also suffered unless the topic of the meeting is crime (in which case the entire community turns out).

Witness after witness pointed to the alarming trend of narcotics addiction among adolescents and teenagers in Harlem. An official of the Youth Services Agency of the City stated their samplings indicated that 10% of Harlem youngsters between the ages of 16 and 21 are heroin users. A significant percentage of youngsters below the age of 16 are experimenting with heroin. Between 10% and 25% of youngsters below the age of 16 are also experimenting with marijuana.

James Bryant, who works in the Addicts Rehabilitation Center in central Harlem, testified that 13 to 15 year old addicts are the rule today rather than the exception. The drug situation in the high schools has become so serious that identified addicts are not permitted to return to public school but, instead, are tutored by volunteers. Ronald Dorsey, a community worker, testified that the heroin traffic has spread from the high schools and junior high schools into the elementary schools.

George Jackson, a 16 year old ex-heroin addict, stated he had become an addict at the age of 14 and had been "shooting" heroin during the hours he was in school. The narcotics traffic in Harlem is so open and notorious that on Jackson's block alone (114th Street) there were at least seven narcotics dealers. Howard Bennet, chairman of the Central Harlem Task Force, testified that there were more youngsters selling narcotics in Harlem than adults, which helps to explain the alarming growth of addiction among the under-21 age group. Reverend Dempsey warned that unless something is done immediately to halt

the traffic among children and teenagers, the present younger generation in Harlem may be doomed.

We cannot afford to ignore the human tragedy revealed in this
message from the ghetto. The warnings from the witnesses are fully
documented in available statistics, especially those of the City's Central
Narcotics Register. It should also be mentioned that there seemed to
be little community confidence in the ability of the State's civil commitment program to make a significant impact on the problem.

More ominously, too many witnesses in the course of these hearings
expressed the belief of the Harlem community that the police were
either passively tolerating the traffic in narcotics or actively cooperating
with the drug traffickers, or both. The digests of the testimony of Rev.
James A. Gusweiler, Vincent S. Baker, State Sen. Basil Paterson, Assemblyman Hulan Jack, Ralph Jackson and John Shabazz all reveal
claims that some police are taking bribes from the drug pushers. If
this represents the common attitude of the Harlem Community,
whether well founded or not, the fact that this attitude exists, represents a real crisis in police-community relations. If in the mind of the
community the police are associated with this condition either as being
tolerant of it or even profiting from it, the resultant distrust and hostility will have broad and deep effects: the community will no longer
support genuine police efforts to stem the drug traffic; police morale
and recruitment will be adversely affected; and a dissatisfied public
will not support the increased taxation necessary to improve police
equipment and salaries. As things now stand, much of Harlem considers the police with distrust, as manifest in the fact that several witnesses at the Committee's hearings looked to the State Police or the
National Guard, rather than to the City's police, for the answer to the
narcotics problem.

An apparent ambivalence in the ghetto attitude toward the police
was observable throughout the testimony before the Committee. On
the one hand, the witnesses were demanding better law enforcement
from the police. Implicit in this demand is a confidence in the ability
of the police to perform their function of effectively and fairly preserving order in the best interests of the community. Yet, on the other
hand, these same witnesses denounced the police for insufficient or
inconsistent protection of the community, and especially for failing to
eradicate the narcotics trade in Harlem. Here the witnesses reflected
either a knowledge of, or belief in, evidence of police corruption, discriminatory law enforcement, or lack of essential concern by the police
for the protection of Harlem's law abiding citizens.

This apparent ambivalence can be reconciled, however. It can be fairly said that the witnesses are expressing confidence in the capacity of a police force, generally, to solve these problems (especially where the laws to be enforced are realistic) but that such capacity is not being demonstrated in Harlem. These witnesses conveyed the message that the Harlem community will fully support any serious concerted police effort directed at stemming the flood of narcotics in Harlem and at making the streets safe. If the police articulate this objective and demonstrate its importance in an actual and effective enforcement program, these witnesses insist that the responsible majority of Harlem citizens will give the police their fullest support.

Conclusion

The demonstrable consequences of organized criminal operations in the ghetto go well beyond mere statistics of gambling, narcotics, or loansharking. From the perspective of the ghetto resident, as revealed by the witnesses before this Committee, the true measure of the impact of organized crime in the ghetto is found in two factors: first, the prevailing fear that the street and home are unsafe due to the depredations of narcotics addicts (sustained by the organized-crime-controlled narcotics trade); second, the distrust and contempt for the police attributable to evidence of corruption and insufficient or discriminatory enforcement of the law.

From the perspective of a state concerned with the just maintenance of law and order in the context of socially healthy communities, the impact of organized crime is likewise clear—narcotics-related crimes are in epidemic proportions; policy and numbers gambling tacitly approved by the community is controlled by organized crime and is drawing revenue from the community to finance further criminal activity; and loansharks prey on hapless indigents and other ghetto residents to compound the crime of usury by forcing its victims into further socially debilitating crimes.

THE CONSEQUENCES
OF CORRUPTION

John A. Gardiner

If you could ever get the opinion-makers—the newspapers and the ministers—off the corruption issue, you might have a civilized election in this town.

—A former Wincanton mayor, 1966

Crime has not only corrupted American government for its own purposes; it has also tended to immobilize government for many other purposes. The problems of the American city . . . are not going to be solved by the dimwits whose campaigns are financed by the syndicates. And is there any reason to suppose that the leaders of organized crime are incapable of perceiving that they will be better off if American municipal government remains fragmented, unco-ordinated, and in the hands, as much as possible, of incompetents?

—Daniel Patrick Moynihan, 1961

The corruption which has been documented in the preceding chapters* led to the violation of many city, state, and national laws. Laws forbidding gambling and prostitution were ignored, city contracts and licenses were awarded to those willing to pay the highest bribes, city jobs went only to those who kicked back part of their salaries, and so forth. Were there *other* consequences of this corruption? Apart from the way in which criminal laws and codes of official conduct are administered, does it make any difference whether a government acts honestly or corruptly? Students of other forms of corruption have concluded that it has a number of beneficial, if indirect, effects: it can serve to permit the coexistence of both gambling and moralistic legislation; to overcome the fragmentation of formal authority in government; and to meet the welfare and socialization needs of

From Chapter Six of *The Politics of Corruption: Organized Crime in an American City,* by John A. Gardiner, © 1970 by Russell Sage Foundation, New York. Pp.70–90, 91–92. Some footnotes deleted.

* Editors' Note: Chapter numbers refer to *The Politics of Corruption.*

immigrants in an alien environment. In modernizing areas, corruption has been viewed as a catalyst for inclining political leaders toward economic development, mobilizing the bureaucracy to aid entrepreneurs, and persuading traditional elites to accept economic and social change. Did Wincanton's corruption have similarly beneficial side effects? In the following pages, an attempt will be made to identify both the individuals and organizations immediately affected by corruption, and the long-range impact which it has had upon governmental policies and political processes in Wincanton. Showing causal relationships will be almost impossible (simply to establish that a corrupt city had incompetent leaders or low expenditures does not *prove* that they are related or that one caused the other), but an exploration of these relationships may aid in evaluating the corruption which Wincanton has known.

The Beneficiaries of Nonenforcement of Gambling Laws

I feel as though I am sending Santa Claus to jail. Although this man dealt in gambling devices, it appears that he is a religious man having no bad habits and is an unmeasurably charitable man.
— A federal judge sentencing slot-machine distributor Klaus Braun to jail in 1948

When I was a kid, the man in the corner grocery wrote numbers. His salary was about $20 a week and he made $25 more on book.
— A candidate for the Wincanton City Council, 1963

Who benefited when the Wincanton police ignored organized gambling? Irv Stern, of course, made a great deal of money from his gambling operations; federal agents believe that he deposited several millions of dollars in numbered Swiss bank accounts. Wincantonites also believe that a number of local politicians have been well rewarded while in office—that Gene Donnelly and Bob Walasek, each of whom was raised in the slums of Wincanton, collected at least a quarter of a million dollars in payoffs from Stern. (Walasek, however, claimed to be penniless when ordered to pay a fine in 1964.) Apart from the gamblers and politicians and the occasional bettor who beat the odds and won more than he lost, the major beneficiaries of gambling were the organizations which relied upon slot machines and bingo to finance their activities, the businesses which accepted bets as a sideline, and the hotels, bars, and restaurants which catered to the gambling trade. Few estimates of their numbers are available (a very rough guess might be that several hundred persons operated the various forms of gambling, five to ten thousand people gambled in one way or another, and a hundred or so profited from the existence of gambling without being directly involved in it), but the following illustrations may be suggestive.

The social life of Wincanton is organized around clubs, lodges, and other voluntary associations. Labor unions have union halls; businessmen have luncheon groups, country clubs, and service organizations such as Rotary, Kiwanis, the Lions, etc. Each nationality group has its own meetinghouse—the Ancient Order of Hibernians, the Liederkranz, the Colored Political Club, the Cristoforo Colombo Society, etc. In each neighborhood, a P.T.A.-type group is organized around the local playground. Each fire hall is the nightly gathering place of a volunteer firemen's association. Each church has the usual assortment of men's, women's, and children's groups. For many of those organizations, gambling was an indispensable means of attracting members and paying bills; thriving when the police tolerated gambling, some organizations were forced to close their doors following periodic crackdowns.

The interest which these organizations had in police enforcement policies was revealed during a conflict over slot machines in the late 1940s. A newly elected district attorney announced on taking office that slot machines were illegal. With the help of the state police and county detectives, he began to seize slot machines in the rural parts of Alsace County. Following local custom, however, he turned to the mayor and city police to act against slot machines within Wincanton city limits. Mayor Jim Watts took a halfway position; while ordering the police to confiscate any slot machines found in public places, he declared that the powers of the city police did not extend to gambling in "private clubs conducted for the benefit of their own members."

Watts' announcement produced a mixed reaction. The clubs, of course, were overjoyed; the slot machines were vital money-makers for clubs with few members or members who were unwilling to pay high annual dues. Indeed, the slot machines had frequently led to the clubs' coming into existence. Stern and Braun often agreed to finance the purchase or remodeling of club buildings simply in return for freedom to install slot machines in them. The privileged status conferred on the clubs by the mayor's declaration of powerlessness was immediately protested by the clubs' competitors, the bars, restaurants, and hotels whose gambling apparatus had been removed pursuant to the district attorney's order. The Retail Liquor Dealers Association publicly complained that continued possession of slot machines was giving the private clubs an unfair advantage in attracting patrons. Under this pressure, the mayor yielded, announcing that police would also act against machines found in private clubs; within a few days, all machines in the city had gone into storage.

Slot machines were unavailable in Wincanton for eleven weeks. In its first issue in 1949, however, the Wincanton *Gazette* proclaimed:

> Alsace County greeted 1949 with the ringing of bells . . . and lemons and cherries and oranges and plums. Old Father Time hardly had his bags packed last Friday night when clubs throughout the city and county were reported oiling their uncovered slot machines in preparation for a Merry New Year's Eve business.

From early 1949 until federal investigators came into town two years later, five hundred slot machines continued to enrich both the clubs and Stern and Braun. The basis for the mayor's new-found tolerance of machines in the private clubs remained a mystery for only a short time, however. Shortly after the machines reappeared, the president of the Volunteer Firemen's Association reported that fire halls had been contacted by representatives of Klaus Braun's syndicate. Fire halls which agreed to purchase $1.25 "Christmas Tree Stamps" for each punchboard lottery, and to contribute 25 percent of their slot-machine revenues to the syndicate, would be guaranteed protection from police harassment. (The fire halls, it might be noted, generally owned their own machines; those clubs which leased machines from Stern or Braun received protection as part of their "lease.") The firemen refused, so far as is known, to buy the stamps or pay for protection, but their immunity continued. While state police and county detectives continued to seize slot machines found in rural areas of the county, the mayor declared that city police would only act against private clubs if citizens complained; he then proceeded to ignore the complaints of the Retail Liquor Dealers Association. One persistent complainant, a restaurant owner active in Republican politics, was harassed by city health inspectors and obscene telephone calls until he threatened to call the newspapers.

The official policy of nonenforcement of gambling laws was thus profitable to many ethnic, political, and firemen's organizations. While seldom displaying slot machines, other city groups took advantage of police leniency, probably without paying for protection. Local playground associations, for example, sponsored bingo games to pay for equipment, Little League uniforms, and so forth, while businessmen used lotteries to advertise "Downtown Wincanton Days." Wincanton churches and charities also benefited, both directly and indirectly, from gambling. Like the other private groups, a number of these churches and charities sponsored bingo, lotteries, etc. In addition, leading gamblers and racketeers have been generous supporters of Wincanton charities. Klaus Braun literally gave away most of his gambling income, aiding churches, hospitals, and the underprivileged. Braun provided 7,000 Christmas turkeys for the poor in 1947, and frequently chartered buses to take slum children to ball games. Brauns' Prospect Mountain Park offered free rides and games for local children (while their parents were in other tents patronizing the slot machines). Irv Stern gave a $10,000 stained-glass window to his synagogue, and aided welfare groups and hospitals in Wincanton and other cities. (Since the residents of Wincanton refused to be treated in the room which Stern gave to Community Hospital, it is now used only for the storage of bandages.) When Stern came into federal court in 1961 to be sentenced on tax-evasion charges, he was given character references by Protestant, Catholic, and Jewish clergy, two hospitals, and a home for the aged. Critics charge that Stern never gave away a dime that wasn't well publicized; nevertheless, his contributions did benefit valued community institutions. (Lest this description be misleading, it should also be stressed that many ministers protested vehemently against gambling and corruption, leading reform movements and launching pulpit tirades against Stern, Walasek, *et al.*)

To conclude this discussion of the beneficiaries of nonenforcement of vice and gambling laws, there was a group of "fringe beneficiaries" whose *legitimate* business increased when vice and gambling laws were ignored by the Wincanton police. Many of the *providers* of gambling, of course, also had legitimate activities; "Mom and Pop" grocery stores often sold bread, milk, and cigarettes to men and women dropping off their bets, and clubs provided drinks and entertainment for their slot-machine and lottery patrons. Examples of *completely* legitimate fringe beneficiaries include the local bus company, which lost business when Mayor Whitton banned bingo in 1964, and the department stores whose gift certificates were awarded as bingo prizes. Several drugstores sold large quantities of cosmetics to local prostitutes. One hotel offered special weekend rates for the gamblers at the dice game, who would gamble at night and sleep during the daytime. Several landlords rented space to Stern for his bookie parlors and accounting offices. One landlord asked, worried that federal investigations might terminate a profitable arrangement, "Who else would pay $150 a month for that basement?" Being the center of gambling and prostitution for a wide area also meant increased business for the city's restaurants, bars, and theaters. One man declared that business at his Main Street restaurant was never as good as when gamblers and bingo players were flocking to the downtown area.

The Beneficiaries of Other Forms of Corruption

We decided to open a new branch of our bank, and needed a traffic light installed. The mayor suggested that the light would be approved more quickly if Architect X drew the plans. His fee was somewhat exorbitant, but we got the job done.—*A Wincanton bank official*

We've built municipal water and sewer systems all over the world, and had done a lot of work for Wincanton. When the time came to award the design contract for a new sewage disposal plant, however, the mayor said that Y would have to get a $10,000 "finders fee." We told him to go to hell. The mayor announced that our firm was "unqualified," and gave the contract to someone else.—*A Wincanton architectural engineer*

Chapter Three noted that toleration of gambling was only one of the forms of corruption practiced by Wincanton politicians, although it probably was the most frequent and rewarding. "Free-lance" corruption also had a number of beneficiaries, although it also produced a number of more directly injured "victims" than did the toleration of gambling. The persons affected by this corruption can be ranked in terms of the willingness with which they participated in the corruption and in terms of the illegality of the transaction (apart from the bribe involved). The most innocent were those who were asked to pay for city privileges to which they were legally entitled. Like the bank official quoted above, businessmen submitting routine applications for building permits often received hints from city officials that approval would come more quickly if the application was accompanied by a "political contribution" or if certain architects, contractors, or lawyers were to do the work. At times, as mentioned earlier, applying for a permit became a cat-and-mouse game, with the official waiting to see how much would be offered, and the applicant waiting to see if he could get his permit without paying for it. In one case uncovered by a reform district attorney, a desperate businessman paid $750 for a permit after his application had lain on an official's desk for three months. Other men, however, said that they received their permits simply by waiting or threatening to call the papers. Where time was important, however, many businessmen considered a $25 or $50 bribe the lesser of two evils.

A more typical participant in official corruption was less innocent, either personally initiating discussions of payoffs or else liberally inflating a contract price in order to cover the bribe. A few examples will suggest the extent to which this type of participant was actively involved in the process of corruption.

—In beginning negotiations for a city purchase of 1,500 parking meters in 1960, Mayor Walasek reminded the salesman that "it costs a lot of money to become a mayor. I'd like to get at least $12 per meter." Hardly shocked, the salesman responded with a counteroffer of $7.50. "I don't think I can get $12 out of my company. There isn't as much money in meters as there used to be." Irv Stern, fearing that Walasek would mess up everything, forced both men to agree to a bribe of $10 a meter. The obvious willingness of the salesman to pay off led a federal judge (trying Stern and Walasek on charges of extortion) to conclude that the salesman should have been on trial as well. "Those in business, the sanctimonious businessmen who pointed fingers of guilt at others, should have sentence imposed on them, and not walk out as free men," the judge said.

—A salesman of fire trucks was called into the mayor's office and asked if he wished to make a contribution to the Democratic Party. The salesman asked how much was expected. "Since the contract is for $80,000," the mayor was reported to have said, "I think $2,000 would be the right amount." After checking with his company, the salesman delivered $2,000 to a designated city councilman. Although no evidence was ever found that the money reached the Democratic Party treasury, a judge refused to conclude that extortion was involved; the salesman freely admitted that the only "threat" present was the loss of a sale if the money wasn't paid.

—A developer renting a large tract of land from the city sought to purchase it. City officials agreed on a sale price of $22,500, with a like amount being quietly distributed among the officials. A few years later, the land was resold for over $100,000.

—To secure a city contract involving an architect's fee of $225,000, one corporation presented a "finder's fee" of $10,700 to an associate of Bob Walasek and Irv Stern.

In all of these transactions, the city received an acceptable result (new parking meters or firetrucks, architect's drawings, etc.) at the cost of inflated prices covering the bribes and kickbacks. In a third set of cases, however, the beneficiaries of corruption secured favors of more questionable value. The operator of a burlesque show, for example, paid at least $25 per week to escape the demands of local clergymen that the show be closed under the state obscenity laws. One real estate developer secured a zoning variance to erect a high-rise apartment building in a single-family residential area, while another arranged for the construction of a shopping center in an area zoned for industrial uses; both men are believed to have paid off city officials before the variances were approved.

In comparison with the number of beneficiaries of nonenforcement of gambling laws, probably far fewer people benefited from the other forms of corruption taking place in Wincanton, and even within the city's business community there was an uneven distribution of profit from official corruption. For some businessmen, corruption presented opportunities to increase sales and profits. If minor building-code violations could be overlooked, houses and office buildings could be erected more cheaply. Zoning variances, secured for a price, opened up new areas in which developers could build. In selling to the city, businessmen could increase profits either by selling inferior goods or by charging high prices on standard goods when bidding was rigged or avoided.

Finally, corruptible officials could aid profits simply by speeding up decisions on city contracts, or by forcing rapid turnover of city-owned curb space through either "10-minute parking" signs or strict enforcement of parking laws. (Owners of *large* stores, however, sought to maximize profits by asking the police to *ignore* parking violations, feeling that customers who worried about their meters would be less likely to stay and buy.)

While corruption aided some businessmen, many Wincanton businessmen were injured by the Stern-Donnelly-Walasek method of operations and fought vigorously against it. Most leaders of the Wincanton business community—bankers, industrialists, the Chamber of Commerce, etc.—fought Walasek and Stern, refusing to kick back on anything, and regularly called upon state and federal agencies to investigate local corruption. In fact, official corruption affected businesses in different ways. Businesses whose markets lay primarily outside the city usually had only to fear that the mayor might force them to pay for building permits. Companies dealing with City Hall, however, were exposed to every extortionate demand that the mayor might impose; agencies usually able to underbid their competitors were ignored if they refused to abide by the unofficial "conditions" added to contracts. Businesses with a local clientele but no government contracts were in an intermediate position, both in terms of their freedom to act against the system and in terms of the impact which it had upon them. Like the others, they suffered when forced to pay for permits or variances. Legitimate businesses, such as liquor stores, taverns, and restaurants, whose functions paralleled those of the clubs, lost revenue when the clubs were permitted to have gambling and slot machines. Those businesses, such as banks, whose success depended upon community growth suffered when the community's reputation for corruption and gambling drove away potential investors and developers. (Interestingly, businessmen disagree as to whether it is the reputation for corruption or for gambling which discourages new industry. Several Wincanton bankers stated that no investor would run the risk of having to bribe officials to have building plans approved, permits issued, and so forth. One architect, however, argued that businessmen *assume* municipal corruption, but won't move into a "sin town"—their employees will not want to raise children in such surroundings.)

A final aspect of gambling and corruption seems trivial in comparison with the factors already mentioned, but it was cited by most of the business leaders interviewed. Simply stated, it was embarrassing to have one's home town known throughout the country for its vice and corruption. "I'd go to a convention on the West Coast," one manufacturer recalled, "and everyone I'd meet would say 'You're from Wincanton? Boy, have I heard stories about that place!' I would try to talk about textiles or opportunities for industrial development, but they'd keep asking about the girls and the gambling." A housewife in her fifties recalled, "Things were so bad [under Mayor Walasek] that you even hated to tell people where you were from. Stern and Walasek gave us a bad reputation." Another housewife apologized after detailing to an interviewer the history of local corruption. "Ain't it awful the way we talk about our city? But honest to God, people move away from here and are ashamed to tell where they are from."

The Indirect Consequences of Corruption

For each of the individuals and organizations discussed thus far, corruption has had an immediate and tangible meaning—"This city contract was won (or lost) because of a bribe," "One-half of our club's revenue came from slot machines or bingo," "I had to pay $25 to get my building permit," and so forth. It is also likely, although the evidence is less clear, that Wincanton's long history of corruption has affected more basic characteristics of the Wincanton political system—the recruitment of city officials and employees, the policies followed by the city government, and the attitudes of city residents. Consideration of these long-range consequences of corruption, however, will require an expansion of the terms on which corruption is evaluated. Even if it is felt that the *short-term* benefits of corruption (satisfying the desires of those who wish to gamble or visit prostitutes, adding to the revenues of stores and restaurants, making possible the survival of marginal businesses and social clubs, and so forth) outweigh the costs (law violations, uneconomic use of funds by gamblers or by the city to cover the cost of payoffs, prolonged survival of obsolete businesses such as "Mom and Pop" stores, etc.), it must be asked whether the short-term net benefits of corruption outweigh its long-range costs. Answers to this question require a number of assumptions as to what recruitment, governmental programs, and citizen attitudes *should* be, but it would appear that Moynihan is correct in asserting that corruption and organized crime can immobilize government far beyond issues of law enforcement.

The process of political recruitment has been affected by corruption in many ways. While there have been surprisingly few charges of election fraud in Wincanton, perhaps because of the use of voting machines and the supervision of elections by county judges, syndicate money has frequently affected elections by giving some candidates the opportunity to "treat" supporters in the neighborhood clubs (see Chapter Two)* and to buy radio and television time during campaigns. Syndicate money and the patronage available at City Hall also made it possible to reward faithful party workers after the campaign was over. Over the years, corruption (or the *issue* of corruption) probably has affected both the type of men who have sought public office and the platforms on which they have run. Simply stated, the history of corruption in Wincanton City Hall has dissuaded competent and energetic men from running for office or working for the city. With the exception of one Socialist mayor during the 1930s, Wincantonites feel that most of their city officials have been of mediocre ability, whether they were honest or corrupt; a few have lived up to Moynihan's definition of "dimwits." A few innovative civil servants (particularly in the fields of planning and urban renewal) have been

---

* Editors' Note: Chapter and table numbers refer to *The Politics of Corruption.*

brought in from other cities, but low salaries and the general practice of rewarding political supporters has meant that there are few rewards for city employees who excel or innovate; it is assumed that every new administration will reorganize city departments to reward their friends. Thus Mayor Walasek's shuffling of the police department after he took office was unusual only in that some new officials had to pay for their jobs, not in the extent of reorganization or the demotion of incumbent department leaders.

This explanation of official mediocrity should not be carried too far, of course, since many factors besides corruption would tend to discourage competent leaders from seeking local office. Salaries have been low (the mayor received $9,500 when this study was conducted, the councilmen $8,500), the commission form of government has required the mayor to share power with councilmen who have almost total autonomy in operating their own departments, and city positions have seldom proved stepping-stones to higher office (since 1945, only Mayor Donnelly was able to win an election—to the state legislature—after serving as mayor). Given the undesirability of the office, it is perhaps not too surprising that weak or temptable men have constituted the majority of local office-seekers, but the tainted image of City Hall has not aided in bringing forth more capable men.

Reinforcing the low caliber of city officials in immobilizing the Wincanton government has been the impact of corruption on the content of political debate and governmental programs. Since the major variation among Wincanton officials has been whether they were honest or corrupt, not whether they responded significantly to urban problems, the issue of corruption has followed a Gresham's Law, driving other issues out of electoral discussion. Should Democratic candidates try to shift the subject to other issues, the Republicans and the Republican-oriented newspapers drag out the history of Democratic thievery and obscure Democratic officials' performances in other areas. While no one can be sure that Wincanton voters would have supported more issue-oriented candidates if they had not been desensitized by forty years of corruption, the former mayor quoted at the beginning of this chapter is probably correct in stating that the issue of corruption has made it impossible to hold "a civilized election" in Wincanton. As James Q. Wilson has noted with reference to official corruption in New York City, "Whatever was good or bad about the official—however competent or incompetent he had been in the conduct of public affairs, however profound or superficial in the analysis of the city's problems—all that was in large measure obscured by the fact, real or imagined, that public power had been used for private purposes."[1]

The same problem of "which comes first" limits analysis of the impact of corruption on the programs which have been adopted by the Wincanton government. In Tables 2.1 and 2.2, it was seen that Wincanton consistently taxes and spends less than other cities with similar social and economic characteristics, ranking *last* in the state in the average ratio of observed to estimated performance on taxation and expenditure policies. Many other factors, of course, have contributed to the depressed level of these policies. The fragmentation of the city's governmental structure and political processes has tended to reinforce the status quo and retard movements for change, and since most of the service-demanding upper-middle classes live in the suburbs, Wincanton may in fact have fewer people who demand a high level of public services than similar cities have. But just as corruption may have made the voters suspicious of candidates who promise new programs, may it not also have reduced popular willingness to support new programs through higher taxes? Many people feel that a city-wide referendum in 1962 to establish a council-manager form of government (which lost by a margin of *six* votes!) was defeated because of fears that a corrupt politician would be given the powerful position of city manager, and thus have greater opportunity to do harm (even though reformers had hoped the plan would *reduce* corruption). It is impossible to say whether Wincanton would have had more expansive and expensive programs if its officials had not been corrupt, but the data in Tables 2.1 and 2.2 leave open the possibility that corruption has reduced the capacity of the government to act on basic revenue and expenditure problems.

Why? The most enduring and damaging consequence of political corruption has been its weakening of public support for local government. It is difficult to make reliable comparisons with other cities, but responses from the 1966 survey suggest that the residents of Wincanton have little interest in local politics, feel their government has done a poor job, and are suspicious of local politicians and officials. The lack of interest in local affairs is suggested by responses to a question in the 1966 survey. When asked about "local politics, the things that the city government does here in Wincanton," only 9 percent said that they were "extremely interested" in local politics; 13 percent were quite in-

1. James Q. Wilson, "Corruption Is Not Always Scandalous," *New York Times Magazine,* April 28, 1968.

terested," 40 percent "moderately interested," and 38 percent said that they were "not much interested at all." Only 30 percent thought that the reform government of Ed Whitton was doing a "good" job, 49 percent thought it was "average," and the rest thought it was "poor" or didn't know.

Other questions in the 1966 survey indicate that Wincantonites are rather cynical about politics and politicians. Forty-four percent of the 180 respondents agreed with the statement that "Most politicians in Wincanton take their orders from a few big men behind the scenes whom the public never really knows" (69 percent of these cited racketeers as the "big men"; 22 percent cited businessmen), 32 percent were undecided, and 21 percent disagreed. They had less cabalistic views of state and national politics: only 26 percent thought "this kind of thing" happened in the state capitol, and 33 percent thought it happened in Washington. Politicians were held in low esteem. Fifty-two percent of the respondents disagreed with the statement, "After politicians are elected to office in Wincanton, they usually keep their promises"; 58 percent felt that "Politicians spend most of their time getting reelected or reappointed." Similar attitudes appeared in other responses. One manufacturer assumed that "the politicians in other cities are better—more aggressive and honest—and want to do more for the people of the city," while a young housewife thought that other cities might have "an idealism that I don't think we have here." A high school teacher added, "There was the crime problem here—that's all people thought about. They were suspicious of the mayor, the district attorney—that was always on the minds of the people." Finally, one young housewife, a newcomer to the city, added, "Where I come from, no politician has ever gone to jail, we've had no madames; somehow they don't quite know what they're doing here. I'm so disgusted with this city and its politics that I don't think I'll ever register or vote."

✿　✿　✿

Conclusions

What difference has it made that Wincanton has been corrupt for most of the last fifty years? On the positive side, it must be admitted that illegal gambling kept alive many private clubs and social organizations, and supplemented the income of a number of marginal shopkeepers. Short-term costs of illegal gambling and corruption include the law violations themselves (if the act of gambling is regarded as a cost), inflated prices paid on city contracts, bribes paid by businessmen to secure legitimate services, and so forth. The long-range, less measurable costs of corruption have included a loss of trust in politicians and respect for the performance of local government, leading to the recruitment of less competent officials and the depression of most municipal revenue and expenditure policies.

Sixty-five years ago, Henry Jones Ford argued that

> It is better that government and social activity should go on in any way than that they should not go on at all. Slackness and decay are more dangerous to a nation than corruption. . . . The graft system is bad, but it is better for a city government to lend itself to the forces of progress even through corrupt inducements than to toss the management of affairs out upon the goose-common of ignorance and incapacity, however honest. Reform which arrests the progress of the community will not be tolerated long by an American city.

True enough. The reformers who have put an end to law-enforcement corruption in Wincanton have generally contributed little else to "the progress of the community." One minister in Wincanton stated the problem neatly: "The Democratic Party often furnishes more creative leadership than the Republican Party does. The housing authority was started by them, and the downtown parking problem was solved, but they were corrupt. The most important thing the Republicans have done is to furnish honest government." But in the long run, the corrupters and corruptees— the Irv Sterns, Gene Donnellys, and Bob Walaseks—have retarded progress more than they have assisted it. The wide-open gambling and the free-lance corruption of the Donnellys and Walaseks have made it harder, not easier, to recruit new industries and investors to replace the declining or departing corporations which built the city at the turn of the century. Progress-oriented officials *could* have used corruption to persuade city councilmen, zoning officials, etc., to acquiesce in projects which might rejuvenate the city, but the more typical pattern has been a conspiratorial sharing of graft for its own sake. Since the areas of Wincanton, as in other metropolitan areas, which are most appealing to industrial developers are the undeveloped suburbs and farmlands, not the decayed, congested, and fragmented parcels of the central city, official corruption has reinforced investors' decisions not to build within city limits. More importantly, as argued by Moynihan earlier, corruption by organized crime has staffed Wincanton City Hall with a series of "incompetents" and "dimwits," men with neither the leadership ability nor the inclination to solve the city's problems of decline and decay. The fact that laws against gambling were not enforced was therefore one of the least significant consequences of corruption; corruption has immobilized the Wincanton political system for other purposes as well.

MUNICIPAL CORRUPTION
Henry Jones Ford

This is a work of a kind that was abundant in England during the eighteenth century but is now extinct there, while it flourishes in this country. Mental growths are no exception to the general laws of growth as regards distribution of species in time and space. Dying out in one region, a species may in another region find favoring conditions and perpetuate the type. In many respects the political ideas of our own times in this country reproduce species which belong to England's past. Mr. Steffens's work belongs to the same class as Burgh's *Political Disquisitions* published in 1774, Browne's *Estimate of the Manners and Principles of the Times* published in 1757, and innumerable tracts and essays now sunk into oblivion.

Mr. Steffens says of the articles collected in his book: "They were written for a purpose, they were published serially with a purpose, and they are reprinted now together to further the same purpose, which was—and is—to sound for the civic pride of an apparently shameless citizenship." Burgh said of his work that it was "calculated to draw the timely attention of government and people to a due consideration of the necessity and the means of reforming those errors, defects and abuses; of restoring the constitution and saving the state." Mr. Steffens

Originally published as Henry Jones Ford, "Municipal Corruption: Review of Lincoln Steffens. *The Shame of the Cities.*" Reprinted with permission from the *Political Science Quarterly*, 19 (December 1904), pp. 673–686. All footnotes deleted.

puts the blame for misgovernment upon the apathy of American character. He says:

> We are responsible, not our leaders, since we follow them. We let them divert our loyalty from the United States to some "party"; we let them boss the party and turn our municipal democracies into autocracies and our republican nation into a plutocracy. We cheat our government and we let our leaders loot it, and we let them bribe and wheedle our sovereignty from us. . . . We break our own laws and rob our own government, the lady at the custom house, the lyncher with his rope, and the captain of industry with his bribe and his rebate. The spirit of graft and of lawlessness is the American spirit.

In the same style Browne argued that virtue was rotting out of the English stock from the development of a sordid commercialism which was corroding all the moral elements which are the true foundations of national greatness. The thought flows in the same channels, the same ideals preside over opinion, and the resemblance extends even to details of suggestion.

> All we have to do [says Mr. Steffens] is to establish a steady demand for good government. The bosses have us split up into parties. . . . If we should leave parties to the politicians, and would not vote for the party, not even for men, but for the city and state and the nation, we should rule parties and cities and states and nation.

All this goes back to the time of Addison. In the *Spectator*, Number 125, Tuesday, July 24, 1711, he recommended the honest men should

> enter into an association for the support of one another against the endeavors of those whom they ought to look upon as their common enemies, whatsoever side they may belong to. Were there such an honest body of neutral forces, we should never see the worst of men in the great figures of life because they are useful to a party; nor the best unregarded because they are above practising those methods which would be grateful to their factions. We should then single every criminal out of the herd and hunt him down, however formidable and overgrown he might appear.

One difference should be noted. It relates to temperament. American self-confidence and optimism make a distinctive mark lacking in the extinct English literature of this species. Mr. Steffens ends his sermon by saying:

> We Americans may have failed. We may be mercenary and selfish. Democracy with us may be impossible and corruption inevitable; but these articles, if they have proved nothing else, have demonstrated with-

out doubt that we can stand the truth; that there is pride in the character of American citizenship; and that this pride may be a power in the
land.

This is a small set-off for such tremendous defects, but the tone of
sentiment is hopeful and buoyant as compared with the gloomy fore-
bodings which Burgh expressed in his closing reflections. He said:

> I see the once rich and populous cities of England in the same condi-
> tion as those of Spain; whole streets lying in rubbish, and the grass
> peeping up between the stones in those which continue still inhabited.
> I see the harbors empty, the warehouses shut up, and the shopkeepers
> playing draughts, for want of customers. I see our noble and spacious
> turnpike roads covered with thistles and other weeds, and scarce to be
> traced out. I see the studious men reading the "State of Britain," the
> magazines, the "Political Disquisitions," and the histories of the eigh-
> teenth century, and execrating the stupidity of their fathers, who, in
> spite of many faithful warnings given them, sat still, and suffered their
> country to be ruined by a set of wretches whom they could have
> crushed.

Such were the opinions of English reformers on the eve of the wonderful outburst of national energy which created the British empire and
brought to England wealth and prosperity beyond the imagination of
the wildest dreamer. And yet the forecast was not wholly mistaken, for
corruption and mismanagement lost England the American colonies
and brought her to deep abasement before the evil generated its cure
and the constitution was brought into accord with the needs of the
state. But historians of English political development point out that the
transformation was accomplished by the politicians themselves, without the adoption of the nostrums prescribed by the reformers and by
the very means which the reformers denounced as the essence of corruption. The reformers sought means of administration by the people;
the politicians denied them that, but unwittingly provided means of
control by the people through the formation of an agency of legislative
direction and management possessing plenary authority and hence
complete responsibility. This went to the root of the trouble; for in
retrospect it is plain enough that the systematic political corruption was
the result of political confusion. The doctrine of the separation of the
powers of government had obstructed the development of any such
agency or organ of sovereignty, clothed with power to provide a
proper division of the functions of government and to correlate the
exercise of those functions. The actual embodiment of sovereignty
which gradually took shape came not by deliberate intention but

through the constraint of hard necessity. The formation of the English parliamentary type of government may be described, in the terms of American politics, by saying that boss rule grew up inside the government until it acquired complete authority, thus bringing within reach of public opinion, through the suffrage, competent apparatus of control over the behavior of the government and creating conditions of political activity which gradually substituted the leader for the boss. The forces which sustained constitutional development did not proceed from reform agitation but from the phlegmatic common sense of the British people, more interested in results than solicitous about means and not prone to extravagant expectations from the every-day human nature which forms the stuff of politics. To take things as they are and make the best of them, to deal with situations as they arise by the means that are available, to endure what cannot be cured, to look upon the bright side and to cultivate a habit of cheerfulness—these are the traits of which sound politics are compounded and by which constitutional progress is sustained. National hypochondria is a worse evil than national corruption. Happily the American people are free from that at any rate; they are disgusted but not dismayed by the situation, and they have a deep conviction that they will eventually find ways and means of dealing with it.

Meanwhile it must be admitted that Mr. Steffens' book does not exaggerate the facts of the case. What he says about the condition of affairs in our cities is true, and much more might be said to the same purport. In this book he confines himself to municipal graft. The graft system extends to state administration also. The "organization" judge who "takes orders" is another feature of the graft system, the more dangerous since its virus penetrates the very marrow of our institutions. The facts with which Mr. Steffens deals are superficial symptoms. Hardly any disguise of them is attempted in the ordinary talk of local politicians. One of the first things which practical experience teaches is that the political ideals which receive literary expression have a closely limited range. One soon reaches strata of population in which they disappear and the relation of boss and client appears to be proper and natural. The connection between grafting politicians and their adherents is such that ability to levy blackmail inspires the same sort of respect and admiration which Rob Roy's followers felt for him in the times that provided a career for his peculiar talents. And as in Rob Roy's day, intimate knowledge finds in the type some hardy virtues. For one thing, politicians of this type do not indulge in cant. They are no more shamefaced in talking about their grafting exploits to an appreciative audience than a mediæval baron would have been in discussing the produce of his feudal fees and imposts. Mr. Steffens has really done no more than to put together material lying about loose upon the surface of municipal politics and give it effective presentation. The general truth of his statement of the case is indisputable. But the same might have been said of the exhibits of the eighteenth century English reformers; and yet the impression made by them of decay and disease in the body politic has since been shown to be erroneous. The three stout volumes of Burgh's *Disquisitions* are crammed with accounts of bribery and corruption, making a more startling showing than that made by Mr. Steffens because more inveterate and extensive. Every part of the structure of government was involved, so that there appeared to be no spot of soundness where reform might find a lodgement and a starting point. Probably in every period of political transition, when an old order is giving place to a new, evidence of corruption has confronted the scrutiny of moralists. The formation of modern nationality itself originally wore the appearance of corruption to observers prepossessed by the ideals of the past. History has vindicated feudalism as a reparative process in the organization of society after the collapse of imperial rule. May it not be that the new feudalism which has developed in American politics, despite all its gross exactions of tribute, is also a natural development from constitutional conditions? When the English reform excitement was at its height, Hume acutely remarked that "those who complain of corrupt and wicked ministers, and of the mischiefs they produce, do in fact most severely satirize the constitution of the state, for a good constitution would exclude or defeat the bad effects of a corrupt administration." This is no more than saying that if a business is well organized, employees cannot steal without being found out and dismissed; but propositions which are obvious as applied to ordinary business affairs do not appear to be readily apprehended in relation to the public business, although there is no essential difference. Hume's opinion that the corruption of his times was due to bad conditions rather than to bad men turned out to be correct. It may be worth while to examine our own situation from this point of view.

Mr. Steffens gives blunt expression to the opinion that the typical American business man is the great source of municipal corruption. "He is a self-righteous fraud, this big business man. He is the chief source of corruption, and it were a boon if he would neglect politics." In his article upon "Tweed Days in St. Louis," Mr. Steffens says that "when the leading men began to devour their own city, the herd rushed into the trough and fed also." But in the same article, referring to the traffic in franchises, he remarks: "Several companies which refused to pay blackmail had to leave." In other words, conditions existed to which business interests had to submit or perish. The case does not suggest business initiative of corruption, but rather compliance with it upon the universal principle that if you want to do business you must meet established conditions.

The nature of those conditions is not difficult to understand if one is able to separate fact from fiction with regard to the suffrage. From the psychological principle of association of ideas it is difficult to separate anything in thought from the use it has served, and such has been the instrumental value of the suffrage that intrinsic qualities are habitually attributed to it of the most absurd character. The increase of literacy and the spread of agencies for diffusing information have imparted to the body politic in modern times a nervous organization unknown before, developing a public consciousness which is the true source of what is known as the democratic movement. The suffrage has played a wonderful part in serving the activities of this public consciousness, but it is merely a vehicle of impulse and its utility is strictly regulated by conditions. Want or desire does not alter in moral quality nor gain in real authority because it happens to be expressed through the suffrage. The right of the majority is a useful fiction as a rule of practical convenience, but if it is manipulated so that it is a pernicious humbug the appearance of corruption may be a healthy manifestation. Instead of being the betrayal of democracy it may be diplomatic treatment of ochlocracy, restraining its dangerous tendencies and minimizing its mischiefs. If any of our large cities should be preserved like Pompeii to remote ages, the archæologists of that period, even without any historic record, would be bound to conclude that the society which evolved such structure was not deficient in great qualities of character; and if some of the lamentations of our reformers should be disinterred, telling how the men of affairs in our times corrupted the government in securing opportunities of enterprise, most assuredly those archæologists would rejoice that they had done so. It is better that government and social activity should go on in any way than that they should not go on at all. Slackness and decay are more dangerous to a nation than corruption.

In order to appreciate the functional office of the suffrage, a clear distinction must be drawn between administration and control. As an instrument of administration the suffrage, from the nature of things, is of very limited value. What can be more absurd than to think that the average citizen, who finds it hard to judge of the qualifications of a clerk or a salesman or to pick out a competent servant for his household, can by any sort of political hocus-pocus be invested with the ability to make a real choice of governors, mayors, judges, clerks of court, district attorneys, sheriffs, constables, tax-collectors, assessors and school commissioners? It is obvious, when one discards cant and exercises common sense, that government by direct administration of the people cannot really be carried on except in small communities, having common and well understood needs quite level with the ordinary capacity of citizenship. Communities in such a situation might just as well choose their officers by lot as by election, as was demonstrated in ancient Greek communities. But in any growing and progressive community diversity of needs and interest is inevitable and specialization of functions becomes necessary. Administration of the government by election then collapses, and the pretence that it is retained is constantly contradicted by actual facts. To assign to the people a power which they are naturally incapable of wielding is in effect to take it away from them. And this is the concise philosophy of boss rule. Genuine democratic government becomes impossible when the suffrage is applied to uses of which it is not capable; the practical result of the system of filling administrative posts by popular election is ochlocracy; and boss-rule is an expensive antidote for ochlocracy provided by the instinctive good sense of the American people. The system is as firmly based upon social necessities under existing conditions as the old feudalism which it resembles in its essential character. So long as those conditions, now inherent in our constitutional arrangements, continue to exist, so long will the boss system endure; and it will secure its revenues and emoluments, no matter how greatly they may be reprobated under the name of graft.

The general tendency of attacks made upon the system is to confirm it by aggravating the conditions which produce it. There are lower depths of corruption than those so far reached; and the movement for what is known as the direct nomination system is likely to sound those lower depths. That movement proposes to parallel the present system of filling a long list of administrative posts by popular election, by choosing party nominees also by popular election. It is seriously preached as a moral duty that the average citizen shall take the time to inform himself upon the personal qualifications of the various candidates, sometimes numbering fifty or more at a time. How does the obligation arise? If sociologists are not mistaken, the paramount duties of the individual man are grouped about the functions of subsistence and reproduction. Or, in every day speech, the chief duty of every man, as a member of society, is to earn his living and provide for his family. What political obligation can contravene this fundamental obligation? Are institutions made for the people or are the people made for the institutions? The latter appears to be the view of those laboring for direct administration, but no such palpable humbug can be foisted upon the people. The mass of the people will quite properly hold that they have more important things to attend to than electioneering. They will leave that to those to whom it offers rewards. In practice the system will mean the legal establishment of gang rule. The law may provide equal terms but cannot provide equal conditions. It is obvious that if there were rewards for all comers two miles up in the air, only those able to get balloons would share in the distribution. Any free-for-all terms which election laws may make as regards nomination to office will be just as closely restricted to class opportunity. The crowning touch of absurdity and immorality is put upon the whole scheme by the assertion, sometimes made, that after the selection of candidates has been put in the hands of the people there will be nobody to blame if results are bad, since the people are entitled to bad government if they want it. Here is, indeed, a doctrine such as Burke would have called "a digest and an institute of anarchy." What is government for but the maintenance of justice? No more besotted claim of prerogative was ever advanced than that any body of men, however high they may heap voting papers in ballot boxes, have a right to perpetrate iniquity. A constitution which produces bad government is a bad constitution, and nothing can give it moral sanction. The extent to which such anarchic ideas prevail among reformers is a far more serious symptom of moral degeneracy than grafting. It is an aphorism of practical politics, for which a biologic explanation might be given, that the offices must bear the cost of filling them. The more elective offices the greater the cost of the government. So long as the people tolerate the system they will have to bear the expense, call it graft or what you will.

These views may appear cynical since they antagonize the political mythology now in vogue. The thought of the day is indoctrinated with the idea that, back of the real people one sees in the shop, the factory or the office, there is an ideal citizenship of great purity and intelligence which if brought into political activity would establish the integrity of our institutions. This hallucination energizes the direct nomination movement. The underlying purpose is to open free channels for the activity of that ideal citizenship. It is also traceable in the absurd importance attached to studies in the technique of government. The assumed existence of that ideal citizenship implies the need of educating it in its duties. Hence great effort is being made to spread the study of civics. Even lads whose chief interest in life is centered in their tops and marbles are considered fit subjects for cramming with civics. In this direction, the great superstition that education can create character as well as train faculties goes to its most extravagant length. But if we regard statecraft as an activity analogous to other social activities, we shall not consider it an imputation upon the competency of the people to say that they are unfit to select their administrative officers, any more than it disparages the business capacity of the shareholders in a stock company to say that as a body they are unfit to appoint the clerks, book-keepers, salesmen and other administrative agents of the company. No sensible man will dispute the latter proposition. The essential principle of business control is universally recognized to be the delegation of administrative duties to a responsible management which, having full power, is subject to full responsibility for results. The notion that people should fit themselves for government by the study of civics is as if shareholders should qualify themselves in the practical management of the business of the corporation in order to secure proper administration of their interests. All that is necessary is an intelligent standard of requirement with a proper organization of responsibility, and the conduct of public business involves no different principles. Instead of the people themselves assuming the impossible task of looking after their servants and being continually fooled and bamboozled, they can turn that business over to a head servant and let him hire the rest and be responsible for them. We do this in the federal government but not in state or municipal government, and here the situation beautifully illustrates the Spanish proverb that the more you grasp the less you hold.

While the suffrage is incapable of serving as an organ of administration, it is capable of serving as an agency of control; but to be an efficient instrument of control, it must act upon some organ of government possessing administrative authority so complete that it may be held to full accountability for results. It is just because such an authority exists in Switzerland that that country is able to maintain such an advanced type of democratic government. Executive authority is so concentrated, and the connection between the executive and legislative departments is so simple, direct and immediate, that not even the mediation of party organization is needful to secure popular control over the conduct of the government. It is the principle of concentrated responsibility with which we are familiar as the basic principle of all business organization. In our governmental arrangements we have deviated from that principle by using the suffrage for administration. We have split up executive authority among a number of independent and coördinate administrative servants, who are practically irresponsible during their term of office if they are shrewd enough to keep out of the clutches of the criminal law. Thus they are put in a position to control the people instead of being controlled by the people. And in employing the suffrage in its proper use for representation, we make it ineffective by disconnecting legislation from administration. We elect a mayor to represent the community as a whole, but we do not give him the right nor do we make it his duty to present the public business to the legislative branch or to bring it to decision. That is left to the good-will and favor of the representatives of localities. Why should we wonder if they turn such irresponsible power to lucrative advantage?

The growth of an extra-legal system of connecting the disconnected functions of government for administrative purposes certainly entails corruption, but it does not follow that under such circumstances it is disadvantageous although founded upon venality. Our ordinary system of municipal government is so opposed to all sound principles of business organization that it is highly creditable to our practical capacity for government that we are able to work it at all. The graft system is bad, but it is better than the constitutional system as established by law. Mr. Steffens himself supplies evidence upon this point. In Chicago, after a reform movement had triumphed, he says:

> I found there was something the matter with the political machinery. There was the normal plan of government for a city, rings with bosses, and grafting interests behind. Philadelphia, Pittsburg, St. Louis, are all governed on such a plan. But in Chicago it didn't work. "Business" was at a stand-still and business was suffering. What was the matter?

Mr. Steffens goes on to say:

> I spent one whole forenoon calling on the presidents of banks, great business men, and financiers interested in public utility companies. . . . Those financial leaders of Chicago were "mad." All but one of them became so enraged as they talked that they could not behave decently. They rose up, purple in the face, and cursed reform. They said it hurt business; it had hurt the town. "Anarchy" they called it; "socialism." They named corporations that had left the city; they named others that had planned to come there and had gone elsewhere. They offered me facts and figures to prove that the city was damaged.

It is possible that these business and financial magnates knew what they were talking about, and that it is better for a city government to lend itself to the operation of the forces of progress even through corrupt inducements than to toss the management of affairs out upon the goose-common of ignorance and incompetency, however honest. Reform which arrests the progress of the community will not be tolerated long by an American city. On the other hand, it is quite possible that public men who have done great things by methods which have brought obloquy upon them may be esteemed when the results of their activity are appreciated. The people of Washington city now regard as a public benefactor a boss of this type and have recently erected a statue to his memory. Historians speak respectfully of one Julius Cæsar, who rose to eminence not upon the recognized lines of the constitution but as a popular boss. He is now credited with having done a great deal for his city and its dependent territories.

If these considerations are sound it may be fairly argued that they raise a greater mystery than they explain away. How is it possible to reconcile with the good sense and business capacity of the American people the growth of governmental arrangements so antagonistic to rational principles of organization? I confess that this phase of the problem has often puzzled me. Ordinary political theory is certainly oblivious of political fact to an astonishing degree. For instance, popular election of public treasurers is ordinarily justified upon the ground that it is necessary for the safety of the public funds to put them in the custody of an independent official not subject to removal by any other authority save the people themselves. The facts are all the other way. The public is not exposed to loss by the appointed treasurers of the United States, but it has lost millions through the elected treasurers of state and municipal governments. Although the growth of suretyship as a systematic branch of business enterprise is reducing risks of loss through absolute defalcation, yet those on the inside of affairs know that the manipulation of public funds in connection with elective fiduciary offices is an extensive department of the graft system, while this particular development of graft is unknown under the federal government. And yet those notorious facts do not perceptibly affect public adherence to the theory. At this very time the appointment of federal postmasters by popular election is receiving organized and influential support as a reform measure, despite every day experience of the fact that in practice this would mean irresponsible appointment by local bosses. A satirist might extract from American politics many fresh instances in confirmation of Robert South's opinion expressed nearly three centuries ago: "The generality of mankind is wholly and absolutely governed by words and names, without—nay, for the most part, even against—the knowledge men have of things. The multitude or common rout, like a drove of sheep or an herd of oxen, may be managed by any noise or cry which their drivers shall accustom them to."

But satire loses in comprehension what it gains in point. The persistence of ideas is an essential feature of the principle of social continuity which gives stability to political conditions. The ideas which have shaped our governmental arrangements are of the same class as those which were at the bottom of the past corruption of English politics. The derivation is distinctly traceable in our political origins. The check and balance theory of government which still controls our political thought was a colonial importation. Some perception of the true principles upon which democratic authority may be founded is shown in the Federalist; but at that stage of constitutional development exact appreciation of those principles was impossible. Popular government was still undeveloped, and the principle of the separation of powers was not construed in its true significance as relating to the functions of government, but as an apportionment of power among classes and interests so as to confine prerogative upon the one hand and popular influence upon the other. The chief concern of the framers of the constitution was to erect barriers against democratic tendencies, and they used the check and balance theory for that purpose. As democratic tendencies gathered strength, they also settled upon the check and balance theory·by natural momentum of thought, applying it to their own advantage. The class control which the gentry enjoyed under the closely restricted suffrage of the first period of the Republic was broken down by the extension of the suffrage and by the conversion of appointive posts into elective offices. The precautions taken by the framers of the constitution to secure executive unity proved so effectual that the latter movement was frustrated so far as the national government is concerned, but it has swept through state and municipal constitutions with increasing vigor until all the functions of government have been both disconnected and disintegrated in a way which leaves public opinion with no embodiment of authority capable of giving it complete representation or of assuming full responsibility for results. The stages of the process were not wholly disadvantageous so long as they were steps in the acquisition of power by the exponents of democratic tendencies, through partition of authority originally aristocratic in its tenure. But with the triumph of democratic principles of government, the partitions of power now useless as shelters from the class oppression against which they were reared, became obstructions which defeat democratic control by preventing its efficient exercise. No one now disputes popular sovereignty, but the people are in the position of the Grand Turk, who can cut off the head of an offender but whose affairs are so out of control that he is robbed right and left by his servants. What makes the situation more exasperating is that it is becoming a matter of common knowledge that democratic control is more complete and effective in some other countries than in our own; but the usual inference that we have somehow lost what our institutions were intended to secure is a fallacy. Our institutions have not lapsed from democracy into plutocracy; they never were democratic, and their present plutocratic character arises from the substitution of money power for the original aristocratic control. In other countries where democracy has arrived, it has not had to devise its constitutional apparatus but has had the far simpler and easier task of attaining control over that already in existence, whereas American democracy has never had a competent organ of authority. In developing such an organ we shall have to work out a constitutional application of the principle that division of the functions of government must be associated with administrative efficiency. The final result may be the formation of a new type of government. The exact form which it will assume it is now impossible to anticipate, but we can at least be certain from the very nature of sovereignty that there will be an organic connection of the executive and legislative functions. So long as the legal frame of government does not provide for that connection, it will take place outside of the legal frame; in which case we are in the habit of calling in the "machine" or the "ring" and of regarding it as a malignant excrescence upon constitutional government, whereas it is in fact the really constituted government, and the formal constitution is but a pretence and a sham.

The municipal situation is not really so desperate as one might think from a perusal of works like that of Mr. Steffens. Genuine improvement is going on through the undermining of our traditional constitutional principles under stress of practical necessity. In such charters as those of New York and Baltimore, the disconnection of the executive and legislative functions which is the root of ring rule is being practically overcome by the creation of boards of estimates and apportionment, which really unite executive and legislative powers in the same organ of government. Such appliances of government will gradually spread to other cities from the effect of example. In most cities, however, matters are likely to be worse before they are better; but even at the worst there are mitigating circumstances. Just as mediæval feudalism was a powerful agency in binding together the masses of the people into the organic union from which the modern state was evolved, so too our party feudalism performs a valuable office by the way it establishes connections of interest among the masses of the people. To view the case as a whole, we should contrast the marked European tendency towards disintegration of government through strife of classes and nationalities with the strong tendency shown in this country towards national integration of all elements of the population. Our despised politicians are probably to be credited with what we call the wonderful assimilating capacity of American institutions. They are perhaps managing our affairs better than we are able to judge. We certainly do not know how to manage the politicians, but that is a branch of knowledge which no people acquires save as the result of a long course of education in the school of experience. There is no royal road to learning even for the sovereign people of the United States.

SOME FUNCTIONS OF
THE POLITICAL MACHINE
Robert K. Merton

Without presuming to enter into the variations of detail marking different political machines—a Tweed, Vare, Crump, Flynn, Hague are by no means identical types of bosses—we can briefly examine the functions more or less common to the political machine, as a generic type of social organization. We neither attempt to itemize all the diverse functions of the political machine nor imply that all these functions are similarly fulfilled by each and every machine.

The key structural function of the Boss is to organize, centralize and maintain in good working condition "the scattered fragments of power" which are at present dispersed through our political organization. By this centralized organization of political power, the boss and his apparatus can satisfy the needs of diverse subgroups in the larger community which are not adequately satisfied by legally devised and culturally approved social structures.

Reprinted with permission of Macmillan Publishing Co., Inc. from *Social Theory and Social Structure* by Robert K. Merton, pp.72–82. © Copyright The Free Press, a Corporation 1957. Some footnotes deleted.

To understand the role of bossism and the machine, therefore, we must look at two types of sociological variables: (1) the *structural context* which makes it difficult, if not impossible, for morally approved structures to fulfill essential social functions, thus leaving the door open for political machines (or their structural equivalents) to fulfill these functions and (2) the subgroups whose distinctive needs are left unsatisfied, except for the latent functions which the machine in fact fulfills.[1]

Structural Context: The constitutional framework of American political organization specifically precludes the legal possibility of highly centralized power and, it has been noted, thus "discourages the growth of effective and responsible leadership. The framers of the Constitution, as Woodrow Wilson observed, set up the check and balance system 'to keep government at a sort of mechanical equipoise by means of a standing amicable contest among its several organic parts.' They distrusted power as dangerous to liberty: and therefore they spread it thin and erected barriers against its concentration." This dispersion of power is found not only at the national level but in local areas as well. "As a consequence," Sait goes on to observe, "when *the people or particular groups* among them demanded positive action, no one had adequate authority to act. The machine provided an antidote."[2]

The constitutional dispersion of power not only makes for difficulty of effective decision and action but when action does occur it is defined and hemmed in by legalistic considerations. In consequence, there developed "a much *more human system* of partisan government, whose chief object soon became the circumvention of government by law. . . . The lawlessness of the extra-official democracy was merely the counterpoise of the legalism of the official democracy. The lawyer having been permitted to subordinate democracy to the Law, the Boss had to be called in to extricate the victim, which he did after a fashion and for a consideration."[3]

Officially, political power is dispersed. Various well-known expedients were devised for this manifest objective. Not only was there the familiar separation of powers among the several branches of the government but, in some measure, tenure in each office was limited, rota-

1. Again, as with preceding cases, we shall not consider the possible dysfunctions of the political machine.

2. Edward M. Sait, "Machine, Political," *Encyclopedia of the Social Sciences,* IX, 658 b [italics supplied]; *cf.* A. F. Bentley, *The Process of Government* (Chicago, 1908), Chap. 2.

3. Herbert Croly, *Progressive Democracy,* (New York, 1914), p.254, cited by Sait, *op. cit.,* 658 b.

tion in office approved. And the scope of power inherent in each office was severely circumscribed. Yet, observes Sait in rigorously functional terms, "Leadership is necessary; and *since* it does not develop readily within the constitutional framework, the Boss provides it in a crude and irresponsible form from the outside."[4]

Put in more generalized terms, *the functional deficiencies of the official structure generate an alternative (unofficial) structure to fulfill existing needs somewhat more effectively.* Whatever its specific historical origins, the political machine persists as an apparatus for satisfying otherwise unfulfilled needs of diverse groups in the population. By turning to a few of these subgroups and their characteristic needs, we shall be led at once to a range of latent functions of the political machine.

Functions of the Political Machine for Diverse Subgroups. It is well known that one source of strength of the political machine derives from its roots in the local community and the neighborhood. The political machine does not regard the electorate as an amorphous, undifferentiated mass of voters. With a keen sociological intuition, the machine recognizes that the voter is a person living in a specific neighborhood, with specific personal problems and personal wants. Public issues are abstract and remote; private problems are extremely concrete and immediate. It is not through the generalized appeal to large public concerns that the machine operates, but through the direct, quasi-feudal relationships between local representatives of the machine and voters in their neighborhood. Elections are won in the precinct.

The machine welds its link with ordinary men and women by elaborate networks of personal relations. Politics is transformed into personal ties. The precinct captain "must be a friend to every man, assuming if he does not feel sympathy with the unfortunate, and utilizing in his good works the resources which the boss puts at his disposal."[5] The precinct captain is forever a friend in need. In our prevailingly impersonal society, the machine, through its local agents, fulfills the important social *function of humanizing and personalizing all manner of assistance* to those in need. Foodbaskets and jobs, legal and extra-legal advice, setting to rights minor scrapes with the law, helping the bright poor boy to a political scholarship in a local college, looking after the bereaved—the whole range of crises when a feller needs a friend, and, above all, a friend who knows the score and who can do

4. Sait, *op. cit.*, 659 a. [italics supplied].
5. *Ibid.*, 659 a.

something about it,—all these find the ever-helpful precinct captain available in the pinch.

To assess this function of the political machine adequately, it is important to note not only that aid *is* provided but *the manner in which it is provided* After all, other agencies do exist for dispensing such assistance. Welfare agencies, settlement houses, legal aid clinics, medical aid in free hospitals, public relief departments, immigration authorities —these and a multitude of other organizations are available to provide the most varied types of assistance. But in contrast to the professional techniques of the welfare worker which may typically represent in the mind of the recipient the cold, bureaucratic dispensation of limited aid following upon detailed investigation of *legal* claims to aid of the "client" are the unprofessional techniques of the precinct captain who asks no questions, exacts no compliance with legal rules of eligibility and does not "snoop" into private affairs.

For many, the loss of "self-respect" is too high a price for legalized assistance. In contrast to the gulf between the settlement house workers who so often come from a different social class, educational background and ethnic group, the precinct worker is "just one of us," who understands what it's all about. The condescending lady bountiful can hardly compete with the understanding friend in need. In *this struggle between alternative structures for fulfilling the nominally same function* of providing aid and support to those who need it, it is clearly the machine politician who is better integrated with the groups which he serves than the impersonal, professionalized, socially distant and legally constrained welfare worker. And since the politician can at times influence and manipulate the official organizations for the dispensation of assistance, whereas the welfare worker has practically no influence on the political machine, this only adds to his greater effectiveness. More colloquially and also, perhaps, more incisively, it was the Boston wardleader, Martin Lomasny, who described this essential function to the curious Lincoln Steffens: "I think," said Lomasny, "that there's got to be in every ward somebody that any bloke can come to—no matter what he's done—and get help. *Help, you understand; none of your law and justice, but help.*"[6]

The "deprived classes," then, constitute one subgroup for whom the

6. *The Autobiography of Lincoln Steffens,* (Chautauqua, New York: Chautauqua Press, 1931), 618. Deriving largely from Steffens, as he says, F. Stuart Chapin sets forth these functions of the political machine with great clarity. See his *Contemporary American Institutions,* (New York: Harper, 1934), 40–54.

political machine satisfies wants not adequately satisfied in the same fashion by the legitimate social structure.

For a second subgroup, that of business (primarily "big" business but also "small"), the political boss serves the function of providing those political privileges which entail immediate economic gains. Business corporations, among which the public utilities (railroads, local transportation and electric light companies, communications corporations) are simply the most conspicuous in this regard, seek special political dispensations which will enable them to stabilize their situation and to near their objective of maximizing profits. Interestingly enough, corporations often want to avoid a chaos of uncontrolled competition. They want the greater security of an economic czar who controls, regulates and organizes competition, providing that this czar is not a public official with his decisions subject to public scrutiny and public control. (The latter would be "government control," and hence taboo.) The political boss fulfills these requirements admirably.

Examined for a moment apart from any moral considerations, the political apparatus operated by the Boss is effectively designed to perform these functions with a minimum of inefficiency. Holding the strings of diverse governmental divisions, bureaus and agencies in his competent hands, the Boss rationalizes the relation between public and private business. He serves as the business community's ambassador in the otherwise alien (and sometimes unfriendly) realm of government. And, in strict business-like terms, he is well-paid for his economic services to his respectable business clients. In an article entitled, "An Apology to Graft," Lincoln Steffens suggested that "Our economic system, which held up riches, power and acclaim as prizes to men bold enough and able enough to buy corruptly timber, mines, oil fields and franchises and 'get away with it,' was at fault."[7] And, in a conference with a hundred or so of Los Angeles business leaders, he described a fact well known to all of them: the Boss and his machine were an *integral part* of the organization of the economy. "You cannot build or operate a railroad, or a street railway, gas, water, or power company, develop and operate a mine, or get forests and cut timber on a large scale, or run any privileged business, without corrupting or joining in the corruption of the government. You tell me privately that you must, and here I am telling you semi-publicly that you must. And that is so all over the country. And that means that we have an organization of society in which, *for some reason,* you and your kind, the ablest, most

7. *Autobiography of Lincoln Steffens,* 570.

intelligent, most imaginative, daring, and resourceful leaders of society, are and must be against society and its laws and its all-around growth."[8]

Since the demand for services of special privileges are built into the structure of the society, the Boss fulfills diverse functions for this second subgroup of business-seeking-privilege. These "needs" of business, as presently constituted, are not adequately provided for by conventional and culturally approved social structures; consequently, the extra-legal but more-or-less efficient organization of the political machine comes to provide these services. To adopt an *exclusively* moral attitude toward the "corrupt political machine" is to lose sight of the very structural conditions which generate the "evil" that is so bitterly attacked. To adopt a functional outlook is to provide not an apologia for the political machine but a more solid basis for modifying or eliminating the machine, *providing* specific structural arrangements are introduced either for eliminating these effective demands of the business community or, if that is the objective, of satisfying these demands through alternative means.

A third set of distinctive functions fulfilled by the political machine for a special subgroup is that of providing alternative channels of social mobility for those otherwise excluded from the more conventional avenues for personal "advancement." Both the sources of this special "need" (for social mobility) and the respect in which the political machine comes to help satisfy this need can be understood by examining the structure of the larger culture and society. As is well known, the American culture lays enormous emphasis on money and power as a "success" goal legitimate for all members of the society. By no means alone in our inventory of cultural goals, it still remains among the most heavily endowed with positive affect and value. However, certain subgroups and certain ecological areas are notable for the relative absence of opportunity for achieving these (monetary and power) types of success. They constitute, in short, sub-populations where "the cultural emphasis upon pecuniary success has been absorbed, but where there is *little access to conventional and legitimate* means for attaining such success. The conventional occupational opportunities of persons in (such areas) are almost completely limited to manual labor. Given our

---

8. *Ibid.*, 573–3 [italics supplied]. This helps explain, as Steffens noted after Police Commissioner Theodore Roosevelt, "the prominence and respectability of the men and women who intercede for crooks" when these have been apprehended in a periodic effort to "clean up the political machine." *Cf.* Steffens, 371, and *passim*.

cultural stigmatization of manual labor, and its correlate, the prestige of white-collar work, it is clear that the result is a tendency to achieve these culturally approved objectives *through whatever means are possible.* These people are on the one hand, "asked to orient their conduct toward the prospect of accumulating wealth [and power] and, on the other, they are largely denied effective opportunities to do so institutionally."

It is within this context of social structure that the political machine fulfills the basic function of providing avenues of social mobility for the otherwise disadvantaged. Within this context, even the corrupt political machine and the racket "represent the triumph of amoral intelligence over morally prescribed 'failure' when the channels of vertical mobility are closed or narrowed *in a society which places a high premium on economic affluence [power] and social ascent for all its members.*"[9] As one sociologist has noted on the basis of several years of close observation in a slum area:

> The sociologist who dismisses racket and political organizations as deviations from desirable standards thereby neglects some of the major elements of slum life. . . . *He does not discover the functions they perform for the members* [of the groupings in the slum]. The Irish and later immigrant peoples have had the greatest difficulty in finding places for themselves in our urban social and economic structure. Does anyone believe that the immigrants and their children could have achieved their present degree of social mobility without gaining control of the political organization of some of our largest cities? The same is true of the racket organization. *Politics and the rackets have furnished an important means of social mobility for individuals, who, because of ethnic background and low class position,* are blocked from advancement in the "respectable" channels.[10]

9. Merton, "Social structure and anomie," chapter IV of [*Social Theory and Social Structure*].

10. William F. Whyte, "Social organization in the slums," *American Sociological Review*, Feb. 1943, 8, 34–39 (italics supplied). Thus, the political machine and the racket represent a special case of the type of organizational adjustment to the conditions described in chapter IV.* It represents, note, an *organizational* adjustment: definite structures arise and operate to reduce somewhat the acute tensions and problems of individuals caught up in the described conflict between the "cultural accent on success-for-all" and the "socially structured fact of unequal opportunities for success." As chapter IV indicates, other types of *individual* "adjustment" are possible: lone-wolf crime, psychopathological states, rebellion, retreat by abandoning the culturally approved goals, etc. Likewise, other

* Editors' Note: Chapter numbers refer to *Social Theory and Social Structure*.

This, then, represents a third type of function performed for a distinctive subgroup. This function, it may be noted in passing, is fulfilled by the *sheer* existence and operation of the political machine, for it is in the machine itself that these individuals and subgroups find their culturally induced needs more or less satisfied. It refers to the services which the political apparatus provides for its own personnel. But seen in the wider social context we have set forth, it no longer appears as *merely* a means of self-aggrandizement for profit-hungry and power-hungry *individuals,* but as an organized provision for *subgroups* otherwise excluded from or handicapped in the race for "getting ahead."

Just as the political machine performs services for "legitimate" business, so it operates to perform not dissimilar services for "illegitimate" business: vice, crime and rackets. Once again, the basic sociological role of the machine in this respect can be more fully appreciated only if one temporarily abandons attitudes of moral indignation, to examine in all moral innocence the actual workings of the organization. In this light, it at once appears that the subgroup of the professional criminal, racketeer or gambler has basic similarities of organization, demands and operation to the subgroup of the industrialist, man of business or speculator. If there is a Lumber King or an Oil King, there is also a Vice King or a Racket King. If expansive legitimate business organizes administrative and financial syndicates to "rationalize" and to "integrate" diverse areas of production and business enterprise, so expansive rackets and crime organize syndicates to bring order to the otherwise chaotic areas of production of illicit goods and services. If legitimate business regards the proliferation of small business enterprises as wasteful and inefficient, substituting, for example, the giant chain stores for hundreds of corner groceries, so illegitimate business adopts the same businesslike attitude and syndicates crime and vice.

Finally, and in many respects, most important, is the basic similarity, if not near-identity, of the economic role of "legitimate" business and of "illegitimate" business. *Both are in some degree concerned with the provision of goods and services for which there is an economic demand.* Morals aside, they are both business, industrial and professional enter-

---

types of *organizational adjustment* sometimes occur; the racket or the political machine are not *alone* available as organized means for meeting this socially induced problem. Participation in revolutionary organizations, for example, can be seen within this context, as an alternative mode of organizational adjustment. All this bears theoretic notice here, since we might otherwise overlook the basic functional concepts of functional substitutes and functional equivalents, which are to be discussed at length in a subsequent publication.

prises, dispensing goods and services which some people want, for which there is a market in which goods and services are transformed into commodities. And, in a prevalently market society, we should expect appropriate enterprises to arise whenever there is a market demand for certain goods or services.

As is well known, vice, crime and the rackets *are* "big business." Consider only that there have been estimated to be about 500,000 professional prostitutes in the United States of 1950, and compare this with the approximately 200,000 physicians and 350,000 professional registered nurses. It is difficult to estimate which have the larger clientele: the professional men and women of medicine or the professional men and women of vice. It is, of course, difficult to estimate the economic assets, income, profits and dividends of illicit gambling in this country and to compare it with the economic assets, income, profits and dividends of, say, the shoe industry, but it is altogether possible that the two industries are about on a par. No precise figures exist on the annual expenditures on illicit narcotics, and it is probable that these are less than the expenditures on candy, but it is also probable that they are larger than the expenditure on books.

It takes but a moment's thought to recognize that, *in strictly economic terms,* there is no relevant difference between the provision of licit and of illicit goods and services. The liquor traffic illustrates this perfectly. It would be peculiar to argue that prior to 1920 (when the 18th amendment became effective), the provision of liquor constituted an economic service, that from 1920 to 1933, its production and sale no longer constituted an economic service dispensed in a market, and that from 1934 to the present, it once again took on a serviceable aspect. Or, it would be *economically* (not morally) absurd to suggest that the sale of bootlegged liquor in the dry state of Kansas is less a response to a market demand than the sale of publicly manufactured liquor in the neighboring wet state of Missouri. Examples of this sort can of course by multiplied many times over. Can it be held that in European countries, with registered and legalized prostitution, the prostitute contributes an economic service, whereas in this country, lacking legal sanction, the prostitute provides no such service? Or that the professional abortionist is in the economic market where he has approved legal status and that he is out of the economic market where he is legally taboo? Or that gambling satisfies a specific demand for entertainment in Nevada, where it constitutes the largest business enterprise of the larger cities in the state, but that it differs essentially in this respect from motion pictures in the neighboring state of California?

The failure to recognize that these businesses are only *morally* and not *economically* distinguishable from "legitimate" businesses has led to badly scrambled analysis. Once the economic identity of the two is recognized, we may anticipate that if the political machine performs functions for "legitimate big business" it will be all the more likely to perform not dissimilar functions for "illegitimate big business." And, of course, such is often the case.

The distinctive function of the political machine for their criminal, vice and racket clientele is to enable them to operate in satisfying the economic demands of a large market without due interference from the government. Just as big business may contribute funds to the political party war-chest to ensure a minimum of governmental interference, so with big rackets and big crime. In both instances, the political machine can, in varying degrees, provide "protection." In both instances, many features of the structural context are identical: (1) market demands for goods and services; (2) the operators' concern with maximizing gains from their enterprises; (3) the need for partial control of government which might otherwise interfere with these activities of businessmen; (4) the need for an efficient, powerful and centralized agency to provide an effective liaison of "business" with government.

Without assuming that the foregoing pages exhaust either the range of functions or the range of subgroups served by the political machine, we can at least see that *it presently fulfills some functions for these diverse subgroups which are not adequately fulfilled by culturally approved or more conventional structures.*

Several additional implications of the functional analysis of the political machine can be mentioned here only in passing, although they obviously require to be developed at length. First, the foregoing analysis has direct implications for *social engineering*. It helps explain why the periodic efforts at "political reform," "turning the rascals out" and "cleaning political house" are typically (though not necessarily) short-lived and ineffectual. It exemplifies a basic theorem: *any attempt to eliminate an existing social structure without providing adequate alternative structures for fulfilling the functions previously fulfilled by the abolished organization is doomed to failure.* (Needless to say, this theorem has much wider bearing than the one instance of the political machine.) When "political reform" confines itself to the manifest task of "turning the rascals out," it is engaging in little more than sociological magic. The reform may for a time bring new figures into the political limelight; it may serve the casual social function of re-assuring the electorate that the moral virtues remain intact and will ultimately triumph; it may actually effect a turnover in the personnel of the political machine; it may even, for a time, so curb the activities of the machine as to leave unsatisfied the many needs it has previously fulfilled. But, inevitably, unless the reform also involves a "re-forming" of the social and political structure such that the existing needs are satisfied by alternative structures or unless it involves a change which eliminates these needs altogether, the political machine will return to its integral place in the social scheme of things. *To seek social change, without due recognition of the manifest and latent functions performed by the social organization undergoing change, is to indulge in social ritual rather than social engineering.* The concepts of manifest and latent functions (or their equivalents) are indispensable elements in the theoretic repertoire of the social engineer. In this crucial sense, these concepts are not "merely" theoretical (in the abusive sense of the term), but are eminently practical. In the deliberate enactment of social change, they can be ignored only at the price of considerably heightening the risk of failure.

A second implication of this analysis of the political machine also has a bearing upon areas wider than the one we have considered. The paradox has often been noted that the supporters of the political machine include both the "respectable" business class elements who are, of course, opposed to the criminal or racketeer and the distinctly "unrespectable" elements of the underworld. And, at first appearance, this is cited as an instance of very strange bedfellows. The learned judge is not infrequently called upon to sentence the very racketeer beside whom he sat the night before at an informal dinner of the political bigwigs. The district attorney jostles the exonerated convict on his way to the back room where the Boss has called a meeting. The big business man may complain almost as bitterly as the big racketeer about the "extortionate" contributions to the party fund demanded by the Boss. Social opposites meet—in the smoke-filled room of the successful politician.

In the light of a functional analysis all this of course no longer seems paradoxical. Since the machine serves both the businessman and the criminal man, the two seemingly antipodal groups intersect. This points to a more general theorem: *the social functions of an organization help determine the structure (including the recruitment of personnel involved in the structure), just as the structure helps determine the effectiveness with which the functions are fulfilled.* In terms of social status, the business group and the criminal group are indeed poles apart. But status does not fully determine behavior and the interrelations between groups. Functions modify these relations. Given their distinctive needs, the several subgroups in the large society are "integrated," whatever their personal desires or intentions, by the centralizing structure which serves these several needs. In a phrase with many implications which require further study, *structure affects function and function affects structure.*

GOSNELL'S CHICAGO REVISITED VIA LINDSAY'S NEW YORK

Theodore J. Lowi

To evaluate the machine we must ask whether, by surviving, machine politics, Chicago model, in any way distorted Chicago's growth and development. How much change would there have been in Chicago's history if the nationalization of politics had made possible in Chicago, as it did in virtually every other big American city, ways of "licking the ward boss" and altering precinct organization, means of loosening the hold of the county organization on city hall, power for freeing the personnel and policies of the professional agencies of government? We cannot answer these questions for Chicago because the basis of machine strength still exists, and the conditions for its continuity, as Gosnell so accurately captures them, may continue through the remainder of the century. We might be able to answer them, however, at least better than before, by looking at Gosnell's Chicago through the contemporary experience of New York.

New York city government, like government in almost all large American cities except Chicago, is a product of Reform. It is difficult to understand these cities without understanding the two strains of ideology that guided local Reform movements throughout the past

From Theodore J. Lowi, "Gosnell's Chicago Revisited via Lindsay's New York," in Foreword to the second edition of Harold F. Gosnell, *Machine Politics: Chicago Model* (1937; 2d ed., 1968), pp.vii–xviii. Copyright © 1968 by The University of Chicago. Reprinted with permission of The University of Chicago Press. Most footnotes deleted.

three-quarters of a century. *Populism* and *efficiency*, once the foundations of most local insurgency, are now, except in rare holdout cases like Chicago, triumphant. These two tenets are now the orthodoxy in local practice.

Populism was originally a statement of the evils of every form of bigness and scale in the city, including big business, big churches, and big labor as well as big political organizations. Decentralization was an ultimate goal. In modern form it has tended to come down to the charge to eliminate political parties, partisanship, and, if possible, politics itself.

Efficiency provided the positive program to replace what populist surgery excised. The doctrine calls essentially for a new form of centralization; that is, centralization and rationalization of government activities and services to accompany the decentralization of power. Some assumed that services do not constitute power. Others assumed the problem away altogether by defining a neutral civil servant who would not abuse centralized government but could use it professionally to reap the economies of scale and specialization. That was the secret of the business system; and, after all, the city is rather like a business. ("There is no Republican or Democratic way to clean a street.")

While there are many inconsistent assumptions and goals between these two doctrines, they lived well together. Their coexistence was supported by the fact that different wings of this large, progressive movement were responsible for each. Populism was largely the province of the working-class, "progressive" wing. Doctrines of efficiency were very much the responsibility of the upper-class wing. Populism resided with the politician-activists. Efficiency was developed by the intellectuals, including several distinguished university presidents, such as Seth Low, Andrew Dickson White, Harold Dodd, and, preeminently, Woodrow Wilson, who wrote a classic essay while still a professor of political science proclaiming the virtues of applying Prussian principles of administration in the United States.

These two great ideas were, by a strange and wonderful chemistry, combined into a movement whose influence is a major chapter of American history. Charters and laws have consistently insulated government from politics (meaning party politics). It became increasingly necessary with each passing decade to grant each bureaucratic agency autonomy to do the job as its professional commissioner saw fit.

On into the 1960's the merit system extends itself "upward, outward and downward," to use the Reformers' own dialectic. Recruitment to the top posts comes more and more often from the ranks of lifetime careerists in the agencies, party backgrounds increasingly signifying automatic disqualification. Reform has succeeded in raising the level of public morality and in making politics a dirty word. "Good press" for mayors consists of a determination to avoid intervening in the affairs of one department after another. The typical modern mayor is probably eager to cooperate, because this is a release from responsibility. Absolution-before-the-fact has become part of the swearing-in ceremony.

Reform has triumphed, and the cities are better run than ever before. But that, unfortunately, is not the end of the story, nor would it have been even without a Negro revolution. The triumph of Reform really ends in paradox: Cities like New York are now *well run but ungoverned.*

Politics under Reform is not abolished. Only its form is altered. *The legacy of Reform is the bureaucratic state.* Destruction of the party foundation of the mayoralty cleaned up many cities but also destroyed the basis for sustained, central, popularly based action. This capacity, with all its faults, was replaced by professionalized agencies. But this has meant creation of new bases of power. Bureaucratic agencies are not neutral; they are only independent. The bureaucrat may be more efficient and rational and honest than the old amateur. But he is no less political. If anything, he is more political because of the enormously important decisions so willingly entrusted to his making.

Modernization in New York and other modern cities has meant replacement of Old Machines with New Machines. The bureaucracies —that is, the professionally organized, autonomous career agencies— are the New Machines.

Sociologically, the Old Machine was a combination of rational goals and fraternal loyalty. The cement of the organization was trust and discipline created out of long years of service, probation and testing, slow promotion through the ranks, and centralized control over the means of reward. Its power in the community was based upon services rendered.

Sociologically, the New Machine is almost exactly the same sort of organization. There are more New Machines in any given city. They are functional rather than geographic in their scope. They rely on formal authority rather than upon majority acquiescence. And they probably work with a minimum of graft and corruption. But these differences do not alter their definition; they only help to explain why the New Machine is such a successful form of organization.

The New Machines are machines because they are relatively irresponsible structures of power. That is, each agency shapes important public policies, yet the leadership of each is relatively self-perpetuating and not readily subject to the controls of any higher authority.

The New Machines are machines in that the power of each, while resting ultimately upon services rendered to the community, depends upon its cohesiveness as a small minority in the midst of the vast dispersion of the multitude.

The modern city is now well run but ungoverned because it now comprises islands of functional power before which the modern mayor stands impoverished. No mayor of a modern city has predictable means of determining whether the bosses of the New Machines—the bureau chiefs and the career commissioners—will be loyal to anything but their agency, its work, and related professional norms. Our modern mayor has been turned into the likeness of a French Fourth Republic premier facing an array of intransigent parties in the National Assembly. The plight of the mayor, however, is worse: at least the premier could resign. These modern machines, more monolithic by far than their ancient brethren, are entrenched by law and are supported by tradition, the slavish loyalty of the newspapers, the educated masses, the dedicated civic groups, and, most of all, by the organized clientele groups enjoying access under existing arrangements.

The Reform response to the possibility of an inconsistency between running a city and governing it would be based upon the assumption of the Neutral Specialist, the bureaucratic equivalent to law's Rational Man. The assumption is that if men know their own specialties well enough they are capable of reasoning out solutions to problems they share with men of equal but different technical competencies. That is a very shaky assumption indeed. Charles Frankel's analysis of such an assumption in Europe provides an appropriate setting for a closer look at it in modern New York: "[D]ifferent [technical] elites disagree with each other; the questions with which specialists deal spill over into areas where they are *not* specialists, and they must either hazard amateur opinions or ignore such larger issues, which is no better. . . ."[1]

During the 1950's government experts began to recognize that, despite vast increases in efficiency flowing from defeat of the machine, New York City government was somehow lacking. These concerns culminated in the 1961 Charter, in which the Office of Mayor was strengthened in many impressive ways. But it was quickly discovered

1. Charles Frankel, "Bureaucracy and Democracy in the New Europe," *Daedalus* (Winter, 1964), p.487.

that no amount of formal centralization could definitively overcome the real decentralization around the mayor. It was an organized decentralization, and it was making a mockery of the new Charter. The following examples, although drawn from New York, are virtually universal in their applicability:

(1) Welfare problems always involve several of any city's largest agencies, including Health, Welfare, Hospitals, etc. Yet, for more than forty years, successive mayors of New York failed to reorient the Department of Health away from a regulative toward more of a service concept of organization. And many new aspects of welfare must be set up in new agencies if they are to be set up at all. The new poverty programs were very slowly organized in all the big cities—except Chicago.

(2) Water pollution control has been "shared" by such city agencies as the Departments of Health, Parks, Public Works, Sanitation, Water Supply, and so on. No large city, least of all New York, has an effective program to combat even the local contributions to pollution. The same is true of air pollution control, although for some years New York has had a separate department for such purposes.

(3) Land-use patterns are influenced in one way or another by a large variety of highly professional agencies. It has proved virtually impossible in any city for any one of these agencies to impose its criteria on the others. In New York the opening of Staten Island by the Narrows Bridge, in what may be the last large urban frontier, found the city with no plan for the revolution of property values and land uses in that Borough.

(4) Transportation is also the province of agencies too numerous to list. Strong mayors throughout the country have been unable to prevent each agency from going its separate way. For just one example, New York pursued a vast off-street parking program, at a cost of nearly $4,000 per parking space, at the very moment when local rail lines were going bankrupt.

(5) Enforcement of civil rights is imposed upon almost all city agencies by virtue of federal, state, and local legislation. Efforts to set up public, then City Council review of police processes in New York have been successfully opposed by professional police officials. Efforts to try pairing and busing of school children on a very marginal, experimental basis have failed. The police commissioner resigned at the very suggestion that values other than professional police values be imposed upon the Department, even when the imposition came via the respected tradition of "legislative oversight." The superintendent

of education, an outsider, was forced out. He was replaced by a career administrator. One education journalist at that time said: "Often . . . a policy proclaimed by the Board [of Education], without the advice and consent of the professionals, is quickly turned into mere paper policy. . . . The veto power through passive resistance by professional administrators is virtually unbeatable. . . ."

The decentralization of city government toward its career bureaucracies has resulted in great efficiency for the activities around which each bureaucracy was organized. The city is indeed well run. But what of those activities around which bureaucracies are not organized, or those which fall between or among agencies' jurisdictions? For these, as suggested by the cases above, the cities are suffering either stalemate or elephantitis—an affliction whereby a particular activity, say urban renewal or parkways, gets pushed to its ultimate success totally without regard to its balance against the missions of other agencies. In these as well as in other senses, the cities are ungoverned.

Mayors have tried a variety of strategies to cope with these situations. But the 1961 mayoral election in New York is the ultimate dramatization of their plight. This election was confirmation of the New York system in the same way the 1936 election was confirmation of Gosnell's Chicago. The 1961 New York election will some day be seen as one of the most significant elections in American urban history. For New York it was the culmination of many long-run developments. For the country it may be the first of many to usher in the bureaucratic state.

The primary significance of the election can be found in the spectacle of a mayor attempting to establish a base of power for himself in the bureaucracies. The mayor's "organization" included the following persons: his running mate for president of the City Council had been commissioner of sanitation, a position which culminated virtually a lifetime career in the Department of Sanitation. He had an impressive following among the sanitation workers, who, it should be added, are organized along precinct lines. The mayor's running mate for comptroller had been for many years the city budget director. As a budget official he had survived several administrations and two vicious primaries pitting factions of the Democratic Party against one another. Before becoming director he had served a number of years as a professional employee in the Bureau. The leaders of the campaign organization included a former, very popular fire commissioner who retired from his commissionership to accept campaign leadership and later to serve as deputy mayor; it also included a former police commissioner who had enjoyed a strong following among professional cops as well as in the local Reform movement. Added to this was a new and vigorous party, the Brotherhood Party, which was composed in large part of unions with broad bases of membership among city employees. Before the end of the election most of the larger city bureaucracies had political representation in the inner core of the new Administration.

For the 1961 election Mayor Wagner had put his ticket and his organization together just as the bosses of old had put theirs together. In the old days the problem was to mobilize all the clubhouses, districts, and counties in the city by putting together a balanced ticket about which all adherents could be enthusiastic. The same seems true for 1961, except that by then the clubhouses and districts had been replaced almost altogether by new types of units.

The main point is that destruction of the machine did not, in New York or elsewhere, elevate the city into some sort of political heaven. Reform did not eliminate the need for political power. It simply altered what one had to do to get it. In the aftermath of twenty or more years of modern government it is beginning to appear that the lack of power can corrupt city hall almost as much as the possession of power. Bureaucracy is, in the United States, a relatively new basis of collective action. As yet none of us knows quite what to do about it.

These observations and cases are not supposed to indict Reform cities and acquit Chicago. They are intended only to put Chicago in a proper light and to provide some experimental means of assessing the functions of the machine form of collective action. Review of Reform government shows simply and unfortunately that the problems of cities, and the irrational and ineffectual ways city fathers go about their business, seem to be universally distributed without regard to form of government or type of power base.

All cities have traffic congestion, crime, juvenile delinquency, galloping pollution, ghettoes, ugliness, deterioration, and degeneracy. All cities seem to be suffering about equally with the quite recent problems of the weakening legitimacy of public objects, resulting in collective violence and pressures for direct solution to problems. All cities seem equally hemmed in by their suburbs and equally prevented from getting at the roots of many of their most fundamental problems. Nonpartisan approaches, even approaches of New York's Republican mayor to Republican suburbs and a Republican governor, have failed to prevent rail bankruptcy in the vast Eastern megalopolis, to abate air or water pollution, to reduce automobile pressure, or to ease the pain of the middle-class Negro in search of escape.

The problems of the city seem to go beyond any of the known arrangements for self-government. However, low morality and lack of what Banfield and Wilson call "public-regardingness" may be a function simply of mass pressure, poor education, and ethnic maladjustment. The old machine and its abuses may have been just another reflection of the same phenomena. If that is so, then the passage of more time and the mounting of one sociocultural improvement after another might have reformed the machines into public-regarding organs, if they had not been first too much weakened to be repaired.

Are there any strong reasons to believe that real reform could have come without paying the price of eliminating the popular but unseemly base of political action? Intimations can be found in the last of the machine-recruited leaders of Tammany, Carmine DeSapio and Edward Costikyan. Each was progressively more public-regarding than any of his predecessors. Costikyan was a model of political responsibility for whom the new New York had no particular use. For this question, however, the best answers may lie in looking afresh at Gosnell's Chicago. With a scientific rigor superior to most political analysis of the 1960's, his book goes further than any other single work to capture what political behavior was like under machine conditions. The sum total of his findings, despite Gosnell's own feelings, does not constitute a very damning indictment of the Chicago machine—if contemporary experience is kept clearly in mind.

Even amidst the most urgent of depression conditions the machine in Chicago does not seem to have interfered with the modest degree of political rationality distributed throughout the United States. Gosnell's data strongly suggest that the New Deal did not win by purchasing masses of the electorate with favorable public policies. Nor did the hungry local Democratic candidates. Persons who benefited most by Roosevelt's relief policies were already Democrats before 1932, certainly before 1936 when the true character of the New Deal was beginning to be grasped by the masses. Party tradition was important in Chicago, as it is everywhere in the United States. Democrats gained an important margin in Chicago through the general disaffection voters were experiencing with parties in power during economic reverses; but again this is typical. Another marginal gain to the Democrats came from the prohibition issue, certainly a rational basis at that time for choosing between the two parties nationally and locally.

What of voting behavior on referendum proposals, the most issue-laden situation an electorate ever faces? Gosnell's criticism of the referendum as subject to fraud and other types of abuse constitutes damnation of the practice everywhere, even though it must have been particularly true of Chicago referenda during the 1920's and '30's. But even so, his figures show that the electorate, despite the machine, did not behave indiscriminately. The theory that universal suffrage provides no check against irresponsible acceptance of financing schemes that pass the real burden on to future generations is simply not borne out in Chicago. Conservative and propertied appeals were effective. Over a twelve-year period, including six fat years and six lean years, sixty-six local bond issues were approved and forty-eight rejected. Those rejected included some major bond issues offered for agencies whose leaders had been discredited. Other issues showed responsiveness to appeals other than those of the local precinct or county organizations. As the anti-prohibition campaign began to grow, so did the vote on the prohibition repealer. Clear irrationalities tended to be associated primarily with highly technical proposals involving judicial procedure or taxation; but even so, there were clear variations according to education, class lines, and other factors that suggest sensitivity to things other than the machine.

In a bold stroke, Gosnell also tried to assess the influence of the newspapers, the best source for rational—at least non-machine—voting decisions. For this particular purpose Gosnell's data were weak, but fortunately he was not deterred from asking important questions merely for lack of specially designed data. Factor analysis helped Gosnell tease out of census tract data and newspaper subscription patterns a fairly realistic and balanced sense of the role of the local newspapers. Gosnell was led to conclude that the influence of news media is limited but that this was a limitation imposed far less by the machine than by the limitations on the distribution of readers. Newspaper influence on issues was measurably apparent wherever daily readership was widely established—*the machine notwithstanding*. Here again is the possibility that real machine domination rested upon a level of education and civic training that was at the very time of Gosnell's research undergoing a great deal of change.

Taking all the various findings together, and even allowing for abuses that were always more frequent in cities than in towns, and probably more frequent in Gosnell's Chicago than in other cities, we can come away from Gosnell's analysis with a picture not at all contrary to Key's notion of the "responsible electorate." It was, in fact, sufficiently self-interested to subdivide into hostile constituencies, and for this phenomenon Gosnell offers his only positive statement about the machine: "On the credit side of the ledger should be placed the success of the bosses in softening class conflicts." This single proposition, antic-ipating by more than a decade Merton's famous essay on the "latent functions" of the machine, tends to confirm, in a perverse way, the existence and the problems of rational voters. It also suggests that ma-chine politics is a special phase in the development of all American cities, a solution to problems that tends to pass when the problems for which it is appropriate pass.

In the end Gosnell may have felt his book to be indictment of ma-chine politics. Perhaps it is only a sad commentary upon our loss of innocence that we can look at his data a generation later and come away morally uplifted.

Suggestions for
Further Reading

This bibliography on local corruption is necessarily selective. A complete list would be quite voluminous since, as demonstrated throughout this book, the subject of urban corruption cannot easily be separated from other aspects of local politics. The works listed below are offered for readers interested in learning about topics not treated in this book and for students who wish to pursue additional research on the subject. In addition to the information to be found in the growing literature on urban politics and social systems generally, valuable insights into the problem of corruption may be gained from studies dealing with the areas of municipal politics in which corruption most often occurs, e.g., crime and law enforcement, campaign finance, machine and reform party structures, urban growth, zoning, taxation, construction, the procurement of goods and services. We encourage readers who are interested in reading further on urban corruption to consult the following:

Braibanti, Ralph. "Reflections on Bureaucratic Corruption." *Public Administration Review* 40 (1962):357–62.
Brooks, Robert C. *Corruption in American Politics and Life.* New York, 1910.
Callow, Alexander B., Jr. *The Tweed Ring.* New York: Oxford University Press, 1966.
Carlin, Jerome. *Lawyers' Ethics: A Survey of the New York Bar.* New York: Russell Sage Foundation, 1966.
Chalmers, David M. "The Muckrakers and the Growth of Corporate Power." *American Journal of Economics and Sociology* 18 (1959):295–311.
Chambliss, William J. "Vice, Corruption, Bureaucracy and Power." *Wisconsin Law Review* 4 (1971):1150–73.
Dorman, Michael. *Payoff.* New York: McKay, 1972.
Flynn, Edward J. *You're the Boss.* New York: The Viking Press, Inc., 1947.
Friedrich, Carl J. "Political Pathology." *Political Quarterly* 37 (1966):70–85.

Heidenheimer, Arnold J. *Political Corruption: Readings in Comparative Analysis*. New York: Holt, Rinehart and Winston, 1970.

Hutchinson, John. *The Imperfect Union: A History of Corruption in American Trade Unions*. New York: E. P. Dutton, 1972.

Ingersoll, John E. "The Police Scandal Syndrome." *Crime and Delinquency* 10 (1964):269–75.

Kefauver, Estes. *Crime in America*. Garden City, N.Y.: Doubleday, 1951.

Landesco, John. *Organized Crime in Chicago*. Chicago: University of Chicago Press, 1968.

Lasswell, Harold D. "Bribery." *Encyclopedia of the Social Sciences*, vol. 1, pp.690–92. New York: Crowell, Collier, Macmillan, 1930.

Maas, Peter. *Serpico*. New York: Viking, 1973.

McKitrick, Eric L. "The Study of Corruption." *Political Science Quarterly* 72 (1957):502–14.

McMullan, M. "A Theory of Corruption." *Sociological Review* 9 (1961): 181–201.

Moynihan, Daniel P. "The Private Government of Crime." *The Reporter*, July 6, 1961.

New York State Commission of Investigation. *Delinquent Real Estate Taxes in Albany County*. Albany, 1961.

Nye, J. S. "Corruption and Political Development: A Cost-Benefit Analysis." *American Political Science Review* 61 (1967):417–27.

"Organized Crime: A Bibliography." *The Police Chief* 38 (1971):48–55.

Peterson, Virgil W. "Obstacles to Enforcement of Gambling Laws." *Annals of the American Academy of Political and Social Science* 269 (1950): 9–20.

———. *Barbarians in Our Midst: A History of Chicago Crime and Politics*. Boston: Little, Brown, 1952.

President's Commission on Law Enforcement and Administration of Justice. *Task Force Report: Organized Crime*. Washington, D.C.: Government Printing Office, 1967.

Price, Barbara R. "Police Corruption: An Analysis." *Criminology* 10 (1972): 161–76.

Ruth, Henry S., Jr. "Why Organized Crime Thrives." *Annals of the American Academy of Political and Social Science* 367 (1967):113–22.

Scott, James C. "An Essay on the Political Functions of Corruption." *Asian Studies* 5 (1967):501–23.

———. "Corruption, Machine Politics, and Social Change." *American Political Science Review* 63 (1969):1142–59.

———. *Comparative Political Corruption*. Englewood Cliffs, N.J.: Prentice-Hall, 1971.

Sherman, Lawrence, ed. *Police Corruption: A Sociological Perspective*. New York: Anchor Press, 1974.

Siegan, Bernard H. *Land Use Without Zoning*. Washington, D.C.: Heath, 1972.

Sufrin, Sidney C. "Graft: Grease for the Palm and Grease for the Wheels." *Challenge* 13 (1964):30–33.

Sutherland, Edwin H. "Crimes of Corporations," in Gilbert Geis, ed., *White Collar Criminals*. New York: Atherton, 1968.

Tyler, Gus. *Organized Crime in America: A Book of Readings*. Ann Arbor: University of Michigan Press, 1962.

Williams, Robert H. *Vice Squad*. New York: Crowell, 1973.

Wraith, Ronald, and Edgar Simkin. *Corruption in Developing Countries*. London: George Allen and Unwin, 1963.

Zink, Harold. *City Bosses in the United States*. Durham, N.C.: Duke University Press, 1930.